FRUITS & VEGETABLES PROCESSING HAND BOOK

FRUITS & VEGETABLES PROCESSING HAND BOOK

Written By

EIRI Board of Consultants and Engineers

ENGINEERS INDIA RESEARCH INSTITUTE

4449, Nai Sarak, Main Road, Delhi - 110006 (India)
Ph: +91-11-23918117, 23916431, 45120361, 23947058, 64727385
* E-Mail: eiribooks@yahoo.com & eiriprojects@gmail.com
*Website: www.eiriindia.org & www.industrialprojects.in

PRINTED & PUBLISHED BY

ENGINEERS INDIA RESEARCH INSTITUTE

4449, Nai Sarak, Main Road, Delhi - 110006 (India)
Ph: +91-11-23918117, 23916431, 45120361, 23947058, 64727385
* E-Mail: eiribooks@yahoo.com & eiriprojects@gmail.com
*Website: www.eiriindia.org & www.industrialprojects.in

Distributors:

EIRI Project Consultants and Publishers
Roop Nagar, Delhi-110007
and
Industrial Technologies, India
Nai Sarak, Delhi-110006

3rd Edition

ISBN: 9788186732328

Printed in New Delhi (INDIA)

₹ 900/-

Printed & Published by Sudhir Gupta for "Engineers India Research Institute", 4449 Nai Sarak, Main Road, New Delhi -110006

Preface

The purpose of this book is to guide small-scale processors in the Ugandan fruits and vegetables sector to optimize their processing methods and implement quality assurance schemes and GHP (Good Hygienic Practices) and GMP (Good Manufacturing Practices) programmes thus building their technical capacity for improved market access and competitiveness. In general, fruit and vegetable processing offers good opportunities for small-scale businesses.

Processing fruits and vegetables is intended to do two things:

1. To preserve them by slowing down the natural processes of decay caused by microorganisms, enzymes in the food, or other factors such as heat, moisture and sunlight.
2. To change them into different foods, which are attractive and in demand by consumers. Like chefs and caterers, processors should use their skills to develop attractive recipes and make products that consumers want to eat. By doing this successfully, they can increase sales and earn an income.

Processors must choose their products very carefully. It is not enough to assume that processing can be a successful business simply because there is plenty of cheap fruit available. There must be a good demand for the processed food and this must be clearly identified before a business is set up. The best types of products for small-scale production are those that have a high 'added-value' as well as a good demand. A high added value means that cheap raw materials can be processed into relatively expensive products. It also means that this can be done at a small scale of processing using equipment that is affordable.

India is advantageously placed to ensure the viability of food processing units. The cost of production and post-harvest handling of most agricultural, horticultural and animal products is low putting us to advantage in comparison to other countries. The varied agro-climatic conditions can facilitate production of the same stuff at different places at different times to aid availability. This makes it possible to develop cottage, small and medium scale units.

The book '***Fruits and Vegetables Processing Hand Book***' covers almost all the basic and advanced details to setup own unit of fruits and vegetables processing products. The chapters covering in this book are *Preservation Principles, Canning in Commercial Scale, Packing Containers, Syrups & Brines for Canning, Canning of Fruits, Canning of Vegetables, Spoilage In Canned Foods, Fruit Juices, Squashes & Cordials, Fruit Beverages, Jams & Jellies, Tomato Products, Pickles, Sauces & Chutneys, Canned Fruits & Vegetables, Canning of Fruits, Cashew Fruit Juice, Dehydration of Fruits & Vegetables, Frozen Foods, Fruit Juices Making & Packaging, Fruits & Vegetables Juice with Other Products, Guava Jam and Jelly, Lemon Juice Squash* etc.

At the end of the book the last but not the least chapter project profiles have also been included for the benefits of the new entrepreneurs.

The book has been written for the benefit and to prove an asset and a handy reference guide in the hands of new entrepreneurs & well established industrialists.

Author

CONTENTS AND SUBJECT INDEX

EIRI PROCESS TECHNOLOGY BOOKS

03 Paint, Pigment, Solvent, Coating Emulsion, Paint Additives & Formulations
04 Technology Of Coating, Resins, Pigments & Inks Industries
05 Manufacturing Technology & Formulations Hand Book On Thinners, Putty, Wall & Industrial Finishes And Synthetic Resins
06 Technology of Synthetic Resins and Emulsion Polymers
07 Technology of Paints and Coatings with Formulations
08 Powder Coating Technology Hand Book

PLASTIC/POLYMER PROCESS, COMPOUNDING, INJECTION MOULDING, ROTATIONAL MOULDING, PLASTIC FILM, FIBRE GLASS, PLASTIC WASTE RECYCLING, MOULDS, PET & RESINS INDUSTRIES

01 Moulds Design & Processing Hand Book
02 Hand Book Of Plastic Materials & Processing Technology
03 Injection Moulding Of Plastics
04 Plastic Processing and Packaging Industries
05 Plastic Waste Recycling Technology
06 Technology Of Plastic Films
07 Rotational Moulding Technology Hand Book
08 Plastic Compounding, Master Batches, Pet & Other Plastics
09 Synthetic Resins Technology With Formulations
10 Technology Of PVC Compounding And Its Applications
11 Hand Book of Polymer And Plastic Technology
12 Hand Book of Fibre Glass Moulding
13 Technology of Reinforced Plastics
14 Plastic Additives Technology Hand Book
15 Technology of Pet Bottles, Preform and Pet Recycling
16 Modern Technology of Extrusion & Extruded Products
17 Technology of Synthetic Resins & Emulsion Polymers
18 Technology of Plastic Additives with Processes and Packaging
19 Technology of Disposable Medical Products

BAKERY, CONFECTIONERY & BREAKFAST, PASTA & CEREALS

01 Hand Book Of Bakery Industries
02 Hand Book Of Confectionery With Formulations
03 Breakfast, Dietary Food, Pasta & Cereal Products Technology
04 Hand Book Of Modern Bakery Products
05 Modern Bakery Technology & Fermented Cereal Products With Formulae
06 Technology of Confectionery, Chocolates, Toffee, Candy, Chewing & Bubble Gums, Lollipop and Jelly Products with Formulations

AGRO CULTIVATION, ANIMAL FARMING, AGRO PLANTATION & AGRO CHEMICAL/ PESTICIDES/ FLORICULTURE & BEE KEEPING

01 Poultry Farming & Feed Formulations
02 Hand Book of Pig Farming
03 Agro Based Hand Book of Plantation, Cultivation & Farming
04 Agro Based Plantation Cultivation & Farming
05 Agro Chemical Industries (Insecticide & Pesticides)
06 Modern Bee Keeping & Honey Processing

EIRI PROCESS TECHNOLOGY BOOKS

07 Technology Of Modern Rice Milling And Basmati Rice

08 Hand Book Of Goat Farming

09 Floriculture Hand Book (Flowers Growing Technology)

10 Aloe Vera Cultivation, Processings, Formulations And Manufacturing Technology

11 Poultry Farming, Hatchery and Broiler Production

DAIRY FARM, MILK PROCESSING AND ICE CREAM

01 Hand Book of Dairy Formulations, Processes & Milk Processing Industries

02 Milk Processing And Dairy Products Industries

03 Hand Book Of Dairy Farming to Produce Milk with Packaging

04 Hand Book Of Ice Cream Technology And Formulae

05 Hand Book Of Milk Processing Dairy Products And Packaging Technology

06 Dairy Farming for Milk Production Technology

07 Commercial Dairy Farming with Project Profiles

HERBS & MEDICINAL CULTIVATION

01 Herbs, Medicinal & Aromatic Plants Cultivation

02 Aushidhi And Sungndhit Paudho Ka Vaysayik (Hindi)

03 Hand Book Of Aromatic & Medicinal Plants And Biodiesel (Jatropha)

04 Hand Book Of Medicinal & Aromatic Plants (Cultivation, Utilisation & Extraction Processed)

FOOD & AGRO PROCESSING, PRESERVATION, SNACK FOOD, DEHYDRATION, FRUIT BEVERAGE, POTATO, MAIZE, MEAT PROCESS

01 Fruits & Vegetables Processing Hand Book

02 Fruit Beverage & Processing With Mango

03 Food Processing & Agro Based Industries

04 Manufacturing Technology of Snacks Food, Namkeen, Pappad & Potato Products

05 Preservation & Canning Of Fruits and Vegetables

06 Hand Book of Food Dehydration & Drying

07 Meat Processing & Meat Products Hand Book

08 Technology of Food Preservation & Processing

09 Hand Book of Food Packaging Technology

10 Agro Based & Processed Food Products

11 Potato & Potato Processing Technology

12 Technology of Maize & Allied Corn. Products

13 Technology of Food Processing Industries

14 Technology of Sweets (Mithai) with Formulae

15 Modern Technology of Frozen Food Products

16 Technology of Water and Packaged Drinking Water

17 Complete Hand Book on Frozen Food Processing and Freeze Drying Technology

18 Technology of Sweets (Mithai), Namkeen and Snacks food with Formulae

19 Complete Book on Banana Cultivation Dehydration, Ripening, Processing, Products and Packaging Technology

EIRI PROCESS TECHNOLOGY BOOKS

20 Technology of Chicken Meat and Poultry Products
21 Agro Food Processing and Packaging Technology
22 Modern Technology of Tomato Processing and Dehydration (Ketchup, Juice, Paste, Puree, Soup and Drying)
23 Modern Technology of Agro Processing and Food Packaging Products with Project Profiles
24 Start Your Own Coffee and Coffee Processing

SOAPS & DETERGENTS

01 Household Soap. Toilet Soap & Other Soap
02 Profitable Small Scale Manufacture Of Soaps & Detergents
03 Synthetic Detergents With Formulations
04 Modern Technology of Acid Slurry, Surfactants, Soap and Detergents with Formulae

ORGANIC FARMING AND FOOD

01 Hand Book Of Organic Farming And Organic Foods With Vermi-Composting And Neem Products

FISH FARMING & FISHERY PRODUCTS

01 Hand Book Of Fish Farming And Fishery Products

COSMETIC (SYNTHETIC & HERBAL)

01 Cosmetics Processes & Formulations
02 Herbal Cosmetics & Beauty Products With Formulations
03 Profitable Small Scale Manufacture Of Cosmetics (Synthetic & Herbal)
04 Hand Book Of Synthetic & Herbal Cosmetics (How to Make Beauty Products)
05 Technology Of Herbal Cosmetics & Toiletries Products With Formulae

OIL AND FATS

01 Hand Book of Oils, Fats And Derivatives With Refining & Packaging Technology
02 Technology of Oilseeds Processing, Oils & Fats and Refining

ESSENTIAL OILS & AROMATIC

01 Essential Oils Manufacturing & Aromatic Plants
02 Modern Technology Of Essential Oils
03 Technology Of Perfumes, Flavours & Essential Oils
04 Essential Oils Processes & Formulations

PERFUMES AND FLAVOURS

01 Hand Book Of Flavours & Food Colourants Technology
02 Hand Book Of Perfumes & Flavours
03 Hand Book of Perfumes With Formulations
04 Technology Of Perfumes, Flavours & Essential Oils
05 Hand Book Of Flavours Technology

BUILDING MATERIALS & CHEMICALS

01 Technology Of Building Materials & Chemicals With Processes

EIRI PROCESS TECHNOLOGY BOOKS

TEXTILE, GARMENTS, DYEING

01 Modern Technology Of Bleaching, Dyeing, Printing & Finishing Of Textiles
02 Technology Of Textiles (Spinning & Weaving, Dyeing, Scouring, Drying, Printing And Bleaching)
03 Garments Manufacturing Technology

SPICES & COLD STORAGE

01 Spices & Packaging With Formulaes
02 Start Your Own Cold Storage Unit

PULP & PAPER TECHNOLOGY

01 Hand Book Of Pulp & Paper, Paper Board & Paper Based Technology

NON WOVEN TECHNOLOGY

01 Complete Technology of Nonwovens Fabrics, Carry Bags, Composite, Geotextiles, Medical Textiles, Fibres, Felts, Apparels, Spunlace and Absorbent Nonwoven

TEXTILE AUXILIARIES & CHEMICALS

01 Textile Auxiliaries And Chemicals With Processes And Formulations

PHARMACEUTICALS & DRUGS

01 Pharmaceuticals And Drugs Technology With Formulations

LEATHER & LEATHER PRODUCTS

01 Hand Book Of Leather & Leather Products Technology

BIOTECHNOLOGY

01 Hand Book Of Biotechnology

CERAMICS

01 Hand Book of Ceramics and Ceramics Processing Technology

TREE FARMING

01 Hand Book Of Tree Farming

MUSHROOM CULTIVATION/ PROCESS

01 Hand Book Of Mushroom Cultivation, Processing and Packaging

BIOFERTILIZERS & VERMICULTURE

01 Hand Book Of Biofertilizers & Vermiculture

MINERAL AND MINERALS

01 Hand Book Of Minerals And Minerals Based Industries

RUBBER CHEMICALS, COMPOUND & RUBBER INDUSTRIES

01 Rubber Chemicals & Processing Industries
02 Modern Rubber Chemicals, Compounds & Rubber Goods Technology
03 Technology Of Rubber & Rubber Goods Industries

AYURVEDIC MEDICINES

01 Ayurvedic & Herbal Medicines With Formulaes
02 Hand Book Of Ayurvedic Medicines With Formulations (A

EIRI PROCESS TECHNOLOGY BOOKS

Complete Hand Book Of Ayurvedic & Herbal Medicines)

STEEL, S.S., NON FERROUS METALS, ROLLING MILL

01 Modern Technology of Non Ferrous Metals and Metal Extraction

02 Processing Technology of Steels and Stainless Steels

03 Modern Technology of Rolling Mill, Billets, Steel Wire, Galvanized Sheet, Forging & Castings

04 Manufacturing Technology of Non-Ferrous Metal Products

WOOD, VENEER, PLYWOOD, PARTICLE, BOARD, FIBREBOARD, BAMBOO & FOREST PRODUCTS

01 Modern Technology Of Wood, Veneer, Plywood, Particle Board, Fibreboard, Bamboo & Forest Products

BIO GAS PRODUCTION

01 Modern Technology of BIOGAS Production

WASTE BASED PRODUCTS INCLUDING INDUSTRIAL, AGRICULTURE, MEDICAL, MUNICIPALITY, ORGANIC & BIOLOGICAL

01 Technology Of Products From Wastes Industrial, Agriculture, Medical, Municipality, Organic & Biological

02 Products from Waste Technology Handbook

FOOD CHEMICALS, FOOD ADDITIVES, PIGMENTS, AROMA, SWEETENERS AND FOOD EMULSIFIERS

01 Technology of Food Chemicals, Pigments and Food Aroma Compounds

02 Modern Technology of Food Additives, Sweeteners and Food Emulsifiers

SOYBEAN

01 Technology of SOYBEAN Products with Formulae

02 Technology of Soya Milk, Tofu, Hydrlyzate and allied Soyabean Products with Project Profiles

EIRI Multiple Project Reports in CD ROM

01 92 New Lucrative Project Reports In Cd

02. 45 Infotech/It, Hospitality, Hospital, College, School & Club

03. 23 Profitable Construction Projects

04. 56 Agro Based & Food Processing Projects

05. 52 Food, Dairy, Bakery, Confectionery & Snacks Foods

06. 45 New Chemicals & Allied Project Reports

07. 100 Profitable Plastic, Polymers & Allied Projects

08. 44 Textile, Garments, Hosiery & Allied Products In Cd

09. 23 Dairy Farming (Buffalo & Jersey Cow, Dairy Products & Other Milk Processing Ind.

10. 42 Paper, Pulp & Paper Converting Products Reports

EIRI Multiple Project Reports in CD ROM

11. 31 Essential Oils, Perfumes, Flavours & Aromatic Compounds
12. 28 Surgical And Disposable Medical Projects
13. 36 Profitable Printing & Allied Projects Reports
14. 63 Profitable Packaging & Allied Project Reports
15. 99 Profitable Printing & Packaging
16. 42 Electroplating, Anodizing & Allied Projects
17. 31 Profitable Plantation & Cultivation Projects
18. 55 Profitable Products From Agro And Other Industrial Wastes
19. 35 Profitable Gums, Adhesives, Sealants And Resins Projects
20. 54 Paint, Varnish, Solvents, Lacquers, Resins, Enamel, Pigments, Thinners & Powder (54 Project Reports In Cd)
21 43 Iron, Steel, Casting, Fabrication, Wire Drawing & Rolling Mills Projects
22. 26 New Educational Projects (Schools, Colleges, Training/ Management Institute, Hostels Etc.)
23. 12 Mosquitoes Preventive Projects (Coils, Mats, Liquids, Agarbatti, Nets, Spray Etc.)
24. 21 Bakery And Allied Products
25. 67 Rubber And Rubber Goods Industries
26. 37 Aluminium And Aluminium Based Industries
27. 14 Potato And Potato Based Industries
28. 50 Electrical, Electronics And Computer Based Industries
29. 52 Cosmetics (Herbal & Synthetics) Technology Projects (52 Project Reports)
30. 10 Molasses Based Lucrative Projects
31. 24 Fruits/Veg. & Allied Food Dehydration Projects
32. 7 Power Plant Projects (Thermal, Hydro, Solar, Wind Energy And Lignite Coal Based)
33. 35 New Profitable Industries
34. 160 New Export Oriented And Profitable Projects (160 Project Reports In Cd)
35. 5 Ginger & Ginger Processing Industries
36. 13 Fish Farming And Fishery Products
37. 6 Agarbatti And Allied Projects
38. 28 Fruit Juices, Food Dehydration And Allied Products
39. 9 Tea Plantation And Processing Based Industries
40. 14 Roasted/Salted Cashew Nuts, Almonds, Namkeens, Spices Projects
41. 23 Injection Moulded Plastic Products (23 Project Reports)
42. 38 Biofertilizer, Biofuel, Enzyme, Organic Farming & Manure, Protein And Allied Lucrative Projects
43. 10 Maize & Corn Processing Projects
44. 11 Profitable Solar & Solar Based Products
45. 11 Infotech/It Projects
46. 42 Hospitality, Building Material, Power Steels, Alcohol & Other Food Products
47. 24 Soap & Detergents (Scouring Powder, Toilet Cleaner, Laundry Soap, Detergent Cake & Powder, Toilet Soap, Enzyme Based Detergents, Phenyl & Soap Coated Paper)
48. 10 Coconut And Coconut By Products
49. 22 Alcohol, Beer, Imfl, Country Liquor, Wine & Other Related Projects

1

Preservation Principles

The modern methods of food preservation in general and of fruit and vegetable preservation in particular may be broadly classified as follows:

I. Physical Methods

(a) By removal of heat (preservation by cold)	i. Refrigeration ii. Freezing preservation iii. Dehydro freezing preservation iv. Carbonation
(b) By addition of heat (thermal processing)	i. Stationary pasteurization ii. Agitating pasteurization/ sterilization iii. Flash pasteurization/HTST processing etc.
(c) By removal of water (evaporation or dehydration)	i. Sun drying ii. Dehydration iii. Low temperature evaporation or concentration iv. Freeze-drying v. Accelerated freeze-drying vi. Foam-mat drying vii. Puff drying etc.
(d) By irradiation	Dosing with U.V. or ionizing radiation etc.

II. Chemical Methods

(a) By addition of acid such as vinegar or lactic acid	Pickled vegetables, fish & meat
(b) By salting or brining	Vegetable/fruit pickles, salted fish, etc. salt-cured meat and pork etc.

(c) By addition of sugar and heating — Fruit preserves, jams, jellies, marmalades, etc.

(d) By addition of chemical preservatives —

i. Using water soluble salts salts of sulphur dioxide, benzoic acid, sorbic acid and a few like hydrogen peroxide, etc. which are permitted as harmless in foods.

ii. By means of substances of bacterial origin such as tylosin, resin, etc. which are permitted to a limited extent, in some cases as harmless additives.

III. By Fermentation

Alcoholic & acetous fermentation as in the case of fruit wines, apple cider, fruit, vinegar, etc.

IV. By Other Methods

A judicious combination of one or more of the methods mentioned above for synergistic preservation.

Although all the main classes of preservation have been employed in varying extents in the case of a variety of fruits and vegetables, some of them are of particular significance now in view of their economic importance. They are efficient, comparatively simple in operation, have universal application and as such have attained commercial importance.

Some of the more important applications of the different methods are mentioned briefly in the following section. More detailed applications of such methods will be described in the subsequent chapters. Preservation by addition of heat in various ways is perhaps the earliest and the most common method of preservation. It is generally known as preservation by canning or heat processing in hermetically sealed containers made of tin plate or glass, or more recently of heat-resistant plastic materials. Both solid and liquid foods are preserved on a very large scale by this method.

Next in importance is the drying or dehydration method. Sun-drying is extensively employed in many parts of the world to dry a variety of fruits and vegetables and sometimes fish and meat. Dehydration or artificial drying of fruits and vegetables is extensively employed, and many improvements have been introduced to obtain dried products of excellent quality. Low temperature drying, freeze-drying, accelerated freeze-drying foam-mat drying, etc. are refinements in the technique of dehydration.

Freeze preservation, which is an extension of the well-known method of increasing the storage life of fresh fruits and vegetables, and similar other fresh food-stuffs, is extensively employed more in the case of fish and meat, although it is being employed to a limited extent in the case of some fruits and vegetables such as peach, pear, peas, beans, etc. With the introduction of deep-freeze cabinets at home and facility for transport in the frozen state and the resulting convenience to the housewife, this method of preservation is likely to develop rapidly in the near future, especially in the more advanced countries, with a highly sophisticated way of living It cannot, however, completely substitute or replace the conventional canning of foods which, in spite of its drawbacks, continues to hold the field on account of its numerous advantages and conveniences.

Preservation by addition of sugar and application of heat is a highly important method in the case of fruits which are utilized in a very large quantities to make jams, jellies, marmalades and preserves. This method is simple, cheap and easy to adopt, and hence its universal popularity.

The use of chemical additives, which are permitted as harmless, within limits is fairly widespread in the case of a variety of squashes, cordials and other beverages. At present, only sulphur dioxide and its salts and benzoic acid and some of its ester derivatives are permitted in foods. Sorbic acid or sorbates are also permitted only in some cases. Product of bacterial origin such as nisin, tylosin, etc. are still in the screening stage. A large number of other chemicals such as formaldehyde, bromo-acetic acid, salicylic acid, etc. which were once used as preservatives, have now been prohibited in foods on account of their harmful nature.

Preservation by fermentation is a very ancient and well-known method. Yeast-fermented fruit wines, which contain ethyl alcohol as a natural preservative have been prepared and used for hundreds of years. Such alcoholic liquids undergo further acetic acid fermentation into vinegar, which is an acidulant and is widely employed in pickling. Other well-known fruit wines besides grape-wine are apple cider, berry wines, etc.

Preservation by salting or brining of vegetables such as cucumber, cabbage, bamboo shoots etc. and of unripe fruits such as those of mango, lime, lemon, etc., is very common in many parts of the world where Indian pickles are well known. Sometimes, pickled vegetables, onion etc. are preserved in clear vinegar to get products having attractive appearance. Such vinegar pickles are highly prized in western countries.

Preservation of fruits and vegetables by application of U.V. and ionizing radiation is of recent origin. There is considerable interest in this technique, especially in view of the fact that cheap sources of irradiation have become freely available as a result of development of atomic energy installations in some parts of the world. Although, the results appear to be promising, it will take quite sometime before it could be guaranteed as completely harmless and free from any health hazard. There is 'however' a great deal of interest at present in the subject.

FRUITS & VEGETABLES CANNING & BOTTLING

It is a common experience that fruits, vegetables, meats, and many other articles of food spoil rapidly unless unless specially cared for. Various methods for preserving in sugar or honey etc. have been developed since time immemorial. Canning is however, comparatively a modern technique.

FOOD PROCESSING PRINCIPLES

The fundamental principle of preserving foods by heat is known as Processing. It consists basically in the application of heat in varying degrees to the food in closed conttainerrs, for a sufficiently long time to sterrilize the contents before these are hermetically sealed. The method of processing varies from food to food.

In the early days of canning, the 'open-bath' processing in boiling water was the one commonly used. By this method, fruits which were naturally acidic, and more acid vegetables like rhubarb and tomato could be satisfactorily preserved as most of the spoilage organisms present in them were easily destroyed at the temperature of boiling water. Non acid vegetables however required processing at higher temperature to get rid of the more resistant organisms present in them. In earlier times, prolonged processing in boiling water for 5 to 6 hours, or heating the canned food for short periods on 3 to 4 successive days to sterilize the product completely, was adopted in the case of non acid vegetables. This was, however, cumbersome. In 1861, Issac Winslow used calcium chloride in the openbath to raise the temperature as high as 121°C. Calcium chloride, however, discoloured the tin can and made it look unattractive. In 1873, a pressure cooker or retort, in which steam is let into a closed vessel under pressure, was invented by A.L.Shriver a canner of Baltimore. This was a big step forward in the technique. Several improvements have since been introduced in this highly useful equipment. Pressure cookers are now available in various designs and capacities to suit different requirements. Some of them can operate continuously for processing foods under pressure.

The original sample open bath method also has been improved greatly. The continuous type open cooker is a notable addition. In earlier days the cooker consisted of a long iron or wooden tank, sometimes as long as 30 meters containing boiling water through which sealed cans were moved in crates suspended from a moving over-head conveyor. These being bulky and inconvenient, continuous agitating sterilizers were introduced. In these, the sealed cans were conveyed on a continuous belt passing through a closed steam chamber with a device to constantly roll and agitate the cans. Bitting estimates that in these sterilizers the processing time is reduced by as much as 75 per cent. These sterilizers are in common use in many of the modern canneries. A recent innovation is the introduction of the spin pasteurizer in which the cans rotate on their own axis during pasteurization as well as subsequent cooling. This type of pasteurizer, first developed in Australia, has been found highly useful in the canning of pulpy and viscous materials such as passion fruit pulp, which have a mild flavour easily affected by strong heating for even short periods. The rock and roll type of pasteurization in an open cooker has been found satisfactory in the case of canned orange segments which have a delicate flavour easily adversely effected by longer heating as in conventional stationary processing technique. Hydrostatic cooker where the can travels through a column of water is a more recent introduction to processing techniques.

In the case of spin processing of even viscous materials, the time can be very short. For instance spin processing is possible for fruit pulp like mango pulp, tomato paste, fruit purees, concentrates, syrups canned fruits, juices and ready-to- serve beverages. It has also been reported that in case of passion fruit juice employing a rotation of 150 rpm, atmospheric steam at 96°C to 97°C and the time of spin heating for safe canning can be as low as one minute, the time of spin-cooling being 1½ minutes, at 150 rpm under sprays of water at the rate of 45 liters per minute.

There is much scope for extending this type of processing to a variety of other heat-sensitive viscous products like custard apple pulp, mango pulp etc.

2

Canning in Commercial Scale

Before dealing with the various processes involved in the canning of fruits and vegetables on a commercial scale, it is necessary to consider certain important factors such as investment site, building, water supply, staff, labour, etc. which are essential for the successful running of a small to large scale cannery.

INVESTMENT

The capital outlay includes investment on land, factory building and machinery. The running or operational expenses include the cost of raw material, labour, processing, storage, transport, and distribution. As a first step, the entrepreneur should plan carefully the type and size of production which would be most advantageous. He should then decide about the plant and other requirements. The entrepreneur may approach to *Engineers India Research Institute, Delhi* for getting loan & project report assistance.

FACTORY SITE

In selecting site for the factory, the following points should be considered carefully.

1. Adequate quantities of the right type of fruits and vegetables should be readily available in the locality, because fruits and vegetables are highly perishable and deteriorate in long distance transport.

2. There should exist proper transport facilities for the movement of raw materials and finished products.

3. The environment should be clean and free from debris, dust etc. as far as possible. The site should be at a considerable distance from other industrial factories spreading soot, smoke, and disagreeable odours, which would affect adversely the quality of the canned product. There should also be facilities for disposal of the cannery wastes.

4. There should be scope for future orderly expansion of the factory.

CANNING IN COMMERCIAL SCALE

FACTORY BUILDING

The factory building may be single storeyed or multi storeyed. Where the plant is a comparatively small one and works for short periods during the year, a single-storeyed building of light construction will do. In the case of larger plants, that have to run almost throughout the year, multi-storeyed construction is desirable as it would facilitate and cheapen the movement of raw as well as finished products. Flooring should be firm and of good cement to withstand the constant use of water and the movement of heavy wheeled trucks. A slope of about one quarter of an inch per foot is necessary for proper drainage. All doors, windows and ventilators should be provided with fine wire-gauze to prevent entrance of flies, wasps and other insects. The roof of the building should be high and well ventilated to provide outlet for vapours and steam. The windows should have large glass panes, and part of the roof should be of ground glass to permit a gentle light inside. There should be provision for efficient artificial lighting as the cannery will have to work at night quite often.

A sufficient number of dressing and toilet rooms should be provided separately for man and women workers in the factory premises. The workers should be taught the importance of personal hygiene. These are important considerations for handling food stuffs for human consumption.

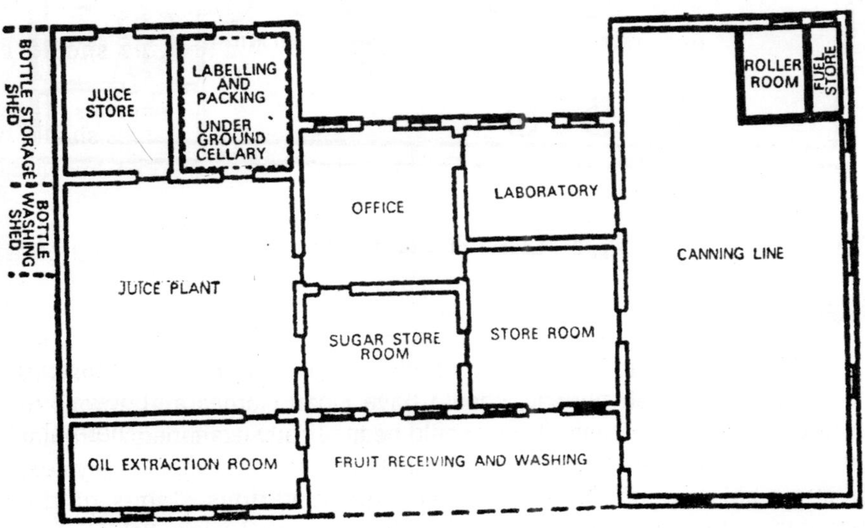

Fig. 1. Plan of a fruit preservation factory

WATER SUPPLY AND DRAINAGE

There should be abundant supply of potable water. Large quantities of water are required for cleaning fruits and vegetables, making syrup and brine, washing floors and machinery, etc. The water system should work at sufficiently high pressure so that supplies can be made at different points in the cannery without a break. The water should not be alkaline or very hard, and should be free from organic matter. Presence of iron and sulphur compounds in it renders it unsuitable for making syrup or brines. Saltish water should be avoided as it would affect the taste of the products. If supplies of the desired quality are not available it would be necessary to install a water softening plant. Further, the boiler feed water requires ion-exchange treatment to bring it to the desired pH and freed from scale forming ions.

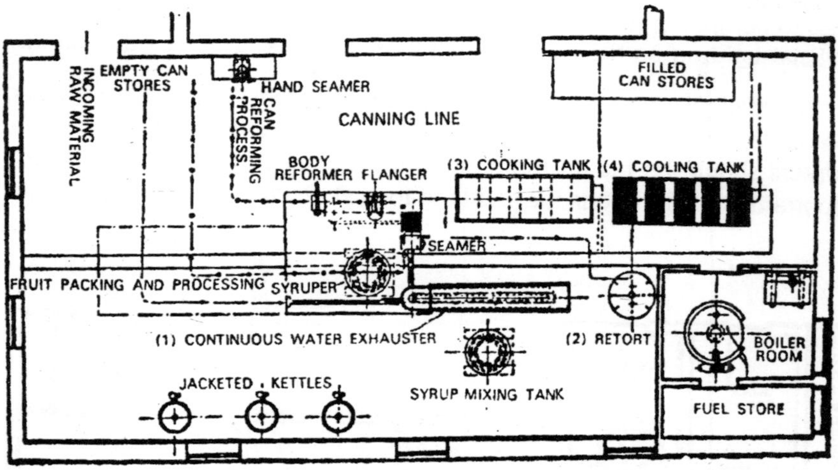

Fig. 2. Layout of a canning line

LABOUR

All the workers in the factory, whether employed on regular basis or recruited during rush periods, should have clean clothes and aprons to ensure hygienic conditions. They should be medically examined at regular intervals as a precaution against infectious diseases. An efficient system of chemical and microbiological control at various stages of the manufacturing process should be maintained to guard against the risk of contamination and food-poisoning. There should be a trained chemist with assistant to supervise the work and to ensure the desired standard of production.

MACHINERY AND EQUIPMENT

While seleeting plant & machinery great care is needed in the selection of machinery and other equipments. Different types of units are in use, but every manufacturer will have to determine his own requirements. However, as a rough guide, layout plant of a small fruit preservation factory with a canning line having output of about 2,000 A 2 1/2 cans per day and a juice plant with a capacity of about 1,000 bottles are given in Figs. 1,2, and 3.

The whole equipment should be arranged in a proper order so that minimum time and effort are needed in handling the products at all stages of manufacture. In short, the raw product should move practically in a straight line till it emerges as finished product, ready for labelling and packing. During the off-seasons, the entire machinery should be overhauled, greased and painted.

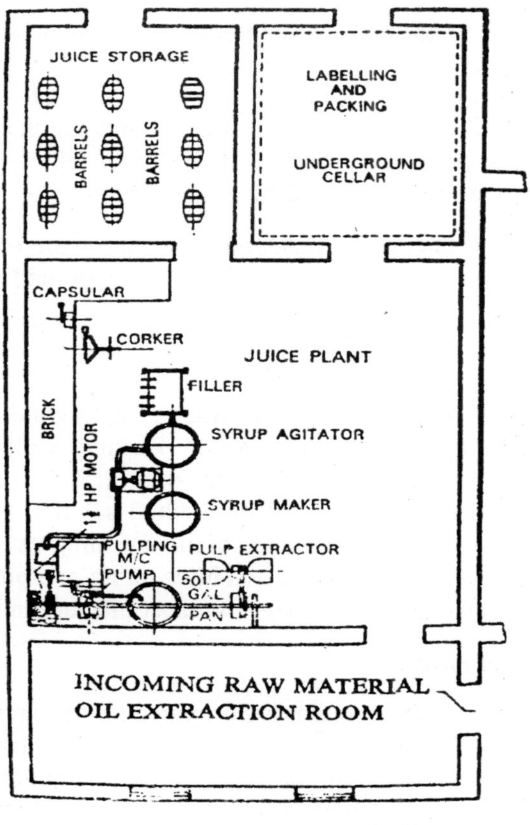

Fig. 3. Layout plan of a juice plant

CANNING PROCESS

For canning, fruits and vegetables should be absolutely fresh. An hour from the field to the can is the accepted ideal. The fruit should be ripe, but firm, and evenly matured. It should be free from all unsightly blemishes, insect damage and malformation. Over-ripe fruit is generally infected with micro organisms and would yield a pack of poor quality. Under ripe fruit will generally shrivel and toughen on canning. The vegetables should be tender and reasonably free from soil, dirt, etc. Tomatoes should however, be firm, fully ripe and of deep red colour.

The fruits and vegetables selected for canning pass through several processes before they are turned out as finished products. The main processes are briefly described here.

Sorting and Grading

After preliminary sorting, the fruits and vegetables are graded. This in necessary to obtain a pack of uniform quality as regards size, colour, etc. It is done by hand or with the help of grading machines. There are several mechanical graders, such as screen graders, roller graders, rope or cable graders, etc. Screen graders, which are fitted with vibrating screens of copper with circular openings, are most commonly employed. A set of about six screens is generally provided to deal with different sizes. Soft and berry fruits are generally graded by hand picking.

Fruits like berries, plums, cherries, and olives are graded whole while peaches, apricots, pears, mangoes, etc., are generally graded after cutting them into halves or slices.

Washing

The graded fruits and vegetables are washed with water in different ways, such as soaking or agitating in water, washing with cold or hot water sprays, etc. A through wash is very essential for good results. Vegetables may preferably be soaked in a dilute solution of potassium permanganate to disinfect them. Agitation of the washing water is effected generally by means of compressed air or a force pump or a propeller-type equipment. Spray washing is, however, the most efficient method.

Peeling, Coring and Pitting

The washed fruits and vegetables are prepared for canning by peeling, coring, blanching, etc. Fruits and vegetables are peeled in a variety of ways : (1) by hand or with knife, (2) by machine, (3) by heat treatment and (4) by lye solution. Cores and pits in fruits are removed by hand or by machine.

Hand Peeling. Many of the fruits and vegetables are peeled and cut by hand with the help of special knives. The peeling knife with curved blade and special guard to regulate the depth of peeling is of special interest as it can be universally employed for many of the fruits and vegetables.

Peeling, Coring and Pitting by Machine

Recently, mechanical peeling, coring and cubing machines for pears, apples and other fruits and vegetables have been introduced. There are also automatic machines for peaches and cherries. Mechanical peelers are also used for root vegetables like carrots, turnips, potatoes, etc.

Peeling by heat. Some fruits and vegetables, particularly certain varieties of peaches and potatoes, are scalded in steam or boiling water to soften and loosen the skin, which is subsequently removed easily by hand. The latest development of this method consists of exposing the fruit or vegetable to a high temperature of 40°C for 10 to 60 seconds, whereby the skin bursts and retracts facilitating its easy removal by means of pressure sprays. For work on large-scale, a furnace fitted with a variable speed conveyor and temperature control device is employed. To get good results, the fruits or vegetables should be of uniform size and maturity. It is claimed that in this method there is practically no loss of flavour, and the product is of uniform colour, free from any blemish. The heat-peeled fruit absorbs sugar more readily than fruit peeled by other methods. Recently, infra-red heating has been successfully employed in Canada and elsewhere for peeling apples, tomatoes, etc.

Lye peeling. Fruits and vegetables like peaches, apricots, quinces, sweet orange and tangering sections, carrots and sweet potatoes are generally peeled by dipping them in boiling caustic soda or lye solution of 1 to 2 per cent strength, for short periods ranging from 30 seconds to 2 minutes (depending on the nature and maturity of the fruit or vegetable). The strength of the boiling lye is adjusted from time to time. The hot lye loosens the skin from the flesh underneath. The peel is then removed easily by hand. Any trace of alkali is removed by washing the fruit or vegetable thoroughly in running cold water, or preferably by dipping it for a few seconds in a very weak solution of hydrochloric or citric acid. This method is quick and reduces wastage as well as cost of peeling.

The lye-dipping equipment varies from a simple open iron pan for the lye solution, with iron baskets or cages for holding the fruits or vegetables, to fully automatic machines. The use of aluminium in the lye dipping equipment should be avoided as it reacts with sodium hydroxide. Recently, stainless steel equipment has been introduced for lye-peeling of fruits such as orange segments, peaches, etc.

Blanching

Treatment of fruits and vegetables with boiling water or steam for short periods, followed by cooling prior to canning, is called "blanching". This loosens the skin, which process is of particular importance in the case of beetroot and tomatoes. It facilitates close filling in the can and drives out the air from the tissues. Further, it helps to clean the fruit or vegetable and to eliminate micro organisms. It also inactivates the enzymes, thus preventing the possibility of discolouration. By removing undesirable acid elements and astringent taste of the peel, it also improves the flavour.

In a small cannery, the fruit or vegetable to be blanched is placed in a wire of perforated basket, which is first dipped in hot water for a short period, ranging from 2 to 5 minutes, and then dipped in cold water. Hard water should not be used for blanching, as it toughens the tissues and destroys the natural texture. In large conneries, blanching is done on belt conveyors passing through boiling water or steam, or in rotary horizontal cylinders.

Can Filling

The cans are washed with water or subjected to a steam jet to remove any adhering dust or foreign matter. In large canneries, the cans are washed with jets of compressed air or water. In India where the canning industry has not developed so much as to warrant the use of costly machines, washing an empty can in open tanks containing hot water is the usual practice. In some factories, however, simple devices have been made to sterilize the cans in steam, before use. Plain cans are used generally, although in the case of coloured fruits like and plums, black grapes, strawberries, etc. it is desirable to employ fruit-lacquered cans. Automatic can filling machines are in use in large canneries in many countries, but choice grades of fruits are generally filled by hand to prevent bruising and also ensuring a properly graded pack. In India, filling by hand using rubber gloves is the common practice.

Syruping or brining. The cans are filled with hot sugar syrup for fruits and with hot brine for vegetables. The object of adding syrup or brine is to improve the taste of the canned product to fill up the interspace between the fruits or vegetables in the can, and to facilitate further processing. The syrup or brine should be added to the can at a temperature of 79°C to 82°C, leaving suitable head space in the can so that when the filled can is closed on the double seaming machine, the space left inside ranges from 0.32 cm to 0.47 cm.

In some of the large canneries in other countries, syruping or brining is done on automatic machines. These machines are available in various designs and capacities. A simple syruper consists of 227 liters capacity tank of stainless steel or aluminium metal fitted with a closed steam coil inside and provided with a delivery valve for filling the cans. In other type, the syrup is drawn into the cans through a horizontal pipe having a row of small holes. The cans travel on a continuous belt in an inclined position below the syrup pipe and get filled, the overflowing excess syrup being pumped back into the syrup tank by a centrifugal pump.

Lidding or Clinching. Formerly, the cans after being filled, were covered loosely with the lid and passed through the exhaust box. In large scale practice this had certain disadvantages such as spilling of the contents, toppling of the lids, etc. Lidding has now been modernized by the clinching process in which the lid is partially seamed to the can by a single first roller action of a double seamer. The lid remains sufficiently loose to permit the escape of dissolved as well as free air from the contents and also the vapour formed during the exhaust process. Counting and coding devices are also generally incorporated in the clinching machine.

Exhausting. Before sealing the cans finally, it is necessary to remove practically all air from the contents. The process by which this is achieved is known as 'exhausting'. By removing air from the containers, risks of corrosion of the tin plate and pinholing during storage, as also of discolouration of the product, are reduced, because oxidation is prevented. To be effective, the temperature of syrup or brine in the can should be at least 79°C to 82°C. Removal of air also helps in better retention of vitamins especially of vitamin C. Since some of the fruits and vegetables have a tendency to expand or shrivel during heating, the exhaust process will be assistance in avoiding over-filling or under filling of the can. For instance, corn and peas expand when boiled in brine and straw berries shrivel when heated in sugar syrup. The other advantages of the exhaust process are prevention of bulging of the can when stored at high altitudes or in hot climates; reduction of chemical reaction between the container and the contents; and prevention of excessive pressure and strain during sterilization. Fruits and vegetables sometimes react slowly with the metal of the can producing hydrogen gas which builds up pressure. If there is no vacuum inside the can to start with, bulging will take place before long and the marketability of the canned product would suffer.

The vacuum in the can, after exhaust, depends on several factors, such as the time and temperature of exhaust the headspace in the can, altitude etc. The higher the temperature of exhaust, the more the volume of the water vapour formed, and consequently the greater the vacuum left inside the can. It is however, preferable to exhaust the cans at a lower temperature for a longer time to secure uniform heating of the contents without softening them into a pulp. The headspace left after sealing the can affects the vacuum; the smaller the headspace the greater the vacuum. Further, the vacuum in a can, which is governed by the difference in pressure outside and inside, is affected by the altitude of the place. A can sealed at a lower altitude will show a lower vacuum inside at a higher altitude and vice versa. Cans with a low vacuum generally become springers at high altitudes, though the contents remain fit for consumption.

Containers are exhausted either by heat treatment or by mechanical means. The heat exhaust method is generally used in the case of cans. The can is passed through a tank of hot water at about 82°C to 87°C or on a moving belt through a covered steam box. In the water exhaust box, the cans are placed in such a manner that the level of water is 1.3cm to 2.5cm below their tops. The time of exhaust varies from 5 to 25 minutes, depending on the nature of the product. At the end of the exhaust, the temperature at the center of the can should be about 79°C. In the case of glass jars, vacuum closing machines are generally used. The jar is placed in a closed chamber in which a high vacuum is maintained.

Sealing. After exhausting, the cans are sealed by special closing machines known as double seamers. These are of various designs and capacities. There are hand-operated as well as semi-automatic and fully automatic seamers. All these machines are now available in India.

PROCESSING

The term processing as used in canning technology, means heating or cooling of canned foods to inactivate bacteria. Absolute sterilization is difficult to attain as many bacteria can form very minute and highly heat-resistant bodies called 'spores', which can be killed only by either very high or very low temperature treatment or prolonged cooking. Such a drastic treatment, however, injures the quality of the canned product. Processing consists in determining just the temperature and the extent of cooking that would suffice to eliminate all possibilities of bacterial growth. Over-cooking should be avoided as it spoils the flavour as well as the appearance of the product. Since fruits and vegetables vary considerably in their composition and texture, it is difficult to lay down any hard and fast rule about the temperature and time required for processing. Generally speaking, however, almost all fruits can be processed satisfactorily at a temperature of 100°C, i.e. in boiling water, as the presence of acid retards the growth of bacteria and their spores. Further, they do not thrive in heavy sugar syrups which are normally used in canning fruits. Vegetables (except the more acidic once like tomato and rhubarb) which are non-acidic in nature, however, require to be processed at higher temperatures of about 115°C to 121°C. The center of the can should reach these high temperatures. The processing time in their case is, therefore, of great importance. The temperature and time center of the can should be maintained for a sufficiently long period to destroy the spores of the more resistant bacteria. The temperature and time of processing, therefore, vary with the size of the can the larger the can, the greater the processing time and vice versa.

Heat Penetration in Cans

Before a process for any particular product can be adopted, it is necessary to study the rate of heat penetration in the. This is done by means of a thermocouple fixed to the center of the can. In the U.S.A. extensive studies have been carried out with special reference to the size and kind of the containers, the nature of the filler, i.e. sugar syrup or brine and the consistency of the product. Based on these studies, processing times of many kinds of non-acid vegetables have been worked out by the National Canners Association, Washington. Ball, Olsen and Stevens also have done useful work in determining the time for which a given size of a can of a particular food should be processed at a temperature at which all the heat resistant spores are destroyed. Similar work has been done in England also at the Fruit and Vegetable Preservation Research Station at Campden. The processing time and temperature for any canned product can be worked out, making use of heat penetration data, either by the simpler integrated graphic method or by the more sophisticated mathematical procedure based on Thermal Death Time of a typical spoilage organism practically similar to Clostridium botulinum.

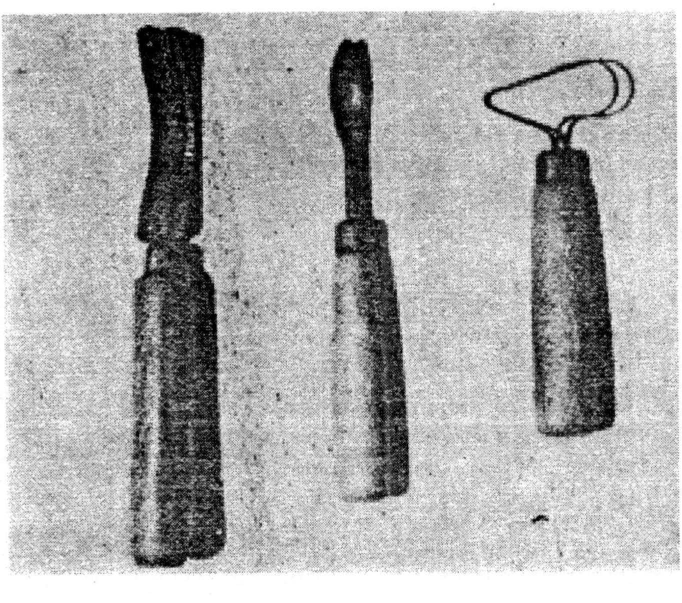

Fig. 4. Peeling, pitting and coring knives

Cruess, Fong and Liu, who investigated the role of acidity in vegetable canning, have shown that brines, acidified with a small amount of acetic or citric acid, greatly reduced the resistance of the heat resisting spores of bacteria, and that in acidified brines, the time and temperature required to sterilize vegetables could, therefore, be reduced considerably. This process, however, is not to be recommended for home-canning of vegetables as there is always an element of uncertainty in the strict application of the conditions prescribed. Pressure processing is the safest course.

Methods of Processing

Fruits and acid vegetables. There are generally three types of cookers used for canning of fruits. They are the open type cookers, continuous non agitating cookers and continuous agitating cookers.

1. *Open cookers.* These cookers are very simple in construction and consist essentially of wooden tubs or galvanized iron tanks of any desired capacity. The sealed cans are placed in crates of galvanized iron and immersed in jets of steam through perforated pipes placed underneath the false bottom of the tank. An improved type of this cooker is a galvanized iron tank with a cover, false bottom of perforated galvanized plate, and perforated steam pipe for jets of steam.

2. *Continuous non-agitating cookers.* In these cookers, the cans travel in boiling water in crates carried by over head conveyors in a single file, on a continuous moving belt. The cookers are fitted with temperature controlling and recording devices also.

3. *Continuous agitating cookers.* These cookers are of various designs and are generally used in big production units. The sealed cans move as in the non-agitating cookers, but are at the same time rotated by special mechanical devices to agitate the contents of the cans. By this technique, the processing time is reduced considerably. These cookers may either be filled three-fourths with water which is kept hot by steam or processing may be carried out in steam itself. They are fitted with automatic temperature control devices so that they can easily be adopted for water. These cookers have an advantage over other types in that they accelerate the output of the factory to a considerable extent. They are in general use in large conneries in the United Kingdom, the U.S.A. and some other countries.

Non-acid vegetables. Due to lack of acid, hard texture, and proximity to soil which infect them with spore bearing organisms, vegetables require much severer sterilization than fruits do. They require to be processed at temperatures much above 100 C, under steam pressure in closed retorts. The retorts vary in shape and size, with capacities ranging from 50 cans to nearly 2,000 to 3,000 cans. They are generally of the batch type. The more modern ones, which are known as automatic pressure cookers, operate continuously. The retorts are either vertical or horizontal. In the U.K. vertical retorts are generally used, but in the U.S.A. horizontal retorts predominate, some of them being as long as 18 meters, and in these trucks are wheeled out at one end as the fresh batch enters through the other end. To the large commercial retorts automatic stream and temperature controlling and timing devices with recording equipment are fitted to avoid any human slip. Bitting has described various types of open cookers and pressure retorts generally used in the U.S.A.

In India, small vertical stationary retorts are generally used (frontispiece). They are made of cast iron cylinders of varying sizes, and are fitted with a lid which can be bolted steam-tight. Necessary steam and water feeds, air vent, drain cock, safety valve, pressure gauge and thermometer are fitted. The sequence of operating these retorts is as follows: The sealed cans are arranged in crates, which are then placed inside the retorts. The lid is placed in position and tightened. The vent and drain cocks are opened and steam let in Unit it blows freely through the vent hole there by removing all entrapped air. The vent and the drain are then partially closed till the temperature reaches 100°C. The exits are then closed, leaving only a small opening for a fine jet of steam to escape, and the steam pressure and temperature allowed to rise to the desired extent. During the cooking period, the thermometer and pressure gauge records should show close agreement. For instance, if the cooking temperature is 115°C the steam pressure should be a little above 0.7kg/sq. cm (Table 1). If at this temperature, the pressure is higher than 0.7kg/sqcm, the presence. of entrapped air is indicated. On the completion of the cooking period, steam is cut off and the release valve at the top opened gradually to let off steam, avoiding any sudden release as it is likely to burst the cans inside. When the pressure becomes normal, the retort is opened and the cans are removed for subsequent cooling to prevent any overheating of them.

TABLE 1. RELATION OF STEAM PRESSURE TO TEMPERATURE OF CANNING RETORTS (CRUESS, 1948)

Pressure		Temperature	
Pounds per sq. inch	Kilograms per sq. cm	F°	C°
1	0.07	215.2	101
2	0.14	218.3	103
3	0.21	221.3	105
4	0.28	224.2	106
5	0.35	228.9	107
6	0.42	229.5	109
7	0.49	231.9	110
8	0.56	233.3	111
9	0.63	236.6	113
10	0.70	238.8	114
11	0.77	241.0	116
12	0.84	243.0	117
13	0.91	245.3	118
14	0.98	247.3	119
15	1.05	249.1	120

Effect of Altitude on Processing Time

The boiling point of water decreases with increase in altitude. The processing time for different kinds of fruits and vegetables, as standardized at places about 152 metres above sea level, has to be relatively increased with further increase in the alttitude. As a rule, for every increase of 152 metres in altitude, the boiling point of water decreases by about 1°C and the normal processing time has to be increased by about two minutes. Table 2 gives the additional time required at different altitudes, over and above the normal period processing at sea level for canned fruits and vegetables.

Thus, an A 2½ size can of pears which requires processing for 30 minutes at sea level, will require a total processing time of 30+25=55 minutes at an altitude of about 1830 metres above sea level.

Effect of Altitude on Processing Pressure and Temperature

As the altitude above sea level increases, the pressure required to maintain the specified processing temperature, say 115°C or 121°C will also increase, Since process time schedules are based on the exposure of the canned food to specified temperature in steam, it may be necessary to maintain higher gauge pressure if the processing is done at altitude substantially greater than 305 metres above the sea level. Table 3 gives details of increased gauge pressure necessary to attain a specified temperature at various altitudes.

TABLE 2. EFFECT OF ALTITUDE ON BOILING POINT OF WATER AND STERILIZATION TEMPERATURE OF CANNED FRUITS AND VEGETABLES

Elevation : above sea level		Boiling point of water in		Extra time in minutes for boiling water	Extra pressure added to pressure given	
ft	metres	°F	°C		Pound per sq inch	Kg per sq cm
500	152	211	99	2	1	0.07
1,000	305	210	98	4	1	0.07
2,000	610	208	97	8	1	0.07
3,000	915	206	96	12	2	0.14
4,000	1220	204	95	16	2	0.14
5,000	1525	202	94	20	3	0.21
6,000	1830	201	93	25	3	0.21
7,000	2135	199	92	30	4	0.28

Effect of Acidity on Sterilization

Acids in solution owe their acidic properties to the hydrogenion concentration of which is a measure of the intensity or potential of acidity rather than of its quantum. It is generally expressed in terms of what is known as the pH value. The pH value of a solution is equal to the logarithm of the number of litres of solution which contains 1 gram of hydrogen ion. The pH value of water, which is neutral, is 7 on this scale. The pH values rising above 7.0 indicate increasing acidity. The more acidic the substance, the lower is its pH value. The acid property or sourness of fruits is due to the presence of hydrogen ions.

The pH value has a great influence upon the destruction of micro organisms. The lower the pH the greater is the ease with which a product can be processed or sterilized. According to Cameron and Esty, foods can be classified as follows:

TABLE 3. GAUGE PRESSURE CORRESPONDING TO SPECIFIED PROCESS TEMPERATURE AT VARIOUS ALTITUDES

Temperature		Sea level	Metres above sea level					
°F	°C	lb./sq. inch (kg/sq. cm)	305 (1000)	610 (2000)	915 (3000)	1220 (4000)	1525 (5000)	1830 (6000)
212	100	0.0 (0.0)	0.5 (0.94)	1.0 (0.07)	1.5 (0.11)	2.0 (0.14)	2.4 (0.17)	2.9 (0.20)
220	104	2.5 (0.18)	3.0 (0.21)	3.4 (0.24)	3.9 (0.27)	4.4 (0.30)	4.9 (0.34)	5.3 (0.37)
230	110	6.1 (0.43)	6.6 (0.46)	7.1 (0.49)	7.6 (0.53)	8.0 (0.56)	8.5 (0.60)	9.0 (0.63)
240	115	10.3 (0.72)	10.8 (0.76)	11.3 (0.79)	11.7 (0.82)	12.2 (0.85)	12.7 (0.89)	13.1 (0.92)
250	121	15.1 (1.06)	15.6 (1.09)	16.6 (1.13)	17.1 (1.16)	17.5 (1.20)	17.5 (1.23)	18.0 (1.26)

(Fig in brackets represent pressure in kg/cm^2 against pressures in lb./sq. inch and feet).

1. *Low acid pH 5.0 and higher.* This class includes peas, beans, corn, asparagus, etc. These are subject to spoilage by all the three groups of thermophilic and mesophilic putrefactive anaerobes, including Clostridium botulinum.

2. *Medium acid pH* 5.0–4.5. Meat and vegetable mixtures, spaghetti, soups and sauces, whose ingredients produce a partially acid product, come under this category. These also are subject to spoilage by the same organisms as in group 1. The thermophilic anaerobes (not producing hydrogen sulphide), which may cause flat, sours, of increasing importance in this group.

3. *Acid pH* 4.5–3.7. In this group are included tomatoes, pears, figs, pineapple, nectarines and other fruits subject spoilage by non-sporing aciduric types, butyric anaerobes of the Clostridium pasteurianum and Winogradskyi types and thermophilic anaerobes.

4. *Highly acid-pH* 3.7 and below. This group includes sauer kraut, pickles, berries, citrus juices, grape fruit and rhubarb.

To be more precise, bacterial spores are much more easily destroyed in fruits at pH 3.0 than in vegetables at pH 5.0 to 6.0. These spores do not germinate and grow at pH values much below 4.5. They do not, there fore, do any harm even if they are not destroyed in canned fruits. Thus, pH 4.5 is regarded as a dividing line between the acid and the non acid foods. A canned product, having pH value of less than 4.5 can be processed in boiling water at 100°C, but a product with a pH value above 4.5 requires processing under pressure of 0.70 to 1.05 kg/cm^2 (10-15 lb. per sq. inch).

Effect of Processing on Strain in Can

When a can is closed, the pressure inside it is equal to that of the atmosphere, irrespective of the temperature of closing. Any increase in the temperature after the closing of the can developer pressure inside the can. This internal pressure depends upon several factors of which the following are important :

1. Pressure due to water vapour inside the can.
2. Pressure due to expansion of any enclosed air.
3. Pressure due to the expansion of the contents of the can.
4. Pressure due to liberation and expansion of gases inside the vegetable.
5. The expansion of the can by the doming of the ends and the compensating effect of the expansible rings on the lid.

Among these, water vapour produces the greater effect. Water vapour has a pressure of 0.2 kg per square centimeters at 60°C, 1.75 kg/sq. cm at 115°C. This would indicate that very high presdirsures develop at higher temperatures.

The pressure inside the can during processing can be regulated by taking into consideration the following points.

1. Internal pressure in the can is equal to the vapour pressure at the processing temperature minus the vapour pressure at the closing temperature.

2. The nearer the closing temperature to the processing temperature, the less the internal pressure during processing.

3. Small cans withstand greater internal pressure than large cans.

4. To avoid buckling, cans, larger than No. A 2½ should be cooled under pressure.

5. To get a good vacuum, the closing temperature of the can should not be less than 71°C.

Cans closed at 71°C and processed at 115°C show a maximum pressure above that of the atmosphere, i.e. 1.40/kg/sq. cm to 1.47/kg/sq. cm. These pressures are close to the theoretical value for water vapour alone.

Cooling

After processing, the cans are cooled rapidly to stop the cooking process and to prevent stack-burning, especially in cans at the center of large stacks where they may remain hot for several hours, if not for several days. Prolonged heating results in an inferior and uneven pack. In extreme cases, peaches and pears become dark in colour, tomatoes turn brownish and become bitter in taste, while peas become mashy with a cooked taste. In the case of many of the vegetables, prolonged heating due to improper cooling may result in the development of 'flat sour' by the heat resistant spore forming bacteria, which survive ordinary commercial processing. In this case the cans do not show any bulging, but the contents will be sour.

Cooling is done by (1) immersing or passing the hot cans in tanks containing cold water (2) by spraying with jets of cold water (3) by turning in cold water into the pressure cooker in the case of canned vegetables or (4) by exposing the cans to air in small lots when water supply is scarce. The cooling equipments, varies with the method as well as the output Various types of equipments, from simple open galvanized iron tanks to the complicated automatic coolers, are available. A simple cooling tank useful in this country is an ordinary galvanized iron tank fitted with water connections for constant over flow of water. The cans are placed in crates for cooling in this tank, where the circulating water is fairly cold. In very hot places, it may even be necessary to cool the water by adding ice. Simple cement cisterns, with overhead travelling crane for moving crates of cans from the retorts to the cooling tank, have been found highly satisfactory in medium size canning factories.

Testing for Defects

In a factory, batches of finished cans should be finally tested for leak or imperfect seals. A simples way of doing this is to tap the top of the can with a short steel rod. A clear ringing sound indicates a perfect seal, while a dull and hollow sound shows a leaky or imperfectly sealed can. This method is very rapid, and an experienced workman seldom fails to detect a defective seal.

The other method commonly used for testing the vacuum inside the cans is by means of a simple vacuum gauge fitted with a sharp point, which is protected with a thick rubber gasket. The sharp point is pierced into the lid of the can, and a short twist given, when the rubber gasket presses against the puncture made and gives an air tight seal. The vacuum in the can is directly read on the dial of the gauge. Faulty cans do not show any vacuum. The vacuum can also be determined with a vacuum tester without puncturing the can and losing the contents of the can. This is a non destructive type of testing vacuum in the can. It is based on the measurement of the concavity of the lid of the can, which is proportional to the degree of vacuum inside the can. A battery operated electrical circuit with a ringing bell facilitates the measurement of concavity and hence the vacuum inside. A Flip Tester can also be employed to determine the vacuum in the can by placing the can in a glass chamber and evacuating it. The can lid will give a Flip sound when the vacuum outside becomes slightly more than that inside the can. This tester can be used for non destructive testing of canned products for internal vacuum. It can be operated with ease either on the mains or with an ordinary dry cell. It is portable and handly.

Labelling, Storing and Packing

The outer surface of the cans should be perfectly dry as even small traces of moisture are likely to induce rusting. When canning is done near the sea or in damp and moist regions, it is advisable to lacquer the can on the outside to prevent rusting during storage. The cans are then labelled by hand or by machine, and packed in strong wooden cases or corrugated cardboard cartons, in standard packings. Till they are diespatched, they should be stored in a cool and dry place. In a hot country like India, where the atmospheric temperatures are high during summer months in a year, basement stores are useful, especially during summer months, as the temperature in these is lower by about 6 to 8°C, compared to the outside temperatures. Storage of cans at high temperature should be avoided, as it shortens the shelf life of the product, and often leads to the formation of hydrogen swells and perforations during extended storage.

3

Packing Containers

Tin and glass containers have so far been successfully employed for packing foods. A great deal of development has since taken place in the manufacture of both types of the containers. Jars and bottles of clear white glass that can withstand heating and can give perfectly air tight seal, are now available in a wide variety of designs and capacities. In recent years, plastic containers and heat sealable pouches are being tried in various research and development laboratories as possible substitutes for the familiar tin and glass containers. The results appear to be promising to some extent.

The open top or sanitary tin can is made of sheet metal with a thin coating of tin.

Cans made from black steel plate have been successfully employed for packing several processed foods, especially non acid foods. This development like several others, had its origin in the Second World War, when there was shortage of tin. The black plate cans are coated on both sides with a special type of lacquer.

In order to overcome difficulties due to world shortage of tin, various attempts have been made in recent years either to reduce the amount of the coating or substitute it with other metals like chromium, silver, etc. Stamped cans made of aluminium also are being considered. The electrolytic tin plate with the tin coating as low as 0.113 kg per base box has been employed in the U.S.A. for certain non critical packs. Electrolytic plate with 0.227 to 0.340 kg coating, which is more uniform than ordinary hot dip coating has, however, been extensively employed for a large number of products where storage condition such as length of storage or climatic factors are not very critical.

To reduce the amount of tin in plating, differentially coated electrolytic plate with a higher coating on the inside of the can and with a much thinner coating on the external surface of the can has also been successfully employed and extensive storage studies conducted under severe Mexican conditions. Where the tin coating is as low as 0.113 kg. comparative studies carried out by in connection with the canning of drinking water, have indicated the possibility of using the stamped aluminium can for some other non acid products also.

The chromium plated can, developed in Japan and reported to be suitable for packing a variety of fruits, vegetables, and meats, during comparatively short periods of storage, requires further development before it can be a substitute for a familiar tin can.

In India, most of the tin plates employed for the fabrication of cans for the canning industry are imported from abroad. Since canning industry is an industry of strategic importance, attempts have been made recently to develop a suitable type of hot dipped as well as electrolytic tin plate, utilizing the base plate being manufactured in the large steel mills in the country. Although the base plate is to be made from phosphorus-rich ore, which is a disadvantage for making tin plate of high quality, with the least amount of tendency of corrosion in the can, extensive trials carried out at the C.F.T.R.I. Mysore, by the expert and his colleagues have shown that when proper selection is made on the basis of ladle analysis of the molten steel, good quality tin plate could be produced within the country. The Rourkela plate is one such and has proved useful to the canning industry. Further work would certainly lead to great improvement in the quality of the plate.

In addition to the tin and glass containers, other new type of containers have also been introduced. One of these is the plywood container which has been recently used successfully for packing dairy products like butter, sweetened milk, milk powder and a variety of other products like lemon cheese, minced meat, confectionery etc. These containers might also be useful for packing jams, jellies and marmalades. Quite recently, an Indian patent has been granted to the Council of Scientific and Industrial Research, for containers made from modified shellac laminated plastic. Although these containers have been found suitable for packing fruit and vegetable products in dried or semi dried conditions, it is too early to predict whether they can replace the tin containers entirely for packing all kinds of products. Aluminium and silver lined containers entirely foı packing all kinds of products. Aluminium and silver lined containers have also been used for packing certain kinds of foods. The tin container, however, still continues to be the most important in the field.

In recent years, a metal box company in this country has developed a new string opening composite container, which is easily opened by sharply pulling a rip cord fixed to the body of the containers. This type of container is said to be the ideal for packing only such products as baby foods and invalid foods, custard powders, confectionery, biscuits etc.

TIN AND GLASS CONTAINERS

Both tin and glass containers are employed in the canning industry, although the tin containers are more common in use on account of the following reasons. These are fabricated readily and are strong enough to withstand processing, they are light in weight, easy to handle, and fairly cheap, they can be handled on high speed machines.

Glass containers are fragile and require extra care in handling and during processing. They, however, possess two definite advantages over tin cans; the contents being visible can be easily displayed; and the containers can be used over and over again. Further, since glass of high quality does not contaminate the contents, glass containers are preferred for packing baby foods.

Tin Containers

Tin cans are made of thin steel plate of low carbon carbon content, lightly coated on either side with tin metal to a thickness of about 0.00025 cm. The composition of the steel used is generally us follows.

Elements	Per cent
Carbon	0.040-0.120
Sulphur	0.015-0.050
Phosphorus	0.015-0.060
Copper	0.020-0.200
Manganese	0.200-0.600
Silica	Trace-0.080

Since corrosion behaviour, strength and durability of the tin plate depend in some measure on the chemical composition of the steel base, the base plate is made according to the specific use for which it is intended. In the U.S.A. the following designations have been adopted.

Type L	Low metalloid steel for critical and highly corrosive packs
Type MR.	Similar in metalloid content to Type L, but less restricted in residuals
Type MC	Rephosphorised or Bessemer steel to give higher temper (all the above are cold-reduced)
Type M	Similar to MC, but hot rolled

Tin Plates

Tin plates are of several grades. The usual weight of tin coating is 0.681 kg of tin per base box, which gives a thickness of tin coating of 0.000225 cm. However, variation in weight from 0.454 to 2.268 kg of tin per base box is common. One base box is equivalent to 112 sheets, each 50.0 cm x 35.0 cm or 19.6 square metres of tin plate weighing 48.8 kg net. These are called I.C. plates. Plates thinner than I.C. are called lights, and those thicker than I.C. crosses.

There are several types of tin plates, such as coke, best coke and charcoal. Cokes are ordinary coated plates. Best cokes are graded between cokes and charcoals. The charcoals are coated with a heavier layer of tin than common charcoal plates.

Lacquering

It is difficult to coat steel plate uniformly with tin during the process of manufacture. Small microscopic spaces are always left uncoated, although the coating may appear perfect to the eye. The contents of the can may react with these exposed parts and cause discolouration of the product or corrosion of the tin-plate. When corrosion is severe, the steel is attacked and black stains of iron sulphide are produced. It is necessary, therefore, to coat the inside of the can with some material like lacquer. which would prevent discolouration, but would not impart its own flavour or injure the wholesomeness of the contents. This is achieved by lacquering the tin plate.

There are two types of lacquers : (a) acid resistant, and (b) sulphur resistant.

The acid resistant lacquer is ordinary gold coloured enamel, and the cans when treated with it, are called R-enamel cans. These cans are used for packing fruits of the acid group with soluble colouring matter. Acid fruits are of two kinds : (a) those in which the colouring matter is insoluble in water, and (b) those in which it is water soluble. In the first group are included fruits like peach, pineapple, apricot, grape fruit etc. and in the second, fruits like raspberry, strawberry, red plum and coloured grapes. Fruits of group (a) are packed in plain cans, and those of group (b) in lacquered cans.

The sulphur resistant lacquer also is of a golden colour, and the cans coated with it, are called C enamel cans or S.R. cans. These cans are used for non acid products like peas, corn, lima beans, red kidney beans, etc. to present discolouration of the contents and the stairing of the inside of the container. They are meant for non acid foods only and should not be used for any highly acid products as acid eats into the lacquer.

Type	Weight kg (lb.)	Rounded off to first decimal place (kg)
IXL	55.338 (122)	55.3
IX	61.668 (136)	61.7
IXX	68.039 (150)	68.0
IXXX	70.760 (156)	70.8
IXXX	89.832 (196)	89.8

Manufacture of Cans

Tin plate is cut into proper size with a trimming and slitting machine. The pieces provide body blanks. After notching and slitting, the flat canbody is passed through an edging machine where hooks are formed. It is then bent into a cylindrical shape, and the side seam soldered. Flanging is done next. Can ends are stamped out from the plates, and the edges curled. A rubber gasket is mounted on the curled edge of the can end. The lining is generally a water emulsion of rubber or rubber composition in benzene or toluene. Sometimes paper gaskets and plastic gums are also used.

One end of the can is fixed to the flanged can body by means of a double seaming machine. The action of the double seamer is shown in Fig.8 Sometimes, to cut down transport costs, can bodies are flattened and supplied to the cannery along with the can-ends. These together can be made into cans readily at the factory by using a set of machines consisting of a can body reformer, flanger, and double seamer. The finished cans should be stored upside down in a clean dry place.

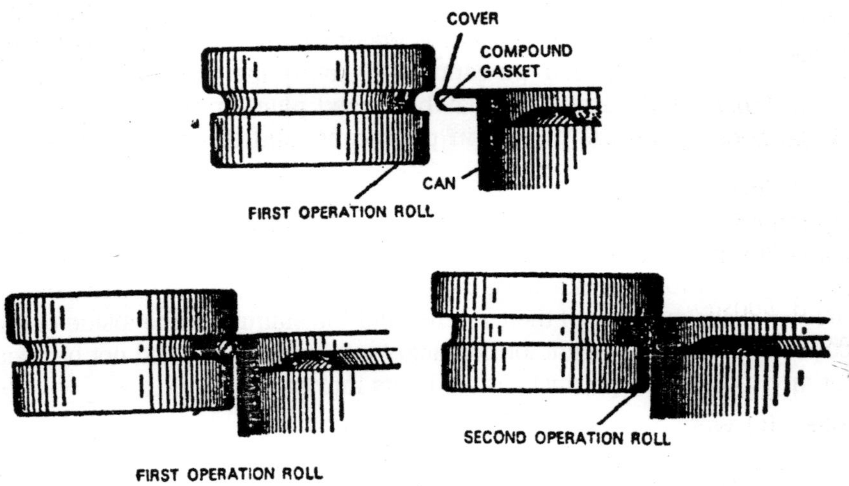

Fig. 8. Roller action of a double seamer

Testing of Cans

The finished cans are tested for leaks with a vacuum or air pressure tester. When working on a small scale, hand testing equipment will suffice.

Several types of mechanical defects may be found in cans. These are given briefly below.

Mechanical Defects

1. *Long seam with normal countersink.* It is due to (i) insufficient first operation, and (ii) short cover hook.

2. *Long second seam.* It may be due to (i) insufficient first operation allowing second operation roller to flatten the seam too much; (ii) second operation roller being too tight and thus flattening the seam too much; (iii) worn out chuck; (iv) worn out second operation roller; (v) excessive base pressure; (vi) grease or dirt on the base plate causing the can to slip during seaming process; (vii) uneven spread of the lining compound in the lid; (viii) chuck being off centre dur to worn machine bearings.

3. *Narrow rounded seam.* It may be due to (i) excessive first operation resulting in a strong curl being formed which resists subsequent pressure of the second operation roller; (ii) not enough second operation to press seam down full length; (iii) countersink too deep.

4. *Lined seam.* It may be due to worn or scoured second operation roller.

5. *Cut seam.* It may be due to (i) too much base pressure; (ii) rollers too high in relation to chuck; (iii) too tight second operation roller ; (iv) excessive solder on the side seam; (v) slipping of can or spinning on chuck.

6. *Fractured or polished seam.* It may be due to (i) Slopping of rollers (ii) flat spots on rollers (iii) too tighy rollers; and (iv) lack of lubrications.

7. *Partial false seam or knockdown.* It may be due to (i) damaged cans; (ii) dented and damaged lids; (iii) bent down flange on the can; (iv) can not centering on chuck.

8. *Loose first seam.* It may be due to (i) loose first operation roller; (ii) worn first operation roller.

9. *Loose second seam.* It may be due to (i) loose second operation roller; (ii) worn second operation roller.

10. *Uneven seam.* It may be due to (i) worn roller, roller pins of other parts of the machinery, (ii) excessive first and second operation.

11. *Wrinkled first seam.* It may be due to (i) loose first operation roller; (ii) worn first operation roller.

12. *Wrinkled second seam.* It may be due to (i) loose second operation roller; (ii) worn second operation roller.

13. *Short an hook.* It may be due to (i) insufficient base pressure; (ii) too tight first operation roller; (iii) too loose second operation roller; (iv) excessive clearance between roller and chuck.

14. *Long can hook.* It may be due to excessive base pressure. It always results in a corresponding decrease in cover hook. spurs may be formed.

15. Short cover hook. It may be due to (i) insufficient first operation not turning sufficient cover took into the seam; (ii) insufficient second operation which will not flatten the cover hook to its full length; (iii) short covers; (iv) body hook normal, spurs may occur.

16. *Long cover hook.* It may be due to (i) excessive first operation; (ii) shallow countersink; (iii) insufficient base pressure. There may be cut overs at top inside of seam.

17. *Wrinkled cover hook.* It may be due to insufficient second operation. Seam may be loose and hooks curved.

18. *Deep countersink.* It may be due to (i) short cover hooks; (ii) chuck being too low for the rollers; (iii) excessive base pressure; (iv) excessive clearance between rollers and chuck; (v) chuck flange too thick; (vi) vertical play in seaming head allowing rollers to rise up from the chuck; (vii) base plate setting not parallel with the chuck; (viii) base plate worn more on one side than on the other thus causing uneven countersink (deep on one side).

19. *Shallow countersink.* It may be due to (i) chuck being too high for rollers, which would cause the rollers to wear away the face of the chuck making it thinner, thus affecting the countersink; (ii) chuck flange being worn.

20. *Lips or spurs.* These frequently occur at overlap. Cover hook is deficient at the side of the spur. It may be due to (i) insufficient first operation; (ii) excessive second operation; (iii) too much base pressure; (iv) worn first operation roller; (v) too much solder at the overlap; (vi) tough plate.

21. *Skidding and spinners.* Sometimes a portion of the seam becomes unduly wide and very loose. This may be due to (i) worn chuck; (ii) insufficient base pressure; (ii) greasy base plate or chuck; (iv) excessive first and second operations; (v) worn serration on base plate.

22. *Cut overs.* Sharp edges or cuts on the top inside edges of the seam are known as cut overs. They are found especially at the overlap. They may be due to (i) worn chuck; (ii) worn rollers; (iii) excessive first operation roller; (iv) excessive base pressure; (v) side seam having too much solder; (vi) spinning of the can due to slip between cover and the chuck; (vii) maladjustment of second operation roller, especially due to the chuck being too low in relation to rollers. when plate is cut through completely with the result that leak occurs.

23. *Bell mouthed or oval cans.* They may be due to excessive base pressure.

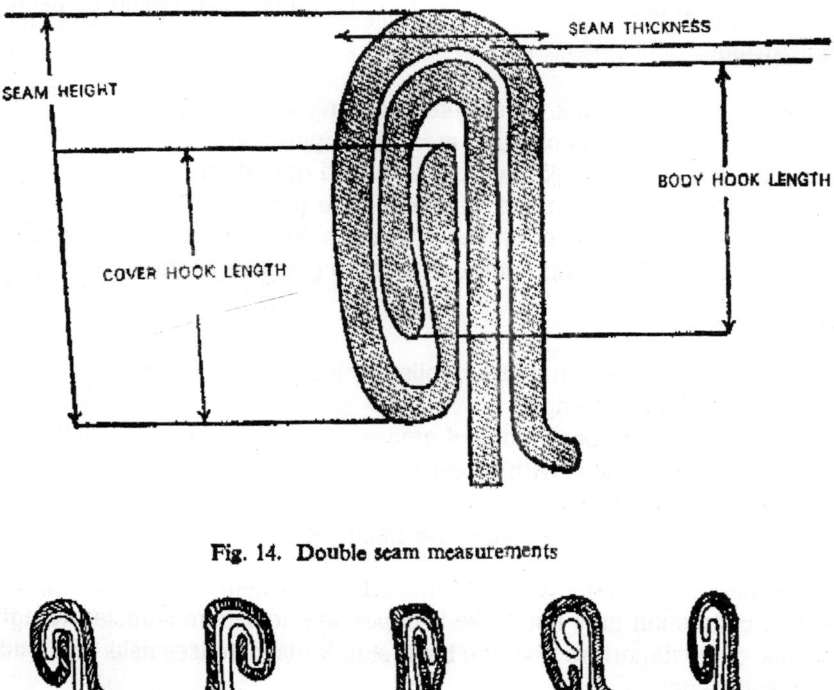

Fig. 14. Double seam measurements

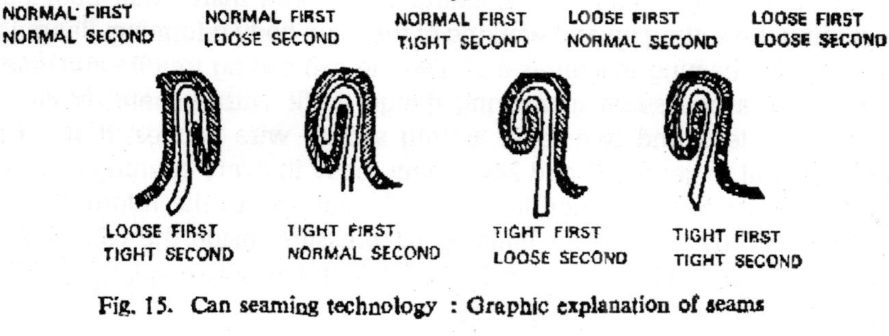

Fig. 15. Can seaming technology : Graphic explanation of seams

24. *Over rolling*. In the case of excessive roller pressure, whether in first operation or second operation or both, there is an over loading of the machine causing excessive wear on bushes, chucks, rollers and all working parts. The life of the spindle bearing is shortened by as much as 50 per cent resulting in bad seaming, frequent replacements, and necessitating complete overhaul of the machine after a much shorter production life than normal.

Since perfect seaming of the can is importance in any cannery, It is essential that the rollers in the seamer should be in correct order. If the setting is not correct, a thorough check up must be carried out to determine the correction needed (Figs 14 and 15). The hints given would be useful.

To correct

1. Short can hook, give more base pressure.
2. Short cover hook, give more first operation.
3. Wrinkle in hook, give more second operation.
4. Contersink too deep, give less base pressure.
5. Seam too wide or broken down at point meeting body side seam, give less second operation or base pressure as the case may be.

Don'ts

1. Don't use worn chucks, rolls or pins
2. Don't roll too tight
3. Don't use poor grades of grease
4. Don't proceed with production if seam is doubtful
5. Don't neglect to keep parts clean
6. Don't attempt to seam over filled cans

Experience has shown that although minor neglect in observing the above instruction may not make it impossible to secure sufficiently tight seams, every departure from the basic standards increases risks and leads to insufficiency.

A metal box company in Kolkatta has issued instruction booklets regarding the setting up and working of their can body reforming, flanging and double seaming machines and also the can coding treadle machine. They have a can seam measuring gauge outfit with a metal scale, a magnifying lens and two roller setting setting wire gauges. It will be highly useful to get these and keep them ready in every canning factory. The can seam testing gauge for detecting any leak in the reformed can using an ordinary pump for building up pressure inside the can, is the most essential equipments, which should be frequently employed while reforming cans from flattened bodies.

TABLE 4. WEIGHT OF TIN PLATE REQUIRED FOR FABRICATION OF 1,000 CANS

Size of can	Weight of tin plate
A 2 1/2 (401x411)	0.1572 ton
A 2 (307x408)	0.1172
0.45 kg (1 lb.) Butter (401x300)	0.1249
0.34 kg (12 oz.) Butter (401x207)	0.1162
0.45 kg (16 oz.) Milk 301x406	0.0946
0.45 kg (14 lb.) Jam (301x309)	0.0863
0.31 kg (11 oz.) Jam (301x303.5)	0.0798
0.23 kg (8 oz.) Flat (301x206)	0.0724
509x709	0.3154
700x900	0.5139

As jellies are made from aqueous extracts, ordinarily it is not necessary to peel the fruit. For example, fruits like guavas and apples do not require peeling. Pluge from berries need not be removed. In the case of oranges and lemons, it is necessary to remove the outer yellow portion of the peel, i.e. the flavedo, to get jellies free from excessive bitterness. Fruits are cut into thin slices so that the and pectin in them can be extracted easily.

TABLE 5. STANDARD SIZES OF OPEN TOP (PACKED) CANS AVAILABLE IN FLATTENED FORM

Trade name	A 1	1-lb Jam	AI-T	A 2	1-lb Butter	2-lb Jam	A 2 1/2	7-lb Jam	A 10
1. Size									
in inches	2.11/16×4	3.1/16×3 9/16	3.1/16×4 11/16	3.7/16×4 8/16	4.1/16×2 12/16	4.1/ 6×4	4.1/16×4 11/16	6.3/16×5 13/16	6.3/16×7
in millimetres	68 × 102	78 × 90	78 × 119	87 × 114	103 × 70	103 × 102	103 × 119	157 × 148	157 × 178
2. Trade-size	211 × 400	301 × 309	301 × 411	307 × 408	401 × 212	401 × 400	401 × 411	603 × 513	603 × 700
3. Approx. freight measurement factor	.1371	.1446	.1701	.1994	.1632	.2172	.2384	.5311	.7125
4. Capacity									
in fluid oz	11.13	12.53	16.87	20.39	16.56	25.41	29.89	89.59	108.12
in cubic cm	316	356	479	579	470	721	848	2543	3069
5. Approx. No. of ends per carton	270	350	355	180	337	225	200	65	65
6. Approx. No. of ends per case	6000	4800	4800	3600	2800	2800	2800	1600	1600
7. Approx. gross wt. per 1000 bodies									
in lb	105	109	140	162	139	188	213	450	565
in kg	48	50	64	74	63	85	97	204	256

TABLE 5 (*Contd.*)

Trade name	A 1	1-lb Jam	A1-T	A 2	1-lb Butter	2-lb Jam	A 21/2	7-lb Jam	A 10
8. Approx. net wt. per 1000 bodies									
in lb	97	100	131	147	127	170	193	417	500
in kg	44	45	60	67	58	77	83	189	227
9. Approx. gross wt. per 2000 ends									
in lb	51	63	63	90	120	120	120	280	280
in kg	23	29	29	41	55	55	55	127	127
10. Approx. net wt. per 2000 ends									
in lb	45	55	55	80	106	106	106	248	248
in kg	21	25	25	37	48	48	48	113	113

TABLE 6. TYPES OF CANS USED FOR VARIOUS PRODUCTS

R = enamel cans		C = enamel cans		Plain cans
Fruits	Vegetables	Vegetables	Fruits	Vegetables
Black berries	+Beets	Corn, whole		Asparagus
Dew berries	*Pumpkin	kernel,	Apples baked	*Beans green
Logan berries	Rhubarb	cream,	Apples butter	or wax
Raspberries		style	Apples, cider	*Beans,
		on the cob,		red kidney
				Carrots
Cherries	+Squash	Succotash	Apricots	Cauliflower
Grapes			Blue berries	Corn and
(coloured)				tomatoes
Strawberries			Figs	Egg plant
				(brinjal)
			Grape fruit	Mustard green
			Goose berries	Spinach
			Guavas	Turnip green
			Litchis	*Hominy
			Oranges	Mushrooms
			Mangoes	Okra
			Papaya	*Peas
				(black eyed)
			Peaches	* Peas (English)
			Pears	Potatoes (sweet)
			Pineapple	+Sauerkraut
			Plums (yellow)	Soup, mixed
			Prunes	Tomatoes
				Tomato juice
				Tomato paste
				Vegetable soup

* These products may also be packed in C-enamel cans

\+ These products may also be packed in R-enamel cans

For fruit juice, use the same type of can recommended for the fruit from which the juice is made.

Size of Cans

According to the American system, which is widely followed in trade, cans are usually referred to by a letter and number, and the size is denoted by a digital symbol. The first number of the symbol denotes the diameter and the second the height of the can. The first digit represents integral inches and the succeeding two digits indicate measurement in sixteenths of an inch. Thus, an A 2½ size can which has a diameter of 10.32 cm (4.1/16 inch) and a height 11.90 cm (4.11/16 inch) would be shown as A 2½ (401x411). The most popular sizes of cans in use are given in Table 5.

Recently, the 0.16 kg (5½ oz.) Midget can (202x308) has become highly popular for canning fruit juices, mango nectar etc. It contains 165 ml of the beverage and is a fast selling picnic pack. A standard case (equivalent to 24 A 2½ cans) holds 96 of these cans.

Project Reports

Engineers India Research Institute, 4449 Nai Sarak, Main Road, Dellhi - 6 (India) Provides Project Report for settingup Unit of Fruits & Vegetables Processing Unit. If entreprenur want to get the Report then he may directly approach to them and take their assistance to setup the Unit.

4

Syrups & Brines for Canning

For canning fruits and vegetables, different covering liquids are employed. Syrup of sugar, glucose or corn is used for fruits, and brine or salt solution for vegetables. The process of preparing these for different requirements, on commercial as well as domestic scale, are dealt.

SUGAR SYRUPS

In canning fruits, sugar in the form of syrup is used to bring out the full flavour of the fruits, care being taken not to make the contents excessively sweet. Strength of the syrup would depend on the kind and variety of fruit. Generally, the more acidic fruits require denser syrups.

Only pure white crystalline sugar should be used. Chemically, this sugar is known as sucrose ($C_{12}H_{22}O_{11}$) and is found to the extent of about 99.5 per cent in cane and beet sugars. In some canneries in the U.S.A. corn syrup or glucose syrup is also used for canning the cheaper grades of fruit and in preparing jams and jellies. Until Hirst and Adam of the Fruit and Vegetable Preservation Research Station, Campden, U.K. showed that beet sugar was as satisfactory as cane sugar for canning purposes, it was not popular.

In India, only cane sugar is employed. However, the possibility of using glucose and corn syrups should also be explored as these are being manufactured in the country nowadays. In the case of Indian cane sugar, several brands have been found to contain appreciable amounts of sulphur dioxide. When these are used for canning, fairly profuse black deposits due to hydrogen sulphide, are formed inside the can during storage. These spoil the appearance of the canned product. Cane sugar made by the carbonation process is, therefore, to be preferred.

Preparation

Syrups can be made either by the cold process or by the hot process. **In the cold process,** sugar is placed in a tank and cold water poured over it and stirred. The solution is then filtered through a thick flannel bag, muslin cloth, or fine brass wire gauze to remove insoluble impurities. Sometimes warm water may also be added to facilitate the dissolving of the sugar. In the hot process, sugar and water are placed in a steam jacketed kettle, boiled and the scum removed. The syrup is clarified further by nitration. Steam helps to sterilize the syrup and to prolong its keeping qualities of sugar and water required to prepare syrups of a given Brix are given in Table.

In commercial practice, syrups of desired Brix are prepared either according to a formula by which a known weight of sugar is added to a given volume of water, or by adding sufficient water to a known weight of sugar to get the desired volume of syrup. For example, addition of 23 litres of water to 23 kg of sugar will produce 36 litres of syrup of 50 degrees Brix. Similarly, to get 23 litres of syrup of 50 degrees Brix, using 13.98 kg sugar, sufficient water is added to obtain the required quantity. Generally, to avoid unnecessary weighings, a 100 kg bag of sugar is taken as the unit and a known volume of water, gallons or litres as the case may be, added to the sugar to prepare the desired syrup.

Testing Syrup Strength

Uniformity of the canned product depends on the accuracy of measuring and increasing the syrup, because any mistake in syrup making cannot be rectified later. Since the cost of syrup forms an important item in the total cost of the finished product, it is essential to control the syrup strength and thereby avoid any wastage. Accurate thermometers and hydrometers are necessary for this. The different kinds of hydrometers used are the Brix or Balling, Baume, specific gravity and Twaddell hydrometers. A refractometer can also be more conveniently employed. The Brix or Balling hydrometer gives directly at the percentage of sugar by weight, in the syrup. It is calibrated at 20°C, and corrections are needed for other temperatures (Table). On the Baumes hydrometer, the divisions range from 0 to 70 degrees. The relation between the Brix and Baume scales is given in Table. Specific gravity in the case of Baumes reading may be deduced by adopting the formula :

$$\text{Specific gravity} = \frac{145}{145 - \text{Baume reading}}$$

Twaddell hydrometer is usually calibrated at 15°C, the divisions ranging from 0 to 200 degrees. One degree Twaddell corresponds to 1.005 specific gravity. Relationships between different types of hydrometers are shown in Table.

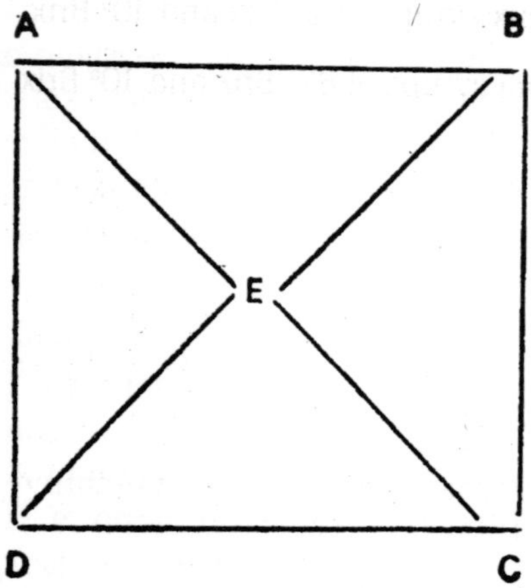

Fig. 16. Square method

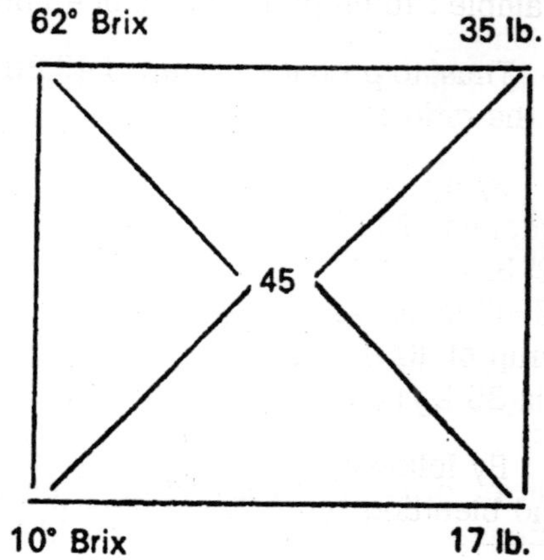

Fig. 16a.

Temperature Corrections

The syrup is placed in a tall glass cylinder, the hydrometer is lowered into, it and the reading on the scale noted carefully at the lower meniscus of the syrup. The temperature of the syrup is also noted. Corrections for temperature are made according to data given in Table. Thus, a syrup testing 30 degrees Brix at 20°C, will test only 26.88 degrees Brix at 55°C. For syrup temperatures above 20°C, corrections have to be added. while for those below 20°C, these have to be subtracted from the observed readings.

Syrup Calculation

Sometimes, it will be found necessary in practice to dilute a syrup or increase its strength. This is facilitated by what is known as the square method which is described.

Draw a square ABCD with the centre marked E. At A, note the Brix reading of the heavy. syrup and the pounds of sugar present per gallon of the syrup. At D write the Brix degree of the light syrup and the pounds of sugar per gallon of syrup. This is marked zero when water only is to be added for dilution, and 100 when sugar is to be added. At E, write the Brix degree and the sugar present per gallon of the desired syrup. Now work diagonally across the square. Subtract the smaller number from the larger and write the difference at the opposite corners C and B. These numbers represent the ratio in which the two syrups are to be mixed by volume, to get the desired strength of syrup noted at E.

Example : To prepare a syrup of 45 Brix, mix syrup of 62° Brix and 10° Brix.

Thus, to prepare a syrup of 45 Brix from syrups of 62° Brix and 10° Brix in the ratio of 4.38 : 2.63, by volume (Fig 16b).

Syrup can be mixed by weight also as illustrated in the following example. Thus, to prepare a syrup of 45° Brix starting with syrup of 62° Brix and 10° Brix mix 45 -10=35 lb. of syrup of 62° Brix with 62-45=17 lb. of syrup of 10° Brix to obtain 52 lb. syrup of 45° Brix. With 17 kg syrup of 10° Brix to obtain 52 kg syrup of 45° Brix using metric weights mix 35 kg syrup of 32° Brix. This is shown in the diagram.

By following this procedure different types of problems in preparing and blending syrups can be easily solved.

In measuring syrup volumes, a calibrated dip stick will be highly useful. The Brix of the syrup can be quickly determined by means of a packet refractometer with sugar scale.

Brines

Brines are used in canning vegetables. Brines containing 1 to 2 per cent of common salt are generally used. Only salt of good quality should be used. It should be free from iron, alkaline impurities such as sodium sulfate, calcium chloride, magnesium sulphate, and their bi-carbonates. The maximum solubility of common salt in water is about 26.5 per cent.

Strength of brine is measured by a salometer (also called salinometer) or a Baume hydrometer. The salometer is calibrated from 0 to 100 degrees at 15°C. A brine testing 100 degrees salometer contains 26.5 per cent of salt. In other words, each degree corresponds approximately to 0.25 per cent of salt. The Baume scale directly representIy the percentage of salt in the brine. One Baume scale reading is approximately equal to four salometer degrees.

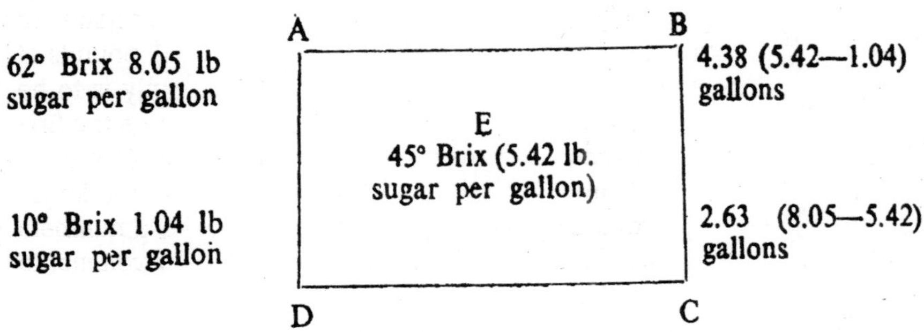

Fig. 16b.

TABLE 7. RELATIONSHIP BETWEEN BRIX READING AND COMPOSITION OF SYRUP

Degree Brix at 20°C (68°F)	Weight of sugar to be added to each gallon of water (one gal = 4.5 litres) (lb)	Volume of syrup from one gallon of water (one gal = 4.5 litres) (gal)	Weight of sugar contained in one gallon of syrup (1 lb = 4.54 g) (lb)
10	1.11	1.067	1.04
11	1.23	1.076	1.14
12	1.36	1.085	1.25
13	1.49	1.093	1.36
14	1.63	1.101	1.47
15	1.76	1.111	1.58
16	1.90	1.119	1.70
17	2.04	1.127	1.81
18	2.19	1.137	1.93
19	2.34	1.146	2.04
20	2.50	1.157	2.16
21	2.66	1.167	2.28
22	2.82	1.176	2.40
23	3.00	1.187	2.52
24	3.17	1.198	2.64
25	3.34	1.208	2.76
26	3.52	1.220	2.89
27	3.70	1.231	3.01
28	3.89	1.243	3.13
29	4.09	1.256	3.26
30	4.30	1.269	3.38
31	4.50	1.281	3.51
32	4.72	1.294	3.64
33	4.94	1.309	3.77
34	5.17	1.323	3.90
35	5.40	1.338	4.03
36	5.64	1.353	4.17
37	5.89	1.369	4.30
38	6.14	1.384	4.44
39	6.41	1.401	4.58
40	6.69	1.419	4.71
41	6.97	1.437	4.85
42	7.26	1.454	4.99
43	7.56	1.474	5.13
44	7.88	1.494	5.27
45	8.20	1.514	5.42
46	8.55	1.536	5.57
47	8.90	1.558	5.71
48	9.26	1.580	5.86

TABLE 7. *(Contd.)*

Degree Brix at 20°C (68°F)	Weight of sugar to be added to each gallon of water (one gal=4.5 litres) (lb)	Volume of syrup from one gallon of water (one gal=4.5 litres) (gal)	Weight of sugar contained in one gallon of syrup (one gal=4.5 litres) (lb)
49	9.64	1.604	6.01
50	10.03	1.628	6.16
51	10.44	1.654	6.31
52	10.86	1.681	6.45
53	11.31	1.710	6.61
54	11.77	1.739	6.77
55	12.36	1.770	6.93
56	12.77	1.803	7.08
57	13.29	1.837	7.23
58	13.85	1.871	7.40
59	14.43	1.907	7.57
60	15.05	1.948	7.73
61	15.69	1.988	7.89
62	16.37	2.032	8.05
63	17.08	2.077	8.31
64	17.84	2.124	8.39
65	18.62	2.174	8.57
66	19.47	2.229	8.75
67	20.39	2.287	8.92
68	21.32	2.344	9.10
69	22.23	2.411	9.27
70	23.40	2.480	9.44

TABLE 8. COMPARISON OF (DEGREES) BRIX, BAUME, TWADDELL AND SPECIFIC GRAVITY SCALES AND REQUIREMENTS OF SUGAR

Degree Brix (per cent sugar by weight) at 20°C (68°F)	Degree Baume' at 20°C (68°F)	Degree Twaddell at 20°C (68°F)	Specific gravity 20°C (68°F)	Approximate weight of sugar to be added to each gallon of water (one gal = 4.5 litres) (1 lb = 454 g) lb	oz
10	5.6	8	1.040	1	2
11	6.1	9	1.044	1	4
12	6.7	10	1.048	1	6
13	7.2	11	1.053	1	8
14	7.8	12	1.057	1	10
15	8.3	12	1.061	1	12
16	8.9	13	1.065	1	14
17	9.5	14	1.070	2	1
18	10.0	15	1.074	2	3
19	10.6	16	1.078	2	5
20	11.1	17	1.083	2	8
21	11.7	17	1.087	2	11
22	12.2	18	1.092	2	13
23	12.7	19	1.096	3	0
24	13.3	20	1.101	3	3
25	13.8	21	1.106	3	5
26	14.4	22	1.110	3	8
27	14.9	23	1.115	3	11
28	15.5	24	1.119	3	14
29	16.0	25	1.124	4	2
30	16.6	26	1.129	4	5
31	17.1	27	1.134	4	8
32	17.7	28	1.139	4	11
33	18.2	29	1.143	4	15
34	18.7	30	1.148	5	3
35	19.3	31	1.153	5	6
36	19.8	32	1.158	5	10
37	20.4	33	1.163	5	14
38	20.9	34	1.168	6	2
39	21.4	35	1.173	6	7
40	22.0	36	1.179	6	11
41	22.5	37	1.184	7	0
42	23.5	38	1.189	7	4
43	23.6	39	1.194	7	9
44	24.1	40	1.199	7	14
45	24.6	41	1.205	8	3
46	25.2	42	1.210	8	9
47	25.7	43	1.215	8	14

TABLE 8. (*Contd.*)

Degrees Brix (per cent sugar by weight) at 20°C (68°F)	Degrees Baume' at 20°C (68°F)	Degrees Twaddell at 20°C (68°F)	Specific gravity at 20°C (68°F)	Approximate weight of sugar to be added to each gallon of water (one gal=4.5 litres) (1 lb=454g) lb	oz
48	26.2	44	1.221	9	4
49	26.8	45	1.226	9	11
50	27.3	46	1.232	10	0
51	27.8	47	1.237	10	7
52	28.3	49	1.243	10	14
53	28.9	50	1.248	11	5
54	29.4	51	1.254	11	12
55	29.9	52	1.260	12	4
56	30.4	53	1.265	12	12
57	30.9	54	1.271	13	5
58	31.5	56	1.277	13	14
59	32.0	57	1.283	14	7
60	32.5	58	1.288	15	1
61	33.0	59	1.295	15	11
62	33.5	60	1.301	16	6
63	34.0	61	1.307	17	1
64	34.5	63	1.313	17	15
65	35.0	64	1.319	18	10
66	35.6	65	1.325	19	8
67	36.1	66	1.331	20	6
68	36.6	67	1.337	21	5
69	37.1	69	1.343	22	5
70	37.6	70	1.350	23	6

TABLE 9. TEMPERATURE CORRECTIONS FOR CHANGING PERCENTAGE OF SUCROSE BY DENSITY OF AQUEOUS SOLUTION TO TRUE VALUE AT 20°C.

Temperature °C	Observed percentage of sugar													
	0	5	10	15	20	25	30	35	40	45	50	55	60	70
SUBTRACT FROM OBSERVED PERCENTAGE														
0	0.30	0.49	0.65	0.77	0.89	0.99	1.08	1.16	1.24	1.31	1.37	1.41	1.44	1.49
5	.36	.47	.56	.65	.73	.80	.86	.91	.97	1.01	1.05	1.08	1.10	1.14
10	.32	.38	.43	.48	.52	.57	.60	.64	.67	.70	.72	.74	.75	.77
11	.31	.35	.40	.44	.48	.52	.55	.58	.60	.63	.65	.66	.68	.70
12	.29	.32	.36	.40	.43	.46	.50	.52	.54	.56	.58	.59	.60	.62
13	.26	.29	.32	.35	.38	.41	.44	.46	.48	.49	.51	.52	.53	.55
14	.24	.26	.29	.31	.34	.36	.39	.40	.41	.42	.44	.45	.46	.47
15	.20	.22	.24	.26	.28	.30	.32	.33	.34	.36	.36	.37	.38	.39
16	.17	.18	.20	.22	.23	.25	.26	.27	.28	.28	.29	.30	.31	.32
17	.13	.14	.15	.16	.18	.19	.20	.20	.21	.21	.22	.23	.23	.24
17.5	.11	.12	.12	.14	.15	.16	.16	.17	.17	.18	.18	.19	.19	.20
18	.09	.10	.10	.11	.12	.13	.13	.14	.14	.14	.15	.15	.15	.16
19	.05	.05	.05	.06	.06	.06	.07	.07	.07	.07	.08	.08	.08	.08
ADD TO OBSERVED PERCENTAGE														
21	0.04	0.05	0.06	1.06	0.06	0.07	0.07	0.07	0.07	0.08	0.08	0.08	0.08	0.09
22	.10	.10	.11	.12	.12	.13	.14	.14	.15	.15	.15	.16	.16	.16
23	.16	.16	.17	.17	.19	.20	.21	.21	.22	.23	.24	.24	.24	.24
24	.21	.22	.23	.24	.26	.27	.28	.29	.29	.21	.32	.32	.32	.32
25	.27	.28	.30	.31	.32	.34	.35	.36	.38	.38	.39	.39	.40	.39
26	.33	.34	.36	.37	.40	.40	.42	.44	.46	.47	.47	.48	.48	.48

TABLE 9. *(Contd.)*

Temperature °C	Observed percentage of sugar													
	0	5	10	15	20	25	30	35	40	45	50	55	60	70
27	.40	.41	.42	.44	.46	.48	.50	.52	.54	.54	.55	.56	.56	.56
28	.46	.47	.49	.51	.54	.56	.58	.60	.61	.62	.63	.64	.64	.64
29	.54	.55	.56	.59	.61	.63	.66	.68	.70	.70	.71	.72	.72	.72
30	.61	.62	.63	.66	.68	.71	.73	.76	.78	.78	.79	.80	.80	.81
35	.99	1.01	1.02	1.06	1.10	1.13	1.16	1.18	1.20	1.21	1.22	1.22	1.23	1.22
40	1.42	1.45	1.47	1.51	1.54	1.57	1.60	1.62	1.64	1.65	1.65	1.65	1.66	1.65
45	1.91	1.94	1.96	2.00	2.03	2.05	2.07	2.09	2.10	2.10	2.10	2.10	2.10	2.08
50	2.46	2.48	2.50	2.53	2.56	2.57	2.58	2.59	2.59	2.58	2.58	2.57	2.56	2.52
55	3.05	3.07	3.09	3.12	3.12	3.12	3.12	3.11	3.10	3.08	3.07	3.05	3.03	2.97
60	3.69	3.72	3.73	3.73	3.72	3.70	3.67	3.65	3.62	3.60	3.57	3.54	3.50	3.43
65	4.4	4.4	4.4	4.4	4.4	4.4	4.3	4.2	4.2	4.1	4.1	4.0	4.0	3.9
70	5.1	5.1	5.1	5.0	5.0	4.9	4.8	4.8	4.7	4.7	4.6	4.6	4.6	4.4
75	6.1	6.0	6.0	5.9	5.8	5.8	5.7	5.6	5.5	5.4	5.4	5.3	5.2	5.0
80	7.1	7.0	7.0	6.9	6.8	6.7	6.6	6.4	6.3	6.2	6.1	6.0	5.9	5.6

TABLE 10. RELATIONSHIP BETWEEN DENSITY, SALT PER CENT AND SALOMETER READING

Density	Per cent salt (wt./wt.)	Salometer reading	Salt per gallon of water (one gal = 4.5 litres) (1 lb. = 454 g)	
			lb.	oz.
1.017	2.5	9.5	0	4.3
1.034	5.0	18.9	0	8.5
1.052	7.5	28.3	0	13
1.071	10.0	37.7	1	2
1.090	12.5	47.1	1	7
1.109	15.0	56.6	1	12
1.128	17.5	66.0	2	2
1.148	20.0	75.5	2	8
1.169	22.5	84.9	2	15
1.190	25.0	94.5	3	5
1.204	26.5	100.0	3	10

5

Canning of Fruits

The methods of canning of various types of fruits are described in this exclusive chapter.

Apple

Apples are not canned to any great extent, since they can be kept in refrigerated or controlled atmosphere storage for practically the whole year from one season to another. Canned apples, which are usually available in the larger sizes of cans, are generally used in pies. The varieties commonly employed for canning are : Yellow Newton, Pippin, Spitzenberg, Winesap, Baldwin, Russet, Jonathan, Delicious, and Rome Beauty.

The fruits are first washed in warm dilute hydrochloric acid to remove any lead or arsenic spray residue and then rinsed in cold water. Next they are peeled by hand or by machine and cut into slices, 0.31 to 0.63 cm thick. The slices are placed in 2 to 3 per cent common salt solution to prevent their darkening due to enzyme action. They are then blanched at 71°C to 82°C for 3 to 4 minutes in plain boiling water or in three per cent boiling brine. Blanching is essential to remove oxygen from the tissues and thus prevent pinholing in the cans during storage. The blanched slices are filled into cans, covered with either hot water or thin sugar syrup, exhausted and processed. Pinholing of cans during prolonged storage, especially in warmer climate, is a serious problem in the case of canned apples.

Apricot

In India, these grow mostly in Kashmir, Simla Hills and Uttar Pradesh, where considerable scope exists for their canning.

Apricots are of two kinds; white and yellow. In other countries, the Blenheim variety, which is of moderate size, deep yellow in colour, and has good flavour, and can stand processing well, is popular for canning. The Tilton and Hemskirk varieties are also canned. The white sweet varieties like the Charmagz and Shakarkand have been found to be quite good for canning.

Apricots are not peeled for canning. They are merely cut into halves and the stones removed. Sometimes, they are canned whole. According to Cruess, on as average, a ton of apricots yields about 55 cases of 24 A 2½ size cans.

Banana

Banana is one of the most important fruit crops of India. More then 200 commercial varieties are grown over an area of about 1,60,000 hectares. Experts worked out a method for canning the fruit alone or in combination with other fruits in the form of salad. According to them, only a few varieties are suitable for canning. Of the 20 south Indian varieties which they tried, Pachabale, Chandrabale, Nendran, Chenganapurikodan, Poovan, and Vannan yielded satisfactory canned products.

Fully ripe fruit is peeled by hand and cut laterally into slices of 1.27 cm to 1.89 cm thickness. Sugar syrup of 25 to 30° Brix, containing 0.2 per cent citric acid is used as covering liquid. The pH of the banana has been found to vary from 4.5 to 5.3. Butter size cans (1 lb. squat) are processed for 15 minutes in (1) boiling water (100°C), if the pH of the fresh fruit is 4.8 or less, and (ii) in a pressure cooker at 5 lb. psi (0.35 kg per cm^2) steam pressure (sea level), if the pH is higher than 4.8. Cooling after processing should be quick and thorough to prevent pink discolouration of the slices in the can during storage.

Cloudiness of the syrup in the can and slight discolouration of the slices are serious problems in the case of canned bananas. The market for the product is also exclusive and limited, because banana in the green state can be had practically the year round, as a result of recent advances in their harvesting, storage and distribution. Indian bananas such as the Cavendish variety are being exported recently to other countries. There is however, still scope for canning good varieties by improved methods.

Black berries

Black berries are canned to some extent in the U.S.A. and in the U.K. They are not available in any large quantity in India for commercial canning. Evergreen Mammoth and Himalaya are the more important canning varieties. The berries should be handled without any delay after harvesting.

Cherries

Charries are grown mostly in Kashmir valley. There are three kinds of cherries sweet, sub acid and acid varieties The sweet varieties are light coloured with pinkish flesh or of deep red or black colour.

TABLE 11. CANNING TIME TABLE FOR FRUITS AND TOMATOES

Fruit	Type of can	Strength of syrup (Degree Brix)	Exhaust	Processing time (min) in boiling water at 100°C				
				No. 2	No. 2½	No. 10	Pint Jar	Quart Jar
1. Apple	Plain	Water or light syrup	Exhaust can at 180 to 212°F (82°C to 100°C) for 7-10 minutes or until the temperature in the centre of the can reaches at least 165°F (74°C)	10	12	25	15	15
2. Apricot	Plain	55	,,	25	35	50	25	35
3. Banana	,,	30+0.2% citric acid	,,	—	20	—	—	—
4. Blackberry	Fruit lacquered	55	,,	15	20	30	20	25
5. Cherry, (sweet)	,,	40	,,	15	20	25	20	30
6. Cherry (sour)	,,	45	,,	15	20	25	20	30
7. Fig	Plain	55	,,	10	15	35	15	20
8. Grape, (coloured)	Fruit lacquered	40	,,	12	12	15	15	20
9. Grape (white)	Plain	40	,,	10	12	15	15	20
10. Grape fruit	,,	60	,,	—See recipe—				
11. Greengage	,,	40	,,	15	20	—	15	15
12. Guava	,,	40	,,	20	20	—	25	30
13. Jack fruit	,,	50	,,	25	30	—	—	—
14. Litchi	,,	40	,,	25	30	—	—	—
15. Loganberry	Fruit lacquered	45	,,	10	12	25	—	—
16. Loquat	Plain	40	,,	25	30	—	—	—
17. Mango	,,	40	,,	25	30	—	—	—
18. Mulberry ('coloured')	Fruit lacquered	40	,,	10	12	—	—	—
19. Musk Melon	plain	40+0.3% citric acid	,,	25	30	—	—	—
20. Orange	,,	50	,,	— See recipe —				
21. Papaya	,,	45	,,	25	30	—	—	—

*TABLE 11. CANNING TIME TABLE FOR FRUITS AND TOMATOES (*Contd.*)

Fruit	Type of can	Strength of syrup (Degree Brix)	Exhaust	Processing time (min) in boiling water at 100°C				
				No. 2	No. 2½	No. 10	Pint Jar	Quart Jar
22. Peach	Plain	55	,,	25	30	50	25	35
23. Pear	,,	40	,,	25	35	60	25	30
24. Pineapple	,,	40	,,	20	30	60	25	30
25. Plum, red	Fruit lacquered	40	,,	15	20	30	15	15
26. Raspberry	,,	45	,,	10	12	25	—	—
27. Strawberry	,,	50	,,	10	15	20	15	15
28. Tomato	Plain	only tomato juice in the case of standard pack	,,	25	30	70 (air cooled)	—	—
29. Fruit cocktail (Fruit salad)	,,	45	,,	25	30	90 (water cooled)	—	—

According to Siddappa and Mustafa, the White Heart Cherry which is of fairly big size and has a creamy white flesh, and the Red cherry which is rather small in size and has a creamy white flesh, are good for canning. The Royal Anne, the Napoleon Bigarreau and the kentish Bigarrecau are good foreign varieties for canning. These are bright red in colour and taste good. Morello, which is a large cherry of bright reddish purple colour, is important among the acid varieties. It is canned in heavy syrup, Maraschino cherries are canned for mixing with other fruits, fruit cocktails, ice creams, etc. For this, slightly under pipe Royal Anne cherries are generally used.

The cherries. are packed in barrels of brine containing calcium hydroxide, sulphur dioxide, and occasionally alum. The Brine fro this purpose is made up of about 0.75 to 1.0 per cent SO^2 and about 0.4 to 0.6 per cent of slaked lime in Oregon, approximately 1.5 per cent of SO^2 and about 0.9 per cent of lime are used. The brined cherries are stored for 4 to 6 weeks for curing. During this period, the colour of the cherries to white or pale yellow. The cured cherries are washed well in water and dyed with a red dye such as Erythrosin, and the colour fixed with citric acid. These coloured cherries are used for canning or for candying.

Fig

Figs are usually canned as preserve. They should be allowed to ripen on the tree to give a good canned product. Kadota, Celeste, Magnolia and Smyrna are the more important canning varieties. After grading, the figs are wilted by placing them in hot water at 82°C for 2 to 3 minutes. They are sometimes lye peeled and washed with water to remove the waxy coating and the adhering lye. They are then blanched in boiling water for 10 to 20 minutes, depending upon their size and degree of ripeness, and canned in syrup of 45° to 55° Brix. Addition of about 0.5 per cent citric acid to the syrup improves the blend and the keeping quality.

Grape

Muscat and Thompson seedless are good canning varieties. Only large sized berries are used for canning. Syrup of 20° to 40° Brix is used. Loss in canning is nearly 20%. The Seedless Kishmish and the Seeded Haitha grapes give good canned products. Coloured grapes should be canned in lacquered cans.

Grape Fruit

Grape fruit should preferably by tree ripened. Marsh Seedless, Duncan and Foster are good canning varieties. Marsh Seedless and Foster varieties are the best for canning.

To remove the thick outer peel, the fruit is immersed in hot water at 93°C to 96°C for 2 to 5 minutes, so that the peel becomes soft and can be easily removed by hand. The peeled fruit is then either lye peeled or hand peeled further. After peeling, the whole fruit is immersed for 20 to 30 seconds in a bath of hot dilute lye containing 1.5 to 2.0 per cent caustic soda. It is then thoroughly washed with cold water and the segments are separated. A clean stainless steel knife of special design is employed to lift the segments one by one from the membranes without breaking them. When all the segments are separated, the membranes will be in the form of the leaves of a book. In Florida, sections of peeled fruits are carefully removed by means of a special blunt knife or a knife made of bamboo or some other hard wood. The segments are filled carefully into plain cans; and sugar is added in layers, or in the form of 60 Brix syrup. Syrup gives a better product. If dry sugar is used, about 56 g would suffice for an A 2 size can. Unlike several other fruits, the filled cans of grapefruit are given a long exhaust of 25 to 30 minutes at 82°C to 87°C, and processed for 30 to 40 minutes at the same temperature to retain the full aroma and texture of the fruit. The cans are cooled immediately after the processing. Canned grape fruit becomes slightly firmer if kept for some time after canning. The cans should, therefore, be retained for some weeks before marketing.

According to Loesecke, 36 kg of grape fruit yields about 33 cans of A 2 size, when lye peeling is adopted, and 24 to 27 cans when peeling is done by hand.

Greengage

Greengages are canned in syrup containing about 0.5 per cent citric acid. The canned product has, however, a tendency to turn brown and become soft and acquire a bitter flavour during storage. True greengage is fairly satisfactory for canning.

Guava

Guavas of good quality are found in abundance in Uttar Pradesh, Madhya Pradesh, and some parts of south India. Canned guava often have a taste and aroma better then those of even the fresh fruit. The pulp although soft in texture, stands processing well, and does not darken during storage. Fully ripe fruit, preferably with white flesh and few seeds, is selected for canning. It is peeled with knife or sometimes with hot lye, and cut into halves. The seeds are scooped out with a spoonshaped knife. The peeled and cored fruit is kept immersed in 1 to 2 per cent common salt solution to prevent it from browning. Peel and core can be used for making guava jelly or guava cheese.

Jack fruit

Jack fruit *(Artocarpus integrifolia)* is available in plenty in Maharashtra, Bihar, Orissa, Karnataka, Kerala and some parts of Tamil Nadu. It is an important staple food for certain sections of the people in these areas. The tree bears annually 60 to 75 fruits, each weighing 10 to 20 kg. In exceptional cases, the fruit weighs even 35 to 40 kg. The unripe green and immature fruit is prized as a vegetable. Experiments have shown that green jack fruit can be canned as a curried vegetable. The crisp bulbs (seeds removed) of the ripe fruit are used for canning in syrup. The yield of bulbs varies from 25 to 40 per cent of the weight of the fruit.

After cutting the fruit into several large pieces, the bulbs are removed with hand. As the fruit contains a white, highly sticky latex, a little gingelly or til oil, or hydrogenated fat (commonly known in India as vanaspati) is smeared on the hand and knife to prevent the latex from sticking to them. The latex is soluble in oil. The seeds are removed from the bulbs, which are then canned whole or as halves or quarters. Syrup of 50° Brix with 0.5 to 0.75 per cent citric acid should be used as the pH of the fruit is quite high, i.e. about 5.2. The method of canning jack fruit has been standardized at the Central Food Technological Research Institute, Mysore.

The canned product has an exotic flavour and is quite likable, although considered strong by some people. There is scope for large scale canning of this fruit for internal consumption as well as for export to other countries. It hhas been studied extensively the possibility of canning the fruit along with other fruits of India such as mango, banana, etc. in the form of a fruit cocktail. Highly acidic fruits have been successfully utilized by them to minimize the addition of citric acid to the canning syrup to lower the pH to a safer level for normal processing in boiling water.

The outer rind of jack fruit is rich in pectin and can be used for making pectin. A good jelly can be out of the rind and also the inner perigones. The seeds can be used as a vegetable, or ground into a flour which can be blended with wheat flour for making chapatis. The seeds contain a trypsin inhibitor which can be removed by boiling the seeds in salt water. This is by the way the normal practice of eating the seeds. The nutritive value of jack fruit, fresh as well as canned, with or without honey, as supplements to the normal rice diet. The fruit is a valuable one in every respect, and the exotic strong flavour can be reduced considerably by processing and the product made acceptable to a large section of people. There is a growing interest in the fruit in several quarters.

Litchi

Litchis are found in Uttar Pradesh, Uttaranchal, Jharkhand, Bihar and Orissa. For canning, the fruit should be tree ripened. The outer shell is first cracked, then the pulp inside is separated, and finally the stones are removed. Plain can and 40° Brix syrup with 0.5 per cent citric acid are used. Prompt and thorough cooling of the cans after processing is necessary to prevent development of pink colour in the product. Canned litchis from China are well-known in foreign countries.

Loquat

Loquat can be cut into halves and canned to get an attractive product.

Mango

India is the home of mangoes. A large number of varieties are found in almost all parts of the country. Uttar Pradesh, Tamil Nadu, Karnataka, Bihar and West Bengal lead in mango growing.

Among the numerous varieties, 'Safaida' and 'Dusehri' of U.P. 'Alphonso' of Ratnagiri, 'Badami' of Mysore, 'Benishan' of East. Coast, and 'Raspuri' 'Neelum and Mulgoa' of Tamil Nadu and Karnataka are the most important varieties for canning. The 'Bangalora' or 'Totapari' mango which is an assured and heavy annual bearer, and also yields an excellent pulp or juice, is sometimes canned to give a fairly good canned product. Juicy and fibrous varieties are not quite suitable for canning. They are mostly used for making juice, squash, nectar, chutney and pickles

Firm ripe mangoes that are just developing colour are picked and ripened in straw. As they ripen, canning ripe fruits are selected daily from the lot. They are washed in water and peeled with hand, and the pulp cut into 6 to 8 longitudinal slices For canning as halves, the cheeks or the two broad sides are taken. The slices are placed in 2 per cent common salt solution to prevent their enzymic browning. Plain cans are used. As some of the table varieties have a pH slightly higher than the critical pH of 4.2, it is necessary to add 0.3 to 0.5 per cent Citric acid to the syrup for safe processing of the cans in open cookers. Nowadays, the practice is to sterilize the cans first in open cookers and then sterilize them in closed retorts at 1 to 2 pound steam pressure (psi) i.e. 0.07 to 0.14 kg per sq. cm. as an additional safety measure. About 0.6 kg of the fruit would be required to prepare slices to fill a 0.4 kg butter size can. The trimmings of the slices and the pulp adhering to the stone can be utilized profitably for the preparation of mango squash and mango jam.

Mango being the most important and unique commercial fruit of India and known as the king of fruits, it is essential to develop large scale canning and preservation of the fruit. Considerable amount of scientific and developmental work has been done in the Central Food Technological Research Institute, Mysore, on various problems concerning the mango including the storage and long distance transport. Mango products are likely to find increasing markets in many countries of the world. Canned mango would, in many respects, compare well with the well known canned peach of commerce.

Orange

Oranges are canned to a limited extent only. 'Satsuma' and 'Mandarin' and 'Unshu' of Japan are the important canning varieties. Being practically seedless unlike the Indian Mandarin oranges, such as the loose jacket Mandarin oranges of Nagpur Coorg, Assam and a few other regions, they are preferred for canning. The segments are easier to handle without much breakage, which would otherwise occur while attempting to remove the seeds. Malta and Sathgudi oranges which are tight skinned like the Valencia orange (Citrus sinensis) and the loose jacket Nagpur and Coorg oranges (Citrus aurantium reticulata) have been found to yield comparatively good canned products. There is a considerable export potential for canned Mandarin orange segments. A great deal of care and sophisticated techniques for peeling, exhausting, processing and cooling the cans needed to get readily good canned product.

The peel of the loose jacket orange is removed easily with hand. In the case of the tight skinned orange, prior dipping of the fruit in boiling water as in the case of grape fruit, is necessary to loosen the skin. The segments are separated and the adhering fibers removed. They are then dipped in boiling lye solution of 1 to 2 per cent strength for 20 to 30 seconds, rinsed in warm water, dipped in dilute HCI of 0.5 to 1.0 per cent strength to remove traces of alkali, and finally rinsed well in cold water. Any adhering membrane and also seeds are removed by hand. The segments are then carefully filled into plain cans containing some water, to prevent undue breakage of the segments during filling. The filled cans are then drained. A small amount of orange flavour may be added to the syrup. The cans are closed preferably on a vacuum double seamer. Alternatively the filled cans are exhausted for 15 to 20 minutes at 82°C to 87°C and then processed for 15 to 20 minutes also at 82°C to 87°C, in a rocking type pasteurizer in an open tank of water. After processing, the cans are cooled in a rocking type cooler. The precautions are necessary to prevent undue breakage of segments and minimize the loss of the delicate flavour of the orange. Orange segments can also be canned as salad along with other fruits like mango, pineapple, jack fruit, banana, etc. Canning of sliced orange instead of segments, without removing the covering membrane of the segments, to give a novel product. This approaches the new concept of using the whole fruit as in the case of comminuted fruit drinks. Broken segments can be profitably utilized for orange jam, juice, squash, etc.

At present, the internal market for canned oranges is rather limited. There is, however, scope for developing an export market for the product.

Papaya

Papaya slices or cubes, can be used for canning. About 0.5 per cent citric acid should be added to the syrup to counteract the high pH of the fruit. Papaya could be canned along with other fruits like pineapple, mango, banana, etc. to get a product similar to the one commercially packed in Australia. Papaya, being a quick growing fruit, can form the basis for a thriving canning industry. It also yields valuable by-products such as the enzyme papain and jelly-forming pectin. An integrated approach to the utilization of this fruit has been investigated by an expert and his co-workers at the Central Food Technological Research Institute, Mysore.

Peach

There are two types of peaches, the Cling-stone and the Free stone. Among the former, the Tuscan, which is an early ripening variety, and the mid-summer varieties, Palora, Sims and Peaks, are important canning varieties. Phillips Cling is a good late variety. Elberta, Lovell and J.H. Hale are free-stone peaches suitable for canning, while Muir is good for drying only. Crawford and Salway do not yield good canned products.

Almost all the canning varieties have a uniform yellow colour. The white-fleshed varieties, which are soft and juicy like those of Quetta, are not suitable for canning. The Peshawari 6-A peach, which is similar to Elberta, is a good canning variety.

The fruit is cut round the suture and the pits removed by inserting a spoon-shaped knife from the stem end turning it till one end of the fruit separates off. The other helf is freed of the stone with the same knife. In large canneries, the pits are cut by a rapidly revolving buzz saw and the pits removed by mechanically-operated crescent-shaped knives. The cut halves are peeled by immersing them in boiling lye of 1 to 2 per cent strength, for 1/2 to 1 minute and then washing away the loosened peel in water. A moving belt, with the peach halves kept inverted, passing under sprays of hot lye solution, is often employed in the larger units. Free stone peaches are sometimes peeled by steam. They are then placed in cold water to prevent darkening. A ton of Cling stone peaches 41.2 cases, each case average 45 cases and a ton of Free stone peaches will yield on an containing 24 A 2½ size cans.

Peaches are generally canned in the form of halves. Sometimes they are canned in the form of sliced fruit also. While halves are filled by hand into cans, the thinner slices are filled by machine from a shallow circular hopper. Peaches form an important constituent of fruit cocktail. Broken halves and slices can be utilized for the preparation of pulp, nectar, jam. etc.

Pear

Pears are grown in abundance in Kullu and Kashmir valleys, and to some extent in the hilly areas of south India. The fruit is harvested when it attains full size, but is still green. Pears of Kullu should be picked at a pressure of about 0.91 to 0.98 kg per sq. cm. These are subsequently ripened at 23°C to 26°C, when they develop a light yellow colour, and the white pulp becomes fairly soft and develops the characteristic, pleasant taste and aroma.

The fruit is peeled with a knife from stem end to blossom end, cut longitudinally into two halves, and the cora removed with a double edged coring knife. The peeled and cored fruit is placed in 1 to 2 per cent common salt solution to prevent browning. The halves are then filled into cans, covered with hot sugar syrup, exhausted, seamed and processed as usual. Prompt and thorough cooling of the cans is necessary to prevent development of pink discolouration of the fruit during storage. Broken halves can be used for making jam.

Pineapple

Pineapples are grown mostly in Assam, Bengal, the West Coast of India and the Godavari district in Andhra Pradesh, Recently, pineapples of an excellent quality in regard to texture, taste and flavour and canning quality have been grown on an increasing scale in the Coorg area of Karnataka state. They have been found to yield a canned product of premium quality. Giant kew and Queen are the two important varieties. In India, Kew is, however, preferred for canning, and the area under it is steadily increasing to meet the mounting demand for canned pineapples within the country.

In Hawaii, West Indies, Australia, and Malaysia where pineapple canning is a big industry, the graded fruit is peeled, cored and sliced simultaneously on a Ginaca machine, which has a large output capacity. In India, however, power driven slicing machines and punches, corers and eye removers which work with hand are generally employed. As the fruit contains highly active proteolytic enzymes, injurious to the skin, the workers should wear rubber gloves. The fruit, which is at the canning ripe stage, is sliced on a power driven slicing machine and the slices fed to the workers, who remove the outer peel with a cured knife fixed to the edge of the work table. It is, however, preferable to slice the unpeeled whole fruit and then punch out the rings from the slices. From the peeled slice, a circular ring is punched out using stainless steel punches of different diameter ranging from 5.6 to 8.8 cm. The core is then removed with a corer and any remaining eyes and hard portions in the outer periphery of the ring trimmed off carefully without breaking it. The rings thus prepared are graded visually for size, by stringing them on to a stick, dipped in water to remove adhering broken bits etc. and them filled into cans. Eight to 9 slices of 1.2 cm thickness are generally filled into an A 2½ size can to give the correct fill and drained weight according to standard specifications for the canned product. A 2½ can and also No. 1 Tall (0.45 kg) and 0.4 kg Butter size cans are employed for canning the slices. Sometimes broken rings are cut into segments of suitable size and canned as tit bits or chunks. Both slices and tit bits are highly popular among the consumers.

Broken slices and smaller segments can be passed through a screw type crusher to get pineapple pulp popularly known as pineapple crush. This can be canned either in A 2½ or in Dalda size cans (0.85 kg and 2.6 kg contents respectively) for use in the ice cream and confectionery trade. From the pulp, pineapple juice of high quality can be extracted by passing it through a hydraulic basket type centrifuge. After blending the juice to proper Brix acid ratio it can be canned. Canned pineapple juice in the small 5½ oz. (165 g), Midget cans has recently become highly popular in many parts of India. The extracted juice can also be utilized for the preparation of pineapple squash. The pulp forms a highly useful base for the preparation of pineapple jam. The juice as well as the jam are fast selling items in the country. Canning of pineapples is developing quickly as an important fruit canning industry in the southern states. The juice can also be concentrated.

Food technologists have conducted extensive canning trials on three varieties of pineapple, namely Giant Kew, Kew, and Mauritius. They found that the percentage recovery of 'A' grade material fit for canning ranged from 24.0 to 32.0 13.7 to 20.8 and 9.7 to 11.4 respectively for the three varieties. They have reported that their ascorbic acid content ranges from 14.0 to 16.6, 5.2 to 8.6 and 19.3 to 24.5 mg per 100 g respectively; the percentage of refractometeric solids from 12.8 to 15.3, 9.3 to 15.4 and 10.4 to 13.4 and the pH from 3.3 to 3.5, 3.4 to 3.6 and 3.2 to 3.3 respectively. He also found that the retention of ascorbic acid in canned pineapples after 12 months storage at room temperature (24° to 30°C) was as high as 72.3 per cent.

The outer peel of the fruit, which is removed from the slices prior to punching out the ring, and the central core are both being discarded as wastes. Experiments have however shown that the core can be converted into pineapple candy as in the case of bamboo shoots. The peel could be pressed and the juice fermented into fruit vinegar. It can also be suitable treated and dehydrated to form a useful component for stock feed. Recently, there has been considerable interest in the country in developing such products.

Plum

A few varieties of plums are grown in some part of north India and in some hilly tracts in the South. Plums are canned largely in the U.K. The Red Victoria and the Vellow Pershore plums are important canning varieties. Purple Pershore, Early Laxton, Magnum Bonum, Evesham, Wonder, Czar, etc. are other varieties that are moderately good for canning. The Alubukhara plum of north India gives a fairly good canned product.

Plum jam is an important by product in the canning of plums and is quite popular in the U.K. It is highly acceptable to the Indian consumer also.

Berry Fruits

Among the numerous berry fruits found in many parts of the world, strawberry, loganberry, black berry, blue berry, raspberry, mulberry, and small fruits like black and red currants are popular for canning. John Paxton, Royal Sovereign, and Oberschlesien strawberries are good for canning

Ponceau 2 R colour is added to the syrup used for canning strawberries. Food technocrats have reported that the white mulberry known as Shahthuth gives a good canned product. A considerable amount of work has been reported in their annual reports and miscellaneous bulletins by Hirst and Adam of Campden Research Station. U.K. who have systematically studied a variety of berry and small fruits for their suitability for canning. These fruits are also very well suited for making jams and preserves. Cranberry is attracting much scientific attention in the U.S.A. in recent years on the basis of findings regarding Cranberry sauce.

MISCELLANEOUS MINOR FRUITS

Some of the findings are briefly summarized here.

BER *(Ziziphus jujube Mill)*

There are two kinds of this fruit, namely small (chota) and large (mota) ber. They are rich in ascorbic acid. They can be canned as well as candied.

DATE *(Phoenix dactylifera L.)*

After reducing the pH by adding acid to the covering syrup, the dates can be canned satisfactorily.

POMEGRANATE *(Punica granatum L.)*

The Kandhar variety is the most popular one. The purplish juice of 16° to 18° Brix. 0.8 to 1.2 per cent acidity and 0.12 to 0.18 per cent tannin content, can be preserved as juice, syrup and a thick sauce like product known as Anar rub. The seeds can be dried into anardana which is used as an acidulant in cooking.

MULBERRY *(Morus sp.)*

Both the white and bleck mulberry juices can be preserved and bottled by pasteurization.

MUSKMELON *(Cucumis melo L.)*

Muskmelon slices and cubes can be canned alone or along with other fruits, as mixed fruit cocktail. Melon jam of golden yellow colour and excellent flavour can be prepared and the flavour further enhanced by imcorporating lemon or ginger slices during the preparation of the jam.

WATER MELON *(Citrullus lanatus)*

The thick rind of the fruit can be candied or made into chutney. The mildly flavoured pinkish juice of the fruit, which is of about 8° Brix can be converted into a syrup of 60° Brix and 1.5 per cent acidity and preserved with 1,000 ppm of sodium benzoate.

AMLA *(Phyllanthus emblica L.)*

Amla which is nutritionally and medicinally important on account of its high vitamin C content and the stabilizing tannis, has been the subject of a series of investigation in recent years. Amla preserve is an important candied product highly valued in the indigenous system of medicine just like Harar (myrobalan) and apple preserves. Amla preserve has a beneficial effect in reducing the cholesterol content of blood. Amla juice concentrate and Amla syrup are other important products.

CHALTA FRUIT *(Dillenia indica Lim).*

The possibility of processing this fruit which is available in Assam.

BANEGARA FRUIT *(Randia dumetorum Lam.)*

This fruit which is found in Karnataka is boiled to remove excess tannis and then eaten as a vegetable. Food technologists have analysed the fruit for its nutritive value.

Garcinia xanthochymus *(Hook. f)*

Experts have determined the proximate composition and standardised methods for the preservation of this fruit. which is found in Karnataka.

AMATEKAYI OR INDIAN HOG PLUM *(Spondias mombin L)*

This fruit which is valued for its vitamin C content is employed for pickling and preserving just like Amla.

PALMYRA PALM KERNEL *(Borassus flabellifer L)*

The palm kernel which is of soft texture and mellow flavour, and known as Nungu in south Indian is prized as a cooling food. Food technologists have shown that it can be preserved by canning and candying.

CARAMBOLA *(Averrhoa caramboia L)*

Both the sweet and acidic types of the fruit can be used in the preparation of squash, jam, jelly and candy.

AVOCADO *(Persia americana Mill)*

This fruit has been introduced in a small way. Freeze dried avocado powder is of considerable interest in view of the relatively high oil content.

CUSTARD APPLE *(Annona squamosa L)*

The fruit grows wild in the South. The juicy pulp is creamy white and possesses a sweet taste and characteristic pleasant aroma. Canning has not proved quite successful as the pulp develops bitterness and a pinkish tint on heating. Preliminary work on freeze drying on the pulp has been encouraging. There is scope for utilizing the pulp for processing in different ways. Sastry and co workers at CFTRI, have done a considerable amount of fundamental work on the preservation of the pulp.

KARONDA *(Karonda carondis L)*

This fruit, which is available in fairly large quantities in some regions of the country, can be candied just like cherry.

DURIAN *(Durio zibethinus Murr)*

LONGSAT *(Lansium domesticum L)*

These exotic fruits, whose cold storage behaviour has been studied might be useful for processing into products, just as in the case of jack fruit, etc. More work in necessary in this respect.

HARD PEAR *(Pyrus spp.)*

Hard pear varieties are not as good as the William and Barlett pears for canning. Modified methods have been standardized by for utilizing them in the preparation of canned halves and quarters. preserve, juice candy and jelly.

LITCHI *(Litchi chinensis Sonn)*

The fleshy pulp of this highly prized fruit can be canned in acidified syrup. The segments are well as the fruit in shell can be dried, as is being done in China. Litchi squash, which has a characteristic taste and flavour, has become popular recently. There is much scope for developing a variety of preserved products from this fruit as in the case of passion fruit.

6

Canning of Vegetables

Vegetables such as pea, beans, carrot, beetroot, tomato, asparagus, etc. are canned in large quantities in different parts of the world. In India, there is a good market for canned peas, green as well as processed ones. Carrot, cabbage, potato, cauliflower, tomato, etc. are canned in the brine in their natural form, or in curried style, using spices, fat, etc., as the covering liquid. Indigenous vegetables like brinjal, lady's finger green jack fruit, bittergourd (kerala), pointed gourd (parwal) etc. are being canned in increasing quantities to meet mostly the requirements of the Armed Forces. The demand from the general public is at present rather limited. Details regarding the type of can, strength of brine, processing conditions, etc. for the canning of some important vegetables are summarized in Table. Now a days, there tremendous demand in india and abroad fro canned Vegetables especially for export.

Asparagus

Canned asparagus is a highly prized delicacy. Green and white asparagus shoots of tender texture are used for canning. Growing of the right type of asparagus requires a great deal of attention. Immediately after removal from the field, the shoots are washed to prevent subsequent discolouration. They are then graded for size, and cut into lengths according to the height of the can. The pieces are then blanched carefully for 2 to 3 minutes in boiling water with the bundle placed, tips up inside a wire cage to prevent undue breakage. Sulphur resistant cans of the round or square type, and 2.0 per cent brine are used for canning. Green asparagus is filled into the cans with the tips down, whereas the white ones are filled with the tipe up.

Asparagus is canned to a limited extent in Kashmir. A slight bitterness in the canned product and metallic taste are pointed out sometimes by the sophisticated consumers.

Beans

Tender stringless beans known as French beans in India, are preferred for canning. They are cut into slices about 2.5 cm in length. The pieces are then blenched in boiling water, drained and filled into plain cans. A two per cent brine is generally employed as covering liquid. The filled cans are exhausted, closed and processed under pressure in retorts. Lima and wax beans are also canned in a similar manner in some countries. The use of copper salts which was once in vogue to fix the green colour of the beans, is now strictly prohibited. Diced beans together with diced carrots and garden peas are sometimes canned as mixed vegetables in macedoine style.

TABLE 12. CANNING TIME TABLE FOR NON-ACID VEGETABLES

Vegetables	Type of can	Strength of brine	Exhaust	Processing time min. at 0.7 kg per cm* steam pressure				
				No. 2 can	No. 2½ can	No. 10 can	Pint jar	Quart jar
Asparagus	Plain	2.25% common salt solution	Exhaust the cans at 192–212 °F (90–100°C) for 7–10 min. or until the temperature in the centre of the can reaches at least 170°F (77°C)	20	24	40	30	35
Bean	Plain	2.25% ,,	,,	40	40	75	35	60
Beet-root	Sulphur resistant	water or 1.5% common salt solution	,,	30	30	40	25	55
Cabbage	Plain	2% common salt solution	,,	—	40	60	—	—
Carrot	Plain	2% ,,	,,	20	25	50	35	40
Cauliflower	Plain	2% ,,	,,	20	20	—	25	30
Curried vegetables	Plain	—	,,	....See recipe....				
Greengram	Plain	2% ,,	,,	40	45	—	40	40
Mushroom	Plain	2% ,,	,,	25	25	40	30	40
Okra	Plain	2% ,,	,,	25	35	—	25	50
Pea, garden	Sulphur resistant	2% common salt & 2.5% sugar solution	,,	40	45	60	40	40
Potato	Plain	2% common salt solution	,,	40	45	—	—	—
Turnip	Plain	2% ,,	,,	30	35	50	35	40

*The data have been taken from : (i) The All American Way of Canning, Wisconsin Aluminium Foundry Co., Inc. Manitowoe Wisconsin ; (ii) The Burpee Way of Home Canning & Cooking, The Burpee Can Sealer Co., 2635, North Kildare Avenue, Cragin Station, Chicago, Illinois; (iii) Lal Singh and Girdhari Lal (1943), Final Report on the workd one under the Fruit and Vegetable Preservation Scheme, Punjab (1934–42) pp. 1–104 and (iv) author's data.

Note : For 0.4 kg butter size cans process time may be taken generally about 5 minutes less than the corresponding values for A 2½ size can

Beetroot

Beetroot is canned in the form of discs or cubes. The top and roots are removed with a stainless steel knife, and the discs or cubes are placed in 1 to 2 per cent common salt solution to preserve the colour prior to canning. Vegetable lacquered cans and 2.0 per cent brine are used for its canning. The purplish red colour pales slightly during storage of the canned product.

Cabbage

Early season cabbage, with tender yellowish leaves is used. The head is either cut into 4 to 8 pieces or shredded into pieces about 2.5 cm thick. The pieces are generally blanched for 5 to 6 minutes in boiling citric or tartaric acid solution of 1.0 per cent strength, and subsequently cooled in 2.0 per cent brine to prevent discolouration. Plain cans and 2.0 per cent brine are used for canning. Pink discolouration in the canned product is a problem which requires more work to determine its cause and prevention.

Carrot

There are two kinds of carrots available in this country, i.e. purple and yellow varieties. The yellow variety is only canned. Tender and small carrots are selected, washed well and the skin rubbed off with coarse cloth or scraped with a knife. For large scale work, mechanical peelers like the potato peeler, which has a revolving emery disc at the bottom of a cylindrical drum, lined with emery, and fitted with sprays for washing off the loosened skin, hair and roots, are used. The peeled carrots are graded for size and canned as such, or are cut into discs or cubes for canning. The pieces are blanched in boiling water for 5 to 13 minutes and packed in plain cans, using brine as covering liquid. Sometimes, a small amount of sugar is also added to the brine.

Cauliflower

Compact flower heads are cut into pieces of suitable size and canned by adopting a procedure similar to that employed in the case of cabbage.

Gram

The white variety of gram (Bengal gram) in the fresh state, as in the case of shelled green peas, is suitable for canning. The pods are shelled by hand. The method of canning is the same as that employed in the case of fresh green peas.

Mushroom

Edible mushrooms which are not poisonous, are canned in the U.K. and the U.S.A. Canned mushroom is a delicacy in India also. As some of the mushrooms are poisonous, great care is necessary in selecting them for canning as such or in the form of soup. Sometimes, they are bleached to a pale colour in a solution of sodium sulphite and citric acid. They are then washed thoroughly and blanched for 4 to 5 minutes in boiling water or in steam, and subsequently dipped in cold water to prevent discolouration. Plain cans and 2.0 per cent brine is used for packing. Sometimes to enhance the flavour, about 28 g of citric acid is added to every 23 litres of brine. To give a friend flavour to the product (when working on a small scale) the mushrooms are cooked in an oven for a few minutes and a little water, butter and salt are added and stirred prior to filling into cans. Mushroom has also got a wide futer scope as the demand of mushroom is growing very fast.

Mushroom cultivation is gaining popularity recently in some parts of India. There is scope for canning as well as dehydration of mushrooms in the country.

Okra (Ladys finger)

Tender green okras of fairly uniform size are selected for canning as whole or as slices. These are blanched for 1 to 2 minutes in boiling water and then cooled in common salt solution of 1.5 per cent strength for about 10 minutes. Plain cans and 2.0 per cent brine are used. The mucilaginous property of the vegetable persists in the canned product also. To overcome this, the slices can be canned in a viscus tomato sauce with suitable spicing. Lady's finger is a highly popular vegetable in India and there is scope for making a good canned product from it.

Peas

Canned fresh green peas stand out prominently among canned vegetables. Peas are canned in several countries of the world such as the U.K. Australia, India etc. which have developed excellent canning varieties. Alaska, Surprise, Thomas Laxton and Lincoln are the more important varieties in the U.K. and the U.S.A. In India, Telephone and Bonnevillae varieties have become popular for canning. Work is continuing to select the right varieties for canning. Safal is a famous brand in india.

Peas for canning should be uniformly ripe and should retain their green colour even after processing. They should possess good texture and flavour. Large size peas are generally preferred for canning, although the Petite Pois the little smooth peas, stand out in a class by themselves in several countries.

Peas are shelled by means of a pea podding machine which consists of a perforated revolving drum with paddles or beaters inside. They are generally graded by size using sieves with mesh sizes ranging from 0.7

cm to 1.0 cm or more. Sometimes, they are graded on the basis of their density by floating them in brine of 1.040 to 1.070 specific gravity. The graded peas are blanched in boiling water for 2 to 5 minutes, rinsed in cold water, and filled into cans manually or by means of a filling machine. Brine containing 1.1 kg of sugar and about 0.67 kg of common salt per 45 litres of water is used as the covering liquid. Sometimes, an edible green colour and mint flavour are also added to the brine. In India a combination of Tartrazine and Blue V.R.S. was being employed successfully till very recently, when the use of Blue V.R.S. was benned as a non permitted food colour. Substitutes in the form of Indigo Carmine have been tried. They have, however, the minor disadvantage in that the green colour of the peas in the can shows up only sometime after opening the can and draining the peas. Experiments are in progress to find a better subsitute from among the harmless green food colours.

After the cans are filled with the peas, they are passed through the exhaust box closed and processed for 40 to 45 minutes (A 2½ cans) in a retort at 10 psig (0.7 kg cm^2) and cooled.

Canned fresh peas are commonly known as garden or 'green' peas. Dried peas, which are soaked in water to imbibe water and then canned, are known as 'processed' peas. These are slightly cheaper than fresh peas, but give an excellent canned product. They can be successfully canned practically throughout the year unlike the fresh peas, which have only a short season of a month or two of canning. For processed peas, the covering liquid should generally contain about 0.5 kg of common salt, 2 kg of sugar, and about 113 to 142 g of a 2.0 per cent solution of a good green food colour for every 45 litres of water. A 2½ cans should be processed for 60 minutes and No. 1 Tall cans (454 g) for 45 minutes, both at 10 psig (0.7 kg/cm2). Large wrinkled Marroufat peas give a superior canned product. Other varieties also may be canned to some extent.

There is a growing demand for canned green as well as processed peas within the country. What is needed is a systematic and intensive drive to evolve and develop the best canning varieties of peas suited to the region on the basis of advance contracts, and scientific advice and supervision at every stage of growing, harvesting and transport, as is being done in several other countries. Peas have a comparatively short season, and they undergo rapid changes during podding, transport, etc. It is, therefore necessary to handle and can them with the least delay, employment automatic machines at strategic poinsts, so that the canned product is of the finest quality.

Potato

Just now, a considerable amount of work has been done in the country with particular reference to variety starchiness, gelatin etc. and some of the references are given under literature cited. Potatoes are canned whole or as slices. They should be sufficiently firm for canning. They are washed and peeled with a knife or in a rotary vegetable peeler lined with an abrasive like emery. Any adhering skin is trimmed. The peeled potatoes are placed in two per cent brine to prevent discolouration. Some of the softer varieties of potatoes have to be placed after blanching in about 2.5 per cent calcium chloride solution for about an hour for firming their texture, so that they do not break up and become meshy in the can. They should be washed well before they are filled into the cans. Plain cans and two per cent brine are used for canning.

Recently, investigations have been carried out at the Central Food Technological Research Institute, Musore, to select varieties suitable for canning. India is an important potato growing country and steps are necessary to develop processing industries based on potato. Some varieties of potato have been observed to turn bitter after canning. They are not suitable for canning.

Tomato

Canned tamatoes are important articles of international trade. Several countries specialise in packing tomato products. For canning, the tomatoes selected should be ripe, of medium size, regular shape and uniform red colour, and should have plenty of pulp and should be free from blemishes. Stone and Sanjose are the two major canning varieties in the U.S.A. Tomatoes have a tendency to split and harbour mould growth. Such varieties are not preferred for canning or for conversion to products such as juice, puree, ketchup, etc.

Tomatoes which are canning ripe are selected washed in water and then scalded in boiling water or steam for 2 to 3 minutes to crach the skin and facilitate its subsequent removal by lifting off. The peeled tomatoes are placed in shallow pans to prevent crushing. According to Siddappa and Mustafa, the loss in peeling and trimming is 30 to 35 per cent. The peeled and trimmed tomatoes are then filled into cans, and common salt is added at the rate of about one per cent, i.e. one tea spoonful of salt for an A2½ can. Sometimes a little sugar also is added. Tomatoes are canned either as a solid pack i.e. without the addition of tomato juice or as a standard pack with the addition of tomato juice. Generally for safe processing long cooking for 45 to 60 minutes in boiling water is necessary. Pressure processing however is not adopted as the tomatoes are fairly acidic with their pH being nearly 4.2.

Turnip

There are three types of turnips-red, white and yellow. White turnips are generally canned. They should be tender and practically free from fibre. They are washed, cut into pieces of about 0.9 cm thickness, and the pieces blanched for 3 to 4 minutes in boiling water and then canned in plain cans using simple brine as covering liquid.

OTHER VEGETABLES

Brussel sprouts (in the U.K.) karela, tinda, parwal, kundree, green jack fruit spinach etc. (in India) are some of the other vegetables that are canned such as green gram, cowpea, Bengal gram. etc. just as in the case of processed peas, as there is a great deal of nutritional interest in these as sources of valuable vegetable protein foods.

The processes for canning karela, tinda and parwal are practically similar to those adopted in the case of turnip, carrot etc. Spinach is canned as puree. The methods are largely as follow.

Parwal *(Coccinia indica)*

It is canned in the form of halves or slices in brine. As already described bhindi (Lady's finger) or okra is canned in its tender form as it would be otherwise highly fibrous and mucilaginous. It is canned whole or as halves or as discs after blanching in dilute brine and washing away most of the mucilaginous matter. It is canned in brine or sometimes in tomato sauce to minimise the muscilaginous character.

Spinach

Canned spinach in the form of its puree, is a popular product. The leaves are blanched in water or in salt solution, made into a puree by passing through a pulper, and the puree canned in plain cans adopting a longer process. Canned spinach has a comparatively short storage life, and the can has a marked tendency to develop pinholes and perforations during storage, especially at elevated temperatures.

KARELA *(bitter gourd)*

Karela is blanched in water and canned in brine whole or in the form of discs or slices in the normal way.

The preservation of Karela (bitter gourd) (momordica charantia, Lin) with particular reference to canning and dehydration and also of tinda, (Citrus vulagaris, Schrad Var. Fistulosus). Medium size karelas are trimmed at both ends and given a deep slit longitudinally. Karelas of other sizes are cut into circular discs of 12 to 22 mm diameter. The prepared material is soaked overnight in 10 per cent salt solution to facilitate removal of excess of bitterness. They are drained the next day, washed in water and blanched for 4 to 5 minutes in boiling water or in steam, and then cooled quickly. They are then canned in plain A 2½ size cans to meet the requirement of the Defence Services in the country and in 0.4 kg butter size or in No. 1 Tall (454 g) cans for the export market. The covering brine contains 2 per cent salt and 0.1 per cent citric acid. The cans are filled with hot brine, exhausted, closed and processed at 116°C for 40, 35 and 35 minutes in the case of A 2½ one pound (0.4 kg) butter and No. 1 tall cans, respectively. On an average every 100 kg of karela yields 200 A 2½ cans or 350 one pound (0.4 kg) butter size cans.

Tinda

Tinda is canned in its whole form. They are pale green in colour and of 3 to 5 cm diameter size are preferred for canning. They are graded, washed and peeled by knife or in a potato peeler fitted with carborundum disc. Small sized tindas are canned whole, while the bigger ones are cut into halves longitudinally. The prepared material is blanched for 4 to 5 minutes in boiling water and canned in plain A 2½ size cans, using covering brine containing 3 per cent salt and 0.1 per cent citric acid. The cans are exhausted in steam for 6 to 8 minutes, closed and processed at 115°C for 45 minutes. In the case of one pound (0.4 kg) butter size (401 x 300) and No. 1 Tall (301 x 409) cans, the process time is 35 minutes. On an average 100 kg of tindas, as received yield 110 A 2½ cans or 175 pound (0.4 kg) butter size cans.

CURRIED VEGETABLES

In the West, vegetables are generally canned in brine. Spices are added to the drained vegetables at the time of serving them. In India, people prefer to add fats, spices, etc. to the vegetable while it is being cooked. A suitable method has been worked out at the Central Food Technological Research Institute, Mysore, for canning 'ready to serve' canned vegetables in curried form. Potato and cauliflower, cauliflower and tomato, potato and peas, potato, peas and cauliflower, are some of the popular combinations. Green jack fruit also has been found suitable for mixing. The vegetables are prepared for canning in the same way as for cooking. A special type of gravy is prepared as follows : For one dozen A 2½ cans of curried vegetables.

	oz. (g).
Mustard (whole)	3/4 (21)
Coriander powder	3/4 (21)
Red chilli powder	1/2 to 3/4 (14 to 21)
Caraway seed	3/4 (21)
Turmeric powder	1½ - 1½ (42-49)
Common salt	31/4 (91)
Vegetable fat (hydrogenated oil)	14 (400)
Water	Sufficient to make up gravy for 12 cans

The fat is heated in a pan and the mustard fried in it for a few minutes till the seeds crack. The other ingredients are then added and frying continued for a few more minutes. The required of water is then added and the whole mass brought to a boil. Sixteen to twenty ounces of the vegetables, depending upon the combination, are filled into each plain a 2 1/2 can. Hot gravy is added to the can and the can closed and processed for 60 to 75 minutes at 10 psig (0,7 kg/cm)2.

Other canned products. Products such as canned plain rice, canned rice etc. which are of Defence interest have been standardised at C.F.T.R.I. Mysore.

7

Spoilage In Canned Foods

Canned foods are liable to spoilage in storage for various reasons. Fruits products often lose their normal and attractive appearance and become unsaleable, although they may remian quite fit for consumption. The two important kinds of spoilage are : (i) spoilage by micro organisms, and (ii) spoilage owing to physical or chemical changes. The former is more important. The appearance and smell of a spoilt can of food is different from that of a good one. Spoilt cans of food should never be tasted, as a precautionary measure, especially when spoilage is suspected to be owing to micro organisms. Various indications of spoilage are as follows :

Swell

In a swelled can, the ends are tightly bulged. The bulge is due to the formation of carbon dioxide or other gases inside the can as a result of decomposition of the contents caused by micro organisms. If the bulged ends are pressed hard, they may go inward, but when the pressure is released, they will get back to their original position and would remian convex. The decomposed food in the can has an offensive and sour odour and is generally discoloured. It is not fit for consumption and may even contain toxins produced by bacilli like Clostridium botulinum.

Hydrogen swell

Hydrogen formed by the action of acids present in the fruit on the tinplate causes the can to bulge at the ends. In such cases, the food remains generally free from harmful micro organisms and is still fit for consumption.

Springer

A mild swell at one or both ends of a can is called a 'springer'. It may be an initial stage of hydrogen swell or may be caused by insufficient exhausting or by overfilling of the can. The bulged ends (or at least one and) can be pressed back to the original position, but will again become convex after sometime. Food in such cans generally remains fit for consumption.

Flipper

A can with a mild positive pressure is called a 'flipper'. It may be an initial stage of swell or hydrogen swell, but more frequently, it is owing to over filling or under exhausting.

Flat sour

This type of spoilage is caused mostly in non acid foods like vegetables by micro organisms without production of gas. It is, therefore, difficult to detect it from the external appearance of the can. It may be caused almost entirely by under sterilization. In that case, thermophilic bacteria would be of special significance. The product has a sour odour, and its acidity will be much higher than that of the normal product. It is not fit for consumption.

Leaker

A very small leak may appear in the can owing to : (i) faulty seam, (ii) fautly lock seam, or (iii) pinholes as a are sult of corrosion from the inside of the can or rusting of the can from the outside.

Breather

There may be a very tiny leak in the can through which air may pass in but not micro organisms. Consequently, air passes back and forth into the can. In this case, the vacuum in the can is always nil, and the pressure inside the can is equal to that of the atmosphere. The food remains fit for consumption. The damage to food in such cases is usually owing to rusting of the can caused by oxygen in the air passing in through the tiny leak.

Bursting of cans

Cans may sometimes burst. This may be due to excess of pressure caused by the gases inside, produced by decomposition of the food by micro organisms, or by hydrogen gas formed by chemical action of the food on the tinplate. In such cases, the canned product becomes a total loss.

8

Fruit Juices Squashes & Cordials

In India, cold drinks are in demand practically throughout the year. Among these, fruit juices have an important place. Being rich in essential minerals, vitamins and other nutritive factors, they are quite popular. Besides, they are delicious and have universal appeal unlike other beverages.

The nutritive value of real fruit beverage is far greater than that of synthetic products which are at present being bottled and sold in large quantities throughout the country. The annual production of carbonated beverages like lemonade, orangeade, strawberry, lime juice, etc. as well as various kinds of sherbet and other artificially flavoured beverage runs into several million bottles. If real fruit juices could be substituted for these synthetic preparations, it would be a boon to the consumer as well as to the fruit grower. There is, therefore, great scope in the country for the production of fruit juices and other fruit based beverage.

With the rapid progress fruit farming that has taken place during the last two decades, fresh fruit juices are being increasingly sold by vendors in some of the larger towns. The demand for fresh fruit juices is on the increase, but these cannot be had easily, when the fruits are out of season. Fruit juices have, therefore, to be preserved in a form in which they can be made available to the public during the off season.

Preparation of fruit beverages on a commercial scale was practically unknown in the country till abut 1930. New products such as squashes and cordials are, however, now being packed to the extent of more than three million bottles annually. If aerated water factories begin to use pure fruit juices insteand of synthetic colour and flavours, that alone will create a steady demand for utilization of several thousand tons of fruit every years.

Nowadays, however, on account of the common use of fruit juices as breakfast foods, a large variety of them is produced on a big scale from fruits such as orange, pineapple, grapefruit, apple, and grape. Small quantities of juices are also produced from sour lime, lemon, tangerine, loganberry, cherry, blackberry, youngberry, apricot, peach, plum, prune, pomegranate, papaya, currents, pear, etc. Several of these tart juices are largely used for preparing mixed drinks and in bakery products. They are now becoming more popular than the carbonated beverages from apples and grapes.

In this country, the pure fruit juice industry is still in its infancy. Preparation of these juices is limited to small scale productions only, because the equipment required for production of the best quality fruit juices is rather sophisticated and costly. Quite recently, however, a few units have come into existence to pack fairly large quantities of pure fruit juices from citus fruits, pineaple, grape, apple etc. Fruits such as apple grape, pomegranate, mulberry, jamun (Eugenia jambolana), phalsa (Grewia asiatica), mango, pineapple, etc. are generally utilized for the preparation of juices. The scope for large scale production of fruit juices is, however, limited at present, as these are not yet included to any considerable extent in the normal dietary of the people. Tomato juice, however, which is in fair demand already, has considerable scope for large scale production.

Sherbet. It consists of sugar syrups flavoured with artificial essences of fruits or herbs, and have been produced in India from times immemorial and are, therefore, well known practically throughout the country.

Of late, large scale manufacture of orange squash, lemon squash, lime juice cordial, pineapple squash and mango squash has made considerable progress in different parts of the country. Methods for the preparation of other fruit beverage like passion fruit squash, pomegranate syrup, mulberry syrup, plum squash, peach nectar, etc. were standardised in the Fruit Preservation Laboratories at Lyallpur and Quetta. There appears to be scope for these beverages also. Proper eduction and publicity of the dietetic value of fruit beverages is necessary to stimulate a general demand for them.

Fruit juices, especially orange, apple and grape juices, are concentrated using modern equipment so that there is practically very little loss in their nutritional properties and flavour characteristics. Sometimes, the recovered flavour is added back to the concentrate to get full fruit taste and flavour on dilution for serving. These concentrates are used as basis for soft drinks, pharmaceutical preparations, baby foods, tonic foods, etc. The frozen orange juice concentrate (four to one) is an excellent example in this case. Concentration is effected by freezing or by application of heat employing high vacuum. Conventional equipments such as climbing and falling film evaporators and more recently, the centri therm or centrifugal evaporators etc. are being employed. Fruit juices and concentrates are further converted into free flowing fruit juice powders by adopting methods such as puff drying foam mat drying, freeze drying etc. Sometimes, sealed in flavours are blended with the powders so as to get natural fruit juices on reconstitution for serving as beverages etc. A considerable amount of work has already been done in recent years at the Central Food Technological Research Institute, Mysore, on several aspects of these products and such work is still continuing. The results promise to be of great scientific as well as industrial importance.

Equipment for fruit juices

Until recently, the equipment used for the extraction of fruit juices was similar to that used in the manufacture of wine, vinegar, etc. There has, however, been a rapid advance in the fruit juice inductry in the U.S.A. the U.K. and several other countries. Consequently, one can now get equipment ranging from the simple household juice ectractor or press, to the fully automatic juice lines capable of handling several thousand bottles daily. Particularly, the development of the citrus juice industry, has been the most important factor in revolutioning the entire juice industry. It is essential that suitable equipment that suitable equipment is employed for the successful operation of this industry.

Washing equipment. For washing apples, citrus fruit, tomatoes berries, etc. different kinds of equipment are available. Tender fruits like berries, tomatoes, etc. are usually washed with fine overhead sprays of water, whereas the fruits travel on a continuous woven wire belt. A rotating rod cylinder with a helical scraw inside to push the fruit along, and fitted with jets of water, forced by a centrifugal pump, has been found highly useful for washing loose jacket mandarin oranges. On a small scale, cement or galvanised iron tanks for holding water are quite useful. A battery of these will be adequate even for a factory of moderate size.

Sorting equipment. In large factories, a continuous broad belt, made of woven metal, is generally employed for sorting the fruits. In smaller factories, however, batch sorting will suffice.

Extraction equipment. There are two types of extractions. In one case, the fruits are crushed and pressed continuously in one operation, whereas in the other, the fruits are crushed or cut into small pieces or comminuted in a mill, and these are subsequently pressed in a suitable press.

In citrus fruits, the juice is enclosed in small natural sacs. Besides there are other adhering tissues also in the fruit. The peel consist of an inner white spongy portion called the albedo, and an outer yellow coloured portion called the flavado. The oil glands are embedded in the flavodo and are easily ruptured even with a gentle pressure. Substances which are responsible for the bitterness of the juice are located chiefly in (i) the fruit tissues in which the juice sacs are embedded, (ii) the inner portion of the flavedo, (iii) the albedo, and (iv) the seeds. The presence of these (containing bitter substances) makes it rather difficult to extract the juice free from bitterness. An ideal equipment would be the one in which the juice is extracted from the juice sacs only without its coming into contact with the other tissues of the fruit. With the existing equipment, the bitter substances also are extracted to varying extents and get incorporated with the juice.

Extraction of juice from peeled segments as such, or from segments dipped in lye solution form removing most of the adhering tissues (Siddappa) helps to minimise the incorporation of bitter substances into the juice, especially in the case of the loose jacket mandarin type oranges such as Coorg and Nagpur oranges. In the Taglith type of press, developed by the Central Food Technological Research Institute, Mysore, the unpeeled orange is cut into halves held against cups in two stainless steel drums revolving towards each other, employing synchronised plungers with conical fluted heads having holes for carrying away the pressed juice down their stem. In this arrangement, a in the case of the small super juicer employing the same principle the inner and outer juices from the cut half of the oranges are colleced into two separate channnels. The inner juice is practically free from the peel emulsion, whereas the outer juice is contains oil rich peel emulsion. The juice is fairly thin in body, unlike the juice got from the screw type ectractor. As such, it is better suited for subsequent concentration (Siddappa). Juice with 'thicker' body' is generally preferred for canning and for making squash. Broadly, there are four types of equipment employed for the extraction of fruit juices.

Halving and burring machines. Malta orange or Sathgudi or mosambi oranges (Citrus sinensis Osbeck), grape fruit (Citrus paradisi var maximan), lemon (Citrus medica var. Limonum) and galgal (Citrus limonia osbeck) are cut by a special machine in which the is placed in a conical cup in a wheel which brings the fruit against a stationary or revolving knife. The fruit is cut into two halves, which drop into a receptacle placed below. The burrs (or roses) are generally made of stainless steel, monel metal, aluminium, nickel, or non odorous hard wood. They are conical in shape and are ribbed. They are driven by a motor. The cut half of the fruit is held against the revolving burr and the reamed juice is collected in a vessel kept below. There are generally two burrs, one each on either side of the shalf. Several single burrs can also be fitted in series. By regulating the speed of the burr and the pressure on the fruit held against it, any excessive tearing of the tissues can be avoided.

Contnuous scraw expeller press. These presses are similar in principle to the familiar household meat mincer. The segments of the fruit are fed through a hopper at one end of a feeding screw, revolving inside a conical jacket, which is perforated in sections or throughout. The diameter of the perforations depends upon the type of fruit. The juice flows out through the perforations and the pomace comes out at the end of the conical jacket. The flow of pomace, and hence the pressing pressure of the screw, can be adjusted to some extent by means of a movable disc at the conical end of the perforated jacket. Small power driven screw type extractors (1/2 to 1 HP) have now been introduced in several factories in the country. Very large units are not, however, in general use at present. The juice extracted is generally thick and cloudy and contains a conciderable amount of mascerated pulp. The juice should be passed through sieves to remove the pulp to the desired extent. Screw type juice extraction are useful in the case of a tomatoes, grapes, etc. In the case of pineaple, however, the pieces of fruit are first crushed in a screw type crusher and and then from the crushed material, the juice is separated effectively in a centrifuge (hydroextractor) which is, by and large, a suspended basket contrifuge widely employed in the sugar and chemical industries. This technique has recently been found hightly effective in pineapple juice production.

Plunger type press. The halved citrus fruit is held on an inverted cup in which it is pressed by an automatic adjustment against a metallic cone fitting into the cup. The clearance between th ecup and the cone is slightly greater than the usual thickness of the peel of the fruit so that very little of the peel oil or emulsion is pressed out. This type of press is being used in one or two factories only in the country.

Roller type press. Roller presses made of hard granite or wood, are specially designed to extract juice from sour limes *(Citrus medica var. acida)* which are popularly known as kagzi or kagdi nimboo. The whole lime is fed through the rollers. These presses are in extensive use in West Indies and Jamaica. They have been introduced in some of the Indian factories also.

Double operation

Fruits like apples, grapes, berries, etc. are first crushed in a grater or crusher or comminuting mill, and the juice then extracted from the crushed material by means of a hydraulic press. In large scale production as in the case of apple juice, the crushing device forms an integral part of the press itself.

Apple grater. The skin and other tissues of apples do not have any undesirable constituents, which adversely affect the taste and flavour of the juice, as in the case of citrus fruits. The entire fruit is, therefore, crushed and pressed. A battery of such graters can be employed for large scale production. The grater consists of a heavy steel cylinder fitted on its surface with short knives which are spring loaded and work against a corrugated plate, attached to the frame of the press by the side of the steel cylinder. The springs give a certain amount of flexibility to the mechanism so that the grater is not damaged in case pieces of wood or stone, etc. get into the press along with the fruit. Gear arrangement is provided for running the rollers at higher speeds. Apples are fed whole into the hopper. They are crushed and grated between the cylinder and the corrugated plate, and the crushed material falls into a receptacle below. The grater can be set to crush the fruit to the desired degree of fineness. Pieces of 0.3 to 1.2 cm thickness are the best for extraction of juice. In recent years, a different type of crusher known as 'Hammer type pulper' has come into use in the U.S.A. and elsewhere.

Crusher for grapes, berries. A grape crusher consists of two fluted or grooved rollers made of wood or metal. These are arranged hortizontally and revolve towards each other. The clearance between the two is adjustable. The fruit which is fed to the hopper at the top falls between the rollers and gets crushed. Strawberries and some other berry fruits which contain gums, are first heated and then crushed. Tomatoes can also be crushed in these crushers.

Pressing

Basket press. In the industry two types of presses are used for pressing the juice from the crushed fruit. They are: (i) the basket press, and (ii) the rack and cloth press. Basket presses which are of various designs and capacities, are worked mannually by hydraulic pressure. The manually operated press consists of a strong cylindrical basket made of wooden slats. It rests ona wooden or matallic base. There is a strong screw at the top of the frams. The crushed fruit is folded in a piece of strong cloth and placed inside the basket. By turning the screw by hand or with a hydraulic pump, the juice is pressed out. It flows out through the slates in the basket into the bottom tray from which it is channelled into a collecting vessel. The basket press has been found useful in the case of apple, grape, pomegranate, phalsa, etc.

Rack and cloth press. In this type of press, the crushed fruit is spread as a layer in coarse woven cloth of cotton or nylon and folded into a square suited to the size of the platform of the press. Several such layers are arranged alternately between racks built of wooden slats. The built up layers are subjected to hydraulic pressure by means of a pump. The juice is pressed out gradually due to increasing pressure in the pile. The released juice is collected at the base of the pile. Various types of these presses, which are in use in several countries, are claimed to give higher yields of clear juice than the basket type presses. In California, however, basket presses are preferred for extraction of juice from grapes. Rack and cloth presses are in use in a few factories in India specialising in the the production of apple juice.

Othe types of extractors. Special devices for extracting juice have been des gned in the U.S.A., Australia, etc. for fruits like pomegranate, passion fruit, etc. It has been described a press for pomeg.'anate in which the whole fruit as such is pressed. Expert has described a special pulper for passion fruit in which the juice is extracted by reaming the halved fruit. A continuously operating device has been employed in Australia to extract the pulpy juice along with the seeds from passion fruit.

Pulping equipment. Fruit juices extracted or pressed by and of the methods described contain suspended matter like coarse fruit tissues, pieces of skin seeds, and finally divided fruit pulp. These are separated from the juice in various ways, depending upon the nature of the product required, e.g. cloudy, sparkling , clear, etc. Three important methods in common use are : (i) straining or screening, (ii) settling or sedimentation, and (iii) filtration.

Straining or screening equipment. Several types of equipment, varying in design and capacity, are in use for straining juices. A pulper made of stainless steel with power driven wooden, metallic or brush paddles, which revolve inside, has been highly useful in the case of citrus, tomato and mango juices. The fruit, which is fed through a hopper, is crushed and pressed by the paddles against the sieve. The juice flows out through the sieve into the jacket and is colllected at the outlet below, while the coarse residue passes out at the lower end of the sieve.

Epuipment for settling and sedimentation. For sedimentation and settling of the juices only a few wooden barrels are required.

Filtration equipment. Finely suspended particles in the juice are removed with a special equipment known as 'Filter press'. Filter presses are of various designs and capacities. The filtering media may be finely woven cloth, canvas, fibre, asbestos pads, cotton or wood pulp discs, porous porcelain wares etc. The frame and fiter press, which is similar to that used in sugar factories, but made of wood, has been highly effective for the clarification of lime juice required for the preparation of lime juice cordial. Seitz filters of various design and sizes are widely employed for filtering wines, spirits, sugar syrups, cordials, apple and other fruit juices, etc.

A simple filtering device, however, is a large conical bag of heavy drill cloth or felt, similar to the ordinary jelly bag. The juice is heated with filter aid and placed inside the bag. Filtration is rather slow, but the output can be increased by having a battery of such filter bags.

Deaerator and flash pasteuriser. Freshly extracted and screened juices contain appreciable quantity of oxygen which should be removed before packing. The special equipment used for the purpose is called a deaerator. The deaerated juice is subsequently heated in a flash-pasteurisation equipment.

Commercial deaerators and flash pasteurisers vary greatly in design, construction and capacity. This process is a combination of deaeration and flash pasteurization and has been successfully employed in the case of citrus, pineapple and tomato juices. Such advanced processes and equipments are not yet in common use in India. They are, however, recommended for improving the quality of the natural fruit juice products.

FRUIT BEVERAGES

Fruit juices are preserved in different forms such as pure juices, squashes, cordials, fermented juices, etc. These are broadly defined as follows.

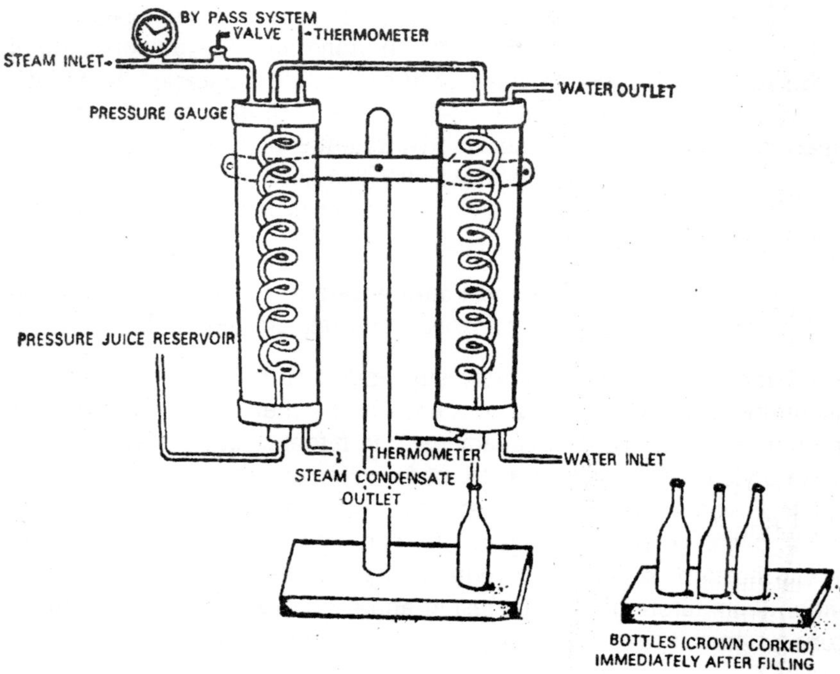

Fig 24. Diagram of a laboratory flash pasteurizer

Unfermented juice or pure fruit juice. This is the natural juice pressed out of the fruit, and remains practically unaltered in its composition during preparation and preservation.

Fruit juice beverage. This is a fruit juice which is considerably altered in composition before consumption. It may be diluted before it is served as a drink.

Fermented fruit beverage. This is a fruit juice which has undergone alcoholic fermentation by yeast. The product contains varying amounts of alcohol. Grape wines, apple ciders, berry wines etc. are typical examples of this kind of beverage.

Fruit juice squash. This consists essentially of strained juice containing moderate quantities of fruit pulp of which cane sugar is added for sweetening e.g. orange squash, lemon squash, pineapple squash, mango squash.

Fruit juice cordial. This is a sparkling clear sweetened fruit juice from which all the pulp and other suspended materials have been completely eliminated, e.g. lime juice cordial.

Sherbet or syrup. This a clear sugar syrup which has been artificially flavoured, e.g. sherbets of sandal, sangtra, almond rose, khuskhus, sarasaparilla, kewra etc.

Fruit juice concentrate. This is a fruit juice which has been concentrated by the removal of water either by heat or by freezing. Carbonated beverages and other products are made from this.

Fruit juice powder. This is fruit juice which has been converted into a free flowing highly hygroscopic powder to which natural fruit flavour in powder form is incorporated to compensate for any loss of flavour in concentration, dehydration, etc. Freeze dried fruit juice powders form the last word among sophisticated fruit juice products. They are reconstituted readily to yield full strength, full fruit, fruit juice drinks.

Preparation and preservation

Fruit juices have their best taste, aroma and colour when they are freshly extracted or expressed. All subsequent efforts to preserve them adversely affect their quality to varying degrees, depending upon the method of preservation employed. The most important problem, therefore, is to adopt only such methods as would help retain their quality to the maximum extent possible.

The most important steps in processing fruits juices are : (i) selecting and preparation of fruit, (ii) extraction of juice, (iii) deaeration, (iv) straining, fitration and clarfication, and (v) preservation. The quality of the juice will depend on the manner in which these several processes are carried out.

Selection and preparation of fruit. All fruits are not suitable for making fruit juice, either because of difficulties in the extraction of juice, or because the juice got is of poor quality. Even some of the juicy fruits are not quite suited as they do not yield juice of good beverage quality. The variety of fruit, its maturity, and the locality in which it is grown, have a marked effect on its flavour as well as keeping quality. The best juice is therefore, extracted from freshly picked, sound and suitable varieties, when they are at the optimum stage of maturity. Fully ripe mid season fruits, particularly citrus fruits, generally yield juice superior to that of fruits picked early or late in the season. Decayed or damaged fruits do not yield good juice. Small cull fruits i.e. undersized, over sized malformed or blemished fruits, which do not fetch a good price in the fresh fruit market, but which are otherwise of good quality, can be profitably utilized for the production of fruit juices.

The fruits should be washed thoroughly with water, and in some cases scrubbed also, while washing to romove any adhering dust and other extraneous matter. Residues of sprays of arsenic and lead should be removed with dilute HCI. Twently three litres of HCI in 455 litres of water is adequate for this purpose. All mouldy and decayed parts should be removed as in the case of fruits prepared for canning.

Juice extraction. The method of juice extraction will differ with the structure and composition of the fruit. Generally, juice from fresh fruits is extracted by crushing and pressing them. In the case of fruits in which the juice is in sace or in cells, during the extraction of the juice, the other tissues of the fruit, in which these sace or cells are embedded, are also broken or crushed, resulting in the incorporation of some undesirable constituents in the juice. The admixture of these extrancous constituents with the juice should be avoided as far as possible by adopting a suitable method of extraction. Further, during extraction, the juice should not be unduly exposed to air, as oxygen of the air will adversely affect the colour, taste and aroma and also reduce the vitamin content of the juice. Citrus juices, tomato juice, and even the more stable juice such is those of apples and grapes, deteriorate rapidly in quality, when they are extracted by adopting methods which expose them to air for unduly long periods. For products like tomato juice, special extraction equipment has been designed recently to reduce incorporation of air to the minimum. The entire process of manufacture of tomato juice should be conducted in an atmosphere of steam to protect the juice from oxidation by air.

Deaeration. In spite of all improvements made so far in the extraction equipment, fruit juices do retain some air. This is due to the difficulty of extracting the juice without some aeration, and also to the presence of air in the inter ccllular spaces of the fruit. Most of the air is present on the surface of the fruit particles, while some is found dissolved in the juice. In the case of citrus juices, particularly orange juice, which is highly susceptible to the adverse action of the residual air, immediately after extraction the juice is subjected to a high vacuum whereby most of the air as well as, others gases are removed. This process is known as deartion. The equipment employed is fairly expensive. It is however, necessary for large scale production of orange and other pure fruit juices. A simple laboratory deaeration unit is therefore desirable.

Straining, filtration and clarification. Fruit juices, after extraction, always contain varying amounts of suspended matter, which consists of broken fruit tissue, seed and skin and also various gums, pectic substances and proteins in colloidal suspension. Usually, coarse particles of pulp, seeds and pieces of skin are removed by means of screens in the case of almost all juices. The presence of these generally causes deterioration in the quality of the final product. In the early years of the fruit juice industry, it was a common practice to remove completely all the suspended matters, including colloidal suspension, before packing the juice in containers. This, no doubt improved the appearance of the product, but quite often resulted in lack of fruit character and flavour. The present trend is to let fruit juices and fruit beverage remain reasonably cloudy or pulpy in appearance. The recent comminuted fruit beverages, employing the whole fruit for extraction, are based on this concept and they are claimed to be more nutritive than the clear juices. Sastry and his colleagues at C.F.T.R.I., Mysore, have done highly useful work on this subject. Some juices and juice beverages like grape juice, apple juice, lime juice cordial are, however, still packed brilliantly clear, employing enzymes clarifying agents, fine filtration etc., to make them remain perfectly clear during storage and distribution. Recently, at C.F.T.R.I., Mysore have made a detailed study of preparation of 'liquid fruits' from guava, banana and other pulpy fruits, adopting enzymatic processing. These liquid fruits are likely to become popular in the near future.

Coarse particles of suspensions in the juice are removed either by straining through sieves of non corrodible metal, or by sedimentation. For sedimentation, the juice is stored in carboys or barrels, adding a chemical preservative to ensure that the juice does not undergo fermentation during storage. The coarse particles settle down gradually over a period of a few days. the supernatent juice, which contains mostly fine suspended particles and colloidal suspensions, is syphoned off for subsequent treatment. The type of equipment used for straining the juice depends upon the kind of juice. It is fitted with screens having holes of varying dimensions. the juice is passed through the sieves soon after extraction. Coarse particles of tissues skins and seeds are separated by vibractory action, and the juice still retaining the desired amount of fine pulp and juice sacs is collected in a vessel. Recently a high speed centrifuge, similar to Sharples centrifuge, and having an automatic sediment discharge device, has been employed for removal of pulp from orange juice prior to its concentration.

When perfectly clear juices are required, complete removal of all suspensions is effected either by filtration or by clarification. For this, enzymes and fining agents are employed. The mothods of clarification, which have been employed for many years by the wine makers, brewers and sugar manufactures, are now being increasingly adopted in the fruit juice industry also.

Filtration is necessary for removing completely all the fine and colloidal suspensions. In this process, which is physical in nature, the juice which has been strained, and from which the coarse particules have already been removed, is forced through a filtering medium. The filtering medium usually consists of woven fibre cloth, asbestos pads, cotton pulp, porous porcelain or wood pulp. The colloidal supension tends to clog the filters in the press. In order to minimise this, filter aids such as diatomaceous or infusorial earth, also known as Kieselguhr, Kaolin, Spanish clay, etc., are added to the juice so that the filtering medium is coated with these, without blocking the fine pores, and thereby facilitating filtration. The use of these filter aids, however, tends to impart to the juice a slight amount of earthy taste, which may be unacceptable to some persons. These aids should, therefore, be used with caution and in small quantities only. Further, they should be kept in uniform suspension by constant agitation when the juice is being forced through the press by means of a pump. They can be ignited and reused a faw times before they are finally discarded.

It is recommended boiling of the filter aid with one per cent of citric or tartaric acid, before use in order to minimise the adverse effect on the taste and aroma of the juice, For clarificationof unfermented apple juice, Expert recommend the use of ignited Kaolin as filter aid at the rate of 1 kg of it to 100 kg of juice. The resulting juice will be clear and sparkling. A variety of equipment like multiple disc filters, freme and plate filters, etc., employing different kinds of filter aids, is available nowadays.

Use of fining agents. This method aims at producing a voluminous flocculent precipitate which settles gradually, carrying down with it finely divided particles and colloidal suspensions that are responsible for cloudiness or haze in clarified juices. A number of substances like gelatin, mixture of tannin and gelatin, milk, white of egg, casein etc., have been used by wine makers and brewers for clarification. The tannin gelatin method is most widely employed for clarifying fruit juices also. Recently, technologist has observed in large scale bottling of clear as well as sparkling apple juice, that prior enzyme treatment of the extracted apple juice is necessary before the tannin gelatin method could give a perfectly clear stable juice.

Finings are of three kinds. (i) enzymes which destroy the colloids present in the juice ; (ii) finings which are purely physical in their action, e.g., infusorial earths; and (iii) chemical findings which act on the gummy and colloidal substancs present in the juice to form insoluble coagulates that settle down easily, e.g., gelatin, albumen and casein.

Enzymes. Various kinds of enzymes, such as proteolytic, pectin decomposing, hyrolytic, starch liquefying enzymes etc. are sometimes used to remove pectin, proteins and starch from fruit juices. In the trade, these enzyme preparations are sold under different brand names such as Pectinol, Filtragol, Ido, Pectasine etc. Each class of enzymes has a different type of action on the colloids present in the juice. The process of clarification differs according to the particular enzyme used.

Pectinol. The natural enzymes being not quite satisfactory, in 1930 Kertesz prepared an effective enzyme which he called pectinol 'A'. Later on Pectinol 'B' and Pectinol 'E' also were produced. Pectinol enzymes are prepared from the mould Penicillium glaucum, which is found growing on grapes. Pectinol breaks down pectin into soluble form, thereby freeing the suspended particles, which subsequently settle down speedily, leaving the solution clear. Pectinol is widely used for clarification of fruit juices. It is sold in different forms in other countries. There are three grades namely (i) W. Grade for grape juice and wine; (ii) A. grade for apple juice; and (iii) M grade for juices of other fruits such as cherries, respberries, prunes, etc. The effectiveness of Pectinol in coagulating colloidal material depends on the following factors :

1. Quantity of Pectinol used : The amount of Pectinol required depends on the quantity of the suspended matter present in the juice. Usually, 0-1 per cent of it is sufficient in the case of apple juice.

2. Composition of the juice, particularly its pH value. Pectinol is more effective in the case of acid juices.

3. Temperature at which the juice is treated. Apple juice can be clarified in about 20 hours at 19°C. At a lower temperature, however, a much longer time is required for clarification of the juice. At 38 to 43°C only a few hours are required. Charley has compared the relative efficiency of Pectinol, Filtragol and Maltolysin (a proteolytic enzyme for clarification of unfermented apple juice).

Fitragol. This is another pectin decomposing enzyme, which has been developed by Messrs. Bayer, Lever Kusen, Germany, for the clarification of juices of kernel fruit, stone fruit and grapes.

In the usual method of clarification by filtration, involving considerable amount of precipitate in addition to the coarse material from the juice a large part of the colour & aromat colloidal matter also are removed with the result that the juice suffers in quality in regard to its colour, taste, and aroma. When Filtragol is used, the pectinous material that holds the precipitate in suspension, is transformed into soluble compounds so that the suspended matter settles down easily. The juice is freed from the slimy matter and is therefore, filtered easily. The colour, taste and aroma of the juice are not affected much. In the case of unfermented apple juice, it has been reported that clarification, using Filtragol, is far superior to that by any other method.

The following are the advantages of using Fitragol.

1. To facilitate filtration, fruit juices have generally to be pasteurised in order to coagulate pectin and other gummy substances in suspension. With Filtragol, however, heating of the juice is not necessary.

2. As Filtragol reduces the quantity of sediment, filtration takes less time.

3. In the presence of Filtragol, the colouring matter of the fruit is solubilised without any heating, which would otherwise be necessary to extract the colour from the fruit tissuce with which it is intimately bound.

4. The efficiency of Filtragol is not impaired by the addition of sulphur dioxide to the juice in concentrations of 30 to 60 ppm. This addition of sulphur dioxide prevents the juice from undergoing any fermentation while the enzyme is at work. The amount of Filtragol necessary for satisfactory clarification of the juice varies with the juice. For juices of kernel and stone fruits. and also for grape juice, 0.5 to 1.5 grams of it per litre of juice will be sufficient. For juices of berries like raspberry, gooseberry, blackberry and currants, 1.5 to 2 grams per litre will be required. If the juice is to be filtered soon after the addition of the enzyme, slightly larger quantity of it should be added.

It is rather difficult to determine the stage of complete breakdown of the pectic substances in the juice, because the juice does not always become crystal clear after the pectic substances have been split up. Further, the estimation of pectin as calcium pectate, which is a standard analytical method, takes a fairly long time to be a useful quick method for determining the end point of enzyme action. The viscosity method on the other hand, is quite rapid. Viscosity of the juice decreases gradually with the progressive breadown of pectin in the juice till it reaches a minimum, which indicates completion of the enzyme action.

After filtration, the juice should be heated to 77°C and maintained at that temperature for about 30 minutes, or it must be flash pasteurised at 88°C to stop fruther enzyme action otherwise the juice may become cloudy again.

Finings having purely physical or mechanical action

Generally, infusorial earths such as Spanish clay, kaolin, bentonite, etc. which are known in the trade as filter cells, are employed for the clarification of fruit juices. Work at the Central Food Technologcal Rescarch Institute Mysore, has shown that a local China clay also is suitable for the purpose. Roasted or ignited filter cells are super cells. Filter cells shoud be immune to the action of acids present naturally in fruit juices. They should not impart any undesirable taste and flavour to the juices. They should not form any colloidal suspensions also. To ensure this, the earths are heated to dull redness to burn away all the organic matter present and likely to cause undesirable changes in flavour of the juice. They are subseqently treated with 1 to 1.5 percent citricor cent tartaric acid to remove all those constituents which are likely to be attacked by the acids present in the juice. They are subsequantly washed thoroughly with water to remove all soluble salts and then dried and ground to a free flowing powder of 80 to 200 mesh size.

Usually, 0.5 to 0.6 per cent of the earth is mixed with the juice and the mixture then passed through the filter gress. In the case of unfermented apple juice kaolin, added at the rate of 1 kg to 100 kg of the juice (one per cent), has been found ot yield a sparkling clear juice.

Absorbing carbons. Absorbing carbons are not generally suitable for clarification of fruit juices, because they not only absorb the colouring matter of the juice, but also remove tannins and flavouring materials thereby rendering the juice insipid. Further, they also go into a coloidal form in the juice with the result that it becomes difficiult to filter the treated juice.

Chemical Finings

The bulk of suspended matter, especially in the case of apple juice, consists of proteins and pectin like substances. The colloidal substances carry on them electrical charge, generally negative, and are precipitated when this charge is neutralised by the addition of positively charged colloids. Gelatin and casein act partly in this manner and partly by forming insoluble precipitates with the consitituents of the juice. For instance, casein combines with the acids, and gelatin with the tannins of the juice. On allowing the treated juice to settle, the precipitates formed carry down with them other suspended particles also.

Gelatin. This is an excellent fining material and as such is widely employed for the clarification of fruit juices. The chemical reaction involved should be adjusted carefully for each juice and for each kind of gelatin used. This requires considerable time and experience. Further, there is also the danger of the treated juice becoming cloudy on account of excessive quantitites of gelatin used, because gelatin forms a stable colloidal suspension.

The quantity of gelatin to be added to the juice is always determined first by carrying out a series of small scale laboratory tests. Sufficient tannin is added to the juice to minimise the bleaching action of gelatin.

In the case of apple juice from Baldwin and Yellow Newtown Pippin varieties, it has been observed that addition of 35 grams of tannin and 70 grams of gelatin per 454 litres of the juice gives maximum clarty. Generally, 14 to 42 grams of tannin and 42 to 170 grams of gelatin are required for every 454 litres of the juice, depending upon the condition of the juice. The juice is stirred well to make it homogeneous and then the tannin solution is added to it and stirred. The gelatin solution is added next. The treated juice is allowed to stand undisturbed for 18 to 24 hours to ensure that the precipitated matter clots together and settles down. The Clarified juice is then syphoned off, care being taken not be disturb the sediment. In the case of lime juice, it has has been found that a dose of 213 grams of tannin and 284 grams of gelatin per 2475 litres of juice, which has been preserved by the addition of about 350 ppm. of sulphur dioxide soon after extraction, gives a brilliantly clear juice. The precipitate formed settles down completely in 4 to 6 days, when the clear supernatant juice can be syphoned off and used for the preparation of lime juice cordial.

Abumen. The white of egg contains albumen which can be liberated by heating it in a small quantity of water. It is sometimes used for clarifying fruit juices. Albumen is also available in solid form in the market and it can be dissolved in water by soaking and agitation. Care should, however, be taken to see that the water used is not very warm or even mildly hot, as otherwise, the albumen will coagulate. The albumen solution is mixed well with the juice, and the mixture heated to a temperature of about 5.5°C higher than the pasteurisation temperature, to ensure complete coagulation of the albumen. If such care is not taken, there would be the risk of further coagulation of the albumen during the process of pasteurisation, and this would spoil the appearance of the juice. Usually, a 2.0 per cent solution of albumen gives satisfactory results. It is, however, advisable to find out by preliminary tests, the exact quantity of the albumen solution required for any particular juice.

Casein. It is prepared from skimmed milk by precipitating it with hydrochloric acid. The precipitated casein is washed throughly with water to remove all traces of acid, and then dried and powdered. It is dissolved in liquor ammonia, diluted with 10 to 20 parts of water and then boiled to remove all traces of excessive ammonia. Finally, it is diluted with water to get a 2.0 per cent solution. This dilute solution is mixed well with the juice which is to be clarified. In about 24 hours, the acids in the juice precipitate to casein, which settles down along with the other colloidal particles. It is however, advisable to find out by small scale trials the exact quantity of the solution of casein required for any particular lot of juice.

Clarification by freezing

Colloidal suspensions when subjected to freezing, are readily precipitated on thawing. Apple juice, particularly, responds very well to this treatment. Freshly extracted grape juice, besides containing the usual suspension of pulp, skin, etc., also carries varying quantities of cream of tartar or potassium hydrogen tartrate. When the juice is bottled in the usual way, the cream of tartar goes on precipitating gradually in the form of fine crystals. The presence of these crystals in the juice is rather objectionable. In order to stop this slow precipitation, the bulk of the juice is subjected to refrigeration for several months to complete the precipitation. The clear juice is then bottled. Grape wines also behave like grape juice and are, therefore treated similarly.

Clarification by heating

It is a well known fact that colloidal material in fruit juices usually coagulates, when the juice is heated and settles down readily. To get good results, the juice is heated to about 82 C for a minute or less, and then cooled down repidly. The heating is effected in flash heaters to aviod oxidation by air and to minimise the loss of flavouring materials. After flash heating and cooling, the juice is mixed with the filter aid and passed through the filter press. One great advantage of this method is that it also removes from the juice those substances which would otherwise be precipitated during pasteurisation of the juice. Clarification of pomagranate juice is a typical example of this process.

FRUIT JUICES PRESERVATION

Freshly extracted juices are highly attractive in appearance and possess good taste and aroma, but deteriorate rapidly, if kept for some time. This is on account of several causes which are stated below.

1. Fermentation may be caused by mould, yeast and bacteria.
2. Enzymes present in the juice may affect the colour and flavour adversely. For example, apple juice turns brown due to the activity of oxidative enzymes present in it.

3. Chemicals present in the juice may react with one another and spoil the taste and aroma of the juice.

4. Air coming in contact with the juice, may react with the glucosidal material in the juice and render the juice bitter. Thus the juices from Naval orange and sweet lime often turn bitter when they are exposed to air even for a short time.

5. Metals from the equipment may get into the juice and spoil its taste and aroma.

To ratain the natural taste and aroma of the juice, it is necessary to preserve it soon after extraction, without allowing it to stand for any length of time. Various methods of preservation are employed, and each has its own merits. The methods generally used are : (1) pasteurisation (2) addition of chemicals, (3) addition of sugar, (4) freezing, (5) drying, and (6) filtration. Other methods such as preservation by pressure, by gases by electric current etc., are not employed generally on any large scale.

Pasteurisation

Preservation of fruit juices by heat is the most popular method. The method consists essentially in heating the juice to 100°C or slightly below for a sufficient time to kill micro organisms, which cause spoilage, and the process of heating is called pasteurisation. The juice is hermetically sealed in containers before being pasteurised. The juice would not spoil as long as the containers remain sealed against the entry of micro organisms from outside. Pasteurisation temperatures do not kill all the micro organisms present in the juice. Some spores and spore bearing bacteria like B. subtilis and B. mesentericus can survive the process and multiply later on. These survivals are, however, generally too weak to cause any spoilage of the juice. Further, these organisms are highly sensitive to acids and cannot grow in acid fruit and acid vegetable juices.

Mould spores are destroyed by heating at 79°C for 5 to 10 minutes. Moulds require oxygen for their growth. Removal of air from the juice by filling the containers completely, or by deaerating the juice under vacuum, or by replacing the air with carbon dioxide, therefore, facilitates their destruction even at lower temperature. Yeast and acid tolerant bacteria are readily killed if the juice is heated for a few minutes at about 66°C. The spore forming bacteria found in tomato juice, however, require processing at a higher temperature i.e. at 88°C for a much longer time. Enzymes also require air for their action and can, therefore, be destroyed at a moderate temperature by removing the air from the juice. Pectic enzymes, which cause changes in flavour and also bring about the clotting of particles in the juice, can be destroyed by heating the juice for about 4 minutes at 82°C or for one minute at 88°C.

Fruit juices are pasteurised at such temperatures and for such periods as would render them sterile, without impairing their flavour. Usually, the juices are pasteurised at about 85°C for 25 to 30 minutes according to the nature of the juice and the size of the container. Acid fruit juices require lower temperature and less time for pasteurisation than the less acid ones. To obtain satisfactory results, it is essential to keep all equipment perfectly clean and to carry out the work under hygienic conditions.

Juices can be pasteurised in two ways : (i) by heating the juice at a low temperature for a long period, and (ii) by heating the juice at a high temperature for a short time only (HTST method).

Bottle method or Holding pasteurisation. This method is commonly used for the preservation of fruit juices on a home scale. The extracted juice is strained, filtered or clarified as the case may be, and filled into bottles leaving proper head space for the expansion of the juice during heating. The bottles are then sealed air light and pasteurised.

Pasteurisation by over flow method. In this method the juice is heated to a temperature about 2.5 C higher than the pasteurisation temperature, and filled into hot sterilized bottles up to the brim, taking care to see that during filling and sealing, the temperature of the juice does not fall below the pasteurisation temperature. The bottles should be hot at the time of filling to safeguard against fall of temperature of the juice and to prevent breakage of bottles. The sealed bottles are pasteurised at a temperature 2.5 C lower than the filling and sealing temperature, After pasterurisation, the bottles are cooled. On cooling, to juice contracts leaving a small head space which does not contain any air. This method is highly suited for grape juice, because it minimises the adverse effect of air on the quality of the juice.

Flash pasteurisation. This is a process in which the fruit juice is heated for only a short time at a temperature higher than the pasteurisation temperature for the juice. The juice is heated repidly to a temperature about 5.5 C higher than the pasteurisation temperature and is held at that temperature for about a minute, and then filled into containers which are sealed air tight under cover of steam to sterilize the seal, and then cooled. It has been developed specially for the canning of natural orange juice which, with ordinary pasteurisation methods, suffers in quality. It can also be adopted for pasteurisation of other fruit juices like apple juice, grape juice, etc.

The degree of heating necessary varies with the type of fruit juice. In order to get the desired effect, the flow of the juice through the pasteuriser is regulated so that it is heated to the desired temperature and held at that temperature for a given interval before it passes out of the pasteuriser.

The rate of heat transfer in these pasteruisers depends on the following factory which must be controlled carefully to get a product of good quality:

1. Viscosity of the juice and the method of its agitation;
2. Material and thickness or consistency of the juice;
3. Circulation of steam and removal of condensate;
4. Specific heat of juice and steam;
5. Temperature differences, initial, final and average.

Flash peasteurisation has the following advantages:

1. It minimises the loss in flavour ;
2. It helps in the retention of vitamins;
3. It effects economy in time and space;
4. It hepls to keep the juice uniformly cloudy;
5. It heats the juice uniformly, thereby reducing to a minimum any cooked taste of the juice.

Preservation with chemicals

Pasteurised squashes and cordials have a cooked flavour. After the container is opened, they ferment and spoil within a short period, particularly in tropical climate. To avoid this, chemical preservations are used. Chemically preserved squashes can be kept for a fairly long time even after opening the scal of the bottle. It is however, essential that the use of chemicals is properly controlled, as their indiscriminate use is likely to lead to harmful resutls. The perservative used should not be injurious to health, and it should be non irritant. It should be easy to detect and estimate.

A 'preservative' is any substance which is capable of inhibiting retarding or arresting the process of fermentation, acidification or other decomposition of food or of masking any of the evidence of any such process, or of neutralising the acid generated by any such process but does not include common salt (sodium chloride), salt peter (sodium or potassium nitrate), sugar, acetic acid or vinegar, alcohol or potable spirits, spices, essential oil or any other substance added to the food by the process of curing known as smoking.

The two important chemical preservatives permitted in many of the countries are : (1) benzoic acid (induding benzoates), and (2) sulphur dioxide (including sulphites). These two are allowed in this country according to the Fruit Product Order of 1955.

Sodium benzoate. This is a salt of benzoic acid and is used in the preservation of fruit juices and squashes. Benzoic acid is the effective agent. As it is sparingly soluble in water, its sodium salt, which is water soluble is generally used. One part of sodium benzoate is soluble in 1.8

parts of water at ordinary temperature, whereas only 0.34 parts of benzoic acid will dissolve in 100 parts of water. Sodium benzoate is thus nearly 170 times more soluble than benzoic acid. Chemically, pure sodium benzoate is practically tasteless and odourless.

The quantity of sodium benzoate required would depend on the extent and type of microbial infection to be overcome and also on the nature of the juice particularly its acidity. In the case of juices having a pH of 3.5 to 4.0, which is the range for the majority of fruits juices, addition of 0.06 to 0.10 per cent of sodium benzoate has been found to be sufficient. On the other hand in case of less acid juices such as those from ripe grapes, at least 0.3 per cent of it is necessary. The acidity of the medium in which sodium benzoate is effective is highly important. The preservative action of benzoic and increases in the presence of carbon dioxide. A typical example is that of Bacillus subtillis which connot survive in benzoic acid solution in the presence of carbon dioxide. Benzoic acid more effective against yeasts than against moulds. It does not stop lactic and vinegar fermentations.

Introduction of substituted groups in the orthometo and parapositions of the benzoic acid molecule increases its germicidal properties, that is to say, as the side chain increases the effectiveness of the compound also increases. In some of the European countries, especially Gennany, esters of pare hydroxy benzoic acid like methyl, ethyl and propyl esters, are generally used. There are known in the trade by brand names. They are however not generly used in this country.

Sulphur dioxide

Potassium metabisulphite (K_2O, 2 So_2 or $K_2S_2O_5$) is commonly used as a stable source of sulphur dioxide. Being a dry chemical, it is easier to use than liquid or gaseous sulphur dioxide. Potassium metabisulphite is a crystalline salt and is fairly stable in neutral of alkaline media. It is, however, decomposed by weak acids like carbonic, citric, tartaric and malic acids. When it is added to the fruit juice or squash, the potassium redical reacts with the acid of the juice forming the corresponding potassium salt, and the sulphur dioxide, which is liberated, forms sulphurous acid with the water of the juice. The reaction involved are as follows :

$$\begin{array}{l} \qquad\qquad\qquad CH_{12}.\ COOH \quad CH_2.\ COOK \\ \text{(i) } 3K_2O.\ 2SO_2 + 2CO(OH).\ COOH = C_1(OH).\ COOK + 6SO_2 + 3H_2O \\ \qquad\qquad\qquad CH_2.\ COOH \qquad\qquad\qquad CH_2.\ COOK \end{array}$$

Potassium metabisulphite + Citric aicd = Potassium citrate + sulphur + Water dioxide

(ii) $SO_2 + H_2O = H_2SO_3$
Sulphur dioxide + water = Sulphurous acid

The preservative effect of sulphuros acid depends not its total quantity, but on the available amount of sulphur dioxide. According to Cruess, combined sulphurous acid has very little antiseptic value against micro organisms, 6000 p.p.m. of the combined form having less toxic action on yeast than 50 p.p.m of free sulphurous acid. It has been shown that it is the undissociated $H_2\ SO_3$ molecule which prevents the multiplication of yeast, and the HSO_3 ion which inhibits the growth of bacteria E. coli in concentration of 10 mg per 100 ml. The growth of yeast is not inhibited by HSO_3 ion. The difference in the efficacy of the undissociated molecule and the ion of the same acid is explained as being due to the difficulty for the ions to permeate living cell membranes.

Pure sucrose does not combine with H2 S03 but many other substances like glucose, unidentified aldehydes and ketones, pectin, perhaps also beackdown products of pectin like arabinose, etc., which are found in fruit juices, have the property of combining with sulphur dioxide with the result that the effectiveness of sulphur dioxide is reduced. This is specially important in the case of syrups and concentrated juices, both of which have a high sugar content. It has been shown that such reaction is reversible and reaches equilibrium according to the following equation.

Sugar (or aldehyde) + bisulphic --sugar (or aldehyde) sulphite.

Although sulphur dioxide can retard the development of yeasts in the juice, it cannot arrest their multiplication once their number has reached a high value. It is, therefore, necessary, to carry out a yeast count in the juice before adding sulphur dioxide to it.

According to the Indian Fruit Product Order, the maximum amount of sulphur dioxide allowed in squashes and cordials, in 350 p.p.m. This corresponds to about 28 grams of potassium metabisulphite to 454 kg of the squash or cordial. The purity of the chemical and the sulphur dioxide content at the time of use require to be known so that the right amount of the preservative can be taken for the preservation of the product.

For preserving raw citrus juices, which are to be stored for some months, for the manufacture of squashes in the off season, generally 700 p.p.m. of sulphur dioxide is used. It is, however, preferable to increase this to nearly 1000 p.p.m. and also add extra citra citric acid in the case of orange juice, when it is to be stored in wooden cases or barrels. These barrels should be topped with additional juice occasionally to guard against spoilage of the juice as a result of some loss of sulphur dioxide during long storage, When the juice is converted into squash, containng 25 to 30 per cent of juice, the higher concertration of sulphur dioxide in the stored juice will be suitably reduced so as to be within the limit prescribed by law.

It is well known that fruit juices with a high percentage of acidity do not undergo fermentation readily. The preservative action of the fruit acid may be due to the hydrogen ion concentration or to the toxicity of the undissociated molecule or to the anion. The toxic effect of a mineral acid is due to the hydrogen ion cencentration, but the toxicity of an organic acid is mainly due to the undissociated molecule or the anion. Moulds grow in the wide pH range of 1.5 to 8.5, yeasts in the pH range of 2.5 to 8.0, and bacteria in the pH range of 4.0 to 7.5. As fruit beverages like citrus squashes and cordials have generally a pH of 2.5 to 3.5, the growth of moulds and yeasts in them connot be prevented or checked by acidity alone. Bacteria, however, cannot grow in this pH range.

The pH value is thus of great importance in the preservation of food products. By regulating the pH of the product, one or more kinds of micro organisms in the beverage can be eliminated, and the preserving quality of the beverage increased. Cruess found that the preservative action of sulphur dioxide increases with decreases in the natural pH of the fruit juce. It has also been noticed that the real antiseptic power of sulphur dioxide in musts and wines is proportional of their acidity. Rahn and Conn have shown that the undissociated sulphurous acid is nearly one hundrad times more efficient as a preservative in strongly acid solutions than in neutral solution. The marked influence of the pH of the medium on the effectiveness of the preservative can be seen from the Table 13 :

The toxicity of sulphur dioxide is markedly increased at higher temperatures.

One great advantage of using of sulphur dioxide to preserve fruit juices and squashes is that its strong effect in retarding oxidation prevents discolouration and loss of flavour in the product. It cannot, however, be used in the case of some of the naturally coloured juices like phalsa, jamun and pomegrenate juices, strawberry pulp, etc., on account of its bleaching action. It cannot also be used in the case of juices which are to be packed in tin containers, because it not only acts onthe tin of the container causing pinholes ultimately, but also forms hydrogen sulphide which has a disagreeable smell and forms a black compound with the iron of the base plate of the tin container. Both of these are highly objectionable defects.

TABLE 13. CONCENTRATION OF SULPHUR DIOXIDE (IN PARTS PER MILLION) REQUIRED TO PREVENT GROWTH OF ORGANISM AT DIFFERENT pH LEVELS

pH value	*Sacchromyces ellipsodeus*	*Mucor* Mould	*Pencillium* Mould	Mixed Bacteria
		p.p.m. of So_2		
2.5	200	200	300	100
3.5	800	600	600	300
7.0	obove 5,000	above 5,000	above 5,000	above 1,000

The following are some of the important considerations to be kept in view while using chemical preservatives :

1. As natural fruit juices contain only small quantities of substances that combine with sulphurous acid, they can be preserved with normal doses of sulphur dioxide, i.e., about 350 p.p.m.

2. In the case of fruit juices of low acidity, extra acid should be added to lower their pH value and thereby increase the preservative action of sulphur dioxide.

3. In concentrated juices, the sulphrous acid fixing substances are high and consquently a higher percentage of sulphur dioxide is necessary for their preservation. Downer suggests that in the case of concentrated juices, the total sulphurous acid to be used should be equivalent to that needed for a normal juice multiplied, by the degree of concentration of the juice. Commercially, concentrated juices are, however, generally preserved with about 1,500 p.p.m. of sulphur dioxide.

4. Since sulphur dioxide has got a selective action and is more toxic to moulds, mould spores and vinegar bacteria than to yeast, its use in conjunction with sodium benzoate, which is more toxic to yeast than to vinegar bacteria, is highly desirable for effective preservation of fruit juices. The use of these two preservatives in combination has been abvocated by joslyn & marh particularly because of the fact that the use of sodium benzoate alone results in the darkening of the product. For effective preservation, the amount of these preservation to be used singly or in combination, depends on the character of the juice, particularly its acidity and sugar content. For instance, according to Lal Singh and Girdhari Lal, the maximum permitted concentration of 350 p.p.m. of sulphur dioxide canbe diminished to 100 to 200 p.p.m. in citrus squashes having an acidity of 2.0 to 2.5 per cent as citric acid, and a sugar content ranging farm 45° to 65° Brix.

5. Sulphur dioxide imparts a slight characteristic taste and odour to a

freshly prepared beverage, but these are not easily discernible when the beverage is suitable diluted for drinking. Further, these adverse effects on taste and edour disappear during subsequent storage of the product. This is particularly true of citrus squashes.

In spite of its shortcomings, the use of sulphur dioxide for preservation of fruit juices and squashes is preferred for the following reasons :

1. It has a better preserving action than sodium benzoate against bacterial fermentation.

2. It helps to ratain the colour of the beverage for a longer time than sodium benzoate.

3. Being a gas it helps in preserving the surface layer of the juice also.

4. Being highly soulble in juices and squashes, it ensures better mixing and hence their preservation.

5. Any excess of sulphur dioxide present in the juice can be removed either by heating the juice to about 71°C, or by passing air through it, or by subjecting the juice to vacuum. This causes some loss of the flavouring materials due to volatilization, but can be compensated for by adding flavours.

The chemical preservatives should never be added in solid form to fruit juice and squashes. They should first be dissolved in a small quantity of the juice or water, and the solution then added to the bulk of the juice. If this care is not taken, the soild chemical may settle at the bottom of the container with the result that fermentation may set in before the preservative dissolves in the juice and exerts its full preserving action. A number of chemicals suchas hydrogen peroxide formaldehyde, halogenated acetic acids, salicylic acid etc. Which were used as preservatives some years ago have now been banned in many countries. In recent years, sorbic acid is being favourably considered on account of its fungistiatic properties. Antibiotics such as Nisin, Tylosin etc., are also being experimented upon as possible preservatives. There is considerable interset in these substances.

PRESERVATION OF ADDITION OF SUGAR

Fruit juices containing 66 per cent or more of sugar do not ordinarily ferment. Sugar absorbs most of the available water with the results that the latter is not available for the growth of micro organisms. Solutions with high total solids have a very low water activity coefficient in regard to growth of micro organisms. Dry sugar does not ferment, and it is very difficult to induce fermentation in highly concentrated sugar solutions.

Sugar syrups containing 66 per cent sugar (sp.gr.1.330) have so little moisture available for micro organisms that their propaagation is inhibited, and also those already present die not gradually. Thus sugar acts as a preservative by osmosis and not as a true poison for micro organisms.

PRESERVATION BY FREEZING

The best way of preserving pure fruit juices is by 'freezing'. The properly frozen juice retains its freshness, colour and aroma for a long time. This method is particularly useful in the case of juices whose flavour is adversely affected by heating. The juice is first deaerated & the vacuum released with nitrogen gas. The Juice is then transferred into containers which are hermetically sealed and frozen. This prevents not only the volatilization of the aromatic elements but also the obsorption of my disgraceable odours and flavours. Experts were able to store apple and berry juices in sealed containers for two years at a temperature of 12 to 10°C. Without any noticeable loss of flavour, aroma and colour. The dehydration and concentration processes, which mechanically separate water as ice at low temperatures, destroy a fair percentage of micro organisms in the juice, although moulds are not affected sometimes.

In filling cans or bottles, an allowance of 10 per cent should be made for the expansion of the juice on freezing. A juice can be kept in good condition for a long time at - 17 to - 12°C. in frozen form by avoiding contact with air. The juice is defrosted before consumption.

PRESERVATION BY DRYING

Process is analogous to the concentration process. It is done in the same way as milk drying. The juice is sprayed in the form of a very fine mist into an evaporating chamber through which hot air is passed. The temperature of the chamber and the blast of the air are so regulated that only dry juice falls on the floor of the chamber in the form of a fine powder. The powder is collected and packed in dry containers, which are then closed air right. The powder when dissolved in water, makes a pleasant fruit drink practically similar to the original fresh juice. Fruit juice powders are highly hygroscopic and require special care in packing. All juices do not however, dry readily without special treatment. Siddappa and Girdhari Lal have developed and patented a process for the preparation of fruit juice powders. In the case of orange juice, the powder which is prepared according to this process, based on 'puff drying' priniciple has good reconstitution properties. It should be packed in free flowing powder form in hermetically sealed containers with in package desiccant to prolong shelf life of the product. Freeze drying, foam mat drying etc. are other recent methods of preparing fruit juice powders. Fruit flovours also can be prepared in free flowing powder form using materials such as gums, sorbitol etc; to seal the flavour in tiny globules. The free flowing flavour powders can be mixed with fruit juice powders to enhance their taste and flavour. There has been in recent years considerable interest in the manufacture of fruit juice powders.

PRESERVATION BY CARBONATION

Carbonation. Moulds and yeasts require oxygen for their growth. As they are areobic, they become inactive in the presence of carbon dioxide. If the yeast cells are filtered off, as in Reuf's process, by passing the juice through a porcelain filter, and then the juice is carbonated under aseptic conditions the juice will keep without fermenting. In the ordinary carbonated drinks the oxygen of the air which is normally present in solution in water, and is sufficient to bring about fermentation, is displaced with carbon dioxide. Although carbonated beverages contain sugar much below 66 per cent, the absence of air and the presence of carbon dioxide in them help to prevent the growth of mould and yeast.

High carbonation should, however, be avoided as it usually destroys the declicate flavours of the juice The keeping quality of carbonated fruit beverages is enhanced by adding 0.005 per cent of sodium benzoate.

PRESERVATION BY FILTRATION

Germ proof filtration or sterilization of cold juices. In this method, the juice which has been clarified by 'settling' or by using ordinary filters, is passed through special filters which are capable of retaining yeasts and bacteria. Various types of Seitz. E.K. 'germ proof' filters are used for this purpose. It requires elaborate precautions to ensure complete sterility in the bottled product. In this country this elaborate process has not yet been in general use in the fruit preservation industry.

OTHER METHODS OF PRESERVATION

In recent years, new methods of sterilization, such as use of electric current ultra violet rays oligodynamic properties of silver etc. have been used. Various patents have been taken out for these e.g. the Schoop Katadyn and Matzka processes. The Schoop process is based on the catalytic acitivity of certain plant substances in the presence of sodium chloride. The oligodynamic properties of silver are made use of in the Katadyn and Matzka process. These processes are not however employed in this country, not are they used to any large extent in other countries.

Glass lined equipment or equipment made of metals like stainless steel, monel metal, nickel aluminium or bronze should be used because such equipment is not readily acted upon the fruit and vegetable juices. A unit of machinery made of different metals should also be avoided because dissimilar metals in the system or unit will lead to the setting up of small electrical couples and consequently corrosion will result. Use of rubber in the equipment should also be avoided as far as possible.

9

Fruit Beverages

Fruits Beverages have got trementdous demand all over the world most commonly used for preparing beverages are sweet orange mandarin (sangtra) loose jacket orange, sour lime (kagzi nimboo or limboo), lemon grape firut grape, apple, mango pomegranate, phalsa (Grewia asiatica) jamun (Eugenia jambolana), mulberry passion fruit pineapple, etc. Tomato juice also has become quite popular. Among the squashes, sweetened orange juice known as orange squash, lemon squash and pineapple squash are the most popular ones.

SQUASHES AND CORDIALS

Fruit juices are most commonly packed as squashes or cordials in this country, although canned pure fruit juices like orange and pineapple juices, and quite recently mango juice are gaining importance. Methods of preparing some of the more important squashes and cordials are dealt with briefly in the following sections.

Orange Squash

Extraction of juice. Orange squash is prepared from tight skinned oranges such as Malte, Sathgudi or chinee, and musambi oranges as well as from loose skinned oranges like Nagpur and Coorg oranges. Tight skinned oranges are cut into halves either with a knife by hand or by means of a halving machine having a circular knife. The halves are pressed by hand against a revolving burr or rose fitted to a rosing machine. These machines are of various sizes and capacities. The reamed juice is collected in a vessel. It contains plenty of coarse tissues, seeds etc. To remove these it is filtered through a net cloth or passed through a sieving machine known as pulper in which the juice gets brushed through a stationary perforated cylinder by revolving paddles of stainless steel wood or fibre brush. The sieved juice is utilized for making squash. Loose jacket oranges are peeled, & the fibrous rag attached to the segments is removed as far as possible as it is responsible for some of the bitterness in the juice. According to Siddappa dipping of the segments in hot lye solution for 1/2 to 1 minute removes most of parchment like material enclosing the juice sace in the segments and the juice obtained from the treaded acid dipped and washed segments is practically free from substances that subsequently cause bitterness in the juice. This juice has been found to be highly satisfactory for canning as pure orange juice as well as for making orange squash. The segments are passed through a screw type juice extractor. Alternatively, the segments may be crushed in a tomato crusher and then passed through a coarse sieve to remove seeds, pieces of tissues, etc. Recently the Taglith type of juice extractor has been found useful for large scale storage of orange juice during the season and also for the manufacture of orange squash and canned orange juice practically free from bitterness.

Preparation of Squash. Sugar, citric acid, flavouring materials, colour and preservative are added to the juice in correct proportions. In large scale manufacture, slight variations in the procedure as well as the propertions of the several ingredients are affected to maintain a standard quality in the product.

Sugar, citric acid and water are mixed and heated. Any dirt is skimmed off. The syrup is cooled slightly and filtered through cloth. The clean syrup is blended with the juice. To improve flavour, peal emulsion of 2 to 4 oranges for every 100 oranges taken or an appropriate quantity of an essential oil and orange essence is added to the squash. The colour of the squash is improved, to satisfy consumer demand, by adding an edible colour like Sunset Yellow F.C.F. Tartrazine, Edicol Orange A.G., etc., in suitable proportions. It is, however, desirable not to resort to the use of colours by gradually educating the public to go in for non coloured squashes in preference to the ones brightly coloured with artificial dyes. Recently, carotenoid colours such carotene, which is the precursor of vitamin A, have become available in water soluble forms. It would be useful to employ these instead of artificial coal tar colours, if it is absolutely necessary to add colour to squashes.

The colour added to the squash should be fairly resistant to the action of sulphur dioxide. Food experts have recently made a thorough study of the stability of added colour in squashes under a variety of preparations as well as storages conditions.

After mixing all the ingredients, a calculated amount of a chemical preservative, namely potassium metabisulphite, approximately about 28 g for every 454 g of squash dissolved previously in a small quantity of the juice or water, is added to the squash. While using stored and SO_2 preserved orange juice for making the squash, allowance should be made for the acid as well as sulphur dioxide added to the juice for preserving it. The amount of sulphur dioxide added to the juice for preserving it. The amount of sulphur dioxide in the final product should not exceed 350 p.p.m. of SO_2

which is the upper limit permitted by law. By careful attention to hygienic conditions the concentration of SO_2 in the squash can be safely reduced to about 250 p.p.m. This will help in minimising the taste of SO_2 in the beverage. The bottles are cleaned and washed in a bottle washing machine fitted with revolving brushes or in a washing machine fitted with jets of hot lye hot water and steam to clean and dry the bottles. The sterile bottles are rinsed with hot water before filling them with the squash leaving about 1.2 to 2.5 cm of head space. The bottles are then closed with crown corks or pilfer proof closures which have been dipped in one per cent potassium metabisulphite solution to sterilize them. The bottles are washed dried and labelled (These machines are easily available in India). On the commercial scale bottle filling machines with two or more filling heads besed on vacuum syphon or plunger action are employed. The labelled bottles are cased and stored in a cool and dry place. The product keeps well for 1 to 1½ years without much change in colour, taste and flvour.

ORANGE SQUASH RECIPE

Ingtedients	25% Juice, 45° Brix, 1.5% acidity		33-1/3% juice 45° Brix, 1.5% acidity		25% juice 65° Brix 2.0 acidity		33-1/3% juice 65° Brix 2.0% acidity	
	lb(kg)	oz(g)	lb(kg)	oz(g)	lb(kg)	oz(g)	lb(kg)	oz(g)
Orange juice, 10° Brix 0.8% acidity	100 (45.4)	0 (0)	100 (45.4)	0 (0)	100 (45.4)	0 (0)	100 (45.4)	0 (0)
Sugar	164 (74)	9 (255)	121 (55)	2 (56)	242 (110)	9 (255)	179 (81)	10 (283)
Citric acid	5 (2)	3 (85)	3 (1)	11 (311)	7 (3)	3 (85)	5 (2)	3 (85)
Essence of orange	2 (1)	8 (225)	1 (0)	14 (390)	3 (2)	5 (141)	2 (1)	9 (255)
Water	127 (57)	8 (226)	73 (30)	2 (56)	46 (21)	11 (311)	12 (5)	7 (198)
Orange colour	q.s		q.s		q.s		q.s	
Preservative (potassium meta-bisulphite)	0	4 (113)	0	3 (85)	0 (0)	4 (113)	0	3 (85)

Grape Fruit Squash

The method of preparation of juice for grape fruit squash is the same as that employed in the case of orange squash.

Lemon Squash

European lemon, Eureka lemon, and galgal (Citrus limonia) are genernally used for the preparation of lemon squash. True lemons are not however yet available in large quantities in India. Lemon squash requires addition of flavour to improve its taste. The method of preparing the juice and squash is practically the same as that employed in the case of tight skinned orange for manufacture of orange squash. The juice is extracted by reaming.

GRAPE FRUIT SQUASH RECIPE

Ingredients	25% juice, 45° Brix, 1.5% aciditj		33 1/3% juice .45° Brix 1.5% acidity		25% juice 65° Brix 2.0% acidity		33 1/3% juice 65° Brix 2.0% acidity	
	lb(kg)	oz(g)	lb(kg)	oz(g)	lb(kg)	oz(g)	lb(kg)	oz(g)
Grape fruit juice 10° Brix, 1.25% acidity	100	0	100	0	100	0	100	0
	(45.4)	—	(45.4)	—	(45.4)	—	(45.4)	—
Sugar	165	0	121	9	243	0	180	1
	(74)	—	(55)	(255)	(110)		(8)	(28)
Citric acid	4	12	3	4	6	12	4	12
	(2)	(340)	(1)	(113)	(3)	(64)	18	(320)
Water	127	8	73	2	46	11	12	7
	(57)	(226)	(33)	(56)	(21)	(311)	(5)	(198)
Essence of grape fruit	2	8	1	14	3	5	2	9
	(1)	(226)	(0)	(396)	(1)	(141)	(1)	(256)
Potass um metabi-sulphite)	0	4	0	3	0	4	0	3
	(0)	(113)		(85)		(113)		(85)

Figures in brackets represent kg against lb and g against oz.

Lime Squash

Kagzi nimboo is widely used for making lime squash. These limes are available in large quantities in Gujarat, Maharashtra, Andhra Pradesh, Karnataka, Tamil Nadu etc. The fruit is cut into halves with a knife and the juice pressed out from the halves by means of small wooden squeezers or by means of stone roller type presses. The juice is sometimes pressed from the cut fruit by means of a wooden basket press. Seeds are removed by sieving through cloth.

Sugar is first made into a syrup which is filtered and added to the juice. The preserved squash is bottled as usual.

LEMON SQUASH RECIPE

Ingredients	25% juice, 45° Brix, 1.5% acidity		331/3% juice 45° Brix 1.66% acidity		25% juice 65° Brix 2.0% acidity		31/3 % juice 65° Brix 1.66% acidity	
	lb(kg)	oz(g)	lb(kg)	oz(g)	lb(kg)	oz(g)	lb(kg)	oz(g)
Juice, 10°Brix, 5% acidity	100 (45.4)	0 —	100 (45.4)	0 (0)	100 (45.4)	0 (0)	100 (45.4)	0 (0)
Sugar	168 (76)	12 (340)	124 (56)	13 (368)	246 (111)	12 (340)	184 (83)	13 (638)
Citric acid	1 (0)	0 (0)	— —	— —	3 (1.3)	— —	— —	— —
Water	127 (57)	8 (226)	73 (33)	2 (156)	47 (26)	8 (226)	13 (6)	2 (54)
Essence of lemon	2 (1)	8 (226)	1 (0)	14 (113)	2 (1)	8 (226)	1 (1)	14 (396)
Preservative (potassium metabisulphite)	0 0	4 (113)	0 (0)	3 (85)	0 (0)	4 (113)	3 (0)	0 (85)

Figures in bracket represent kg against lb and g against oz.

LIME SQUASH RECIPE

Ingredients	25% juice, 45° Brix 1.5% acidity		33 1/3% juice, 45° Brix 2.0% acidity		15% juice, 65° Brix 1.5% acidity		33 1/3% juice, 65° Brix 2.0% acidity	
	lb(kg)	oz(g)	lb(kg)	oz(g)	lb(kg)	oz(g)	lb(kg)	oz(g)
Lime juice 10° Brix, 6.0% acidity	100 (45.4)	0 (0)	100 (45.4)	0 (0)	100 (45.4)	0 (0)	100 (45.4)	0 (0)
Sugar	169 (76)	12 (340)	124 (56)	13 (368)	249 (113)	12 (340)	184 (83)	13 (368)
Water	130 (59)	0 (0)	75 (34)	0 (0)	50 (23)	0 (0)	15 (7)	0 (0)
Preservative (potassium (metabisulphite)	0 (0)	4 (113)	0 (0)	3 (85)	0 (0)	4 (113)	0 (0)	3 (85)

Figures in bracket represent kg against lb and g against oz.

Lime Juice Cordial

Lime juice is stored in large carboys or upright wooden barrels lined with microcrystalline wax. Fifty six g of potassium metabisulphite is added to every 45 kg of the juice to preserve it during storage. The juice settles gradually, and the sediment forms a compact layer at the bottom leaving a clear juice at the top. This process takes 2 to 3 months. The clear juice is syphoned off. This method is rather slow and time consuming. Clarification of the juice can also be achieved quickly by adding gelatin and tannin in proper proprotion, based on preliminary laboratory trials. Sugar, water, colour, if necessary, and preservative are added to the clear juice and the mixture is then filtered by means of a filter press. Filter aids are added in this process to facilitate filtration. The clear cordial is bottled as usual.

Sugar is added in the form of syrup. The quantity of preservative added to the juice for storage taken into account while ádding the required quantity of it to the cordial. Only a small quantity of colour should be added.

Citrus Fruit Barley Waters

The juice from citrus fruit like lemons, limes, etc, is extracted and filtered. A small quantity of barley flour (according to the recipe) is made into a thin paste with a little water. More water is then added to thin the paste. It is then heated to gelatinise the starch of the flour, cooled, filtered and made up to volume.

LIME JUICE CORDIAL RECIPE

Ingredients	25% juice, 35° Brix, 1.5% acidity		33⅓% juice, 35° Brix 2.0% acidity		25% juice, 50° Brix, 1.5% acidity		33⅓% juice, 50° Brix 2.0% acidity	
	lb(kg)	oz(g)	lb(kg)	oz(g)	lb(kg)	oz(g)	lb(kg)	oz(g)
Clarified lime juice, 10° Brix	100	—	100	—	100	0	100	0
6% acidity	(45.4)	—	(45.4)	—	(45.4)	—	(45.4)	(0)
Sugar	129	12	94	13	189	12	139	13
	(58)	(340)	(42)	(368)	(86)	(340)	(63)	(368)
Water	170	0	105	0	110	0	60	0
	(77.1)	—	(48)	—	(50)	—	(27)	—
Colour	q.s.		q.s.		q.s.		q.s.	
Preservative	0	4	0	3	0	4	0	3
(potassium metabisulphite)	(0)	(113)	(0)	(85)	(0)	(113)	(0)	(85)

Figures in bracket represent kg against lb and g against oz.

CITRUS FRUIT RECIPES

Grape fruit Barley Water

Ingredients	25% juice, 45° Brix 1.5% acidity		33 1/3% Juice, 45° Brix 1.5% acidity	
	lb(kg)	oz(g)	lb(kg)	oz(g)
Grape fruit juice 10° Brix, 1.25% acidity	100	0	100	0
	(45.4)	(0)	(45.4)	(0)
Sugar	165	0	121	9
	(75)	(0)	(55.1)	(255)
Citric acid	4	12	3	4
	(2)	(340)	(1)	(133)
Essence of grape-fruit	2	8	1	14
	(1)	(226)	(0)	(396)
Barley water	127	8	73	2
	(57)	(226)	(33)	(56)
	from 21 oz. (578g) of barley flour		from 16 oz (453 g) of barley flour	
Preservative (potassium metabisulphite)	0	4	0	3
	(0)	(113)	(0)	(85)

Lemon Barley Water

Ingredients	25% juice, 45° Brix 1.5% acidity		33 1/3% juice, 45° Brix 1.66% acidity	
	lb(kg)	oz(g)	lb(kg)	oz(g)
Lemon juice 10°Brix, 5% acidity	100	0	100	0
	(45.4)	—	(45.4)	—
Sugar	168	12	124	13
	(76)	(340)	(56)	(368)
Citric acid	1	0	—	—
	(0)	—	—	—
Barley water	127	8	73	2
	(57)	(26)	(33)	(56)
	(from 21 oz. (578 g) of barley flour)		(from 16 oz. of (453 g) barley flour)	
Essence of lemon	2	8	1	4
	(1)	(226)	—	(113)
Preservative (potassium meta-bisulphite)	0	4	0	3
	(0)	(113)	(0)	(85)

CITRUS FRUIT RECIPES

Lime Barley Water

Ingredients	25% juice, 45° Brix 1.5% acidity		33⅓% juice, 45° Brix 2.0% acidity	
	lb(kg)	oz(g)	lb(kg)	oz(g)
Lime juice 10° Brix, 6% acidity	100 (45.4)	0 —	100 (45.4)	0 —
Sugar	169 (77)	12 (340)	124 (56)	13 (368)
Barley water	130 (59)	0 —	73 (33.1)	0 (0)
	(from 21 oz. (578 g) of barley flour)s		(from 16 oz. (465 g) of barley flour)	
Preservative (potassium metabisulphite)	0 (0)	4 (113)	0 (0)	3 (85)

Orange Barley Water

Ingredients	25% juice 45° Brix 1.5% acidity		33⅓% juice, 45° Brix 2.0% acidity	
	lb(kg)	oz(g)	lb(kg)	oz(g)
Orange juice 10°Brix, 0.8% acidity	100 (45.4)	0 (0)	100 (45.4)	0 (0).
Sugar	164 (74)	9 (255)	121 (55)	2 (56)
Citric acid	5 (2)	3 (85)	3 (1)	11 (311)
Essence of orange	2 (1)	8 (226)	1 (0)	14 (396)
Barley water	127 (57)	8 (226)	73 (33)	2 (56)
	(from 21 oz. (578 g) of barley flour)		(from 16 oz. (453 g) of barley flour)	
Orange colour	q.s.		q.s.	
Preservative (potassium metabisulphite)	0	4 (112)	0	3 (85)

In the production of squashes in a factory, it is more convenient to work back the recipes to 100 kg of sugar, because one bag of sugar contains 100 kg of sugar. Juice and water can be easily measured by volume making allowance for their specific gravity. For instance, in the case of orange squash, taking one bag of sugar per batch, and keeping 25 per cent juice in the squash of 45 Brix the recipe would approximately be as follows :

Orange squash (234 kg batch)

Stored orange juice (acidified and sulphited)	58.5 kg
Sugar (bag)	100 kg
Citric acid	1.75 kg
Water	87 litres
Colour 6 % solution	(450-500 ml)
Orange essence	(300-400 ml)
KMS (by difference)	23.4 g

Similarly recipes can be worked out for lemon squash, pineapple squash etc.

Lemon lime squash (250 kg batch, 25 % juice and 45°Brix)

Lime juice fresh	62.5 kg
Sugar (bag)	100 kg
Citric acid	Nil (may be added, if necessary)
Water	84 litres
Flavour	Nil (optional)
Colour 6% solution	Nil (A small quantity may be added)
KMS 0.06%	150 gm

Pineapple squash (250 kg batch 25% juice and 45°Brix)

Pineapple juice (fresh)	62.5 kg
Sugar (bag)	100 kg
Water	86 litres
Citric acid	2.5 (may be varied)
Colour (6% solution)	q.s. (150-200 ml)
Potassium metabisulphite (KMS) 0.06%	150 g.

Jack Fruit Nectar

Fruit squashes with plenty of fruit pulp in them are known as nectars. They generally contain a higher percentage of fruit in them. They are thick in consistency. Typical exemples of fruit necters are peach, apricot and mango nectars. A similar product has been prepared from jack fruit also.

The bulbs are removed from ripe jack fruit and after removing the seeds and the thin tissue enclosing the seed, they are passed through a mincing machine. The minced pulp is mixed with about 10 per cent its weight of water and passed through a pulper fitted with a fine sieve of 1 mm hole. The finely divided pulp obtained is used for preparing jack fruit nectar. Not more than 20 per cent of the pulp should be added to the nectar, because with higher percentages of it, the nectar becomes highly viscous and jelly like.

Jaman Squash or Syrup

Jaman fruit is crushed and heated in its own juice gently for 5 to 10 minutes at about 60°C to extract the rich purple colour. The heated material is pressed in cloth in a basket press and the clear purple coloured juice used for making the squash, which is highly attractive in appearance and possesses a pleasant tasts and flavour with a slight astringency.

JACK FRUIT RECIPE

Ingredients	17% pulp, 50° Brix 1.2% acidity		20% pulp, 50° Brix 1.2% acidity	
	lb(kg)	oz(g)	lb(kg)	oz(g)
Pulp of jack fruit bulbs, 20° Brix, 0.3% acidity	102 (46)	0 (0)	100 (45)	0 (0)
Sugar	272 (123)	5 (241)	224 (101)	0 (600)
Citric acid	6 (3)	14 (196)	5 (2)	11 (311)
Water	218 (99)	6 (170)	170 (77.1)	0 (0)
Preservative (potassium metabisulphite)	0 (0)	6 (170)	0 (0)	5 (141)

Mango Squash

Juicy varieties of mangoes are preferred for making mango squash. Fully ripe fruit is taken and washed well. The stem portion is cut off and four vertical slits given to each fruit to facilitate pulping. The fruits are then passed through a pulping machine to separate the skin and the stones. The fine smooth pulp is used for for making the squash.

Sugar is added in the form of syrup. The squash may be strained through cloth before botting.

JAMAN SQUASH RECIPE

Ingredients	50% juice, 45° Brix 1.5% acidity	
	lb(kg)	oz(g)
Jaman juice, 14°Brix, 0.75% acidity	100	—
	(45.4)	(0)
Sugar	73	0
	(33)	0
Citric acid	2	4
	(1)	(113)
Water	24	0
	(11)	(0)
Preservative (sodium benzoate)	0	3
	—	(85)

MANGO SQUASH RECIPE

Ingredients	25% juice 45° Brix 0.8% acidity		33% juice 40° Brix 0.8% acidity		25% juice 50° Brix 1.0% acidity		33% juice 50° Brix 1.0% acidity	
	lb(kg)	oz(g)	lb(kg)	oz(g)	lb(kg)	oz(g)	lb(kg)	oz(g)
Mango pulp	100	0	100	0	100	0	100	0
18° Brix	(45.4)	(0)	(45.4)		(45.4)	(0)	(45.4)	(0)
0.5% acidity								
Sugar	139	1	99	15	178	4	129	5
	(63)	(30)	(45)	(425)	(80)	(113)	(58)	(141)
Citric acid	2	11	1	14	3	8	2	8
	(1)	(311)	(0)	(396)	(1)	(126)	(1)	(226)
Water	158	0	98	0	118	0	68	0
	(72)	(0)	(40)	(0)	(53)	(0)	(26)	(0)
Preservative	0	4	0	3	0	4	0	3
(Potassium	(0)	(113)	(0)	(85)	(0)	(113)	(0)	(85)
metabisulphite)								

Passion Fruit Squash

With its exotic and delicate flavour, which originally become popular is Australia and South Africa, passion fruit squash is attracting attention in India also. Purple passion fruit of good edible quility (Passiflora edulis Sims) is grown is the Nilgiris and Coorg in south India.

Ripe purple coloured fruits are preferred for making squash. The fruit is cut into halves and the yellow mucilaginous pulp, along with the brownish black seeds, is scooped out with a spoon. The pulp is then passed through a pulper to remove the seeds. On a small scale the pulp can be rebbed through an ordinary stainless steel sieve of 20 to 30 mesh per 25 cm. Pruthi developed recipes for passion fruit squash and blended squashes like Passiola, etc.

Peach Squash

White juicy peaches are good for making squash. The pulp is heated with helf its weight of water for about 15 minutes at 82°C and the juice pressed from the softened pulp in a basket press. The thick pulpy juice is used for making peach squash. Potassium metabisulphite is added as preservative.

Phalsa Squash

The method of preparing phalsa squash is similar to that described for making jaman squash. As the juice itself is sufficiently acidic, extra citric acid is not added to the squash.

PASSION FRUIT SQUASH RECIPE

Ingredients	25% juice, 45° Brix 1.5% acidity		33% juice, 45° Brix 1.5% acidity		25% juice, 65° Brix 2.0% acidity		33% juice, 65° Brix 2.0% acidity	
	lb(kg)	oz(g)	lb(kg)	oz(g)	lb(kg)	oz(g)	lb)kg)	oz(g)
Passion fruit juice								
18° Brix,	100	0	100	0	100	0	100	0
3% acidity	(45.4)	(0)	(45.4)	0	(45.4)	(0)	(45.4)	(0)
Sugar	158	12	155	5	236	12	173	13
	(72)	(340)	(52)	(140)	(107)	(340)	(78)	(368)
Citric acid	3	0	1	8	5	0	3	0
	(1.3)		(0)	(126)	3	(0)	(1)	(0)
Water	138	0	83	0	58	0	23	0
	(62)	(0)	(37)	(0)	(26)	(0)	(10)	(0)
Preservative (potassium metabisulphite)	0	4	0	3	0	4	0	3
	(0)	(113)	(0)	(85)	(0)	(113)	(0)	(85)

Pineapple Squash

Pineapple squash, and pineapple crush, which is similar to squash but with a higher sugar content, have become highly popular in this country in recent years. There is a growing demand for the outer skin peeled off with a curved knife. The peeled slices are cored and then cut into small pieces, which are passed through a screw type crusher and extractor. Broken fruit slices, which are less than quarters, can be used for the preparation of juice for squash. From the crushed material juice is pressed in a basket press, or in a centrifugal extractor known as hydro extractor. The clear juice is used in the preparation of squash.

Plum Squash

Juicy plums like the alucha plum are preferred for the preparation of plum squash. To extract the colour from the skin, the plums are heated at 82 C for about 30 minutes in half their weight of water. The heated fruit is passed through a pulper to extract juice. The juice is made into squash of 45 to 55 degrees Brix. Sodium benzoate is added as preservative.

PINEAPPLE SQUASH RECIPE

Ingredients	25% juice, 45° Brix 1.5% acidity		33 1/3% juice, 45° Brix 1.5% acidity		25% juice, 65° Brix 2.0% acidity		33 1/3% juice 65° Brix 2.0% acidity	
	lb(kg)	oz(g)	lb(kg)	oz(g)	lb(kg)	oz(g)	lb(kg)	oz(g)
Pineapple juice 8° Brix, 0.5% acidity	100 (45.4)	0 (0)	100 (45.4)	0 (0)	100 (45.4)	0 (0)	100 (45.4)	0 (0)
Sugar	166 (75)	4 (113)	122 (55)	13 (368)	244 (110)	4 (113)	181 (82)	5 (315)
Citric acid	5 (2)	8 (226)	4 (1)	0 (0)	7 (3)	8 (226)	5 (2)	8 (226)
Pineapple flavour	2 (1)	8 (226)	1 (0)	14 (396)	3 (1)	5 (141)	2 (1)	9 (255)
Water	125 (56)	8 (226)	71 (32)	2 56	44 (20)	11 (311)	10 (4)	7 (198)
Yellow colour	q.s.		q.s.		q.s.		q.s.	
Preservative (potassium metabisulphite)	0 (0)	4 (113)	0 0	4 (113)	0 0	4 (113)	0 (0)	3 (85)

Water Melon Squash

Ripe water melon is cut into suitable pieces, and the flesh scraped from the rind. From the scraped pulp, juice is extracted by means of a basket press. The pinkish juice, which is of 6 to 7 degrees Brix, is converted into squash. Sodium benzoate is used as a preservative.

WATER MELON SQUASH RECIPE

Ingredients	45° Brix, 1.0% acidity	
	lb(kg)	oz(g)
Juice 6°Brix, 0.1 % acidity	75	0
	(35)	(0)
Sugar	52	8
	(23)	(226)
Citric acid	1	4
	(0)	(113)
Sodium benzoate	0	2
	(0)	(56)

Other Fruit Squashes

Squashes and syrups can also be made from several other fruits like mulberry, raspberry, strawberry, pear, apricot, pumelo, guava, musk melon etc. The methods of preparation are broadly the same as those described in the case of orange, mango, pineapple, etc. Ingredients required can be deducted from basic principle involed in the preparation and preservation of squashes.

JUICES

Pure fruit juices like orange juice, apple juice, pineapple juice, etc., which are highly prized as nutritive breakfast foods, are packed in large quantities in several countries. Apple juice is generally bottled, while other juices are canned.

Apple Juice

Unfermented apple juice is highly popular in Europe. In this country also, it is gaining popularity. With the increase in area under apples, the demand for apple juice is likely to increase in the near future. A method has been standardised for the preparation of juice from Kulu valley apples like the Yellow Newton and Baldwin varieties. The apples are washed with a weak solution of hydrochloric acid (22.7 litres of acid in 454 litres of water) to remove any arsenic and lead spray residues, and are then crushed in an apple grater to pieces of 0.3 cm to 1.2 cm size. The pieces are placed in a basket press and pressed to get the juice. The juice is collected in a non corrodible vessel. Aluminium vessels can be used for small scale production. The juice is strained through coarse cloth to remove fruit tissues, etc., heated to 82° to 85°C filled hot into clean bottles, and pasteurised by the overflow method for 30 minutes at 79°C

Cashew Apple Juice

Cashew apples are available in large quantities on the West Coast, where there is a thriving cashew kernel processing industry. Large areas are being planted with cashew to meet the increasing world demand for the kernel. At present, the fruit, which is the fleshy portion to which the nut is attached, goes practically to waste. The fruit is highly perishable. It is fairly rich in vitamin C, and as such is worth preserving, by organising its collection and processing at convenient centres. Experiments have shown that by suitable preliminary treatment of the fruit to remove the characteristic astringency of the fruit, a juice of fairly good quality can be prepared. Siddappa has described a simple method for its preparation and preservation by blending it with a small quantity of lime juice. Jain, Bhatia, Anand and Girdhari Lal have recommended steaming of the fruit for about 5 minutes at 5 psig. prior to extraction of juice by pressing. The juice is mixed with 0.045 per cent of gelatin by stirring, set aside for about 15 minutes, strained through cloth, and to the strained juice 5 to 6 per cent sugar is added. The resulting sweetened juice has a pleasant taste and the characteristic aroma and flavour of the cashew apple.

Citrus Juices

Among citrus juices, canned orange juice and frozen 4 : 1 orange juice concentrate are the most popular fruit juices on account of their nutritive value, vitamin C content and universal appal in almost all countries. To retain the natural taste and flavour as well as vitamin C content of the juice highly sophisticated processing equipment and technique are employed.

Tight skinned oranges like the malta, sathgudi and mushambi oranges give a good canned juice free from any bitterness. The juice from loose jacket oranges like the Nagpur and Coorg oranges, however, often develop, on heating, a characteristic bitter taste in the can or bottle. This bitterness is not readily acceptable by some people and is thus considered a defect. One has to acquire a taste for this juice, which is otherwise, of excellent quality. The rootstock used for raising budded trees has been found to be responsible for this bitter principle to a major extent in the orange. The trifoliate root stock has been found by them to reduce the bitterness in the orange juice to a great extent. Further work is still in progress to pin point the source and also to overcome its development in canned orange juice. In a practical way, the bitterness in the juice can be reduced considerably by extracting the juice from the segments dipped in 2 per cent boiling alkali for 30 to 60 seconds to remove the outer covering of the segments and the fibrous materials, which cause bitterness in the juice when juice is extracted from the segments in a screw type juice extractor. Addition of 5 to 6 per cent sugar to the juice also helps in reducing the bitter taste of the canned juice. In spite of the slight residual bitter taste, mostly after taste canned orange juice is quite acceptable to the majority of consumers who are awre of the nutritive characteristics of the juice. A certain amount of education and propaganda is required to popularise the juice. Taglith type press yields a juice practically free from bitterness.

To improve its quality and retain its vitamin C content, the juice is generally deaerated and flash pasteurised. Preservation of orange in its pristine purity, with all its natural flavour, is still a technical problem. It develops a characteristic stale or off flavour during storage.

Food technocrat has conducted extensive studies on the effect of different factors such as headspace in the container, sweetening, deaeration, type of container used and the method of preservation employed (i.e. sulphitation, benzoation, holding pasteurzation etc.) on the ascorbic acid content, colour and keeping quality of seven kinds of citrus juices, viz. lime, mosambi, orange, Nagpuri mandarin, grape fruit, sweet lime, khatta (C.auranttum) and galgal (C. limonia). Deaeration combined with flash pasteurization gave the best overall results. Losses in ascorbic acid during processing have been reported to be about 7 per cent in comparatively less acidic juices (i.e. mosambi, orange, Nagpuri sangtra. and sweet lime) and about 3 per cent in more acidic juices (i.e.lime, khatta and galgal). During 7 months' storage at room temperature under ditterent treatments, the losses in ascorbic acid varied from 27.2 to 36.2 per cent in galgal juice, 24.5 to 28.8 per cent in lime juice, 17.0 to 25.5 per cent in grape fruit juice, and from 19.8 ot 21.5 per cent in mosambi orange juice. The falvour and and keeping quality of citrus juices, and the role of pectic enzymes in sedimentation and of ascorbic acid in discolouration of citrus juices have been discusesed by him in detail. Colour deterioration in processed Nagpuri orange juice, grape fruit, and other citrus juices, as affected by factors, has been reported. Addition of cane sugar to the extention about 5 per cent is reported to have accelerated in the juice. Statistical analysis of the data also reveled that addition of sugar did not help in th retention of ascorbic acid in the juice. In most citrus juices, discolouration was noticed within 1½ to 3 months' storage at room temperature (24 to 50°C) and at 37°C. Storage at a low temperature of 0.2°C helped in better retention of ascorbic acid. It also retarded darkening of the juice. Better retention of ascorbic acid as well as colour was noticed when the juice was canned in plain tin cans then when it was bottled. The methods were also standardised for estimating ascorbic acid in unsulphited and sulphited citrus juices and also for measuring the colour by means of a photo electric calorimeter.

By a suitable modification of the method of extraction and preliminary treatment of the juice, it is possible to minimise the development of bitter taste in the preserved juice.

During the main orange season, the juice can be extracted, acidified with citric acid preserved with potassium metabisulphite. The juice can be filled into wooden casks or barrels, or galss or polythene carboys, and stored for subsequent conversion into orange squash as and when there is demend for the product. This technique is widely employed in this country. Care should be taken to see that the barrels are full and there is not any considerable loss of sulphur dioxide during storage. It is desirable to top up the juice in the barrels occasionally. The barrelled juice keep in good condition for more than a year.

Modern equipment comprising of fruit washers, juice extractors, depulpers, deaerators, flash pasteurizers, fillers etc., have quite recently been installed in one or two factories in the country for canning orange juice and manufacture of high density (6:1) orange juice concentrate.

Grape Juice

Coloured as well as white grapes can be used for making grape juice. In the case of coloured varieties, it is necssary to heat the crushed berries for 10 to 15 minutes at 60 to 63°C to extract the colouring matter. White grapes are not heated. Juice is extracted from the crushed grapes by means of a basket press. The extracted juice is filtered through cloth and bottled by the 'over flow' method. In the bottled juice, cream of tartar (argol) gradually settles down during storage. This can be avoided by preliminary storage of the juice for 3 to 4 months, preferably at low temperature, to secure complete separation and setting of the cream of tartar. The clear juice can then be bottled and preserved by pasteurization or by addition of sodium benzoate. Addition of sulphur dioxide is not remommended as it imparts a bitter taste to the juice.

Pineapple Juice

As already mentioned earlier, pineapples are cultivated fairly extensively in Assam, West Bengal, Kerala and recently in Coorg. The production in this area is nearly 95 per cent of the total production of pineapples in the country. Although there are a number of varieties, Kew, Giant Kew, Mauritus, Jaldhoop, Singapore, etc., Kew and Giant Kew are preferred for canning whereas other varieties can be used for preparation of juice. Pineapple juice is generally but not always a by product in the canning of pineapples. Culled or under sized fruit, slightly more ripe fruits then the canning stage of ripeness, soft fruit, broken slices and titbits etc., can be profitably employed for the manufacture of pineapple juice, which is generally canned.

The fruit is peeled, sliced, minced or grated. The minced material is passed through a screw type juice extractor or pulper or hydraulic press, or more recently, through a centrifuge, to separate the juice. The juice is screened through mislin cloth to remove coarse tissue, and than beated to about 82 to 85°C or canning. Plain cans are used. The juice is filled hot. The cans are losed and processed for 25 to 30 minutes at 80 to 82°C (or for 15 to 18 minutes at 100°C) (No. 1 Tall. 448 g cans) and cooled in water. Pineapple juice in the 156 g midget cans (15 minutes process at 1 psig.) is quite popular as a retail pack.

In the HTST process, the juice is quickly heated to 88°C, held at that temperature for 2 to 3 minutes, and then immediately filled into clean and steamed cans, which are closed, inverted for a minute or two and then cooled.

Food technocrat has conducted storage studies on ascorbic acid retention, colour and general keeping quality of pasteurized (canned as well as bottled) and sulphited pineapple juice and pineapple squash stored at room temperature (24 to 30°C) and at 37°C. The retention of ascorbic acid was 80 to 85 per cent at room temperature and only 38 to 47 per cent at 37°C. Colour deterioration, as determined with a photo electric calorimeter and expressed in terms of optical density at 6 different wave lengths ranging from 420 to 640 was three times at 37°C of that stored at room temperature. Canned pineapple juice could be stored for a period of 12 to 15 months without any serious loss in quality or nutritive value.

Pomegranate juice

The kamdhari variety of pomegranate, which contains richly coloured purple grains, gives a highly delicious juice. The fruit is cut into quarters and the grains separated and pressed in a basket press. The juice can also be extracted from the cut quarters as such by applying gentle pressure in a basket press. The juice is filtered through thick cloth. It is then bottled and preserved by pasteurization or by addition of sodium benzoate. The flavour is rather delicate and becomes less intense gradually during prolonged storage. The juice can also be converted into an attractively coloured peleasant tasting squash of 55 to 60 degrees Brix. The well known syrup of grenadine is prepared from pomegranates.

SYRUPS

Syrups of rose, sandal, almond, sarasaparilla, kewra, strawberry, pineapple, raspberry, orange, mulberry, etc., are highly popular as summer drinks in different parts of the country. They are generally prepared from extracts of natural material, or by using artificial colours and syrups of 70 to 75 Brix. To prevent crystallization, sugar is inverted by heating it in water to which a small quantity of citric acid is added.

Many of these synthetic syrups can be gradually replaced with real fruit syrups which are more nutritive.

CARBONATED BEVERAGES

Use of fruit juices in the preparation of carbonated beverages was practically negligible till very recently, although large quantities of aerated waters, iced sherbets, and synthetic drinks containing sweetening agents like saccharin, are consumed all over the country. There products have practically very little or of no nutritive value. If real fruit juices are popularised instead, the nutritive value of these beverages could be increased considerably which is a highly desirable objective.

Juices can be carbonated directly, or they can be stored as such or in the form of concentrates for subsequent carbonation, wherever necessary. Carbonated beverages keep well for about a week without the addition of any preservative. It is, however, necessary to add 0.005 per cent of sodium benzoate to the finished product, if the beverages are to be kept for a longer period.

FRUIT SYRUPS

Ingredients	Orange	Lemon	Pineapple	Raspberry	Straw-berry
Syrup of 70° Brix gallon	1	1	1	1	1
(litres)	(4.54)	(4.54)	(4.54)	(4.54)	(4.54)
Citric acid oz	2.9	4.35	2.9	1.45	0.8
(g)	(82)	(122)	(82)	(40)	(22)
Colour (q.s.)	orange-yellow	yellow	yellow	red	strawberry
Essence (oz)	soluble essence, sweet orange	lemon essence, cloudy	soluble essence, pineapple sweet	essence of raspberry	essence of straw-berry

To prapare orange syrup for carbonation, a heavy syrup is made by mixing 4.5 kg of orange juice, 6.8 kg of sugar and 198 g of citirc acid. Of this, 42 to 56 g are filled into 283 to 340 g bottles for carbonation. Other syrups like those of pineapple, lemon, lime, etc., can also be prepared in similar manner.

FRUIT JUICE CONCENTRATES

At present, several of the fruit juices are made into squashes or syrups by merely adding sugar, water, acid, colour, essence, and preservative as already described. In some of the other countries, concentrates of pure fruit juices are highly popular. They are sometimes frozen also for subsequent thawing and dispensing as drinks. Citrus juice concentrates are in great demand in the U.K., Europe, the U.S.A., and a few other countries for feeding children (as sources of vitamin C), for carbonation and for uses in ice cream, etc. Apple and grape juice concentrates of 68 to 72 Brix are also prepared for use in beverages.

Juices are concentrated either by freezing and centrifuging or by evaporation under reduced pressure at low temperature so that their original flavours are not completely lost. Highly elaborate equipment is necessary in the case of citrus juices. Concentration is carried out at temperatures as low as 5° to 12°C, using multiple effect systems and refrigeration for the condenser. The falvours volatilized and lost during evaporation are recovered and cut back into the concentrates. Recently, a Centri Therm evaporator has been introduced to effect concentration of orange juice. The contact period for the juice is as low as 30 seconds.

In the freezing process, known as Gores process, the juice is frozen into a mushy mixture of ice crystals and juice, or into a solid cake of ice, which is broken up later. On centrifuging the broken mass in a basket type centrifuge, ice crystals are retained in the basket whereas the concentrated juice passes through. Centrifuged and partially concentrated juice is again frozen and re centrifuged to remove more of the water and raise the Brix to about 50 degrees. This concentrate should either be held in cold storage, or pasteurized, to prevent spoilage. The concentrate possesses the flavour of fresh fruit, which is richer than that of the concentrate prepared by other processes. The freezing process is not, however, in general use even in some of the advanced countries.

Linde Kraus process. In the process, this juice is frozen on the external surface of a refrigerated drum which revolves slowly. The lower part of the drum dipe into the juice in a trough placed below. Ice is removed from the drum by a scraper. Owing to continuous removal of water as ice, the juice in the trough gets concentrated gradually to the desired extent. A method has been recently developed for recovering apple flavour during concentration. Eskew and his colleagues have carried out exhaustive investigations on this subject at the Eastern Regional Research Laboratories of United States Departmant of Agriculture. The juice is heated under pressure in a continuous stream to 160°C. allowing the juice to flash vaporise into another part of the apparatus. About 10 per cent of the juice by volume, is vaporised. The vapours are condensed at 21°C. Practically all the apple esters in the juice are found in this distillate, which can be added to he concentrate to give it the rich natural fresh flavour of the apple. It may be possible be extend this technique to other fruit juice concentrates also.

Recently, in connection with a systematic investigation on the concentration of the fruit juices, It has been studied the factors responsible for bitterness and gelation in orange juice concentrate. By modifying the method of extraction of juice, especially from loose jacket oranges like the Coorg and Nagpur oranges, and by centrifuging the juice after flash pasteurization they were able to prepare orange juice concentrate practically free from bitterness and gelation during storage. They also studied the changes in the ascorbic acid content, natural as well as added, during the preparation and storage of the concentrate under different conditions. While there is considerable loss of ascorbic acid during storage at ordinary temperatures, it is very little at 2 to 5°C.

Recently, there has been considerable interest in the country in fruit juice concentrates such as citrus juice concentrate, grape juice and pineapple juice concentrates, etc. in concention with the development of fruit juice based ready to serve drinks which are highly popular in the country. Recovery of flavours just as in the case of apple juice concentrate, is an important factor in this connection. Recently, a modern Centri Therm Concentration Unit has been introduced into the countryfor the large-scale production of orange juice concentrate of high dencity.

Tamarind Juice Concentrate

Indigenous tamariad fruit, which is a highly important acidulant in Indian cookery, requires preliminary soaking, squeezing, draining etc. which is rather a tedious jobs.

Spray dried fruit juice powders are highly hygroscopic and lose much of their original fresh flavour in drying. A method for perparing fruit juice powders from Coorg and Sathgudi oranges, mango, jack fruit, guava, tomato, etc. has been evolved at the Central Food Technological Research Institute, Mysore. This method, which is based on the puff drying technique, employing additives like sugar, glucose, etc. has been patented. The powders can be packed. transported and dispensed cheaply in a highly hygigenic manner. There is much scope for developing these products.

Some experiments have also been conducted to prepare freeze dried powders from guava and other fruits. Guava powder is of excellent quality in regard to flavour and reconstitution properties. These fruit powders prepared from strained fruit juices and pulps can form the basis for or a variety of infant and baby foods. Their nutritive value has been studied by several research workers at the Central Food Technological Research Institute, Mysore. Further work is in progress on several scientific as well as technological aspects of fruit juice powders.

Recently, It has been reported that among the known methods of producing tomato powder such as vacuum drying, spray drying, tower drying, freeze drying and foam mat drying, the drum spray drying tower drying freeze drying and foam mat drying the drum drying method gives a good product when conditions of drying were carefully controlled. To overcome the difficulties encountered in drum drying, a modified design of the Mitchell double drum drier, including provision for vapour removal above and below the drums, and for cooling of the product sheet in the doctor blade zone, was employed. Tomato concentrate of 28° Brix, as such, as well as tomato foam, prepared from the concentrate, using glycerol monostearate and methyl cellulose for stabilizing, and sodium sulphate at a level of 2000 ppm of SO_2 to prevent browning, were employed. The powder prepared had good colour, recontstitution and consistency, with only a small loss in lycopene content. Moisture content varied from 3 to 5 per cent.

For the preparation of the base for soup powder, tomato juice concentrate, admixed with a small amount of cereal flour or starch, has been successfully dried as flakes on a double drum drier at the CFTRI, Mysore. There is scope for developing and extending this technique to other fruit and vegetable powders.

10

Jams & Jellies

Among preserved fruits, jams, jellies and marmalades form and important class of products. Nowadays, such products are being manufactured extensively in several factories in this country, as by products or joint products in fruit canning units. They are also made in many of the homes all over the country. Their production and demand can be increased manifold by making better. use of cull fruit that is being wasted at present.

Jam is prepared by boiling the fruit pulp with a sufficient quantity of sugar to a reasonably thick consistency, firm enough to hold fruit tissues in position. In its preparation, about 20.4 kg of fruit should be used for every 24.9 kg of sugar. It should contain not less than 68.5 per cent soluble solids as determined by refractometer, when cold, and uncorrected for insoluble solids.

Jelly is prepared by boiling the fruit, with or without addition of water, straining the extract, and mixing the clear extract with sugar, and boiling the mixture to a stage at which it will set to a clear gel. A perfect jelly should be transparent, well set, but not too stiff, and should have the origional flavour of the fruit. It should be of attractive colour and should keep its shape when removed from the mould. When cut, it should retain its shape and show a clean cut surface. It should be tender enough to quiver but not flow.

Marmalade is a fruit jelly in which the slices of the fruit or of the peel are suspended. The term 'marmalade' is generally associated with the product made from citrus fruits like oranges and lemons, in which shredded peel is included as the suspended material.

The term fruit jelly covers, in a general sense, jams and marmalades also which possess the consistency of jelly (whether made from clear juice or from pulp).

JAMS

The method of preparing jams is similar to that used for jelly making, cxcept that pulp and pieces of fruit, instead of clear extract, are used. Jams may be made from a single fruit, or from a combination of two or more fruits.

A jam differs from a preserve in that it does not contain pieces of the whole fruit as in the case with a preserve. In preparing the jam, the fruit is crushed, or otherwise finely cut, so that when cooked, the mass is fairly uniform throughout. A jam is more or less a concentrated fruit possessing a fairly thich consistency and body. It is also rich in flavour, because ripe fruit, which have developed full flavour, are used in its preparation. Pectin present in the fruit gives it a good set. High concentration of sugar facilitates preservation. A great advantage in its preparation is that it can be made completely in a single operation, unlike the preserve which has to pass through several over a number of days, before it is complete.

Analytical data for some of the jams from other countries as well as of those made in India are given in the following table.

TABLE 13. ANALYSIS OF DIFFERENT KINDS OF JAMS

Description of jam	Total soluble solids by refracto meter	Acidity as citric acid	Degree of inversion	Remarks
	%	%	%	
Gooseberry jam (Indain)	71.5	0.48	50.0	
	78.0	0.70	55.2	
	72.0	0.74	80.0	
Apricot jam (Indian)	72.0	0.74	80.0	
Peach jam (Indian)	75.5	0.50	54.0	
Mixed fruit jam (Indian)	67.5	0.52	64.0	
Mixed fruit jam (Indian)	69.5	0.68	72.7	
Gooseberry jam (foreign)	73.4	0.53	81.0	
	71.5	0.67	85.1	
Raspberry jam (foreign)	73.8	0.57	59.0	
	72.5	0.81	71.6	
Strawberry jam (foreign)	72.7	0.52	48.6	
Greengage jam (foreign)	74.0	0.50	76.8	Stone included
	73.0	0.62	79.8	Stone excluded
Plum jam, stoneless (foreign)	79.6	0.71	78.6	Data on stone free basis
Plum jam (foreign)	78.3	0.99	75.3	Stoneless jam

A jam manufacturer can choose fruit from among the following five classes :

1. Fresh fruit
2. Frozen, chilled or cold stored fruit
3. Fruit or fruit pulp preserved by heat.
4. Sulphited fruit or fruit pulp i.e. fruit preserved with sulphur dioxide.
5. Dried fruit

Fresh Fruits

Fresh fruits generally give the best jams. There are, however, certain difficulties in using fresh fruits. Firstly, the supply of the fruit has to be regular so that it can be used in fresh and sound condition. Otherwise it is likely to spoil, especially in hot weather. Use of fresh fruit for day to day manufacture of jams is possible only when the factory has its own orchards in its neighbourhood or it is located in an area where the particular fruit required is grown on a large scale. If the fruit has to be transported over long distances, there will be the problem of spoilage during transit. Secondly, due to the short duration of the fruit season, large stocks of the fruit will have to be held in cold storage or frozen or chilled, or preserved with chemicals, or by heat treatment.

As pectin is the main ingredient in the fruit which gives a set to the jam, it is preferable to use some green fruit which is rich in pectin along with the ripe fruit to secure the desirable jellying effect in the jam. Over ripe fruit should not be used as it produces pasty product. In some ceses, where the fruit is deficient in pectin, pectin from other fruits or commercial liquid or solid pectin may be added to supplement it.

Frozen Fruits

In a modern fruit preservation factory, a cold store is considered a necessary adjunct. During the season when the fruits are in glut, they are stored to ensure regular supplies to the factory over a period during the off season. It has been found that the flavour and aroma of the coldstored fruit remain practically unimpaired, and jams prepared from the coldstored fruit are as good as those made from fresh fruit. Fruits which cannot be kept in cold storage for long periods, are kept in the frozen condition. Some fruits such as cherries and plums, discolour badly on freezing and turn brown. Such fruits are frozen after adding sugar or sugar syrup to prevent browning. In this country, fresh fruits are generally employed for the manufacture of jams.

Fruits Preserved by Heat Treatment

The fruit is prepared in the same way as for canning, and heated to a sterilizing temperature in hermetically sealed containers. Some times, a small quantity of sugar is also added to preserve the aroma, colour and texture of the fruit. Plums, apricots, pineapples, and peaches are stored without addition of sugar whereas strawberries and respberries are stored after adding sugar. The added sugar is taken into account at the time of making the jam. This method is not, however, generally used largely for the following reasons:

1. Difficulty of storing the fruit in barrels.
2. Loss of colour in fruits such as strawberries and respberries during the treatment and subsequent storage.
3. A certain amount of loss of pectin while the fruit remains hot for a long period in bulk packing.

Sulphitation for Storing

For preserving fruits in bulk, sulphur dioxide is universally employed in the form of sodium or potassium meta bisulphite, sulphurous acid or calcium sulphite. Calcium sulphite provides an additional advantage in that it hardens the tissues of soft fruit and thereby prevents their disintegration.

The preservative fluid in the fruit should be an aqueous solution containing 0.08 to 0.1 per cent of sulphur dioxide. In general practice, the total quantity of sulphur dioxide in the fruit and liquor is kept at 1,500 to 2,000 p.p.m. as a safeguard against any possible leakage of sulphur dioxide.

Sulphur dioxide temporarily bleaches the red colour of fruits, like red plums, strawberries and raspberries. The colour is, however, restored when sulphur dioxide is driven off at the cookings stage of making the jam.

Although sulphur dioxide causes complete stoppage of enzymic activities the fruit, its presence in soft fruit causes the pectic enzymes to convert pectin into pectic acid, and thereby practically destroys all the jellying power of the pectin of the fruit.

Sulphur dioxide toughens the skin of some fruits such as gooseberries and red currants. These fruits should, therefore, be heated to boiling temperature and then cooled before adding SO_2. This preliminary heating will destroy the enzyme in the fruit that would, otherwise, destroy the jellying power of the pectin present in the fruit.

Preparing the Fruit for Jam making

The fruit is washed thoroughly to remove any adhering dust and dirt. Leaves, stalks and other undesirable portions are removed. The fruit is then subjected to preliminary treatment which varies with the type of fruit. For example, strawberries are crushed between rollers. Raspberries are steamed, crushed and passed through sieves to remove the hard cores. Plums are heated with a small quantity of water until they become soft, and are then passed through a wide mesh sieve to separate the stones. Sometimes, the stones are not removed while making whole fruit plum jam. Cherries are treated in a similar way Gooseberries are whirled in a rotary vertical cylinder lined with carborundum to rub off tope and tails. They are then passed through sieves to separate the stalks. Pears are pooled, cored and cut into small pieces. Peaches are lye peeled, and the stones removed. They are then cut into small pieces. Apricots are cut and the stones removed, unless the jem to be made with the stones is also included. Mangoes are peeled, stones separated, and then sliced. The slices are passed through a pulper. Pine apples are peeled, sliced and the cores punched. The slices are then cut into smaller pieces and passed through a screw type cruesher to get a fairly coarse pulp suitable for making the jam. In the case of loose jacket oranges like Coorg and Nagpur oranges, the segments are separated and lye dipped to remove the outer covering, and then passed through a screw type extractor to get a fairly coarse pulpy juice, fit for making orange jam. Bananas are peeled & crushed in a screw extractor fitted with a coarse sieve. Greapes are heated and passed through a screw extractor fitted with a coarse sieve. Grapes are heated and passed through a screw type juice extractor for getting a coarse juicy pulp. Other fruits are suitably treated to get a fairly coarse pulp suitable for making the jam. The pulp should contain recognisable pieces of fruit. In the case of mixed fruit jam, two or more fruits or fruit pulps are taken in the proportion found suitable for the purpose.

Adding of Sugar

Generally, cane sugar (sucrose) of good quality is used in the preparation of jams. The proportion in which it is added depends not only on the fruit, but also on its acidity and degree of ripeness. Sweet fruits require less sugar then tart fruits do. The quantity added should be adequate to give the maximum strength to the pectin sugar acid gel. To ensure a minimum of 68.5 per cent invert sugar in the jam, generally 24.9 kg of sugar is required for every 20.4 kg of fruit taken. The finished jam should contain 30 to 50 per cent invert sugar, or of glucose, to avoid crystallization of cans sugar in the jam during storage. If the percentage of invert sugar (reducing sugar) is less than 30 cane sugar may crystalize out; if it is more than 50 per cent, the jam will develop into a honey like mass due to the formation of small crystals of glucose. Alternatively, corn syrup or commercial glucose may be used along with cane sugar to avoid crystallization. Sugar in excess of the requisite quantity should not be added because, if the percentage of total soluble solids becomes very high, the jam becomes gummy and sticky. In case excess of sugar has been added, the remedy lies in adding pectin or acid or both, to counteract the effect of excess sugar. If on the other hand, the percentage of soluble solids is low and there is premature setting of the jam, indicating thereby that the material contains excess of pectin, it is advisable to add more sugar. Under exceptional circumstances where sugar is not added, it would be desirable to and a small quantity of sodium bicarbonate to reduce the acidity and thus prevent pre coagulation.

Addition of Acid, Colour and Flavour

Acid. Generally, citric, tartaric or malic acid, which are natural fruit acids, are used to supplement the acidity of the fruit for jam making. Addition of acids to fruits, deficient in it, is a necessity because appropriate combination of pectin, sugar and acid is essantial to give a 'set' to the jam. Tarr is of the view that the pH of the mixture of fruit juice and pectin should be 3.1 before sugar is added. Accoring to Hinton, however, purified pectin gives the best 'set' at pH 2.0. As fruits contain natural buffering salts and other associated materials, the best results are obtained when the pH of the mixture is about 3.0.

Colour. Only permitted edible food colours should be used, if necessary, and these should be added towards the end of the boiling process.

Flavour. Ordinarily, jams do not require the addition of flavours. If desired, they may be added when jam boiling is nearing completion.

Boiling. A steam jacketed pan made of nickel, monel metal, aluminium, stainless steel or copper heavily lined with tin or silver, is generally used for boiling jams. They are of the stationary or of the tilting type. They are highly convenient for rapid boiling of jams. The fruit sugar acid pectin mixture is boiled in these pans, heated by steam at 60 to 80 psig (4.20 to 5.60 kg/cm^2). Each batch of mix is in small lots of 45.3 to 54.4 kg. Sugar and fruit are first weighed separately. The fruit is placed in the boiling pan and, if necessary, a small quantity of water is added to facilitate pulping. It is then cooked sufficiently to liberate the pectin. Sugar is added next. The fruit sugar mixture is then boiled repidly to concentrate the soluble solid to about 68.5 per cent and also to effect the necessary degree of inversion of the sugar. To avoid excessive frothing during boiling, a small quantity of butter or some other brand of edible oil may be added to the boiling mixture. It the fruit does not contain sufficient pectin, commercial pectin may be added to make good the deficiency.

Boiling under Vacuum

Sometimes, jam is boiled in a vacuum pan under reduced pressure at a lower temperature of 65° to 76°C. The advantage of vacuum boiling or cooking is that in minimises the undesirable changes in colour and prevents loss of vitamin C. The disadvantage, however, is that the jam mixture has to be boiled for a longer time to soften the fruit pieces with the result that there is some loss of flavour. This drawback can, however, be over come by recovering the volatile esters and putting them back into the jam.

Proper control of boiling is necessary to avoid over concentration of soluble solids, over inversion of sugar, and hydrolysis of pectin.

End Point

In order to make a product of uniform quality, a definite quantity of fruit and sugar should always yield a definite quantity of the finished jam. This can be determined by carrying out a jelmeter test. Generally, in the case of fruits fairly rich in pectin, the weight of the finished jam is one and a half times the weight of sugar taken. The data in the following Table would serve as a ready reckoner :-

Jam containing 68.5 per cent of soluble solids boils at 106°C at sea level. Correction will, however, be necessary for higher locations as the boiling point decreases with increase in the altitude. Generally, the end point for boiling the jam should be about - 13°C higher then the boiling point of water at any particular place.

When jam is to be packed in cans, it should be filled hot, and the cans closed and pasteurized for about 30 minutes at 82° to 85°C. In the case of A 2½ and larger size cans, it is sufficient to fill the cans hot, seal them and invert them to sterilize the ends for about five minutes and then cool them in water or in air.

TABLE 14. RELATIONSHIP BETWEEN THE AMOUNT OF SUGAR AND THE JAM PRODUCED

Jelmeter test figure on nearest mark	Sugar to be added to each lb (0.4 kg) of cooked fruit		Weight of cooked jam	
	lb (kg)	oz. (g)	lb. (kg)	oz. (gm)
1½	1	8	2	6
	(0.4)	(226)	(0.9)	(170)
1	1	4	2	0
3/4	(0.4 kg)	(113)	(0.9)	0
	1	0	1	10
1/2	(0.4)	0	(0.4)	(283)
	0	12	1	4
	0	(340)	(0.4)	(113)

Storage

Storage of jam in glass jars, which cannot be hermetically sealed, is rather difficult, as the surface of the jam in the jar is susceqtible to mould growth. It should also be remenbered that unless the jars are stored in a fairly cool place, moisture will evaporate from the jam resulting in surface graining and also shrinkage of the jam. According to Tomkins, if storage conditions are such as to allow the mould to draw moisture easily from the substrtum, the atmospheric humidity will have very little effect on their growth. It will, however, have a considerable effect when the movement of water from below is slow, and especially when the surface of the jam is covered with a closely adhering waxed tissue paper. This is true in cases where available water is very low due to the presence of a high concentration of sugar. He further states that most fungi are completely destroyed if they are exposed to humidity less than 90 per cent. As a safeguard, jams should, therefore, be stored preferably at a place having a relative humidity not exceeding about 80 per cent. Hirst, and also Morris, state that jams are rarely spoiled by yeasts because of their jelly consistency in which they cannot grow or thrive. There are however, certain strains of osmosphilic yeast which can tolerate the high concentration of sugar in the jams. They cause occasionally some spoilage in jams.

To prevent spoilage of jams by moulds, the filled jars should be left unsealed, but only covered with a disc of waxed paper on the surface of the jam, because moulds do not grow under open conditions as rapidly as in a closed space. The jars should be inspacted from time to time and if there by any sign of mould growth, the waxed tissue paper should be changed. If desired, the paper may be dipped in alcohol before placing it on the jam. These jars should be finally sealed only at the time of despatch for sale. When the jam is to be packed in glass jars, which can be hermetically sealed or in cans, it should be filled hot and the container sealed air tight and pasteurized at 82 C for 25 to 30 minutes, depending upon their size. This process is rather inconvenient. In the case of 0.4 kg jars which can be sealed air tight by means of an R.O. seal, it has been found that if after filling the hot jam into jars to the brim, they are closed with the R.O. seal and the sealed jars inverted for some time to sterilize the closures and then kept in the upright position to cool down, the chance of mould growth is practically negligble. In the case of cans it is sufficient if the closed cans are inverted for 5 to 10 minutes to sterilize the lid, before they are cooled. In the case of jars with jam made from fresh, unsulphited fruit pulp, it is advisable to add to the jam about 40 p.p.m. of sulphur dioxide in the form of potassium metabisulphite, which is permitted by law. This acts as a safeguard against any possible moulding of the surface of the jam. In the case of cans, addition of sulphur dioxide to the jam should be avoided as it leads to blackening of the internal surface of the can. In the case of R.O. closures for jars, an additional precaution would be to dip them in 1 to 2 per cent potassium metabisulphite solution for 3 to 4 minutes, then drain them for sealing the jars. Siddappa has noticed that the procedures described above given highly satisfactory results (unpublished).

Controlled Manufacture

Analytical control in the manufacture of jams as well as of jellies is highly important to ensure standards of quality. The various methods of control are as follows:

Soluble Solids

Determination of soluble solids is of great importance in the chemical control of jam manufacture. Soluble solids can be determined easily with a retractometer or by means of a specific gravity hydrometer, or even by a thermometer, as the boiling point of the product depends upon the soluble solids in the product.

Refractometer Method.

Percentage of soluble solids can be determined easily with an Able or Zeiss type refractometer of with a pocket retractometer, while the boiling is in progress. As jams and jellies contain other materials like acid, invert sugar fruit salts, etc besides sucrose, the readings are not quite accurate. For all practical purposes, however, minor corrections for other materials may be ignored and the refractometer reading fixed for each type of product. If desired, the refractometer readings may be standardised with other methods based either on trial boiling to the requied output weight, or on a more exact determination of the soluble solids by the specific gravity method.

A sufficient quantity of a representative lot of the sample should be taken and cooled immediately so that the percentage composition of soluble solids may not alter due to evaporation of water. The sample should be homogenized thoroughly before testing. A very convenient way to do this is to squeeze a portion of the jam throgh a piece of muslin cloth directly on to the prism of the refractometer. The percentage of total soluble solids is read directly on the scale. with dark coloured jams and jellies, a projection type refractometer may be used.

Specific Gravity Method. Fifty grams of the product are stirred with a little warm water to dissolve the jelly portion. The solution thus made is poured off from the sediment of fibre and seeds, and collected in a 250 c.c. (ml) volumetric flask. The residue is boiled two or three times with a-small quantity of water, decented, and the clear extract mixed with the first extract. The combined extract is cooled to room temperature and made up to 250 c.c.(ml). It is then filtered through a coarse filter paper. The specific gravity of the solution is determined at 20°C using a specific gravity hydrometer.

Citrus juices like orange juice, lemon juice etc. are extracted during the season and stored in wooden barrels, glass and polythene carboys, etc., for subsequent conversion into squashes, cordials, etc. during the offseason. For effective storage, it is necessary to acidify the orange juice to some extent and preserve it by the addition of about 1000 ppm of SO_2 in the form of its salt, potassium meta bisulphite (KMS). During storage of the juice, especially in the case of wooden casks and barrels, there is gradual loss of sulphur dioxide through the pores in the wood, although the barrel may be kept full by topping it with additional juice occasionally. If there is much loss of sulphur dioxide from the juice during prolonged storage, there will be the likelihood of the juice spoiling due to fermentation. To guard against this, it is necessary to make sure that the sulphur dioxide in the stored juice is not reduced considerably from the initial 1000 ppm. For this, it will be necessary to add occasionally further small quantities of KMS to the juice. To know the sulphur dioxide content in the juice, a quick factory laboratory method will be highly useful. The conventional Monier Williams, distillation and absorption method is rather laborious and time consuming for routine estimation. In the quicker and simpler method, the sulphited juice is titrated against standard N/50 or N/100 iodine solution, (prepared approximately by weighing iodine and dissolving it in potassium iodide solution) using starch solution as internal indicator, starch developing a blue colour with iodine. Iodine solution is got standardised aginst sodium thiosulphate solution, which in turn, is standardised against standard potassium dichromate solution, which is prepared by weighing accurately the A.R. Chemical and making the standard solution.

A known quantity of the filtered juice is pipetted into in Erlenmeyer conical flask (100 ml capacity) and the standard iodine solution is run in from a burette. A few ml. of starch solution (1 per cent) is added to the juice towards the end to determine the end point of titration, any excess of iodine forming a blue compound in the solution in the flask.

Alternatively, a known volume of the standard iodine solution can be pipetted into the conical flack and titrated with the filtered sulphited juice, using starch solution to indicate the end point.

(1 ml of N/100 iodine solution = 0.32 mg SO_2)

Atomic/Molccular weight

Resublimed iodine = 126.9
Sodium thiosulphate $Na_2S_2O3.\ 5\ H_2\ O= 248.18$
Potassium dichromate (AR) $K_2Cr_2O7 = 294.22$
Potassium metabisulphite (KMS) $K_2O_22SO_2 = 222.33$
or K_2S_2O5

SO_2 content in pure potassium metabisulphite $\frac{128}{222} \times 100 = 57.7$ per cent

Note : Generally, potassium metabisulphite purchased in the market will not be cent per cent pure. It is, therefore, necessary to determine the degree of purity sulphur dioxide content.

Total Soluble Solids

The refractometer and specific gravity methods are useful for the determination of soluble solids content of fruit pulps, which is required to work out recipes.

Invert Sugar

Invert sugar is generally determined by the volumetric method of Lane and Eynon. The solution prepared for the determination of specific gravity is further diluted so that the diluted solution contains about 0.2 per cent of soluble solids. It is then titrated with Fehling's solution, using methylene blue as internal indicator. The amount of sugar can be calculated from the corresponding titration value, using a table. Ten c.c. (ml) of standard Fehling's solution is equivalent to 0.05 gram of invert sugar of 0.0475 gram of cane sugar (sucrose).

Sulphur Dioxide

Estimation of sulphur dioxide is highly important when the jam has been made from pulp preserved with sulphur dioxide. According to the Fruit Products Order, the residual sulphur dioxide in the jam should not exceed 40 p.p.m. Sulphur dioxide is generally determined by the distillation procedure of Monier Williams according to A.O.A.C. method. A quick laboratory or factory method for the estimation of SO_2 in sulphited juices and squashes is described here.

Acidity

Ten grams of the sample are dissolved in water and the solution brought to a boil and titrated with standard N/10 sodium hydroxide solution, using phenolphthalein as indicator. When the end point is not sharp, the solution should be diluted further, and phenolphthalein paper used as external indicator.

Regulating pH of the Material

The pH of the material has great influence on the inversion of sugar and the set of jam or marmalade. The pH necessary to produce a good firm set in pectin jelly is 3.30 but in jams, it varies with the kind of fruit used. The relative pH ranges and optimum pH values of a nubmer of jams have been worked out by Cameron, who states that the setting of jams takes place only within certain pH ranges. His data are given in Table 15.

TABLE 15. pH RANGE AND OPTIMUM pH FOR DIFFERENT KINDS OF JAMS

Type of jam	pH range	Optimum pH
Apricot, greengage, damson, plum	3.2 -3.5	3.35
Apple and damson, apple and plum	3.2 -3.5	3.35
Apple and raspberry	3.4 -3.5	3.40
Orange marmalade	3.4 -3.5	3.40
Gooseberry	3.4 -3.5	3.40
Black currant	3.4 -3.6	3.50
Seedless Bramble	3.4 -3.6	3.50
Raspberry	3.5 -3.7	3.60
Raspberry and red currants	3.5 -3.7	3.60
Strawberry	3.7	3.70

Note : Data practically similar to the above hold good in the case of pineapple, mango, orange, mixed fruit jam, etc, which are popular in this country.

Use of Buffer Salts. As the pH is the controlling factor in the setting of jams, it is sometimes necessary to adjust it to the optimum. This is done generally by adding salts of citric or tartaric acids, or alkalies like sodium bicarbonate or calcium carbonate. The addition of about 28 grams of the buffer salt to 45.3 kg of the jam will generally change the pH by about 0.1 unit. The pH can be determined with any standard pH meter having a glass electrode.

Insoluble Solids

The fruit content in a jam can be detemined from the amount of insoluble matter present in it. To determine the insoluble matter, 20 grams of the samples are taken, minced thoroughly, and boiled with 100 c.c. (ml) of distilled water for 30 to 40 minutes. The boiled mixture is filtered through a dried and weighed filter paper. After filtration, the fibre is washed back into the water and boiled again with 100 c.c. of water for 15 to 20 minutes. It is filtered again on the same filter paper. This boiling and filtering process is repeated several times to remove all soluble materials. Finally, the fibre is washed on the filter paper itself with plenty of water and then dried along with the filter paper at 100°C constant weight. Knowing the insoluble matter content of the original fruit, one can work out roughly the quantity of fruit present in the jam.

Estimation of Pectin

Pectin does not have a definite composition, because pectins from different sources behave differently. Even if pectin is determined quantitively, employing elaborate analytical methods, that alone will not be sufficient to guarantee or predict the set of the jam. On the other hand, the alcohol precipitation test for pectin, which in very simple and quick, is highly useful. From the general appearance of the pectin precipitate, one can judge fairly and accurately its sugar carrying capacity and hence the jellying power.

JELLIES

In jelly making, pectin is the most essential constituent. Although there is difference of opinion about the exact nature of pectin, it is generally accepted that pectins jellies, when mixed and boiled with the proper amounts of sugar, acid and water. All these constituents must be present in a particular proportion for making a good jelly.

Fruit for Jelly

Pectin is present in the cell walls of fruits. Its quantity, however, varies with the kind of fruit and even with the variety of the same fruit. Many fruits are rich in pectin as well as acid, and are thus well suited for jelly making. There are other fruits, however, which are either rich in pectin or in acid, or deficient in both. In order to get a jelly from fruits rich in pectin, but deficient in acid, it is necessary to add either fruits rich in acid, or an acid like citric, tartaric or malic.

In the case of fruits deficient in pectin but rich in acid, either fruits rich in pectin or commercial pectin should be added. Both these methods have their own merits. Combining of fruits rich in acid with those rich in pectin is less expensive then using acid or commercial pectin to supplement the deficiency, but the drawback is that the flavour of the jelly is affected. Special care is, therefore, necessary to ensure that the fruits are mixed in proper and juicious proportion. On the other hand, commercial pectin does not have any deleterious effect on the final flavour of the jelly made from any particular fruit.

A classification of some fruits according to their suitability for jelly making, based on their pectin and acid contents, as worked out by Elwell and Dehn, is shown in Table 16.

Selection of Fruits

The fruits should be sufficiently ripe, but not over ripe, and they should have good flavour. Slightly under ripe fruit yields more pectin then over ripe fruit does because as the fruit ripens, the pectin present in it decomposes into pectic acid, which does not form a jelly with acid and sugar. The amount of pectin extracted from a fruit depends on the degree of disintegration of protopectin during the heating. In practice, a mixture of under ripe ripe fruits is used; under ripe fruits fro their pectin content and ripe ones for their flavour.

After picking, the fruits should be used, without undue delay, for jally making becausem, if kept for a long time, degradation of pectin proceeds rapidly. In some cases, artificial ripening of the fruits is also useful.

Preparation of Fruits

Fruits are washed thoroughly with water to romove any adhering dirt. If the fruit has been sprayed with lead or arsenical sprays, it should be washed in a warm solution of one per cent hydrochloric acid and then rinsed in water.

TABLE 16. CLASSIFICATION OF FRUITS FOR JELLY-MAKING
(after Elwell and Dehn, 1939)

Fruits rich in pectin and acid	Fruits containing less pectin and acid	Fruits rich in pectin, but low in acid	Fruits containing acid, but low in pectin	Fruits low in pectin and acid
Apples, sour and crab	Apples, ripe	Apples, kinds low in acid	Apricots, sour	Apricots, ripe
Blackberries, sour	Blackberries	—	—	Elder berries
Cranberries	Cherries, sour varieties	Bananas, unripe	Cherries, sweet varieties	Peaches, ripe pomegranates
Currants	Fejoias	Cherries, sour	Peaches, sour	Prunes
Gooseberries	Grapes, California	Figs, unripe	Pineapples	Raspberries
Guavas, sour	Loquats	—	Rhubarb	Strawberries
Grapes, eastern	Plums	Pears	Strawberries	Overripe fruits
Kumquats	Grapefruits, peel			
Logan-berries	Guavas, ripe			
Lemons	Orange, peel			
Oranges, sour	Quince, ripe			
Plums, sour				

Jams

Apricot jam. Both White and yellow apricots can be used for the preparation of apricot jam. The method is similar to that employed in the case of peach jam except that the quantity of acid added should be increased to 0.5 per cent, especially in the case of the sweeter white varieties. The kernels can be decuticled like almonds and added to the jam to improve its tasts and appearance. Besides fresh apricots, sulphited apricot pulp packed in barrels during the fruit season and also dried paricots, are extencisvely employed for large scale manufacture of apricot jam. Aprirot jam is a popular product in several parts of the country.

Peach jam. White as well as yellow peaches of free and also olingstone type are employed for the preparation of peach jam. The fruit is peeled with a knife or with lye solution and the stones removed. The pulp is softened by heating it with about 1.4 th is weight of water. An equal weight of sugar and 0.2 per cent citric or tartaric acid are added to get a jam having good tasts, set and flavour.

Pear jam. Pears are peeled and cut into small pieces which are then crushed and boiled with 3/4th of their weight of water. To that pulp 0.25 to 0.5 per cent citric acid is added towards the end point of boiling the jam. pear jam forms an important by product in the canning of pears.

Plum jam. Plum jam can be made with or without the stones. The fruit is crushed and boiled with about one third of its weight of water to softenn the pulp. The pulp is screened through sieve to remove the stones and skin. The alucha plum gives a golden brown jam with a fruit sugar ratio of 1:1. If desired, citric or tartaric acid to the extent of about 0.5 per cent of the weight of fruit may be added to improve the taste of the jam. Other yellow and purple varieties of plums also can be utilized for the prepartion of jam. Plum jam is a popular product in the United Kingdom where the yellow pershare plums and the red and purple plums like Victoria, and Czar plums are extensively canned. Plum jam has a fairly tart taste unlike jams made from less acidic fruits.

Other Jams. Jams from cherry, mulberry, strawberry, mushmelon, mango, jack fruit, cashew apple, pineapple, etc. also can be made in the usual way. It may however, be necessary to very slightly the fruit sugar ratio and the precentage of acid added. In some cases, it may be useful to supplement the flavour of the jam by adding extra fruit flavour.

Pineapple jam in cans as well as in jars is a highly popular product in this country. Mixed fruit jam which is made from a blend of fruits like pineapple, mango, orange, banana, etc. in different combinations, is another popular product. Orange jam made from lye peeled segments of the mandarin orange like Coorg orange, is becoming popular in spite of a slight tinge of bitterness. It has, however, full fruit taste and flavour. It is comparatively a new product. Strawberry and respberry jams with attractive purplish red colour and pleasent taste and flavour, sutiably augmented, are quite popular among the jams made and sold in the country. Papaya fruit is sometimes employed in the preparation of mixed fruit jams. Banana jam by itself is not quite popular on account of its texture and astringent taste. Tomatoes are sometimes used for the preparation of tomato jam. Jams can be prepared from several other local fruits on a home scale till they become popular.

In the case of pineapple jam, using fresh pulp from broken slices, it has been found that addition of about 0.5 to 0.75 per cent pectin and about 0.5 per cent citric acid by weight of the pulp taken, and also addition of about 0.1 per cent of pineapple essence, gives an excellent jam. The addition of pectin and acid will be necessary in the case of mango jam. which is made as a by product in the mango canning industry. Some typical recipes found useful in large scale manufacture of jams are given here (Siddappa, unpublished data).

RECIPES FOR SOME IMPORTANT TYPICAL JAMS

Pineapple jam

Pineapple pulp (fresh or canned)	75 kg
Sugar	75 kg
Citric acid	375 g
Pectin, 150 grade	563 g
Pineapple essence	75 ml

Orange jam

Orange pulp (from lye peeled segments)	50 kg
Sugar	50 kg
Citric acid	250 g
Pectin, 150 grade	375 g
Orange sweet essence	50 ml

Mango jam

Mango pulp	40 kg
Sugar	40 kg
Pectin 150 grade	500 g
Citric acid	400 g
Mango essence	70 ml

Apple jam

Apple pulp	40 kg
Sugar	44 kg
Pectin 150 grade	400 g
Citric acid	500 g
Apple essence	60 ml

Mixed fruit jam. Blends of mango, pineapple, orange, apricots, papaya, gurya etc. pulps, as available in different proportions to meet the consumer acceptance.

Sugar. Equal in weight to that of blended pulp taken; citric acid to the extent of about 0.75 to 1.0 per cent by weight of blended pulp; pectin to the extent of 0.5 to 1.0 per cent by weight of blended pulp, depending upon the fruits used.

Essence. Blend of appropriate essences to be added to the desired extent.

Colour. A blend of predominantly red food colours may be added to the extent desired.

Jellies

Guava jell. Ripe guavas, preferably with plenty of pulp and less seeds, are used for the preparation of jelly. The fruit is washed well and cut into thin slices. They are covered with an equal weight of water containing 2 grams of citric acid for every kg of guava taken. The mixture is heated gently for about 30 minutes to extract pectin from the slices. The extract is drained, and to the residue, water equal to 1/4 th of the weight of slices is added, and a second extract is taken. The two extracts are combined and strained through a piece of thick cloth to remove the coarse particles. The strained extract is adowed to settle overnight in a tall vessel. Naxt day, the clear supernatant lieuid is syphoned off without disturbing the sediment at the bottom of the vessel. The extract which is clear, is tested for its pectin content by the alcohol precipitation method or by the jelmeter. The required quantity of sugar (generally on equal quantity) is added to the extract and the mixture boiled down to the desired consistency. The finished jelly is packed in glass jars or in cans. Guava jelly with its attractive purplish red colour and pleasant taste and aroma, is a fairly popular product in this country and also in some other countries. There is at present a limited export market for the product.

Other jellies. By adopting the procedure described for guava jelly, jellies can be prepared from fruits like apple, grape, reselle, jaman, jack fruit, etc., These are generally prepared on a small scale for home consumption.

Jam like products

Apart from the conventional types of jams, other products resembling the jams is several respects are also made occasionally. Some of them have commerical importance also. Guava, cheese and apple butter belong to this category.

Guava cheese. Firm ripe guavas are washed, cut into thin slices, and boiled with an equal quantity of water to soften the pulp. The softened pulp in screened through net cloth to separate the skin and seeds. To every kilogram of the pulp are added 1.25 to 1.50 kg of sugar, 2.2 to 3.3 grams of citric acid and about 56 grams of butter. The mixture is cooked to a thick paste. Small quantities of a permitted red colour common salt may be added towards the end to improve the apprarance of the final product. After boiling is completed, the hot cheese is allowed to set by spreading it as a slab on a greased tray. After cooling, the slab can be cut into small pieces of suitable size and the pieces wrapped in moisture proof paper or polythene sheets. The wrapped pieces can be further packed in jars or cartons.

Apple butter. Apple butter is practically similar to apple jam except that it is made from finely sieved apple pulp to which small quantities of spices consisting of nutmeg, cinnamon, clove etc. are added. The pulp sugar ratio is generally 1:3/4. On account of its mild spicy taste and flavour apple butter is popular among a large number of consumers.

11

Tomato Products

(Tomato Juice, Tomato Paste, Cocktail, Ketchup, Chilli Sauce etc.)

Fresh tomatoes are highly refreshing and appetizing. They are a good source of vitamins, particularly vitamin C. In this country, tomatoes are grown both in summer and winter, but those grown in winter are superior because they contain more solids. Two types of tomatoes more commonly grown in India are the large and the round ones and the small and oval ones. In other countries well known varieties like Marglobe, Sanjose etc., are grown for their better suitability for preserving and processing. In this country, fairly large quantities of tomato sauces and ketchups popular with the public are being manufactured on an increasing scale, mostly in small units. Large tomato processing units employing fully automatic equipment, have not yet come into being, although proposals to set a few such units are being actively considered.

The tomato changes in colour during different stages of its maturity and ripening i.e. from green to pale white, yellow and finally red. The yellow colour is owing to the presence of carotene. The red colour appears when the lycopene is formed in the fibres.

As tomatoes are available practically throughout the year in this country there is scope for setting up a large scale processing industry. Equipment for the purpose is standard and can be obtained without much difficulty. Tomato products are judged by their colour, which in turn, depends on the degree to redness of tomatoes. The red pigment, lycopene, being a highly characteristic and rather unique rigment in tomatoes, can be used as an index of the amount of the real tomato used in a product. In fact some of the analytical methods are based on this concept.

The following rules should be kept in mind to secure a product of high quality.

1. Use only plant ripened red tomatoes as far as possible. The yellow

and greenish portions not only mask the red colour of the fully ripe tomatoes, but also turn brown owing to oxidation.

2. Never use iron equipment at any stage of processing. Lycopene, which is a self oxidizing isomer of carotene, and to which tomatoes owe their red colour, turns brown when it comes into contact with iron. Iron also forms black compounds with the tannin of the tomatoes or of the spices used. Equipment should be glass lined, or made of monel metal or preferably stainless steel. Copper equipment also adversely affects the colour of tomato products. Further, there is a severe legal limitation on the amount of copper in tomato products.

3. Avoid prolonged heating, and cool the product quickly after preparation. Tomato juice, cocktail, ketchup, sauce and soup, and chilli sauce are some of the more important products made from tomatoes. The method of preparing these is described briefly in the following sections.

TOMATO JUICE

For this product, only plant ripened and fully red tomatoes should be used. All green, blemished and over ripe fruits should be rejected as they adversly affect the quality of the product. Juice got from over ripe tomatoes is usually thin and not quite pleasant in its taste and aroma.

The yield, colour and flavour of the juice depend on the degree of ripeness of the tomatoes, the variety and the place where grown. The following points should be kept in view to ensure good quality of the juice.

1. The juice should be of deep red colour. As the red colour is contained in the fibres, and not in the serum of the juice, the fibrous portain as much as possible should be incorporated in the juice in finely divided condition.

2. The juice should possess the characteristic tasteand flavour of tomato.

3. The acidity of the juice as citric acid, should be about 0.4 per cent.

4. The vitamins present in fresh tomatoes should go into the juice during its preparation. Their retention in the juice depends on the method of extraction used. It has been found that while carotene (3carotene) is fairly resistant to heat and oxidation in various processes of preparation; vitamin C (ascorbic acid) is lost papreciably particularly during the sreening of the juice, on account of oxidation.

5. For uniformity in quality either the tomatoes used should be from one stock and place or the juice should be suitably blended.

Washing and Trimming

Mere rinsing of tomatoes in water is not enough, because mould filaments and other micro organisms found in the cracks, wrinkles, folds and stem cavities are not easily dislodged by gently washing alone. For thorough cleaning, tomatoes should be washed in plenty of running water. For commercial production, rotary washers, or trough washers fitted with moving conveyor belt and soft roller brushers, are generally employed.

Great care should be taken in trimming the washed tomatoes. The loss on account of trimming green and yellowish portions, stalk end, and cracked portions etc., varies from 4.0 to 17.0 per cent with an average of about 8.0 per cent, according to data collected over a period under Indian processing conditions. The heavy wastage is mostly owing to absence of standard varieties for defects in picking, packing, and transport and marketing. The loss can be cut down to a bare minimum by adopting gradually improved methods of handling. Recently, considerable work has been done on several of these aspects with the result that tomato products manufactured in the country are of high quality and stand comparison with similar produced elsewhere. Large scale commercial production is, however, necessary for attaining this objective.

Crushing

After trimming, tomatoes are cut into 4 to 6 pieces for boiling to soften the tisses. Alternatively, they may be crushed by means of fluted wooden roller crushers.

Pulping

Tomatoes can be pulped by the 'hot' process or by the 'cold' process described below.

Hot Pulping. The crushed tomatoes are boiled in their own juice in steam jacketed stainless steel pans or in aluminium pans for 3 to 5 minutes to facilitate pulping. This method has the following advantages.

1. The tendency of the juice to separate into liquid and pulp can be overcome if the pectin naturally present in the seed and in the skin can be incorporated into the juice. During the preliminary boiling, this pectin is released and it thickens the pulp. The pectase enzymes which would otherwise hydrolyse the natural pectin present in tomatoes and thereby make the juice thin, are also destroyed during boiling.

2. Boiling sterilizes the juice partly, thereby checking to some extent the growth of micro organisms which cause fermentation etc., in the juice. It also inactivates the oxidative enzymes which are responsible for the destruction of vitamin C in the juice.

3. A light cooking releases the red colour present in the skin.

4. The yield of juice is higher than in cold pulping of the tomatoes.

Cold Pulping. The tomatoes are crushed in the cold and as such passed through a pulper. This method has the following defects :

1. As compared to the hot process, the extraction of juice is somewhat difficult and the yield is less.

2. Air gets incorporated into the juice in the process of extraction and this oxidizes vitamin C in the juice. There are, however, suitable equipments available nowadays which minimise considerably the mixing up of air with the juice.

3. The juice extracted by this method is somewhat lighter in colour, since it is necessary to heat the skin to release the colour from the fibrous tissues.

4. The whole process of crushing pressing etc has to be completed quickly to avoid microbial spoilage, especially during the initial stages of preparation.

Recently, Penfold has pointed out that cold pulping yields a juice whose flavour and consistency are diffenent from those of the hot break juice. The manufacturers have, therefore, to decide about the type of juice most likely to satisfy the market demand. The flavour of the coldbreak juice is much sharper and more acidic than that of the hot pulped juice. This is due to the extra pressure applied in the cold pulping and extraction process, whereby the juice surrounding the seeds, which is richer in acid and poorer in sugars than the other portions of the tomato, is extracted first. On account of this, the cold break juice is also of lighter consistency than that got from hot break methods. It has, however, a better fresh flavour.

Extraction of Juice

There are two types of juice extractors in use, namely the Continuous spiral press and the Cyclone.

Continuous Spiral Press. This consists of a long spiral scraw which presses the tomatoes against a tapered screen of fine mesh having 25 holes per linear lnch, each hole being of a diameter of 20/1,000 of 2.5 cm. The juice passes through the screen, but the skin and seeds are expelled at the lower end of the sieve. When this type of extractor is operated at a speed of about 250 revolutions per minute (RPM), there is practically very little or no incorporation of air into the juice. The crushed tomatoes which are fed to the screw from a hopper at the upper end, should be subjected to a jet of steam to prevent oxidation and destruction of vitamins in the juice.

Cyclone or Pulper. Juice can also be extracted by passing the crushed tomatoes through a Cyclone or Pulper. The main defect in this type of machine is that a considerable amount of air is incorporated into the juice. With special attachments to the Cyclone, this defect can be minimised nowadays. In these machines, the insoluble solids in the juice are very finely divided and stay in suspension in the juice for longer periods.

In small scale production, the tomatoes can be strained through monel metral, nickel or stainless steel sieves having one millimeter diameter holes. Not more than about 60 per cent of the fruit should be recovered as juice, because with higher yields, the juice becomes unduly thick and harsh in flavour.

Total Solids

On an average, juice should have a total solids content of 5.66 per cent (sp.gr 1.0240) at 20°C. The amount of total solids present in the juice can be determined in a number of ways, such as by weighing the dried sample, by noting the refractive index and by using a specific gravity hydrometer. For routine work, the specific gravity method gives fairly satisfactory results. The juice is strained through a piece of thick cloth, and the specific gravity of the strained juice determined with a hydrometer at 20°C. If the specific gravity is measured at a temperature higher than 20°C, a temperature correction is applied to the reading.

The percentage of total soluble solids is deduced from standard tables showing the retationship between specific gravity and the percentage of solids precent in the juice.

Common Salt and Sugar

On an average, 4 to 6 kg of common salt is added to every 1000 kg of the juice to counteract the astringent taste of the juice.

Sometimes, sugar also is added to improve the taste. According to Lal Singh and Girdhari Lal, addition of about one per cane sugar to the juice improves the flavour.

Packing

The juice can be packed in galss in glass bottles or cans. Canned juice has, however, better taste, aroma, colour and keeping quality than the bottled juice. Further, the public has got accustomed to the slight metallic tang in the taste of the canned juice, and like it. This is another typical instance of a product which becomes popular with public through long usage, in spite of the drawback owing to the presence of traces of metal in it. The processing temperature and time for canned tomato juice are given in the Table on the next page.

The juice is generally homogenized to retard separation of liquid from the pulp and to give it a thick consistency and uniform appearance. It is heated to about 66°C and forced through a small orifice under a high pressure of about 70 kg per square cm. This shears the particles and tends to reduce all of them practically to the same size. The juice is afterwards heated 82°C to 88°Cand filled into hot sterilized bottles of 316 to 4548 g capacity. The bottles are then hermetically closed by means of crown corks and sterilized for about 30 minutes in boiling water (100°C).

Size of can	Sterilization time when the juice is filled into can at 82° to 88°C	Sterilization temp.
	Minutes	0°C
No. 1	15	100
No. A2	25	100
No. A 2½	30	100
No. 10	40	100

For canning, plain cans are the best, although enamelled or lacquered cans also may be used. In this cans also, the juice is filled hot into cans at 82° to 88°C leaving practically very little head space, to avoid marked loss in colour, flavour and vitamin C content, which would occur when the headspace is considerable. The cans are then sealed and processed, according to size, as shown in the accompanying Table (above). After processing, the cans are cooled in running cold water.

In the case of the large No. 10 cans, owing to the longer processing time, the juice has generally a slightly cooked taste and flavour.

According to Tressler, Joslyn and Marsh, tomato juice may be presterilized by heating in a continuous heat exchanger to temperatures much above the boiling point of water. The following temperautures much above the boiling point of water. The following temperature time relation ships are considered to be approximately equivalent in sterilizing value.

Temperature of juice (°C)	Holding time (minutes)
116	3.3
118	1.5
121	0.7 standard process
124	0.32
127	0.15
129	0.07

This procedure is effective for destroying the flat sour organism, B. thermacidurans, which often causes trouble in the case of canned tomato juice. Before filling into cans, the juice should be cooled slightly below the boiling point, but should still be sufficiently hot to sterilize the containers also.

Analysis of Juice

Lal Singh and Girdhari Lal have made a comparative analysis of four foreign and two Indian brands of tomato juice, and their data is given in the Table 21.

Tomato Puree

Commercial tomato pulp without skin or seeds, with or without added salt and containing not less than 8.37 per cent of salt free tomato solids, is medium tomato puree. It is further concentrated to heavy tomato puree which contains not less theh 12 per cent solids.

TABLE 21. ANALYSIS OF VARIOUS BRANDS OF TOMATO JUICE OBTAINABLE IN INDIAN MARKET

Serial No.	Brand of juice	Sp. gr. of juice at 20°C	Sp. gr. of filtrate at 20°C	Per cent solids in juice	Salt, as sodium chloride in 100 c.c. of juice	Total acid as malic acid in 100 c.c. of juice
1.	Foreign I	1.0240	1.022	5.66	0.89	0.38
2.	Foreign II	1.0240	1.022	5.66	0.79	0.36
3.	Foreign III	1.0334	1.031	7.99	0.84	0.49
4.	Foreign IV	1.0250	1.023	5.91	0.82	0.38
5.	Indian I	1.0387	1.036	9.27	1.74	0.59
6.	Indian II	1.0292	1.027	6.95	1.11	0.56

Preparation

The first step in the preparation of tomato puree is the preparation of tomato pulp. This pulp is prepared from plant ripened tomatoes in the same manner as tomato juice.

Pulp concentration

Concentration of the pulp is carried out in two types of vessels, namely, (i) open cooker, and (ii) vacuum pan.

Open Cooker. When dealing with small quantities of the pulp, an aluminium patila (vessel) will do. For large scale or commercial production, glass lined tanks or tanks made of stainless steel, monel metal or nickel, and fitted with flash coils are used. The open pen method, although emloyed generally, has obvious disadvantages. During boiling, the juice is exposed to the oxygen in the air, which not only destroys vitamins in it, but also makes the juice brown. Experts have pointed out that unless special equipment is used to prevent the incorporation of air during the entire manufacturing process, a considerable loss of vitamin C occurs. Butter or an edible oil is added to the juice during boiling to prevent it from foaming boiling over sticking or burning. Incidentally, it also helps in lessening oxidation. This method has, however, now been superseded by the vacuum pan method, which gives a product of superior quality.

Vacuum Pan. The installation of a vacuum pan is rather expensive for a small factory. Its main advantage is that the juice can be boiled at a much lower temperature under reduced pressure, i.e., at about 71°C, thereby facilitating the ratention of the original red colour and flavour of the tomato to a marked degree. As air also is removed during boiling, there is very little likelihood of oxidantion or loss of vitamin C. In order to sterilize the product the vacuum is broken towards the end and the temperature raised to 100°C and maintained at that level for about 10 minutes.

Pulp Consistency

The two methods used for the concentration of pulp are as follows.

Method I. Sufficient pulp is transferred to the boiling pan till the heating coils are fully covered. Heating is then commenced. More juice is added and the heating continued till the pan is practically full of pulp. Heating is then stopped and the total solids content of the pulp determined. If the total solids content is higher than the required percentage, more juice is added to lower it; if it is lower, concentration is continued till the desired concentration is reached. Manufacturer generally finds it easy and convenient to follow this method.

Mothod II. In this method, a known volume of the juice is concentrated to a known volume of the finished pulp. The juice is let into the boiling tank and when the heating coils have been fully covered, heating is commenced and the tank is filled to capacity. Heating is continued till the pulp begins to boil vigorously. Steam is then off momentraily and the volume of the hot pulp is measured with a measuring stick. Then a small sample of the pulp is drewn for the determination of the solids by the specific gravity method. When the determination of the solids is being carried out, boiling of the pulp in the tank is continued. By making use of Standard Tables (appendix I) the pulp is boiled down to the desired specific gravity. As both the original and the final measurements of volume are taken at the boiling point, temperature corrention for the readings is not necessary.

The End Point

The total sodils in the juice, in the beginning, during boiling and at the finished point can be determined either with a specific gravity hydrometer or with Abbe' or pocket refractometer, or by drying the juice in vacuum at 70°C. In prectice, the firsh two methods are employed as they are fairly simple.

Packing

Tomato puree can be packed in plain as well as lacquered cans. The puree is filled into the cans, scalding hot, at 82 to 88°C., and the cans closed without exhausting them first. In the case of 453 g cans, they are processed for 20 minutes at 100°C. Larger cans not generally processed, the temperature of the hot puree itself being sufficient to sterilize the cans also.

TOMATO PASTE

A concentrated tomato juice or pulp without skin and seeds, and containing not less than 25 per cent of tomato solids, is known as tomato paste. If the pulp is further concentrated so as to contain 33 per cent and more of tomato solids, it is called concentrated tomato paste. Common salt, basil leaf or sweet oil of basil leaf also may be added. Part of its acidity may be neutralized with sodium carbonate or bicarbonate. Ordinarly, tomato juice can be concentrated to 14 to 15 per cent times solids open pans, but for higher concentration, vacuum pans are required. The initial concentration is generally carried out in open pans and the product is then finished in vacuum pans.

As the product is very thick, the total solids in it are determined with an Abbe' refractometer.

TOMATO COCKTAIL

Tomato cocktail is gaining popularity in many of the high class hotels and restaurants. It is prepared just before serving and sometimes is also servel from stock. In the latter case, the cocktail is preserved by pasteurization in bottles. Although the recipes very, the main constituent is tomato juice to which common salt, Worcestershire sauce, lemon or lime juice, tabasco sauce etc., are added in different proportions to suit the palate. Two typical formulae are given here.

FORMULA I

Ingredient	Quantity
Tomato juice (sp. gr. 1.020)	4.53 kg
Cloves (headless), whole	1.5 g
Cumin, black pepper and cardamon, in equal quantities	4.5 g
Cinnamon, broken	1.5 g
Coriander seeds	1.5 g
Red chilli, finely ground (Kashmiri)	0.25 g
Vinegar (10 per cent acetic acid)	283 g
Common salt	45 g

Simmer the tomato juice with the spices loosely tied in a cloth bag for about 20 minutes in a covered vessel. Then add the lime juice, vinegar and common salt.

FORMULA II

Ingredient	Quantity
Tomato juice (sp. gr. 1.020)	4.53 kg
Cloves, (headless) whole	1.5 g
Cumin	1 g
Black pepper	1 g
Cardamom	1 g
Red chilli finely ground (Kashmiri)	0.25 g
Ginger dried	1.5 g
Lime juice	42 g
Vinegar (10 per cent acetic acid)	212 g
Common salt	45 g

Quality of Ingredients

Tomato juice. If possible use fresh juice, otherwise, use canned juice.

Vinegar. Use only malt or cider vinegar of good quality and not acetic acid.

Lime juice. Only crystal clear lime juice should be used, because any sediment in it will impart in undesirable flavour. Moreover, it gives a 'foreign' taste to the cocktail when it is pasteurized in containers. Citric acid is not a good substitute, as it does not produce as good a taste as natural lime juice does.

Sugar. This should be of good quality.

Pasteurization

When all the ingredients have been mixed and the cocktail is ready for bottling, heat it to 82 to 88°C and fill it into 340 g bottles, which have been sterilized and kept hot for filling. Close the bottles and keep them immersed in boiling water (100°C) for 30 minutes and then cool them.

TOMATO KETCHUP

Tomato ketchup is a fairly common and popular tomato product in this country. It is made by concentrating tomato juice or pulp without seeds and pieces of skin. Spices, salt, sugar, vinegar, onion, garlic, etc., are added to the extent that the ketchup contains not less than 12 per cent tomato solids and 28 per cent total solids.

Raw Material

Select sound ripe tomatoes having deep red colour. Remove all green and yellow portions. Green fruit makes the ketchup inferior in colour and flavour.

Juice Standardisation

The raw juice is a thin watery fluid and its specific gravity varies with the kind of tomato and the duration of boiling. It follows, therefore, that spices to be added each time very in proportion. This would not, therefore, yield a standard product. Standardisation can be achieved by using a recipe based on tomato juice of 1.0220 specific gravity (filtrate of pulp of 5.66 Brix). Keeping the other ingredients constant, an equivalent quantity of juice of any other specific gravity can be conveniently added.

Recipes

There are several recipes which give ketchup of good quality. Recipe I has become popular with the ketchup manufacturers in this country.

RECIPE - I

Tomato juice (sp. gr. 1.022-1.027)	27.27 litres
Onion (chopped)	375 g
Garlic (chopped)	25 g
Cloves (whole) headless	10 g
Cardamon	4 g
Black pepper	4 g
Zira	4 g
Mace (jalvatri) not ground	2.5 g
Cinnamon (broken)	17.5 g
Vinegar 6% acetic acid	0.68 kg
Sugar	0.9 kg
Salt	312 g
Red chilli (powder)	12.5 g

RECIPE - II

Tomato pulp (sp. gr. 1.020)	1498 litres
Sugar	54.4 kg
salt	12.2 kg
Vinegar, 100 grain, white distilled	31.8 litres
Cloves (headless)	425.2 g
Cinnamon broken and sifted	425.2 g
Mace	28.3 g
Cayenne pepper	141.7 g
Garlic (freshly ground) (or onions 708 g and garlic 142 g)	708.7 g

Cook to a finish of 568.2 litres. This makes a mildly spiced product.

RECIPE III

Tomato pulp (sp. gr. 1.022)	2722.6 litres (about 2700 ltr.)
Sugar	136.1 kg
Salt	22.6 kg
Paprika	3.6 kg
Onions (chopped and ground)	4.5 kg
Garlic	0.9 kg
Mace	340 g
Cinnamon (broken and sifted)	283 g
Cloves headless	340 g
Cayenne pepper	368.5 g
Vinegar, 100 grain	54.5 litres

Cook to a finish of 200 gallons or about 900 litres. This makes a spiced ketchup with a good colour, which is partly due ot the paprika.

RECIPE -IV	
Heavy tomato puree (sp. gr. 1.06)	454.6 litres
Salt	793 g
Sugar	3542 g
Chopped onions	708 g
Cinnamon (broken bark)	708 g
Mace	100 g
Clove (whole headless)	425 g
All spice	425 g
Cayenne pepper	100 g
Chopped garlic (optional)	113 g
Vinegar (distilled 10% acetic acid)	54.5 litres
Paprika ground (optional)	0.9 kg

Place all the spices except paprika, onion and garlic in vinegar in a covered kettle and simmer the mass for about 2 hours. Add sugar and salt the vinegar and stir. Add the vinegar extract of spices thus got, after removing the spice residues to the ketchup towards the end of the boiling process. If desired, add the paprika powder directly to the ketchup. This recipe yeilds slightly more than 454.6 litres of ketchup.

Recently using 227.3 litres steam jacketed pans and freshly extracted juice, the following recipe has been found to yield ketchup of good quanlity in every respect (Siddappa unpublished data).

The spices are added by the bag method. Oleoresins and essential oils of some of the spices used may also be employed in the preparation of the ketchup.

RECIPE FOR TOMATO KETCHUP (using fresh tomato juice)	
Tomato juice	120 kg
Sugar	8 kg
Salt	1 kg
Acetic acid (glacial)	400 ml
Red chilli powder	60 g
Ginger (green)	160 g
Onion, (fresh chopped)	1 kg
Clove (headless)	40 g
Cinnamon (broken)	40 g
Cardamom	40 g
Zira	40 g

Black pepper	40 g
Colour (blended 6% solution)	100 ml
Sodium benzoate at 750 ppm. of ketchup (as preservative)	30 g

Yield : approximately 120 x 370 g ketchup bottles.

Note :

1. Chilli powder, spices, onion, ginger should be tied loosely in a muslin cloth bag.

2. Acetic acid and colour may be added towards the end of boiling.

3. One third of the sugar may be added in the beginning to preserve the red colour of the pulp.

4. Instead of clove, cinnmon and cardamon, essences of these spices may be added more conveniently.

According to Campbell, the Table gives the approximate relation between the whole spices and the equivalent essential oils of the spices.

Spices (100 kg)	(Equivalent weight of essential oil (kg)
Cinnamon	0.5
Clove	1.5
Mace	3.5
Pepper	1.0
Cardamom	3.0

It is advisable to standardize the amount of spice, essential oil or oleoresin required as the equivalents very with the brand of the essential oil available in the market.

5. Instead of tomato juice, tomato puree of 15 per cent total soluble solids, which has been canned for use during the off season, may be used for the preparation of the ketchup on an equivalent basis, *vis a vis* the fresh juice.

6. Garlic may or may not be added along with the spices, depending upon consumer acceptance.

7. As the most suitable component for tomato ketchup colour blend, namely Acid Magenta II has now been deleted from the list of permitted food colours, one has to choose other red and orange colours such as Erythrosine, Carmoisine, Sunset Yellow etc. Addition of a yellow component in the form of tartrazine will be useful.

A suitable combination of Carmoisine, Greengage and Ponceau 4 R has also been been suggested.

It is, however, advisable to use the best tomatoes to avoid the nacessity for reinforcing the colour of the ketchup. Ketchup without the addition of any colour would be the ideal product, one should attempt to achieve. This is not impossible. Recently the government has banned the use of any coaltar colour in tomato ketchup. Some varieties of tomatoes have been found to yield ketchup of excellent red colour.

Addition of Ingredients

Spices. The spices should be of good quality and they should be added in the proper proportion to give an agreeable tasts and flavour to the product. The blend should be such that no single spice dominates the natural flavour of tomato. The spices may be used in the following way.

Bag Method. The spices are tied loosely in a muslin cloth bag, and the bag piaced in the tomato juice during boiling. The bag in taken out, and the ketchup in it pressed and then removed before bottling the ketchup. The spice bag can be used for a second batch of juice also. The bag method of adding spices has, however, the following drawbacks.

1. The bag may give way during boiling and spoil the whole product. In that case, even if the pulp is again forced through a fine sieve, particles of the spices will still pass through and darken the ketchup prepared.

2. The taste and flavour of the ketchup may very from time to time, depending upon the variation in the composition of the spices used and the duration of boiling on different occasions.

3. All the flavour of the spice is not extracted in the first boiling itself. Moreover, some of the volatile flavouring substances may be lost during boiling. To counteract these, a quantity of spices greater than what is actually required, will have to be used. This will add to the cost, although the once used spices can be utilized in the preparation of pickles.

In spite of these drawbacks, the bag method gives a ketchup of superior quality.

Use of essential oils. The essential oils of the spices do not contain tannins and do not, therefore, adversely affect the colour of the ketchup, in the way the whole spices containing tannins do. Essential oils of spices may be easily blended. They do not, however, give exactly the same true and characteristic aroma of the whole spice. The equivalent of the essential oil vis a vis whole spice has also been mentioned eariler under the recipe for the ketchup.

Use of oleoresins. There are true aromas of the spices and can be used with advantage in commercial production. They are added to the ketchup for a few minutes before the boiling is complete.

Use of extracts. Spice extracts can be prepared on a large scale by prolonged steeping or boiling of the spices in vinegar. The use of these extracts helps to standardise the proportion of spices and to maintain the same tasts and aroma in the ketchup. This process is now being adopted by some of the ketchup manufacturers in this country also. Spiced vinegar extract is widely employed in several other leading tomato ketchup and sauce manufacturing countries.

Sugar. About one third of the sugar required should be added initially at the time of commencing the boiling. This helps to intensify and fix the red tomato colour. The rest of the sugar is added a little before the ketchup is ready. If the whole of the sugar is added in the beginning itself, the pulp will have to be boiled for a longar time and at a higher temperature with the result that the colour of the ketchup will be adversely affected. In a ketchup manufactured on a commercial scale, the proportion of sugar varies widely from 10 to 26 per cent.

Common salt. Salt bleaches the tomato colour and also dissolves to some extent copper from the kettle or the coil, when the equipment is made of copper and tinned. It is, therefore, desirable to add it towards the end of boiling. Finely powdered salt is evenly sprinkled on the surface of the ketchup in the boiling pan and stirred well. In commercial ketchups, the proportion of salt ranges from 1.3 to 3.4 per cent.

Vinegar. Well matured salt vinegar is essential for the preparation of ketchup of high quality. Spirit vinegar does not produce a good flavour in the product. Cider vinegar although highly pleasant, has rather a mild flavour. Good vinegar should have 5.0 to 5.5 per cent acidity in the form of acetic acid. It is necessary to use vinegar of the same strength and quality ot obtain a ketchup of standard quality. Vinegar should be added when the ketchup has thickened sufficiently, so that the acid does not volatilize away, leaving the ketchup deficient in acid and flavour.

Tomato ketchup generally contains 1.25 to 1.50 per cent acid, expressed as acetic acid. Glacial acetic acid is sometimes used, as it has the following advantages.

1. It is cheaper than vinegar.
2. Being clear and colourless like water, it does not impart any colour of its own to the product.
3. It is 100 per cent acetic and can be added practically at the end of boiling without causing any loss of flavour or acidity.

When spiced vinegar or acetic acid is used, the acidity of the vinegar already present in it should be taken into account at the time of of adding the vinegar according to the recipe.

Thickening Agents

The tendency of tomato ketchup to separate into pulp and clear juice depends largely on the amount of pectin present in it. In order to increase the viscosity of the ketchup and prevent the separation of pulp, pectin is usually added to the extent of 0.1 to 0.2 per cent by weight of the finished product.

Cooking and Concentration

To get a product of uniform taste and flavour and also of fine texture and thickness or body, the total solids in the finished product should be maintained constant at the same level. In commercial ketchups, the percentage of total solids varies from 20 to 37. A ketchup with 28 to 30 per cent total solids has a better flavour than a ketchup having more than 30 per cent solids. A higher proportion of the total solids dilutes the concentration of tomato solids, because it contains more of sugar and vinegar. As a ketchup with 28 to 30 per cent solids does not generally keep for a long time after once opening the bottle, the general tendency is to increase the total solids from 32 to 37 per cent. This increases its keeping quality on account of its higher sugar, salt and vinegar content.

Some well known brands of ketchup have been found to contain 31.5 to 32.6 per cent of total solids.

Total solids in the ketchup can be determined by means of a specific gravity hydrometer. This method is, however, tedious The refractometer method is more convenient, although it does not give highly accurate results due to the presence of salt, acetic acid, etc. There is also a slight deviation in the relationship between total solids and refract meter solids. According to Cruess, in commercial practice, the juice (sp. gr. 1.0220) is concentrated to one third of its original volume as determined with a gauge stick.

Bottling

When the ketchup is ready at the end of boiling, it is passed through a finishing machine fitted with a very fine sieve to remove any tomato fibre, small pieces, of paper, wood, etc., that might have got in through sugar or spices.

The ketchup should be bottled hot at about 88°C to prevent darkening of its colour and loss of vitamin content during subsequent storage and distribution. On cooling, the ketchup shrinks in volume producing thereby a high degree of vacuum in the bottle. Sometimes, a black ring is formed on the surface of the ketchup in the neck of the bottle. This is known as 'black neck'. In is stated to be due to the oxidation of iron compounds which get into the ketchup from the boiling equipment, and from the metal of the cap through the action of acetic acid. When the iron comes in contact with the spice tannate, it forms ferrous tannate the boiling which, on oxidation, forms the black ferric tannate. To overcome this defect, the ketchup should be deaerated and a tin foil faced linear should be inserted under the caps. Recently Siddappa, et al., have studied the beneficial effect of addition of ascorbic acid in preventing 'black neck' formations.

Pasteurization

Even under the most favourable conditions, pasteurization of tomato ketchup in bottles is essential. Some manufacturers are of the view that the hot ketchup may come in contact with the cap and thus sterilize it. This is not a ways safe on account of the wide variation in temperature at different points in the container. The temperature at the centre approaches the filling temperature, whereas that at the bottom, sides and the neck of the bottle is considerably less. Thus it is not possible to know quite definitely whether the cap also will get sterilized by mere contact with the ketchup. It is, therefore, necessary to pasteurize the product in the bottle. Ketchup is filled into bottles at about 88°C. and the bottles sealed with crown corks and pasteurized for 30 to 35 minutes in hot water at 85° to 88°C.

With a modern filling machine, the bottles are filled at 88°C, sealed and washed with warm water to remove any adhering ketchup. The filled and closed bottles are not sterilized, the filling temperature being considered adequate for their sterilization. During filling, the temperature of the ketchup should not be allowed to fall below 88°C at any stage.

A ketchup made from tomatoes of good quality, using sugar, salt, vinegar and spices in the correct proportions, does not generally spoil for a fairly long time even after opening the sealed bottle, if it is kept in a cool and clean place. It, is however, preferable to add 0.025 per cent sodium benzoate to the product before bottling and then pasteuize the bottles as a safeguard against spoilage during 3 to 4 weeks when the ketchup inthe opened bottle will be used in small proportions at a time. The sodium benzoate in the ketchup can be determined by the method given in A.O.A.C. The Fruit Products Order lays down limits for benzoic acid in ketchup and other products.

CHILLI SAUCE

Chilli sauce is a highly spiced product which is prepared from plant ripened and peeled tomatoes. It is mostly used as a flavouring material in cooking, and also as a table relish to some extent.

Preparation

The tomatoes are washed thoroughly, rejecting any blemished or rotton portions. They are then blanched in hot water or in steam till the skin is loosened. They are then dipped in cold water to stop further cooking and softening. They are then dipped by lifting the peel easily by means of pointed end of a knife and chopped. The seeds are not removed. During cooking of the chopped material, spices are added, tied loosely in a muslin cloth bag, just as in the case of tomato ketchup.

The following method of preparation has been recommended by food experts.

To 45.3 kg of peeled tomatoes add 1.0 kg of sugar, 10 g of red chillies (Kashmiri), 0.9 kg of peeled and finely chopped onions and the following spices tied loosely in a muslin cloth bag.

Mace (not ground)	7 g
Cinnamon (broken)	18 g
Cumin cardamom and black pepper in equal quantities	22.5 g
Ground white pepper	10 g
Ground ginger	10 g

Cook the whole mass in a steam jacketed kettle down to about 25.4 kg, crushing the tomatoes with a ladle, if necessary, during the process. Add 2.2 kg of sugar, 0.67 kg of common salt and finally 1.6 kg (10 per cent) vinegar. Continue the cooking of the mass for 5 to 10 minutes and then pack the finished sauce immediately in plain A 2 1/2 size cans. Close the cans and sterilize them for half in boiling water.

According to andon, the following recipe gives a sauce of good quality.

Tomato (peeled)	22.6 kg
Sugar	2.4 g
Common salt	255 g
Chillies (ground)	42 g
Garlic (chopped)	255 g
Onions (chopped)	100 g
Vinegar (5% acetic acid)	8.6 kg

To the tomatoes add all the ingredietns except vinegar, and cook to a thick consistency. Next, add the vinegar and boil for a more minutes. Then pack the product hot into wide mouthed jars, close and sterilize them for

30 minutes in boiling water.

TOMATO SAUCE

This sauce has been found satisfactory also for canning of baked beans in tomato sauce. The composition of tomato sauce is similar in many respects to that of the thicker ketchup.

RECIPE	
Tomato pulp (6% soluble solids)	29.4 g
Cardamom, pepper, cumin (zira) in equal quantities	8.5 g
Cloves (headless)	8.5 g
Cinnamon (broken)	10 g
Mace (not ground)	5.7 g
Common salt	0.67 kg
Onions (chopped)	155 g
Garlic (ground)	18 g
Sugar	2.2 kg
White vinegar, 100 grain	(58 cc of 100% acetic acid)
Red chilli powder	15 g

Cook to about half the volume of the pulp taken, i.e., 26 to 28 per cent refractometer solids, taking necessary precautions as in the case to tomato ketchup. Fill into plain A 2½ cans, close and process for 45 minutes in boiling water.

TOMATO SOUP

Tomato soup is a fairly popular product nowadays. In its preparation, the first step is the preparations of tomato pulp just as in the case of tomato juice. The main constituents of the soup are :

Tomato juice, butter or cream, spices, arrow root starch (for thickening), etc. These are added in different proportions to suit the customer. The following typical formula yields a good soup

Tomato juice (sp. gr. 1.0220)	31.8 litres
Onion finely chopped	368 g
Cinnamon broken	5 g
Cloves whole, headless	5 g
White pepper ground	7 g
Red chillies ground (Kashmiri)	0.7 g
Cumin (zira) cardamom and black pepper in equal quantities	5.3 g
Ginger, dried ground	4.2 g

Cream (30 per cent) or butter 0.55 kg or	191 g
Sugar	481 g
Common salt	318 g
Arrow root starch	120 g

Preparation

Neutralize about 1/6 of the acidity of the juice by adding a thin paste of sodium bicarbonate in water. Place 27.2 litres of the juice in a boiling pan and boil to concentrate it. While it is being concentrated, add the spices in a cloth bag as in the case of tomato ketchup. In the meantine, mix arrow root and butter (or cream) with the remaining 4.6 litres of the juice to form a smooth paste. When the juice in the pan has been sufficiently consentrated, add this paste. Continue boiling to the desired consistency, stirring it continously to prevent clotting of the starch. At the end, add sugar and salt anf boil the mixture for about two minutes to dissolve them. Then fill the soup the cans close them.

Sterilization

Sterilize the cans at 115°C 10.7 kg/cm^3 for 45 minutes in the case of A2 ans and for 40 minutes in the case of 0.45 kg milk cane or o,45 kg jam size cans. Cool in the cans quickly after processing.

MICROBIOLOGY

When tomatoes of poor quality are used in the preparation of tomato products, excessive amounts of moulds, yeasts, bacteria and fregments of insects lower the quality of the product. The insect fragment count also is highly indicative of gross contamination of the fruit and unhygienic conditions during handling and preparation of the raw materials and finished products.

The main ingredient is pumpkin (Cucurbita moscheta). The sauce is slightly thinner in consistency than the normal tomato sauce, but comparable with it in taste and other characteristics. Sodium benzoate is the preservative employed. In the case of Lactobacilli lyropersici even 0.2 per cent sodium is more tolerant than benzoate has very little inhibitive effect in neutral tomato broth. Yeast is more tolerant than L. lycopersici to sodium benzoate and could be inhibited at 0.17 per cent level. A minimum of 10 minutes heating of the sauce with 0.5 per cent acetic acid could ensure the destruction of spore formers & addition of 750 PPm of sodium benzoate to the sauce would prevent spoilage during storage. The present practice of adding sodium benzoate to tomato ketchup and sauce. which contain acetic acid, and then heating them in boiling water for 15 to 20 minutes, is in line with the above findings. Under such conditions, the sauces, rarely undergo any microbial spoilage.

Specifications for Tomato Products

The Government of India have regulated the manufacture of tomato products such as tomato juice, puree, ketchup and sauce, by laying down proper specifications.

12

Pickles, Sauces & Chutneys

Chutneys, sauces and pickles of various kinds are prepared in Indian homes and also on a commercial scale. They find a ready market in many countries. Standard recipes have been modified to suit local taste in the country and consumer acceptability in other parts of the world. Fruits such as apple, peach, plum, apricot and mango and vegetables like turnip, cauliflower, carrot, etc, are the basic raw materials. Onion, garlic, spices, herbs, etc., are added for flavour. Vinegar, common salt and sugar are also used to make the products more palatable. Vinegar serves as a preservative also to some extent.

CHUTNEYS

A chutney of good quality should be palatable and appetising. The method of preparation is similar to that adopted in the case of jams except that spices and vinegar are added. Mango chutney is one of the better known products of its kind in several countries. Apricot chutney is another popular product and so also is apple chutney.

The fruit or vegetable is cut into slices or pieces of suitable size and softened by boiling in water. Slow cooking at a temperature below the boiling point yields a better product than brisk heating at a comparatively higher temperature. Onion and garlic are added at the start to mellow their strong flavours. Spices are coarsely powdered before they are added to the product. Sometimes a vinegar extract of spices is used instead of whole spices. Spices as well as vinegar extract sould be added just a little before the final stage of boiling, because during prolonged boiling, some of the essential oils of the spices as also of the vinegar, are likely to be lost by volatilization.

Cooking Process

Sweet chutneys such as mongo and apricot chutneys are generally cooked to consistency of jam to avoid fermentation of the product during storage. Where vinegar is used in fairly large quantities, the amount of sugar may be reduced correspondingly, because vinegar itself serves partly as a preservative.

Bottling

Only clean and dry bottles and jars earlier sterilized in boiling water should be used and they should be warm at the time of filling. If the bottles and the jars not properly cleaned, fermentation is likely to set in through fermentation organisms adhering to the walls of the containers. It is safer to pasteurize the filled bottles are sealing them at 82°C for about 30 minutes in 0.45 kg size jars.

Equipment

Equipment made of iron and copper should not be used as they are acted upon by vinegar. Further, small amounts of these metals, dissolved in oil act as catalytic agents for development of rancidity in the product. These metals also form black compounds with the tannins of fruits and spices, and thereby adversely affect the colour, taste and flavour of the product. The vessels used should be glass-lined, or they should be made of nickel or stainless steel. Copper utensils freshly tinned adequately can also be used without risk.

Recipes

There are a large number of recipes for chutneys. Apricot, mango, and apple chutneys are, however, of particular interset in this country. A considerable amount of research and development work has been carried on to standardize these products for indigenous as well as export purposes. Recipes for peach, plum, date, tomato chutneys and some mixed chutneys will be found in some books and bulletins on pickle-making and preservation.

Some chutney recipes, which have been tried with some degree of success, are given in the following section :

Apple Chutney

Poultney gives the following two recipes for apple chutney.

RECIPE -I	
Apple	18.1 kg
Sultanans	9.0 kg
Onion powder	226.7 kg
Sugar	13.6 kg
Salt	28.3 g
Cassia ground	28.3 g

Pimento, ground	28.3 g
Nutmeg, ground	14.1 g
Caramel	283.4 g
Acetic acid	0.9 kg
Malt vinegar	13.6 litres

Peel, core and slice the apples. Cook the slices along with the other ingredients, till they become tender. Bottle the product hot. The final acidity of the chutney should not be less 2.4 per cent.

RECIPE -II

Apple	2.7 kg
Onions	to taste
Brown sugar	2.27 litres
Preserving sugar	2 heads
Cayenne (red chilli powder)	1/4 tea spoonful
Garlic	1/2 tea spoonful
Salt	3 tea spoonful
Vinegar	2 tea spoonful

Peel, core and cut the apples into small pieces. Core and cut the onions very finely. Mix all the ingredients with the vinegar and boil gently till the chutney becomes thick. Pick while hot and seal the bottles air-tight. Use wide-mouthed bottles or jars for packing the chutney.

A typical recipe for the preparation of apple chutney to suit Indian taste is as follows :

Apple slices	35 kg
Apple pulp	15 kg
Sugar	55 kg
Salt	1.2 kg
Cardamom	70 g
Cinnamon	70 g
Clove	70 g
Red chilli powder	200 g
Black pepper	70 g
Ginger dried	70 g
Apple essence	5 ml
Sodium benzoate (as preservative)	50 g

Apricot Chutney

Siddappa and Mustafa have recommended the following process for the preparation of apricot chutney :

Take firm, but fully ripe apricots of the white or the yellow variety.

Cut them into slices about 0.3 cm thick. Cover the slices with sugar and allow the mixture to stand for 1 to 2 horus so that sugar partially dissolves in the juice liberated and the mixture becomes fairly thin in consistency. Fill the spices loosely in a muslin cloth bag, tie it up and place it in the mixture in a boiling pan. Boil the mixture to about 105°C (at sea level). Add salt and vinegar to the boiling mixture and continue boiling for another 5 minutes. The chutney will be ready now to be filled hot into sterile hot bottles. Fill into the bottles and close them tight.

RECIPE	
Apricot slices	1.3 kg
Sugar	1.3 kg
Salt	56.6 g
Cardamom, roughly ground	2 g
Black pepper broken grains	2 g
Cumin (zira) whole	2 g
Cinnamon whole	2 g
Red chilli powder (according to taste)	7 g
Cloves, headless	1 g
Mace, broken	0.5 g
Unions, sliced and gently crushed	28.3 g
Vinegar, 4 to 5% strength	226.7 g

This recipe will about 2.2 kg of apricot chutney. It can be sealed up for large-scale production.

Bamboo Chutney

Tender bamboo shoots make a good sweet bamboo chutney. Select, young tender bamboo shoots and remove the outer sheaths. Cut the tender portion into small pieces. Boil the pieces in water twice or thrice, each time for about half an hour to remove the bitter poisonous principle, hydrocyanic acid. Discard the water used for boiling each time. Mince the boiled pieces finely.

RECIPE	
Minced bamboo shoots	1.8 kg
Sugar	1.8 kg
Salt	85.0 g
Caldamom, cinnamon, and cumin mixed in equal proportion	56.6 g
Red chilli powder	28.3 g
Onions, chopped	28.3 g
Garlic, chopped	28.3 g
Vinegar	85.0 g

Add the sugar, salt and a little water to the minced bamboo pieces and warm the mass to dissolve the sugar and salt. Place the spice loosely in a muslin cloth bag, tie it up, and place the beg in mixture in a vessel. Cook slowly until the mass attains the consistency of jam. Remove the spice bag from the pan, and add vinegar to the hot mixture in the pan. Boil again for a short period to ensure that the product is of the desired consistency. Cool the product, fill it into clean wide mouthed glass bottles or jars and seal them tigh. Bamboo chutney is an exotic product of the East.

Mango Chutney

This is a typical product of India. For its preparation, slightly under ripe fruits of seedling varieties are preferable. Fresh as well as brined and peeled mango slices can be used in its preparation. Both types of raw material are employed by the industry. The latter is used to extend manufacture of chutney beyond the mango season. In this case, the slices are preserved in a brine of 15 per cent strength, the percentage of salt being maintained by adding salt from time to time. Some of the manufacturers prefer to add dry salt to the slices. The main drawback in this simple method is that the slices shrivel due to osmosis and do not regain their original size and shape in the final product. Further, the slices also become hard. Usually, 1 kg finely powdered salt is added to every 4 kg of slices. The amounts of sugar, spices, vinegar, etc,. added depend largely on the local taste.

Some typical recipes for mango chutney are given here.

Sweet Mango Chutney

The following recipe has been recommended :

RECIPE

Peeled mango slices	0.9 kg
Sugar	0.9 kg
Salt	56.6 g
Mixed spices (cardamom, cinnamon, cumin etc, in equal quantities	28.3 g
Garlic, chopped	6.0 g
Red chilli powder flnely ground	14.0 g
Vinegar	113.4 g
Onions, chopped	28.3 g
Ginger, green	113.4 g

Take slighly under ripe mangoes, peel and cut into thin slices. Heat the slices in a small amount of water to make them soft. Add sugar and salt. Tie the other ingredients loosely in a cloth bag; place the bag in the slices in a boiling pan and cook the mass to the consistency of jam. Then add vinegar and boil for about 5 minute. Remove the spice bag. Fill the hot product into hot and dry bottles that have been previously sterilized. Seal them air tight. The product is generally of high quanlity and keeps well in storage.

Sliced Mango Chutney

The following recipes are typical ones for sliced mango chutney. Some of the spices, garlic and other ingredients can be varied or omitted.

RECIPES

	I	II	III
Sliced mangoes	3.6 kg	2.2 kg	2.2 kg
Sugar	2.7 kg	2.2 kg	1.92 kg
Almonds (blanched & peeled)	0.45 kg	-	-
Raisins (stemmed)	0.45 kg	-	-
Salt, finely ground	170 kg	141 kg	114 g
Ginger finely ground	227 g	-	-
Vinegar	0.78 kg	0.78 kg	0.67 kg
Red chillies, finely ground	56 g	56 g	28 g
Cinnamon, broken	14 g	-	-
Cumin, black	28 g	14 g	-
Mustard, finely ground	-	-	56 g
Garlic, chopped	-	-	56 g

The method of preparation of the chutney is the same as that for the sweet mango chutney.

A typical recipe for commercial production of mango chutney is as follows (Siddappa) :

Mango slices	25 g
Sugar	25 g
Salt	1 kg
Ginger, dried	125 g
Clove, headless	25 g
Cardamom	125 g
Red chilli	200 g
Acetic acid glacial	250 ml
Sodium benzoate	25 g

Peach Chutney

Sarson gives the following recipe for peach chutney.

RECIPE	
Dried peaches	0.9 kg (equal to 4.5 kg of peeled peaches)
Onion	0.45 kg
Raisin	0.45 kg
Sultanas	0.22 kg
Cinnamon, powder	14 g
Ginger, ground	14 g
Vinegar	1.1 litre

Cut the dried peaches into quartes. Place them in a shallow pan and cover with vinegar. Set aside for 24 hours to allow the fruit to swell. Chop the onions finely and cut the raisins into halves. Then add them along with the spices to the rest of the vinegar. Bring the mass to a boil and let it simmer for about 15 minutes. Transfer the peacher and vinegar into the pan and continus to cook till the product becomes sufficiently thick. Bottles hot.

In the case of fresh peaches, the peeled slices can be cooked directly with the vinegar till they become soft. The rest of the process is the same as for as dried peaches.

Plum Chutney

The following recipe for a good plum chutney has been recommended.

RECIPE	
Plums, fully ripe	1.8 kg
Sugar	1.8 kg
Vinegar	0.45 kg
Mace (jalyatri) not ground	1 blade
Cloves (headless)	6 in number
Pepper, black ground	10 in number
Chillies Kashmiri, finely ground	7.0 g
Salt finely powdered	14.1 g

Wash the plums and place them in a large cooking pan along with the other ingredients except sugar and vinegar. Heat the mixture with a small quantity of water till the plums become soft. Pass the whole mass through a coarse sieve of aluminium or monel metal or stainless steel to remove the stones and skin. Add sugar and boil till the pulp becomes thick. Then add vinegar. Stir well all the time and continue boiling till the chutney is ready. Fill into sterilized bottles and seal them air tight.

Tomato Chutney

The following recipe gives a good tomato chutney.

RECIPE	
Tomato	13.6 kg
Onions, chopped	9.5 kg
Sugar	18.1 kg
Salt	0.9 kg
Ginger	56.0 g
Chillies	14.1 g
Vinegar	20.4 litres
Garlic vinegar	9.0 litres

Peel the tomatoes by blanching. Place all the ingredients except vinegar in a pan and cook to a thick consistency. Add the vinegar, cook for another five minutes and pack the finished chutney in wide mouthed and sterilized dry bottles and seal them air tight.

Chutneys can also be made from fruits like pear, greengage, date, banana, papaya etc., by adopting slight modifications, the above mentioned recipes and following a similar procedure.

THIN SAUCES

Sauces are generally of two kinds, and they are the thin and the thick sauces. Thin sauces mainly consist of vinegar extract of various flavouring materials like spices and herbs. Their quality depends mostly on the piquancy of the material used.

Some sauces are matured by storing them in wooden barrels or casks. During storage, they develop flavour and aroma. Freshly prepared products have sotorage they develop flavour and aroma. Freshly prepared products have often a raw and harsh taste and they should, therefore, be matured by storage. For the preparation of sauces of high quality, the spices herbs, fruits and vegetables are macerated in cold vinegar. Sometimes, they are also prepared by boiling them in vinegar. The sauce is filtered through a fine or coarse mesh sieve of non corrodible metal, according to the quality desired. The skin, seeds and stalks of fruits, vegetables and spices used, should not be allowed to pass through the sieve as they spoil the appearance of the sauce. The usual commercial practice is to prepare vinegar extracts of each kind of spice and fruit separately, either by maceration or by boiling in vinegar and then blending these extracts suitably before filling the sauce into barrels for subsequent maturation.

A few typical recipes for thin sauces are given here.

Soya Sauce

Soya sauce is made from soya beans. The sauce has usually a predominent saltish taste and has a dark brown colour. It is made by cooking soya beans and wheat, and then allowing the mass to undergo mould fermentation for 3 to 4 days. The moudly mass is then mixed with strong brine (15 to 20 per cent) to form a mash which is filled into wooden barrels to bring about bacteriological and chemical changes in the presence of a high concentration of salt. In due course, a thick brown liquid is formed. It is boiled and filtered. To the filtered liquid, molasses are added to improve the flavour. The finished product, which is known as soya sauce, is bottled in the usual way.

The high concentration of salt in the medium prevents any harmful microbial changes taking place in the sauce. Soya sauce is a higly popular product of China, Japan and the Far East and it is considered to be not only a relish, but also a nutritious products on account of the protein hydrolysate of the soya bean, which is rich in protein as well as fat. Soya sauce is becoming popular in a limited way in this country also. There is scope for developing similar products from indigenous materials like horsegram, groundnut, etc., by adopting improved local methods and by introducing the techniques employed in Japan and elsewhere for commercial production.

Worcestershire Sauce

Tamarind, which is a typical acidic material employed widely in south Indian cooking, is an important constituent of this sauce. This sauce is utilized in the preparation of cooktails also.

Tandon has recommended the following recipe for the preparation of the sauce.

RECIPE	
Malt Vinegar	5.6 litres
Tamarind	226 g
Garlic	56 g
Onion	56 g
Essence of lemon	28 g
Essence of vanilla	28 g
Dried ginger	56 g
Common salt	28 g
Cumin	7 g
Cardamom	7 g

Clove, headless	7 g
Sugar	113 g
Lemon juice filtered	0.45 kg
Ethyl acetate	0.5 ml

Macerate tamarined in a small quantity of vinegar and filter the extract through muslin cloth. Prepare an extract in vinegar of garlic, onion, dried ginger, cumin, cardamom, cinnamon and clove, and mix it with the tamarind extract. Then add essence of lemon and vanilla and vanilla and also sugar, salt, lemon juice and ethyl acetate. Place the blended mixture in a wooden barrel for maturing over a period of about two months. After maturation, filter the mixture again through a coarse sieve to get the sauce. Bottle it properly. If desired, a small quantity of caramel may be added to the sauce to give it an attractive colour. There are various popular barnds of worcestershire sauces in the market.

Eaton has evolved the following recipe for Worcestershire sauce. The figures are conventiently expressed as percentages.

RECIPE

	Percentage
Malt vinegar (6% acetic acid)	70.0
Sugar	4.0
Molasses	9.5
Caramel	0.5
Salt	2.5
Mixed spices	3.5
Onion, brined	7.0
Tamarind	2.5
Protex (or meat extract)	0.5

The mixed spices are prepared by mixing the following ground spices.

	Percentage
Capsicum	20
Hungarian paprika	15
Black pepper	25
Clove	10
All spices	15
Ginger	10
Mustard	5

Prepare tamarind extract by simmering it in a portion of the vinegar. Prepare an infusion of the spices and crushed onion, preferably in the cold. Mix all the extracts, place the mixture in clean barrel and allow to stand for about six months for maturing. At the time of bottling strain the sauce. Meat extract may be avoided if it is not desired in the sauce.

Mushroom and walnut ketchup sauces popularly known as ketchups are also produced commercially. Ketchup is generally the name given to tomato sauce of thick consistency. Thick sauces made from other fruits or vegetables are not generally called ketchups or catsups. This is a widely accepted definition and classification.

Mushroom Ketchup (Sauce)

Sarson recommends the following method for the preparation of this product.

Select dry fully grown and unbruised mushrooms of edible harmless variety. Break them into pieces and place them in largers with salt in a deep bowl. Sprinkle salt at the rate of 1 kg for every 8 kg of mushroom. Allow the mushroom to stand in the brine formed for 4 days, stirring the mixture twice a day. Cook the mass genlty for about 45 minutes and strain the liquor. To every quart of the liquid, add the following ingredients.

All spices	1 teaspoonful
Pepper	1 -do-
Ginger	1/2 -do-
Mace	1/2 -do-
Clove	A pinch
Cinnamon	-do-

*A mixture of equal quantities of cumin, cinnamon and cardamon may be used instand of all spices.

Simmer the ketchup in a pan until it is reduced to about a third of its original volume. Bottle hot.

Walnut Ketchup (Sauce)

Sarson recommends the following recipe :

RECIPE	
Tender, green walnuts	100 numbers
Vinegar	2.2 litres
Chopped onions	0.45 kg
Salt	0.22 kg
Pepper corns	28 g
*All spices	14 g
Clove	1/2 teaspoonful
Nutmeg	1/2 teaspoonful

*Instead of all spices, cumin, cinnamon and cardamom mixed in equal proportion may be added.

Cut the walnuts into halves. Crush them and place them in a deep jar. Place the rest of ingredients in the vinegar; bring the mass to a boil and pour it over the crushed walnuts. Allow the mixture to stand for 2 weeks, stirring it daily. Draw off the separated liquid, simmer it for about half an hour and fill it into bottles.

THICK SAUCES

A sauce which does not flow freely and which is highly viscous is called a thick sauce. On the other hand, thin sauces, described earlier are less viscous in consistency. They also contain more of sugar and less of acid. Generally spices and colouring added are practically similar to those in the case of the thick ketchups and sauces. It should contain at least 3 per cent acetic acid to ensure. It should contain at least 3 per cent acetic acid to ensure its keeping quality. The acidity should not however, exceed 3.4 per cent as otherwise the sauce would taste sharp. The sugar content may usually very from 15 to 30 per cent according to the kind of sauce made. Usually malt vinegar is used. In addition to contributing to acidity of the sauce, it also improves its flavour. The sweetness is derived partly from like date, raisin, sultanas, apple and tomato, and partly from the sugar added. The colour of the sauces varies with the raw material used. Sometimes, a little caramel is added.

The manufacturing process is the same as for chutneys. Thickening agents also are added to prevent or retard sedimentation of solid particles in suspension in the sauce. In this country, apple pulp is often used for this purpose. Sometimes, the fruit which is used in the preparation of the sauce is boiled to soften it, then pulped and added as a filter. The starches of maize, potato, arrow root (cassava starch), sago and rye also are used as thickening agents. The use of Indian gum, locust kernel gum, tagacanth, karaya gum, gelatin, Irish moss, pectin and other similar substances have been advised. These are not, however, as good as the cereal and root starches. When using these thickening agents, it is advisable to consult the food laws of the country such as the Prevention of Food Adulteration Act (P.F.A.A.) of the Govt. of India etc. because some of them are not allowed as adjunct in food by some of the importing countries.

There is considerable scope for developing a variety of thin as well as thick sauces, making use of indigenous material and effecting suitable changes in the spices and other ingredients added.

Apple sauce and tomato sauces are quite popular in this country. The following tentative recipes may be adopted in their preparation.

Apple Sauce

RECIPE	
Apple pulp	100 kg
Sugar	28 kg
Salt	750 kg
Red chilli powder	150 kg
Dried ginger, onion, garlic each	250 g
Clove oil	30 ml
Cinnamon oil	10 ml
Cardamon oil	10 ml
Acetic acid	1,200 ml
Malt vinegar	1,200 ml
Apple essence	40 ml
Citric acid	200 g
Sodium benzoate	to the desired extent
Red colour (6 per cent solution preservative (within permitted limit)	50 g

*Fresh ginger, onion and garlic may be used in equivalent quantities instead of the dried materials. The proportion of other ingredients may be varied to suit consumer taste. The sauce is prepared as usual by boiling and is bottled hot.

Tomato Sauce

RECIPE	
Tomato juice	120 kg
Sugar	9 kg
Salt	1.35 kg
Acetic acid, glacial	230 ml
Chilli powder (to suit taste)	60 g
Ginger, green (optional)	-
Onion fresh, chopped	680 kg
Clove, headless	35 g
Garlic dried (optional)	-
Cinnamon	4 g
Cardamom	12 g
Cumin (zira)	12 g
Black pepper	2 g
Colour, red, (6% solution)	as required

Prepare the sauce by boiling as usual 26 to 27 per cent total soluble solids and can it hot. Process A 2½ minutes in boiling water.

The sauce can also be bottled by adding sodium benzoates as chemical preservative within the limits prescribed by P.F.A.A.

The spices added in the case of tomato sauce are considerably less then in the case of tomato ketchup.

Fruit Sauces

Besides tomato and apple sauces, mixtures of various other fruits and starchy vegetables like pumpkin, papaya, ash gourd etc., are sometimes employed in the preparation of fruit sauce to which quite often the characteristic red colour of the tomato is added with the result that the cheaper product passes off as the move expensive tomato product. Legislation is under way to protect the genuine tomato product by insisting that fruit sauces other than genuine tomato sauce, do not have a red colour. They should contain some other colour. Experimental work is needed to recommend a suitable colour for this purpose. Recently addition of colour has been banned in the case of tomato ketchup in this country.

SOUPS AND SOUP MIXES

Ready to serve soups as tomato soup, mushroom soup, mixed vegetable soups, especially dried vegetable mixtures for quick preparation of soupe at home, are gaining popularity nowadays. Liquid soups are generally canned. They are warmed at the time of serving. In the case of typical soup, namely tomato soup, the following soup, the following two recipes; one for home scale preparation and the other for commercial production will be useful as guidelines.

TOMATO SOUP (home scale)

Tomato pulp (6% soluble solide)	5 kg
Water	1.75 kg
Onion, chopped	75 g
Salt, powdered	90 g
Butter,	90 g
Sugar	100 g
Flour	50 g
Garlic, chopped (optional)	5 g
Pepper, ground	5 g
Cinnamon, cardamom and other spices, as desired	2.5 g each

Make the flour into a thick paste, boil and strain it. Place the spices in a muslin cloth as in the case of tomato ketchup. Add the starch paste to the tomato juice in a boiling pan. Add sugar, salt and butter. Place the spice bag in the juice. Heat the juice till it becomes fairly thick. Remove the spice bag and can the soup in plain cans. Process A 1 tall (453 g) cans for 45 minutes at 115°C (10 psig) or 0.7 kg/cm² in a pressure cooker. Cool the cans after processing.

TOMATO SOUP (large scale)	
Tomato juice (5% T.S.S)	50 kg
Water	16 kg
Sugar	1 kg
Salt	800 g
Butter	800 g
Onion, chopped	800 g
Flour (wheat, rice or barley)	450 g
Garlic (optional)	35 g
Pepper, ground	30 g
Cinnamon cardamom and other spices, as desired	15 g each

After the preparation of the soup as in the case of the home scale method, fill into cans at 74°C, close and process at 115°C(10 psig) or 0.7 kg/cm° for 45 minutes in the case No. 1 tall cans (453g).

PICKLES

The process of preservation of food in common salt or in vinegar is called pickling. Spices and edible oil also may be added to the product.

Pickles of various kinds are known throughout India and many parts of the word. Some of the typical Indian pickles made from mango, lime, turnip, cabbage, cauliflower, etc., have become popular in several countries. There is a wide and growing export market for these products which are associated with the well known Indian condiments.

Pickles are good appetizers and add to the palatability of a meal. They aid digestion by stimulating the flow of gastric juice. Very little scientific data is, however, available regarding their nutritive value. Different kinds of pickles contain varying amounts of nutrients depending upon the raw material taken and the method of preparation followed. The food value of cucumber pickle exceeds that of eggs, rice, fresh onions and fresh tomatoes.

Different kinds of pickles are made in several Indian homes in fairly large quantities. Pickles are also manufactured on a large scale and exported to other countries. In Indian pickles in oil, mustard, rape seed and sesamum oils are generally used. Some pickles are made in lime juice. Pickles made to resemble imported pickles are made in vinegar. Onion pickles in cleas spiced vinegar belongs to the latter category.

Problems in Pickling

The changes that take place during pickling on account of the activity of micro organisms depend largely on the composition of the fruit of vegetable. Yeast and mould can grow in the presence of acid. Thus, fruits and acidic vegetables spoil either by yeast fermentation or by moulding. As acidity is not favourable for the growth of putrefactive bacteria, fruits and vegatables are not generally spoiled by them. On the other hand, the decay of vegetables which have little or no acid in them, is always mainly owing to the action of bacteria. In the preparation of pickles, however, the desired fermentation is brought about by the action of lactic acid forming bacteria, which are capable of growing in an acid medium. In this respect, they differ from the putrefactive bacteria, which cause decay of fruits and vegetables.

There are mainly two methods of preserving fruits and vegetables, namely (i) by killing all the micro organisms responsible for spoilage, by heat or other means, and then checking the entry of fresh organisms into the preserved product, and (ii) by making the contitions most unfavourable for the growth and multiplication of micro organisms. The first method is generally employed in the preservation of fruits and vegetables, and the second method in the preparation of pickles.

Action of Preservatives

Salt, vinegar and acetic acid are the three important ingredients used in pickling. These substances when used in sufficient quantities, act as preservatives either singly or in combination.

Salt. Vegetables do not ferment when they are covered with a strong brine, or packed with a fairly large quantity of salt. Spoilage is prevented by adding sufficient common salt, bringing its final concentration in the material from 15 to 20 per cent. At this high salt concentration, mould and even lactic acid forming bacteria do not grow. This method of preservative is applicable only to vegetables which contain very little sugar because sufficient lactic acid cannot be formed by fermentation to act as preservative.

Vinegar. In vinegar pickles, vinegar acts as a preservative. In order to ensure satisfactory results, the final concentration of acid as acetic acid, in the finished pickle should not be less than 2 per cent. To avoid dilution of the vinegar by the water liberated from the tissues, the vegetables are generally placed in strong vinegar of about 10 per cent acidity for several days before final packing. This treatment helps to expel the gases present in the intercallular spaces of the vegetable tissue and also prevents subsequent dilution of the vinegar in the pickle.

Lactic acid. Bacteria prefer for their growth material with little or no acid. The lactic acid bacteria, however, can grow in acid media and can also produce acid through their action on the substrate. They can grow in the presence of 8 to 10 per cent salt. Advantage is taken of these two factors in pickling. The growth of undesirable organisms is inhibited by adding salt, while allowing the lactic fermentation to proceed.

When vegetables are placed in brine, the soluble material present in them diffuses into the salt water owing to osmosis and the liquid penetrates into the tissues. The soluble material, besides containing mineral matter, contains fermentable sugar also. The sugars serve as food for lactic acid bacteria, which convert them into lactic and other volatile acids. In prectice, usually 2 to 3 kg of salt is mixed with every 100 kg of the material and the mixture allowed to stand for 12 -24 hours, when sufficient juice comes out from the material to form the brine. If the vegetables does not contain sufficient juice, it is covered with brine. Containing 5 per cent salt. The soluble material extracted is fermented by lactic acid forming bacteria, which are generally present in large numbers on the surface of fresh vegetables.

When lactic acid is formed in sufficient quantity, the lactic acid bacteria cease to function, and any further change in the composition of the material is prevented. Although the pickle is ready for consumption, preceutions should be taken to save it from spoilage by aerobic micro organisms. The presence of salt and the lactic acid formed preserve the pickle by preventing the growth of putrefactive bacteria provided air is excluded. In the presence of air, however, 'pickle scum' is formed and it destroys the lactic acid and brings about putrefaction. The acid brine formed during pickling acts upon the vegetable tissues and produces the characteristic taste and aroma of pickles.

Temperature is the most important factor for successful lactia fermentation. Lactic acid bacteria are most active at a temperature of about 30°C. It is, therefore, essential that the temperature of the product undergoing lactic acid fermentation shoould be kept as close to 30°C as possible, especially in the beginning.

Raw Materials

Raw materials used in pickling should possess certain definite characteristics.

Salt. For pickling any variety of common salt is suitable, provided it is pure. At any rate, it should not contain more than one per cent of impurities, nor should it contain chemicals like tricalcium phosphate or magnesium phosphate, which are generally added to salt to reduce its tendency to take. Salt should be free from lime (CaO), as it reduces the acidity of the vinegar in which brined vegetables are pickled, and also sometimes causes lime deposits on the bottom of the container. Salt should also be free iron, which in contact with the tanin of the fruit, vegetable and spice, produces blackening of the pickle. It should not also contain magnesium salts which impart a bitter taste to the pickle. Carbonates, being alkalin, lower acidity of the pickle and also make the pickle soft in texture.

Vinegar. Vinegar of good quality should contain at least 4 per cent acetic acid. Vinegars of low acid content or imitation or synthetic vinegars, are not suitable for pickling. For pickles of high standard and quality, the vinegar used should be of good quanlity and should be of 40 to 60 grain strength, that is, should contain 4 to 6 per cent of acetic acid. Usually, malt or cider vinegar is used.

Some manufacturers prefer to use acetic acid, because it is highly concentrated and prectically free from colour and sediment. If a fruit vinegar is used, it should be filtered first to remove any sediment. Vinegar should not come in contact with iron as it leads to the blackening of the pickle. In order to ensure good keeping quality, the final concentration of acetic acid in the pickle should not be less than 2 per cent in addition to the other organic acids naturally present in the raw material.

Sugar. Sugar used in the preparation of sweet pickles should be of high quality.

Spices. Spices are added practically to all pickles, the quantity added depending upon the kind of fruit or vegetable taken and the kind of flavour desired. The spices generally used are bay leaves, cardamom, chillies, cinnamon, clove, coriander, dill herb, ginger, mace, mustard, black pepper, cumin, turmeric, garlic, mint, sage, parsley, thyme, fennel, aniseed etc. These should be of good quality and should be stored in friction top tins in a cool and dry place.

Water. Only potable water should be used for the preparation of brine. Hard water contains salts of calcium, sodium, magnesium etc, which interfere with the normal salt curing of the vegetable. If hard water is to be used, a small quantity of vinegar should also be added to the brine to neutralize its alkalinity. Iron should not be present in the water in any appraciable quantity as it causes the blacking of the pickle.

Colouring and Hardening Agents

Once it was the prectice to heat the vinegar pickle in a copper vessel so that the pickle might acquire a green colour. It has now been shown that the green colour is owing to copper acetate, which is a poisonous compound. The use of copper vessels for making pickles has, therefore, been prohibited in many countries. Colours are not generally added to pickles, although they are used, to some extent, in sauces. Some manufacturers use alum for firmness in pickles. It is, however, a doubtful expedient, because the same results can be obtained by employing proper pickling methods. The use of alum in pickle making is not, therefore, recommended as a normal practice.

Equipment

Wide mouthed stone jars with straight sides are highly suited for making small quantities of pickles. The advantages of such containers are that they can be easily cleaned and they absorb any undesirable flavours and odours to a less extent than wooden containers. For large scale production, 227 litres capacity water tight kegs or barrles are suitable. Before use, the barrels must be washed thoroughly with a strong lye solution to remove any undesirable flavours and odours. To remove traces of lye, they should then be cleaned thoroughly with hot water.

The covers for the kegs should be thick and they should be made of a material that would not impart any colour, taste and flavour of its own to the pickle. They should be 2.5 to 5 cm less in diameter than the inside of the container so that they can be easily placed inside the keg on the top of the vegetable and can be removed, when desired. They should be coated with paraffin wax to fill up any pores in them and thereby facilitate their cleaning.

Weighing Scales

For small scale production, an ordinary country balance would do. A platform balance is, however, essential for large scale work.

Measures for Liquids

Water, brine and other liquids can be measured conveniently and need not, therefore, be weighed. Half litre, one litre, two litres and four litres measures are most suitable.

Cooking Utensils

Metallic vessels should be non corrodible. Vessels made of iron or copper are not suitable. Glass lined vessels, those made of stainless steel, monel metal, inconel, and aluminium are preferable. The ladles, spoons and measuring vessels should also be made of non corrodible materials.

PICKLING PROCESS

Pickling is done is two stages: (i) by curing or fermentation with dry salting or fermentation in brine, or salting without fermentation; and (ii) by finishing and packing.

Dry Salting

In this method, the vegetable is treated with dry salt. The salt extracts the juice from the vegetable and forms the brine, which is fermented by lactic acid forming bacteria. The method of dry salting in general, is as follows.

The vegetable is prepared, washed thoroughly in running cold water, drained and weighed. For every 100 kg of the prepared vegetable, 3 kg of salt is used. The vegetable is placed about 2.5 cm deep in the keg or barrel and is sprinkled with a small quantity of salt from the weighed amount. Another layer of the vegetable is added and again sprinkled with salt. The salt is added, layer by layer, in this manner till the keg is three quarters full. Then one or two folds of cheese cloth are spread over the salted vegetable, tucking in the cloth at the sides, and then placing a wooden board on the top of it. A clean stone, which is not acted upon by salt and organic acids, is placed on the board to press the vegetable so as to form a brine. Generally, a stone weighing about 4.54 kg will be sufficient in the case of a 22.10 litres keg. If necessary, additional weight may be placed, in case brine does not form after the material has stood for sometime. Generally, brine is formed in about 24 hours.

After packing the vegetable, the keg is placed in a warm and dry place and fermentation is allowed to proceed. In a short time, due to osmosis, juice from the vegetable forms the brine covering the whole mass. The weighted board helps to keep the vegetable submerged in the brine.

As soon as the brine is formed, fermentation starts and bubbles of carbon dioxide begin to rise from from the liquid.

Fermentation is usually completed in 8 to 10 days under favourable conditions which are attained in the temperature range of 27° to 32°C. In cold weather, however, it may take 2 to 4 weeks for the fermentation to be complete. When the fermentation is over, gas bubbles cease to form rise. This may be confirmed by tapping the keg gently.

The product may now be preserved and kept by excluding air.
If this is not done, 'pickle scum' a kind of wild yeast, appears on the surface. It soon destroys the lactic and formed by fermentation with the result that the pickle is ultimately spoilt.

According to Round and Lang, air can be exhausted or expelled in the following manner.

Method I. An air seal on the surface of the brine can be made by pouring on top of it an edible oil-like rape seed oil or cotton seed oil. The oil, being lighter than the brine, floats on the surface and thereby prevents the access of air to the pickle below. A layer of oil about a 0.6 cm thick is generally sufficient to keep the pickle indefinitely. The only drawback in this otherwise simple method is that the vegetable cannot be taken out from the container without getting covered with the oil. To overcome this the oil may be removed from the surface by decanting, syphoning or skimming, or making it overflow by addiing more brine to the keg.

Method II. After dry salting and fermentation, the barrel or keg is filled with the vegetable to its maximum capacity, and the cover replaced. A 1.25 cm hole is bored in the head. Then the barrel is filled to the brim with the brine so that very little air is left inside. It is allowed to stand for about 48 hours, or till such time that bubbles of gas cease to rise. If necessary, more brine is added at intervals to keep the barrel full. When the bubbling has stopped, the vent hole is closed tightly and the barrel kept in a cool and dry place. The product packed in this manner will keep indefinitely.

Method III. Hot molten paraffin wax is used to cover the surface of the brine. The barrel is kept in a place where it will not be disturbed until the material is ready for used. Sufficient paraffin wax is melted and poured over the surface of the brine. If it is not enough to warm up the surface of the brine, a smooth and even layer of it will be formed before it cools and hardens. This will give an air tight seal.

There are two advantages in using paraffin wax. They are : (i) it can be easily separated from the fermented brine before removing the vegetable from the barrle, and (ii) it can be remelted, refined and used again. The only disadvantages, however, is that in case any gas is produced in the brine after sealing it, it will rise up and break the seal, and resealing will be necessary. The wax seal should not, therefore, be applied before fermentation is complete and gas formation has ceased.

Fermentation in Brine

Steeping of the vegetable in a salt solution of pre determined concentration for a certain length of time is called brining. This type of treatment is adopted in the case of cucumbers and similar vegetables, which do not contain sufficient juice to form brine with day salt.

Brine Preparation

Brine can be prepared by dissolving common salt in water and filtering it through jelly bags to remove insoluble impurities. The amount of brine necessary to cover the vegetable is usually epual to about half the volume of the material to be fermented. To be more precise, if a keg of 45.4 litres capacity is to be packed, the amount of brine required would be 22.7

litres. It is preferable to make the whole quantity of brine needed for the days in one lot.

Brining is the most important step in pickling. Although no set of conditions, ordinarily practicable in pickle making will destroy or retard the growth of every kind of bacteria, yet the growth of a majority of them is checked in a brine containing 15 per cent salt. Lactic acid bacteria, which are salt tolerant, can flourish in a brine of 8 of 10 per cent strength only.

Fermentation takes place fairly well in a brine containing approximately 5 per cent salt (20° Salometer). In a brine containing approximately 10 per cant salt, fermentation proceeds somewhat slowly. To some extent fermentation takes place up to 15 per cent also, but at 20 per cent strength, all fermentation stops. It is, therefore, customary to place the vegetables in 10 per cent salt solution to allow lactic acid fermentation to take place and then to increase the proportion of salt gradually, so that by the time the pickle is ready, salt concentration would have reached 15 per cent level. It is to be borne in mind that vegetables contain a certain amount of moisture, which exudes from them in the presence of salt and lowers the strength of the brine. The brine strength can, however, be maintained by adding dry salt. The time required for proper fermentation is determined by experience.

Keeping Quality

Properly brined vegetables will keep well in vinegar for a long time. The duration of brining is of importance. If the vegetables are soaked for a short time of about 12 hours only, the curing of the vegetable tissues will be incomplete with the result that the pickle will not have proper texture and taste. Brining has, therefore, to be controled properly. On curing, the vegetables become semi-translucent, and their colour changes from green to dark olive green or yellowish green this is an indication of correct curing. This usully takes 4 to 5 weeds. By this method, the vegetables can be kept more or less for an indefinte period, provided the right storage conditions are maintained. If the vegetable is to be kept in brine of 10 per cent or less, all air should be excluded from the containers. During curing, the vegetables lose their 'raw' flavour and become firm and crisp.

With salt. In this method, vegetables are packed with a large quantity of salt to inhibit fermentation. In practice, generally 25 kg of salt is mixed with every 100 kg of the prepared vegetables.

The cured vegetables are drained and excess salt is removed by soaking them in cold or warm water, as may be necessary. After removing the salt, the vegetables are stored for several weeks in plain vinegar of 10 per cent (100 grain) strength. This treatment reduces the tendency of the vegetable to shrivel when packed in sweetened and spiced vinegar and also helps absorption of vinegar by the vegetable tissues.

Spiced vinegar. Spiced vinegar should always be kept ready so that it is available at the time of pickling. It is made as follows:

Method I. The ground spices are soaked in vinegar and set aside for 2 to 3 months, stirring accasionally. The spices are then squeezed out, and the vinegar allowed to stand. When it has become clear, it is decanted or syphoned from the sediment.

Method II. The spices are boiled with the vinegar till the flavours are extracted fully. The extract is then filtered.

Method III. Essentail oils of spices are used. This, however, does not always impart to the product the original aroma of the spices.

The kind and quantity of spices required depend upon the piquancy desired in the pickle. There are numerous recipes, each having its own adherants. A few of these are given here to serve as guidelines.

Sweet spiced vinegar is made as.

RECIPE	
Sugar	213.1 kg
Clove, hole	4.9 kg
Coriander seed	5.8 kg
Mustard seed	7.2 kg
Cardamom seed	0.67 kg
Celery seed	0.56 kg
Ginger, whole	1.69 kg
Caraway seed	0.22 kg
Vinegar	227.3 litres

The sugar is dissolved in vinegar by heating. The spices placed in linen bags, are suspended in the vinegar. The batch is simmered gently for 6 hours and is then allowed to cool. The bags are removed and the vinegar filled into casks for storage.

Spiced vinegar with essential oils is made as follows:

RECIPE	
Oil of ginger	42 g
Oil of cloves	39 g
Oil of mace	8 g
Oil of coriander	85 g

Oil of mustard	49 g
Oil of cardamom	226 g
Oil of bay	28 g
Vinegar	908 litres

The essential oils are stirred with the vinegar. For proper emulsification a little gum be added. The oils may also be mixed with sugar and then dissolved in the vinegar.

The following recipe gives a good spiced vinegar.

RECIPE

White vinegar (100 grains)	90.9 litres
Water	77.2 litres
Garlic	311 g
Cayenne, finely ground	680 g
Cloves, headless, finely ground	1360 g
Mace, finely ground	226 g
Coriander, finely ground	1360 g
Mustard, finely ground	1360 g
Cardamom finely ground	226 g
Bay leaves, finely ground	680 g
Caraway, finely ground	92 g
Ginger finely ground	907 g

The spices should be leached in the vinegar for about week.

Packing Methods

Pickled onions and mixed pickles should be packed finally into bottles or jars loosely so as not be damage the shape and appearance of the pieces. Fresh vinegar is then added to fill up the spaces between the pieces. The bottles or jars are then allowed to stand for a while, with the lids loosely on, covered again with more vinegar, if necessary and then closed air-tight. They are stored for a few days, the storage period depending upon the vegetable used for pickling, the size of the pieces, condition of the cured vegetable, etc., so as to ensure thorough absorption of the vinegar before the pickles are sent to the market.

Causes of Spoilage

Different kinds of spoilage occur in pickles. They are dealt with briefly in the following paragraphs.

Shrivelling

Shrivelling occurs when vegetables like cucumber are placed directly in a very strong solution of salt or sugar and even in very strong vinegar. To avoid this, weak solutions should be used to start with, increasing their strength gradually.

Bitter Taste

This results from the use of strong vinegar. It can also be caused by cooking the spices for a long time and also by overspicing.

Blackening

This is caused by iron, which enters though the brine or from the equipment. Sometimes, specfic organisms also cause blackening.

Dull and Faded Products

Pickles become dull and faded due to either insufficient curing or use of material of inferior quality.

Softness and Slipperiness

This is owning to the action of bacteria and is the most common form of spoilage. It is invariably owing to inadequate covering with brine or owing to the use of a week brine. By using a brine of proper strength and by keeping the pickle well below the surface of the brine, this kind of spoilage can be eliminted.

Scum Formation

When vegetables are placed in the brine for curing, a white scum is invariably formed on the surface owing to the growth of wild yeast. This scum may be thin or thick in appearance, varying from an almost imperceptible film to a thick wrinkled layer. It retards the formation of lactic acid. As this action may help the growth of putrefactive bacteria, which causes the vegetable to become soft and slippery, it is essential to remove the scum as soon as it is formed. Addition of about one per cent acetic acid helps to prevent the growth of wild yeast on the brine, without in any way hindering the formation of lactic acid. For this reason, some manufacturers add a small amount of vinegar to the brine in the initial stage.

Cloudiness

When vegetables are placed in vinegar, it is generally presumed that the products will not spoil. In the case of onion and some other vegetables, however, sometimes the vinegar becomes cloudy and turbid, thereby spoiling the appearance of the pack. These raw materials being of a very solid structure, the acetic acid in the vinegar may not penetrate deep enough to prevent the activity of bacteria or other micro-organisms that may be present in them with the result that fermentation starts from inside, rendering the vinegar. cloudy. This activity of micro-organisms can only be checked by proper brining. Cloudiness may also be caused by the use of a vinegar of inferior quality or imitation vinegar, or possibly by chemical action between the vinegar and the impurities such as calcium, magnesium and iron compounds, that might be present in the salt used, or by reaction between vinegar and minerals naturally present in the vegetable itself.

Blemishes in Pickled Onions

Blemishes may sometimes occur in the pickles and especially in onion pickles in vinegar. In the case of onions a white blotch is sometimes seen under the first layer of the skin. This appears to be owing either to some kind of fermentation, or non-removal of all the brine prior to the final pickling of cured onion in vinegar.

VARIOUS PICKLES

There are several kinds of pickles sold in the Indian market. Mango pickle ranks first. Then comes cauliflower and turnip pickles followed by those of lime, chilli, bamboo etc. Pickles are classified according to the method of their preparation.

Vinegar pickles are the most important ones in other countries. There are sour, sweet, spiced and mustard pickles. Pickled onions occupy a prominent place among pickles imported into this country. Then come mixed pickles, followed by piccalilli, dill, walnut, beetroot, cabbage and all other kinds of pickles made from different fruits and vegetables.

Fruit pickles are generally preserved in sweetened and spiced vinegar, while vegetable pickles are preserved in salt.

Some recipes for typical pickles are given here.

Apple Pickle

The following recipe for apple pickle is :-

RECIPE	
Sour apples	1.8 kg
Spirit or cider vinegar	0.84 litres
Sugar	0.9 kg
Cinnamon stick	7.5 cm
All spices	1 teaspoonful
Cloves, whole	20 (in number)

Peel, core and slice the apple. Place the slices in water to prevent their browning. Boil the vinegar, sugar and spices for 5 minutes. Then add the slices and simmer the mass till the pieces become soft. Take out the fruit and pack into jars. Reboil the vinegar and sugar to a syrupy consistency, pour it hot on the slices and seal the jars. If desired, the spices may be added to the jars.

Cabbage Pickle

Binstead has given the following recipe :

Take fully mature, solid heads of cabbage. Remove the coarse outer leaves and quarter the heads and then shred them across the grain. Place the shreds in a non corrodible vessel and sprinkle them with a thin layer of salt at the rate of 1 kg of salt for every 40 kg of shreds. Place a heavy wooden board over the mass and let it stand for 24 hours. Next day, drain the brine well for about an hour. Cover the shreds with the spiced vinegar, according to taste and let it stand for another 24 hours mixing occasionally so that the shreds may absorb the vinegar uniformly. Then pack fairly loosely into jars. Cover the shreds with fresh vinegar and seal the jars.

Beetroot Pickle

The following recipe for beetroot pickleis :-

Take young and tender beetroots and blanch them in steam or in boiling water. Care should be taken to see that the tops or roots are not cut too close. After blanching, remove the skin by hand. Cut the peeled beetroot into slices or disce. Fill the pieces into jars, add 10 per cent vinegar to the brim and seal the jars. The vinegar may be flavoured suitable with salt and spices.

Cucumber Pickle

Cucumber pickles are manufactured on a large scale. They are made as follows :

With salt. Small size cucumbers for pickling are known as 'gherkins' and there are size specifications for each grade. Select firm cucumbers of small size and fill them into a cask half full of brine of 40° Salometer. Add more brine to cover the cucumbers. Place a circular wooden head over the cucumbers and keep it in place so that the cucumbers remain submerged in the brine during fermentation. To prevent the growth of putrefactive organisms, maintain the strength of the brine in the cask at 40° Salometer i.e., 10 per cent salt concentration. The cucumbers will gradually acquire a bright green to olive green colour, or yellowish green colour, and the flesh will be translucent without any chalky white and opaque appearance. They can be stored in the brine for a very long time.

With Vinegar

For preparing the vinegar pickle, take out the cucumbers from the brine and steep them in several changes of water at 38° to 54°C to remove the salt. In case the pickle becomes soft, add hardening agents like soda alum or calcium chloride at the rate of 42 g per every 4.5 litres of water. Keep the washed cucumbers for a few days in distilled or white vinegar of 4 to 5 per cent acidity (as acetic acid). Then remove them and pack in fresh 5 to 6 per cent vinegar in glass bottles.

Sweet Variety

For preparing sweet cucumber pickle, remove the cucumbers from the vinegar and add spiced vinegar, which is prepared according to the following recipe.

RECIPE	
Distilled vinegar (8% acidity)	36.3 litres
Brown sugar	4.5 kg
White vinegar	4.5 kg
Clove	28 g
Coriander	28 g
Mustard seeds	28 g
Broken ginger root	28 g
Mace	28 g

Heat the spices in a bag with vinegar at 79° to 94°C for about an hour in a covered vessel. Remove the spice bag and dissolve the sugar in the vinegar. This vinegar will be of about 40° Brix and will contain about 5 per cent acidity as acetic acid. Store the cucumbers in this spiced vinegar for several weeks. Replace the old vinegar with fresh spiced vinegar raised to 55° Brix by adding sugar.

Other sweet pickles like those of onion, green tomato and cauliflower may also be mixed with sweet cucumber pickles, if desired. Pack in glass jars and seal them air tight.

Dill pickles, which are highly popular in some countries, are prepared by fermentation of cucumbers in dilute flavoured with dill herb spices. They are marketed in brine rather than in vinegar. These dill pickles do not, however, keep so well as vinegar cucumber pickles.

All kinds of cucumber pickles and mixed pickles are now successfully canned in heavily lacquered cans.

Jack Fruit Pickle

Tender green jack fruit has been found suitable for pickling. The method of preparation is as follows.

With spices. Select tender green jack fruit Peel the outer spine rind with a knife and cut the peeled fruit into 1.2 to 1.8 cm thick slices. Fill the slices into a glazed jar and cover them with 8 per cent common salt solution Keep the pieces well immersed in the brine by placing a wooden weight at the top. Raise the strength of the brine by 2 per cent daily till the final concentration re ches 15 per cent. Allow the pieces to remain in this brine for 8 to 10 days to make them sufficiently soft.

Take the quantities of the other ingredients for preparing sweet spiced vinegar pickle as :

Sugar	1.3 kg
Vinegar (8 per cent)	1.8 kg
Water	0.67 kg
Clove, headless	
Cinnamon, whole	
Coriander seed	1 g each
Ginger root, ground	
Mace, broken	
Mustard seed, broken	

Plain product. For the plain pickle, 8 per cent vinegar only is used without any addition of sugar or spices. As the vinegar added first gets diluted, it should be replaced with fresh vinegar of the same 8 per cent strength after 2 to 3 days. Pack the pickle in bottle or jars.

Onion Pickle

The following method gives a good product.

Without fermentation. Select fully mature, dry onions which are free from adhering soil and grade them according to size. Remove the outer brown layers, the tope and the tails with a stainless steel knife. For brining without preliminary fermentation, pack the onions fairly tight in a cask and fill the cask with brine of 85° Salometer. After 48 hours, run off the brine and replace it with saturated brine. Add 56 g of potassium metabisulphite to a 204 to 227 kg cask to bleach the onions. The pickle will be ready in about two weeks.

With fermentation. For adopting the fermentation process, Campbell with fernmentation process, Campbell favours the following procedure :

Soak the onions in water for 2 to 3 days and then place them for a further period of 4 to 5 days in 5 per cent brine. This will leach out the strong taste of the onion and make the product wither. Drain the mass the replace with fresh brine of 60° Salometer. Increase this to 80° for longer orage.

Drain the brine from the onions and leach out the salt by soaking in ot water for about 12 hours. Run the water off and pour 4 per cent acetic :id solution over the onions. Allow the mass to stand for 24 hours. Then move the onions from the cask and fill them into wide mouthed bottles. over with 5 per cent acetic acid or white vinegar and seal the bottles air ght.

A few red chillies and small quantity of white mustard seeds may be lded for better appearance. Suitably spiced vinegar also may be used.

The following are quicker methods:

1. Take small onions of about the same size and blanch them in boiling ater till they become tender. Then add dry salt at the rate of 1 kg for very 8 kg of the onions and let them stand for 24 hours, with occasional irring. Drain and pack in cold spiced vinegar accroding to taste.

2. Peel and simmer the onions for about 15 minutes in spiced vinegar ontaining one g of salt for every 0.04 litre of vinegar. Drain and pack in rs. Cover with fresh and hot spiced vinegar.

'alnut Pickle

Tender walnuts, with their shell still soft, are used for pickling. As ey are intensely astringent, they require prolongard curing for a period : 3 to 4 months. To facilitate curing, they should be pricked with stainless eel needles or bamboo spikes or pricks.

Recipe I. To one litre of vineoar add 17 g of salt and 8.5 g each of all oice, whole pepper, clove and ginger. Puncture the walnuts with a fork nd store them in the vinegar for about 4 months. Cook the walnuts in ie vinegar, replacing water lost by evaporation. Drain and fill them into ottles, using fresh hot spiced vinegar to cover them. Seal the bottles. The ickle will be ready for use in about three weeks.

Recipe II. Walnuts can be pickled as follows.

Take green tender walnuts, prick them and cover them in a vessel rith brine containing 1 kg of salt per 2.5 litres of water. Set aside for 3 ays, drain and cover with fresh brine of the same strength. Repeat this rocess twice. Drain the nuts and dry them in the sum till they turn black. repare spiced vinegar by boiling 226 g black pepper, 113 g of all spices nd 113 g of bruised ginger in 4.5 litres of 5 per cent vinegar. Pack the 'alnuts in bottles and cover them with this vinegar.

For preparing spiced vinegar, sugar may be added at the rate of 3 to 5 kg per 10 litres of vinegar.

OIL PICKLES

In india, oil pickles that is pickles which contain some edible oil, are highly popular. Cauliflower, lime, mango and turnip pickles preparaed in this manner are the most important. The preparation of those is described briefly in the following section.

Bamboo Pickle

Tender bamboo shoots can be used for preparing different types of pickles.

Select tender bamboo shoots and remove the outer leaves. Cut the shoots into small pieces and boil them boil them for helf an hour twice with 2 to 3 changes of water to remove the poisonous bitter principle namey, hydrocyanic acid. Drain and rinse well. Dry the pieces for 2 to 3 hours in the sun. Mix them with the usual spices and a small quantity of rapeseed oil or gingelly oil. Fill them into a stone jar. Place the jar in the sun for about a week. To improve its keeping quanlity, add sufficient oil to keep the pieces fully covered.

Cauliflower Pickle

Cauliflower pickle is highly popular in north India. The following method gives a good pickle.

Take fully developed and compact heads of cauliflower. Remove the outer leaves and the central stalk. Cut the flowers into pieces of suitable size, wash, drain and place them in the sun for 2 to 3 hours to remove surface moisture. Take the other ingredients as indicated in the recipe. Take all the spices, except mustard seeds and grind them into a fine powder. Fry them in the oil. When the spices turn brown, add the cauliflower pieces and mix. well. When the pieces turn slightly soft, allow them to cool. When the mass has cooled down to room temperature, add mustard and mix them thoroughly. Place the mixture in the sun for 5 to 7 days. Then add 2.2 kg of vinegar and again place it in the sun for 3 more days.

RECIPE	
Prepared cauliflower	18.1 kg
Salt	1.12 kg
Chilii powder	0.56 kg
Cumin	56 g
Clove	56 g
Cardamon	28 g
Cinnamon	56 g

Ginger, green	0.56 kg
Onion chopped	0.56 kg
Mustard seeds	0.56 kg
Rapeseed oil	2.26 kg

For a sweet pickle, add 4.53 kg of sugar or jarqgery along with the vinegar. The pickle will be ready in about a week.

The following recipe which requires more mustard, also gives a good product.

RECIPE

Prepared cauliflower	37.1 kg
Salt	2.26 kg
Mustard, finely ground	2.72 kg
Red chillies, finely ground	0.90 kg
Turmeric, finely ground	0.22 kg
Dry ginger, finely ground	0.22 kg
Onion, finely ground	0.90 kg
Garlic, finely ground	0.22 kg
Jaggery (gur)	9.07 kg
Rapeseed oil	Sufficient to mix the spices

Blanch the cauliflower pieces for 5 to 6 minutes in boiling water. Mix all the ingredients in a jar and place the jar in the sun. The pickle will be ready in 4 to 5 days. Then add 510 g glacial acetic acid and mix well.

RECIPE

Brined jack fruit slices	9.07 kg
Salt	0.56 kg
Chilli powder	170 g
Cumin (zira)	28 g
Clove	28 g
Cardamon	14 g
Cinnamon	28 g
Dry ginger	14 g
Onion, chopped	283 g
Mustard seed	28 g
Gingelly oil	1.12 kg
Garlic	28 g
Vinegar	1.12 kg
Sugar	1.12 kg

Jack Fruit Pickle

The pre-pickling treatment of the slices of tender, green jack fruit is the same as for the pickle in vinegar. Take the following ingredients.

Fry chopped ginger, onion, garlic and mustard seeds in a little oil till they turn brown. Add these and the rest of the spices to the jack fruit slices and fill the mass into glazed jars. Mix well and jack in the sun for 3 to 4 days, stirring the mass occasionally. Add sugar and vinegar, again mix well and keep jar in the sun. The pickle will be ready in another 3 to 4 days. Fill the pickle into glass or glazed earthen jars and pour sufficient oil on top to cover the pieces well

Lime Pickle (Lime Chilli Pickle)

Take fully ripe limes and wash them well. Give two or four slite to each fruit. Take common salt of good quality at the rate of one kg for every 4 kg of fruit taken. Fill into the jar about two third the quantity of the limes and add the salt, preferably in alternate layers of fruit and salt Squeeze the remaining portion of the limes partially and fill them also into the jar. The juice should now cover the contents of the jar. If necessary, a few more limes may be squeezed and filled into the jar. Place the jar in the sun for about a week. The limes becomes soft and the yellow skin turns light brown.

For preparing lime and green chilli pickle, limes and chillies may be taken in the proportion ranging from 8:1 to 4:4 by weight. The rest of the process is similar to that for lime pickle. Bamboo shoots also can be used alongwith limes and chillies.

Mango Pickle

The method of preparation of mango pickle is different in different parts of India. These are by and large oil pickles. The *'Avakai'* pickle of the Circars in Andhra Padesh is a well known mango pickle in oil. It is very pungent and hot to taste. Oil pickles are generally highly spiced. In north India, repeseed oil is commonly used, but in the south, gingelly oil is preferred. If handled carefully the pickle will keep in good condition for 1 to 2 years. There is a considerable demand in other countries for mango pickles. Mangoes of high quality being almost a monopoly of India, it is desirable to standardize the method of pickling of mangoes to build up an extensive export market for the product.

The following recipe gives a good mango pickle :

Take under ripe but fully developed tart varieties of mango. Wash the fruit in water and slice them longitudinally with a stainless steel knife. Discard the stones. Keep the slices in brine of 2 to 3 per cent strength to prevent blackening of the cut surface. Take spices as indicated in the recipe.

RECIPE	
Mango slice	0.90 kg
Common salt, powdered	226 g
Fenugreek (methi), coarsely ground	113 g
Nigella (kalaunji) coarsely ground	28 g
Turmeric powder	28 g
Red chilli powder	28 g
Black pepper	28 g
Fennel or aniseed (saunf)	28 g

Mix the mango slices with the common salt powder. Place the mixture in a glazed jar. Keep the jar in the sun for 4 to 5 day till slices turn pale yellow. Then mix the other ingredients with the slice and smear them with a little repessed (sarson) oil. Then pack the pickle in glass or glazed jars and cover with a thin layer of sarson oil. The pickle will be ready in 2-3 weeks.

Turnip Pickle

Sweet turnip pickles are highly popular in several parts of north India. The following process gives a good pickle.

Select sound turnips, preferably those with a pink skin. Wash them thoroughly, peel and slice them into pieces of convenient size, preferably 0.63 to 1.25 cm thick. Take the ingredients mentioned in the following recipe.

RECIPE	
Prepared turinps	9.0 kg
Red chillies	226 g
Black pepper	113 g
Mustard	0.45 kg
Spices (caraway and cinnamon)	56 g
Dried dates (chhohara)	226 g
Tamarind (imli)	226 g
Ginger, fresh, chopped	226 g
Onion, fresh, chopped	0.9 kg
Garlic, chopped	0.9 kg
Salt	0.45 kg
Vinegar	0.45 kg
Jaggery (gur)	0.56 kg
Rapeseed oil (sarson oil)	0.90 kg

Blanch the turnip pieces for 5 to 6 minutes in boiling water. Chop the ginger, onion and garlic, and fry them in a little oil. Soak tamarind and dates in water overnight. Prepare a thick extract of the tamarind by maceration and pass it through muslin cloth to remove seeds and coarse fibrous pulp. Remove the stones from the dates and slice them into small pieces. Grind black pepper, red chillies and all the other spices. Mix all these ingredients except gur and rappeseed oil with the prepared turnip slices. Fill the mixture into jars and keep the jars in the sun for 5 to 6 days. Then add gur in the form of a thick syrup and again place the jars in the sun for 3 to 4 days. Add the rapeseed oil and the pickle in stone jars.

OTHER PICKLES

Various types of pickles of exotic nature such as tender bamboo shoot pickles, brinjal pickle, mixed vegetable pickle etc. are highly popular in some parts of the country. The turnip-cauliflower combination is highly favoured in some parts of north India. Mustard, jaggery, gingelly oil are the major constituents in such pickles, apart from a variety of spices. Much work can be done in developing a variety of such pickles to suit local taste. The scientific principles underlying preparation are practically similar in all cases.

General

In recent years, practically all kinds of Indian pickles for which specifications have been laid down by F.P.O., are finding a ready market in many parts of the world. Experiments are in progress to can the pickles with suitable liners inside the cans. Recently, interest in the chemistry and technology of pickles has revived at the CFTRI.

PROJECT REPORT

Engineers India Research Institute, 4449 Nai Sarak, Main Road, Delhi - 110006 (India) provides project report for setting up above unit. If entrepreneur want to get the Report then he may directly approach to them and take their assistance to setup the unit.

13

Canned Fruits & Vegetables

MANUFACTURING PROCESS

CANNING

Apples, Bananas, Grapes, Guavas, Litchi, Mangoes, Oranges, Papaya, Pears & Pineapples among fruits and Cabbage, carrot, cauliflower, Mushroom, Lady's fingers, peas, potato & tomatos are chosen for the canning process. The details of the process is given below.

The whole process can be divided into following step.

1. SORTING AND GRADING

After preliminary sorting, the fruits and vegetables are graded. This is necessary to obtain a pack of uniform quality as regards size, colour, and is done be hand or with the help of grading machines.

2. WASHING

The graded fruits and vegetables are washed with water in different ways, such as soaking or agitating in water, washing with cold or hot water sprays, etc.

3. PEELING, CORING AND PITTING

The washed fruits and vegetables are prepared for canning by peeling, coring, pitting by machines. Some cases it is done by hand, by heat treatment and by lye solution.

4. CAN FILLING

The cans are washed with water to remove any adhering dust or foreign matter. In large canneries, the cans are washed with jets of compressed air, water. The cans are filled by fruits and vegetables a automatic cans filling machine. The cons are filled with hot sugar syrup for fruits and with hot brine is to improve the taste of the canned product, to fill up the inter-space between the fruits or vegetables in the can, and to facilitate further processing. The syrup or brine should be filled at temperature of 175°-180°F and suitable head space should be left in the can so that when the closing end is fitted the space left inside range from 1/8" to 3/16".

After this lid is partially seamed to the can by a single first roller action of a double seamer. Before sealing the cans finally, it is necessary to remove all our from the contents. This is necessary to remove all our from the contents. This is done by heating the cans for 5 to 25 minutes depending on the nature of the product, at the end of the exhaust, the temperature at the centre of the can should be about 175°F. After exhausting, the cans sealed by special closing machines known as double seamers.

5. PROCESSING

After the above process heating of canned foods is done to inactivate bacteria. Fruits can be processed satisfactorily at a temp. 212°F in boiling water. While the vegetables which are non acidic in nature require to be processed at higher temp. of about 240° to 250°F. The temp. and time of processing, therefore, vary with the size of the an. The larger the can, the greater the processing time and vice versa.

6. COOLING

After processing the cans are cooled rapidly to stop the cooling process and to prevent stack-burning especially in cans at the centre of large stacks, where they may remain hot for several hours, cooling is done by immersing or passing the hot cans in tanks containing cold water.

7. LABELLING, STORING & PACKING

After cooling, the cans are labelled by machine, and packed in strong wooden cases. They are stored in a cool and dry place.

SYRUP AND BRINES FOR CANNING

For canning fruits and vegetables different covering liquids are employed. Syrup of sugar, glucose, or corn is used for fruits, whereas brine is suitable for vegetables. The process of preparing these for different requirement, on commercial as well as domestic scale, are dealt with below.

PREPARATION

Syrups can be made either by the 'cold process' or by the 'hot process'. IN the cold process, sugar is placed in a tank and cold ware poured over it and stirred. The solution is then filtered through a thick flannel bag, muslin cloth, or fine brass wire gauze to remove insoluble impurities.

sometimes, warm water may also be added to facilitate the dissolving of sugar. In the hot process, sugar and water are placed in a steam-jacketed kettle ad boiled and the scum removed. The syrup is clarified further by filtration. Steam helps to sterilize the syrup and to prolong its preservability.

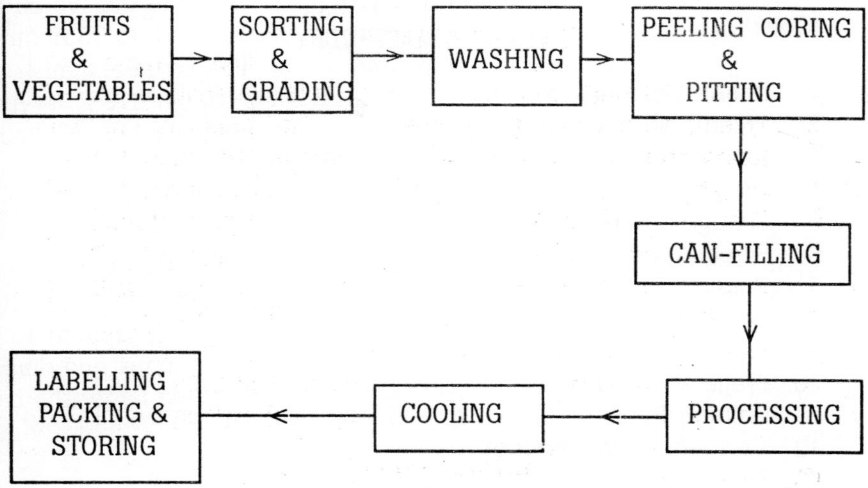

PROCESS FLOW DIAGRAM FOR CANNING

PLANT ECONOMICS

Rated Plant Capacity	=		1.34 MT/day

LAND & BUILDING

Land Area 1000 Sq.. mt.	=	Rs.	6,70,000.00

PLANT & MACHINERY

1. Double Seaming machine,
2. Treadle lid embossing Machine
3. Rotary Fruit & Vegetable washing machine
4. Lye peeling equipment
5. Storage and Mixing tanks
6. Screen grading Machine
7. Rotary type pea grader
8. Pea Auller
9. Fruit and vegetable slicer hand operated
10. Preparation table
11. Chilling Plant
12. Cold storage accessories
13. Pineapple slicer
14. Knife of different types
15. Trolleys, Trays
16. Canning Retorts
17. Boiler
18. Testing Equipments

FIXED CAPITAL

1.	Land & Building	Rs.	6,70,000.00
2.	Plant & Machinery	Rs.	7,32,000.00
3.	Other Fixed Assets	Rs.	25,000.00
	Total	Rs.	14,27,000.00

RAW MATERIALS

1. Fruits (Apple, Banana, Grape, Guava Litchi, Pineapple, litchi, mangoes, etc.)
2. Vegetables (Cabbage, Carrot, Cauli-flower, mushroom, lady's finger, peas & Potato)
3. Miscellaneous : Preservatives i.e. Sodium benzoate
4. Chemical i.e. Sodium Sulphate, NaCl, Sugar, Citric Acid, dil HCL, etc.

5. Packing Materials (Cans)

TOTAL WORKING CAPITAL/MONTH

1.	Raw Material	Rs.	2,85,000.00
2.	Salary & Wages	Rs.	1,01,520.00
3.	Utilities & Overheads	Rs.	44,000.00
	Total	Rs.	4,30,520.00

TOTAL CAPITAL INVESTMENT

Total Fixed Capital	Rs.	14,27,000.00
Total Working Capital for 3 Months	Rs.	12,91,560.00
Total	Rs.	12,91,560.00

TURN OVER/ANNUM

Canned fruits 150 Tonnes		
Canned Vegetables 250 Tonnes	Rs.	82,50,000.00

PROFIT SALES RATIO = Profit/Sales x 100 = 27.43%
RATE OF RETURN = Operating profit/T.C.I x 100 = 83.23%
BREAK EVEN POINT (B.E.P) = 40.18%

14

Canning of Fruits

(PINE APPLES SLICES, LICHEES, CHERRIES, STRAWBERRIES IN SYRUPS)

PROCESS OUTLINES OF CANNING OF FRUITS

The canning of fruit involves several distinct operations which are more or less common to all kinds. The first of these is that of preparation; thus gooseberries have to be snibbed, strawberries plugged, blackcurrants strigged, and so on. For the snibbing of gooseberries and the strigging of currants machines are used, but strawberries have to be plugged by hand. After being prepared, the fruit is graded either by hand or machinery; it is then washed, if necessary, and filled into the cans.

The latter pass to a syruping machine and then to an exhaust box, where the temperature of the contents is raised, and air adhering to the fruits or gases held internally are released. This reduces the oxygen content of the gases in the cans and also ensures a good vacuum when the cans are cooled. As the cans leave the exhaust box they pass on singly to the closing machine, where the lids are spun on. The head-space at this stage should not be too large or vitamin C will be destroyed during processing; on the other hand, it should not be too small or hydrogen swells may form too easily. A good depth of head-space is about 3/16 inch when the lids are spun on.

The remaining processes are sterilising and cooling. Continuous cookers and coolers are largely employed for these processes. The finished article is then stacked to await labelling and casing.

MANUFACTURING PROCESS

CANNING:-

Apples, Bananas, Grapes, Guavas, Litchi, Mangoes, Oranges Papaya, Pears & Pineapples among fruits are chosen for the canning process. The details of the process is given below.

The whole process can be divided into following step.

1. **SORTING AND GRADING:-**

After preliminary sorting, the fruits are graded. This is necessary to obtain a pack of uniform quality as regards size, colour, and is done be hand or with the help of grading machines.

2. **WASHING:-**

The graded fruits are washed with water in different ways, such as soaking or agitating in water, washing with cold or hot water sprays, etc.

3. **PEELING, CORING AND PITTING:-**

The washed fruits are prepared for canning by peeling, coring, pitting by machines. Some cases it is done by hand, by heat treatment and by lye solution.

4. **CAN FILLING:-**

The cans are washed with water to remove any adhering dust or foreign matter. In large canneries, the cans are washed with jets of compressed air, water.

The cans are filled with fruits by a automatic cans filling machine. The cons are filled with hot sugar syrup for fruits and with hot brine is to improve the taste of the canned product, to fill up the inter-space between the fruits in the can, and to facilitate further processing. The syrup should be filled at a temperature of 175°-180°F and suitable head space should be left in the can so that when the closing end is fitted the space left inside ranges from 1/8" to 3/16".

After this lid is partially seamed to the can by a single first roller action of a double seamer. Before sealing the cans finally, it is necessary to remove all air from the contents. This is done by heating the cans for 5 to 25 minutes, depending on the nature of the product, at the end of the exhaust, the temperature at the centre of the can should be about 175°F. After exhausting, the cans sealed by special closing machines known as double seamers.

5. **PROCESSING :-**

After the above process heating of canned foods is done to inactivate bacteria. Fruits can be processed satisfactorily at a temp. 212°F in boiling water. The temp. and time of processing, therefore, vary with the size of the can. The larger the can, the greater the processing time and vice versa.

6. **COOLING:-**

After processing the cans are cooled rapidly to stop the cooling process and to prevent stack-burning especially in cans at the centre of large stacks, where they may remain hot for several hours, cooling is done by immersing or passing the hot cans in tanks containing cold water.

7. **LABELLING, STORING & PACKING:-**

After cooling, the cans are labelled by machine, and packed in strong wooden cases. They are stored in a cool and dry place.

SYRUP FOR CANNING

For canning fruits sugar syrup covering liquids are employed. Syrup of sugar, glucose, or corn is used for fruits. The process of preparing these for different requirement, on commercial as well as domestic scale, are dealt with below.

PREPARATION:-

Syrups can be made either by the 'cold process' or by the 'hot process'. IN the cold process, sugar is placed in a tank and cold ware poured over it and stirred. The solution is then filtered through a thick flannel bag, muslin cloth, or fine brass wire gauze to remove insoluble impurities. sometimes, warm water may also be added to facilitate the dissolving of sugar. In the hot process, sugar and water are placed in a steam-jacketed kettle ad boiled and the scum removed. The syrup is clarified further by filtration. Steam helps to sterilize the syrup and to prolong its preservability. The quantities of sugar and water required to prepare syrups of a given Brix are given in Table.

TABLE
RELATIONSHIP BETWEEN BRIX READING AND COMPOSITION OF SYRUP

DEGREES BRIX 68oF.	WEIGHT OF SUGAR TO BE ADDED TO EACH GALLON OF WATER 1 B.	VOLUME OF SYRUP FROM ONE GALLON OF WATER GAL.	WEIGHT OF SUGAR CO-TAINED IN ONE GALLON OF SYRUP 1 B.
10	1.11	1.067	1.04
11	1.23	1.076	1.14
12	1.36	1.085	1.25
13	1.49	1.093	1.36
14	1.62	1.101	1.47
15	1.76	1.111	1.58
16	1.90	1.119	1.70
17	2.04	1.127	1.81
18	2.19	1.137	1.93
19	2.34	1.146	2.04
20	2.50	1.157	2.16
21	2.66	1.167	2.28
22	2.82	1.176	2.40
23	3.00	1.187	2.52
24	3.17	1.198	2.64
25	3.34	1.208	2.76
26	3.52	1.220	3.01
27	3.70	1.231	3.01
28	3.89	1.243	3.13
29	4.09	1.256	3.26
30	4.30	1.269	3.38
31	4.50	1.281	3.51
32	4.72	1.294	3.64
33	4.92	1.309	3.77
34	5.17	1.323	3.90
35	5.40	1.338	4.03
36	5.64	1.353	4.17
37	5.89	1.369	4.30
38	6.14	1.384	4.44
39	6.41	1.401	4.58
40	6.69	1.419	4.71
41	6.97	1.437	4.85
42	7.26	1.454	4.99
43	7.56	1.474	5.13

44	7.88	1.494	5.27
45	8.20	1.514	5.42
46	8.55	1.536	5.57
47	8.90	1.558	5.71
48	9.26	1.580	5.86
49	9.64	1.604	6.01
50	10.03	1.628	6.16
51	10.44	1.654	6.31
52	10.86	1.681	6.45
53	11.31	1.710	6.61
54	11.77	1.739	6.77
55	12.26	1.770	6.93
56	12.77	1.803	7.08
57	13.29	1.837	7.23
58	13.85	1.871	7.40
59	14.43	1.907	7.57
60	15.05	1.948	7.73
61	15.69	1.988	7.89
62	16.37	2.032	8.05
63	17.08	2.077	8.21
64	17.84	2.124	8.39
65	18.62	2.174	8.57
66	19.47	2.229	8.75
67	20.39	2.287	8.92
68	21.32	2.344	9.10
69	22.23	2.411	9.27
70	23.40	2.480	9.44

In commercial practice, syrups of desired Brix are prepared either according to a formula by which a known weight of sugar is added to a given volume of water, or by adding sufficient water to a known weight of sugared to get the desired volume of syrup. for example, addition of 5 gallons of water to 50-35 1b. of sugar will produce 8.14 gallons of syrup of 50 degrees Brix. Similarly, to get 5 gallons of syrup of 50 degrees Brix, using 30-80 1 b. sugar, sufficient water is added to obtain the required quantity. Generally, to avoid unnecessary weighing a 2 cwt, (224 1b). bag is taken as the measure and a known volume of water added to the sugar.

Table - 2
Canning & Preservation of Fruits & Vegetables

Fruit	lb. of sugar/gallon of Water	Degree Brix
Blackberry	10 to 12	50 to 55.0
Black currant	15 to 17	60 to 64.0
Damson	15 to 17	60 to 64.0
Plums	8 to 9	44.4 to 47.7
Gooseberies	8 to 9	44.4 to 47.7
Raspberries	10 to 12	50 to 55.0
Loganberries	17 to 20	64 to 66.0
Sour Cherries	9 to 11	47.7 to 52.7
Red currant	17 to 20	63 to 66.0
Rhubarb	10 to 12	50 to 55.0
Strawberries	13 to 15	57 to 60.0
Sweet cherries	6 to 8	37 to 44.5

Canning of Pineapple:-

Ripe and juicy fruit with characteristic colour and aroma should be selected and washed in cold water.

Removed the crown, peel and cut the fruit into transverse slices of 1.25 cms. thickness with a stainless steel knife. Prepare the sugar syrup by mixing 1 cup of sugar with one cup of water and bring them to boil. Place the pineapple rings (5-6) in butter size can (plain). Fill the interspace with syrup 1.25 cms. head space. Exhaust, seal pasteurize and cool in dry place.

Canning of Litchi:-

A large number of litchi varieties are grown in different parts of India, most of them are not well established. The same variety may be known under different names in different places and these tend to be deceptive. In Bihar, which has largest area under litchi cultivation in India, the important varieties are China, Deshi, Dehra Rose, Purbi, Bedana, Mclean and Muzzaffarpur. The important varieties grown in Western Uttar Pradesh including Dehra Dun, Punjab and Haryana are Seedless Early, Seedless Late, Early Large Red, Late Large Red, Kolkatta, Rose Scented, Khatti and Gulabi. The varieties recommended for growing in Punjab and Haryana are Saharanpur, Dehra Dun, Kolkatta, Muzaffarpur, Seedless Late and Rose Scented. Among the eight varieties, Muzaffarpur, China, Deshi, Purbi, Elachi early, Elachi Late and Bombai, ave been growing in West Bengal. Bombai, Elachi Early, Elachi Late and China are considered important both for quality and yield.

Cherries Canning:-

Two fairly distinct classes of cherry are canned: the sub-acid red or purple fruit (Morello, May Duke), and the sweet white fruit (Napoleon Bigarreau, Amber Heart). The former are packed in lacquered cans and in a plain syrup of 40° Brix. White cherries are packed in plain cans in syrup containing erythrosine to colour them red. After filling and covering with hot syrup, the cans are exhausted for four to six minutes at 185°F, the lids are spun on, and the cans cooked for 16 to 20 minutes at 210°F, and cooled.

Cherries packed in lacquered cans are prone to rapid hydrogen swell formation (q.v.). It is therefore essential to ensure that they are given a heat process sufficient to inactivate the enzymes in the stones of the fruit. In plain cans, corrosion is not usual and no special precautions need be taken.

Cherries are abnormal in their susceptibility to form hydrogen swells (q.v.), and cool storage of the cans is therefore essential.

Glace, Maraschino, or cocktail cherries are sweet white cherries, with the pits removed, which have been impregnated with sugar syrup to give a total solids content of about 74 percent and coloured with a red or green dye.

Black Currants:-

The chief merits of canned blackcurrants are their high content of vitamin C and their strong and characteristic flavour. Canned blackcurrants generally contain about 100 mg. of vitamin C per 100 g. of canned material. An A. 2 can will thus provide the full daily requirement (30 mg.) of vitamin C for about twenty people.

The fruit should be ripe, and should be prepared by removing the stalks. This is known as strigging, and on a commercial scale is carried out by a machine which consists of an inclined reciprocating screen through the interstices of which mechanical fingers rotate at a very rapid rate. The currants are fed on to the higher end of the screen, and are freed from the stalks by the gentle tapping of the rotary fingers. The stalks, freed from the fruit, are drawn through the screen by the rotating fingers into a receptacle below, while the fruit rolls down the inclined screen into another vessel at the bottom of the machine. Before being filled into cans, the fruit should be carefully picked over to remove small strigs not detached by the machine. The following times and temperatures are recommended:

Can.	Exhaust at 180°-190°F	Cook in Stationary Cookers at 212°F	Cook in Automatic Cookers at 212°F
A.2.	6 minutes	15 minutes	7 minutes
E. 1.	5 minutes	12 minutes	6 minutes

Canning of Straw Berries:-

Strawberries for canning purposes should be firm in texture of good color and flavour, and of large size. The most important requirement is firm texture.

The principal difficulty in the coming of strawberries is the softening of the fruit during sterlization, which result in the Can containing only from one-third to one half its volume of berries.

Strawberries shrival if canned in too heavy a sirup, although a fairly heavy Sirup is necessary to develop and retain the berry flavour.

A sirup of 50° balling is satisfactory.

Strawberries are washed and placed with sugar and little matter in a steam Jacketed pressure Kettle and boiled very rapidly. The partially collapsed berries are then filled into Cans, the syrup is partially evaporated before it is added to the cans. The cans are closed and processed for 10 months (No 2 and 21/2 Cans) in boiling matter and cooled quickly. The cans used are Acid Resistant lacquered Cans.

Processing Details (Canning):-

Mashing :- Washing of strawberries can be made more effective by causing the product to soil during washing with high pressure water sprays.

Filling :- Before filling the Cans are subjected to steam jet remove any adhering dust and subsequently washed with water. Now the strawberries are filled in the cans with hot sugar syrup.

Exhausting :- Exhausting is a process in which air and other intrapped gases are removed from the Cans after filling and before the cans one sealed. In filling, the syrup is normally filled hot as (above 80° or above) to allow air in the head space to expand and get partially displaced by steam from the hot liquid.

Sealing :- Cans are sealed by special can sealing machine known as double seamer.

Processing :-It consist of exposing the under pressure to sterilize the content.

Cooling :- After processing the Cans are cooled rapidly to stop the cooking process and to prevent stock burning especially in cans at the Centre of large stacks, where the remain hot for several hours.

Labelling and Storning :- Labelling serves to indentify the poducts by kind and make and also protect the Cans from rusting.

DATA OF CANNING STRAWBERRIES

Fruit	Types of Can	Strength of of Syrup °Brix	Processing time in minute at 100°C and at 1 atm pressure		
			NO.2	No.21/2	No.of Cans
Strawberries	Lacqured	50	10	15	20

Canning of Gooseberries:-

Gooseberries are best picked underripe, but the berries must not be too immature or they will have little flavour. For canning, green varieties of medium size are preferable, and the following varieties are generally satisfactory: Careless, Keepsa, and Lancashire Lad. Gooseberries which are to be canned must first of all be washed and the stalks and blossom ends removed. On a commercial scale this is done by a machine known as a gooseberry snibber. The interior of this machine is roughened by means of carborundum, and is fitted so that water may be sprayed on to the fruit. The berries are tipped into the machine, the water is turned on, and the belt is moved on to the fast pulley. This causes the base to move at a high speed, the berries are thrown against the roughened surface and the tops and tails are thus rubbed off. The outer skin of the berries is also removed to a certain extent during the operation, and this is an advantage, as it allows the sugar syrup to get into the fruit after canning without the berries wrinkling.

The following times and temperatures are recommended:

Can.	Exhaust at 180°-190°F	Cook in Stationary Cookers at 212°F	Cook in Automatic Cookers at 212°F
A. 2.	6 minutes	10-15 minutes	5-7 minutes
½	6 minutes	2-8 minutes	6-8 minutes
E. 1	5 minutes	10-12 minutes	5-6 minutes

Cans : Types and Sizes:-

The older class of can with the soldered top has now been replaced almost entirely by the sanitary can in which the lid is spun on mechanically. The side of the can is generally lock-seamed, although in certain cases a lap seam is still used.

The method of stating the dimensions of a can, which is used in America and in Great Britain, is to express the dimension of diameter and height each by means of three figures, the first figure representing inches and the next two the number of sixteenths of an inch. Thus a can measuring 3 7/16 by 4½ inches would be given as 307 x 408.

Standard types and sizes of can are now commonly used throughout the fruit and vegetable canning industry and considerable progress has been made towards the agreement of International Standards.

Some Standard Size of Cans

Cans.	Overall Size Inches.	Overall Size Inches.	Conventional Dimensions (1/16 in.)	Capacity
5-oz	$2\frac{11}{16}$	$2\frac{1}{8}$	211 x 202	5.5
8-oz.Bean	3	$2\frac{1}{2}$	300 x 208	8.2
Picnic	$2\frac{11}{16}$	$3\frac{1}{16}$	211 x 301	8.3
A. I	$2\frac{11}{16}$	4	211 x 400	11.1

E. I	$3\frac{1}{16}$	4	301 x 400	14.2
16-oz	3	$4\frac{5}{8}$	300 x 410	16.1
No.1 Tall	$3\frac{1}{16}$	$4\frac{9}{16}$	301 x 409	16.4

PROCESS FLOW DIAGRAM FOR CANNING

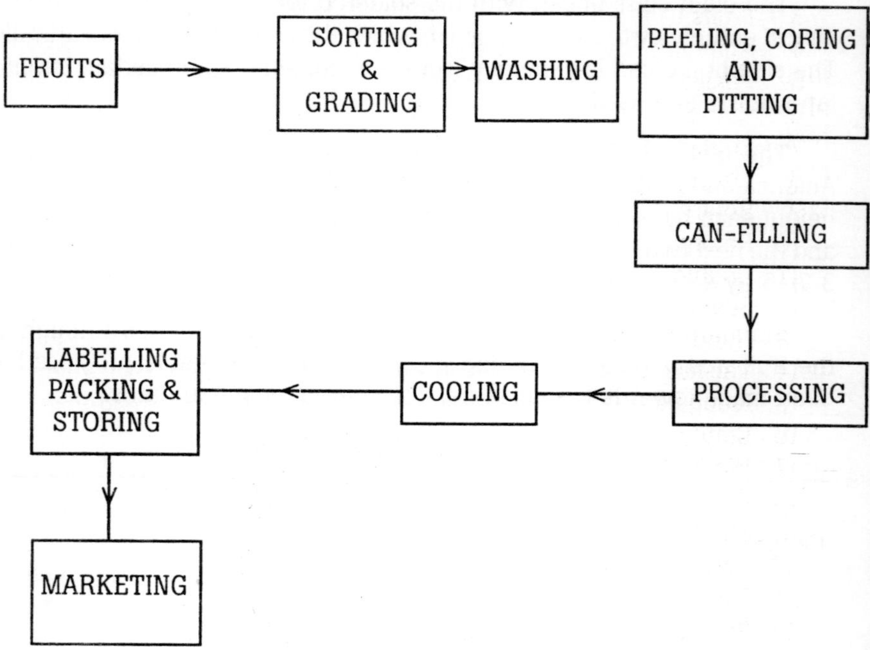

PLANT ECONOMICS

Rated Plant Capacity	=		5000.00 CANS./Day

LAND & BUILDING

Land Area 2000 sq.mt.	=	Rs.	44,00,000.00

PLANT & MACHINERY

1. Rotary Fruits washing machine,
2. Sugar Syrup Making unit
3. Fruits Grader,Rotary type,
4. Aluminium and rest unit
5. Peeler
6. Carborandum
7. Fruits Slicer
8. Fruits Slicer, electrically
9. Rotary Dicing & Cubing machine
10. Reforming unit
11. Double Seaming machine
12. Seam checking Gauge
13. Hand Can Tester
14. Vacuum Tester
15. Flange Rectifiers
16. Empty can washer & steriliser
17. Working table stainless steel
18. Aluminium Trays
19. Storage and Fixing Tanks
20. Syrup filling machine
21. Laboratory Equipments
22. Steam Boiler oil fired

FIXED CAPITAL

1.	Land & Building	Rs.	44,00,000.00
2.	Plant & Machinery	Rs.	31,36,000.12
3.	Other Fixed Assets	Rs.	13,80,000.00
	Total	Rs.	89,16,000.12

RAW MATERIALS

1. Fresh Fruits Viz. Pine apples, cherries, plums, litchis, raspberries,
2. Sugar
3. Packaging materials
4. Misc. Labels cartons

TOTAL WORKING CAPITAL/MONTH

1.	Raw Material	Rs.	19,90,000.00
2.	Salary & Wages	Rs.	2,07,000.00
3.	Utilities & Overheads	Rs.	3,91,000.00
	Total	Rs.	25,88,000.00

TOTAL CAPITAL INVESTMENT

Total Fixed Capital	Rs.	89,16,000.12
Total Working Capital for 3 Months	Rs.	77,64,000.00
Total	Rs.	1,66,80,000.12

TURN OVER/ANNUM

By sale of Canned Fruits
(15,00,000 Cans of 500 gm) Rs. 4,35,00,000.00

PROFIT SALES RATIO = Profit/Sales x 100 = 19.92%
RATE OF RETURN = Operating profit/T.C.I x 100 = 51.96%
BREAK EVEN POINT (B.E.P) = 43.41%

15

Cashew Fruit Juice From Cashew Fruit Apple

USES AND APPLICATION

Cashew apple juice is used as a beverage for drinking purposes.

It is also used for wine manufacturing and cashew-feni manufacturing.

It is consumed by all categories of people.

It is consumed in hotels, restaurants, juices, corners, etc.

It is consumed in picnic parties, excursions, birthday parties, marriage parties and kitty parties etc.

MANUFACTURING PROCESS

The cashew apple is soft and juicy. When tender, it is acidic and highly astringent, but when fully ripe, it is sweet and only slightly astringent. The fruit is edible and yields a delicious beverage.

Each cashew apple yields 20-25 cc, juice.

The cashew apple juice beverage is prepared by following operational steps.

1. Ripe tendered cashew apples are purchased from market.
2. The fruits are inspected to remove insect or bacterial infestation fruits.
3. Then it is weighed in the weighing scale for required quantity.
4. The fruits are washed with clean water several times to remove dusts, soils, pesticides etc.
5. The fruits are now passed through juice extractor to remove out all juices from cashew apples.
6. The juice is collected in the stainless steel tank.
7. The collected juice is filtered, standardized by addition of sugar, citric

acid and edible colour (like beta carotene) etc.

8. The standardized juice is now deaerated by passing through deaeration tank (made of stainless) to remove out all the soluble gas or oxygen to protect the juice from enzymatic changes by aerial oxidation.

9. The juice is now pasteurized by passing through plate heat exchanger to kill all the pathogens present in it.

10. The pasteurized juice is now packed in the clean glass bottle and crown cork is fitted on the same.

11. The bottled juice is now sterilized in an autoclave for 15-30 seconds at 121°C temperature.

12. The sterilized bottles are bring out from the autoclave and left for cooling. The bottles are labelled with requisite information.

13. These juice bottles are now packed in corrugated cardboard boxes, stored and send for marketing.

PROCESS FLOW SHEET FOR CASHEW APPLE FRUIT JUICE

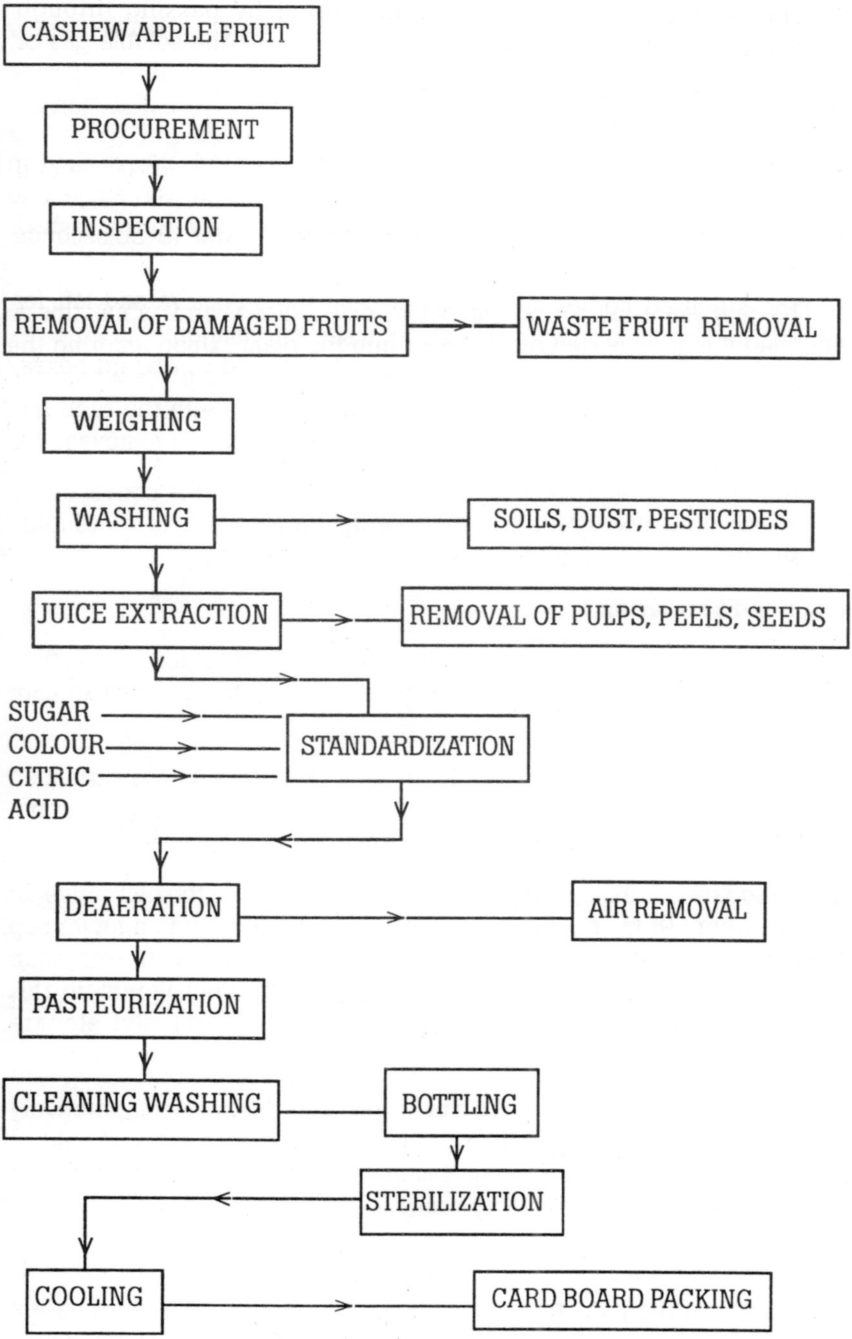

PROCESS OF MANUFACTURING

The processing operations are taken into consideration, while cashew apple juice preparations.

Storage of Material & Cleansing :

While the cashew apple raw material can be stored and stocked in storage bins, it is necessary to give due consideration to the subject so that no changes in form and shape as well as no damage to the cashew apples will occur during storage by loads.

The raw material is first subject to dirt removal and while this is performed it is transported by conveyor into the plant. Upon entering the plant, while it is led to the cleaning conveyor, it is at this place where the earth and sand attached to the raw material, together with the soot, and remnants of agricultural chemicals, among others, must be removed.

While in the cleaning conveyor, a brush attached to the conveyor roll rotates and the raw material, while being transported, is thoroughly cleansed using edible detergents and fresh clean water.

Sizing and Extraction :

While many and various methods exist in regard to juice extraction, the method being widely utilized at the present time is the In-Line Extractor System.

In this system which employs the In-Line Extractor, in juice extraction is effected by a cup matching the size of the cashew apple, the raw material is separated, in advance, according to size.

The separated cashew apples the Feeder Hopper from the belt conveyor in a row where they are, one by one, accurately thrown into a lower cup by the feeder flipper when next an upper cup is lowered with extraction taking place in the lower sector's strainer tube. In other words, in this process, the juice and the solid substances such as fruit rind etc. are separated.

Due to the fact that cashew apple among fruits, are comparatively easier to extract juice, from the average juice extraction ratio, is said to range between 25% - 35% when this In-Line Extractor is utilized for the purpose of obtaining good quality cashew apple juice.

Screening :

Included in the juice that emanates from the squashing machine are to be found fragments and segments or film of rind together with coarse pulp. For the purpose of removing these substances, they are first screened and separated by a 0.5 mm punching screen in a Finisher.

Next, coping with requests, the pulp is separated by decanter and disk centrifuge. Should the pulp not be thoroughly removed, the juices are viscous and in the concentration process get scorched leading to a decline in flavor. Also in the event that the pulp is extremely small in quantity, the coloring of the juice deteriorates and the taste also becomes light and watery.

While it is stated that the most appropriate pulp volume is in the range of 3% to 5%, it is nevertheless possible to adjust this pulp volume by controlling the centrifuges.

Pre-heating & Cooling :

The extracted juice is then heated to temp. 90°C for inactivation of enzyme, after which it is cooled to 40°C.

Sugar Syrup Preparation :

In this stage, sugar, citric acid and water as shown in the formulation are mixed homogeneously with warning to form sugar syrup. This sugar syrup is filtered and mixed with cashew apple juice to make homogeneous product.

To this homogeneous product the rest ingredients like colour, essences are added. Then the whole product is mixed homogeneously for 30 minutes. In this stage the RTS-orange juice beverage is ready for bottling.

The beverage (RTS) is now filled in the cleaned glass bottle. Then crown cap is fixed and sealed on the bottle. The packed cashew apple juice bottle is now pasteurized/sterilized in the continuous bottle sterilizing machine.

As soon as the cashew apple juice bottles are coming out of the sterilizing machine, it is cooled and placed in the crates and despatched for marketing to the consumer.

FLOW DIAGRAM OF READY TO SERVE BEVERAGES

Cashew Apple Beverage

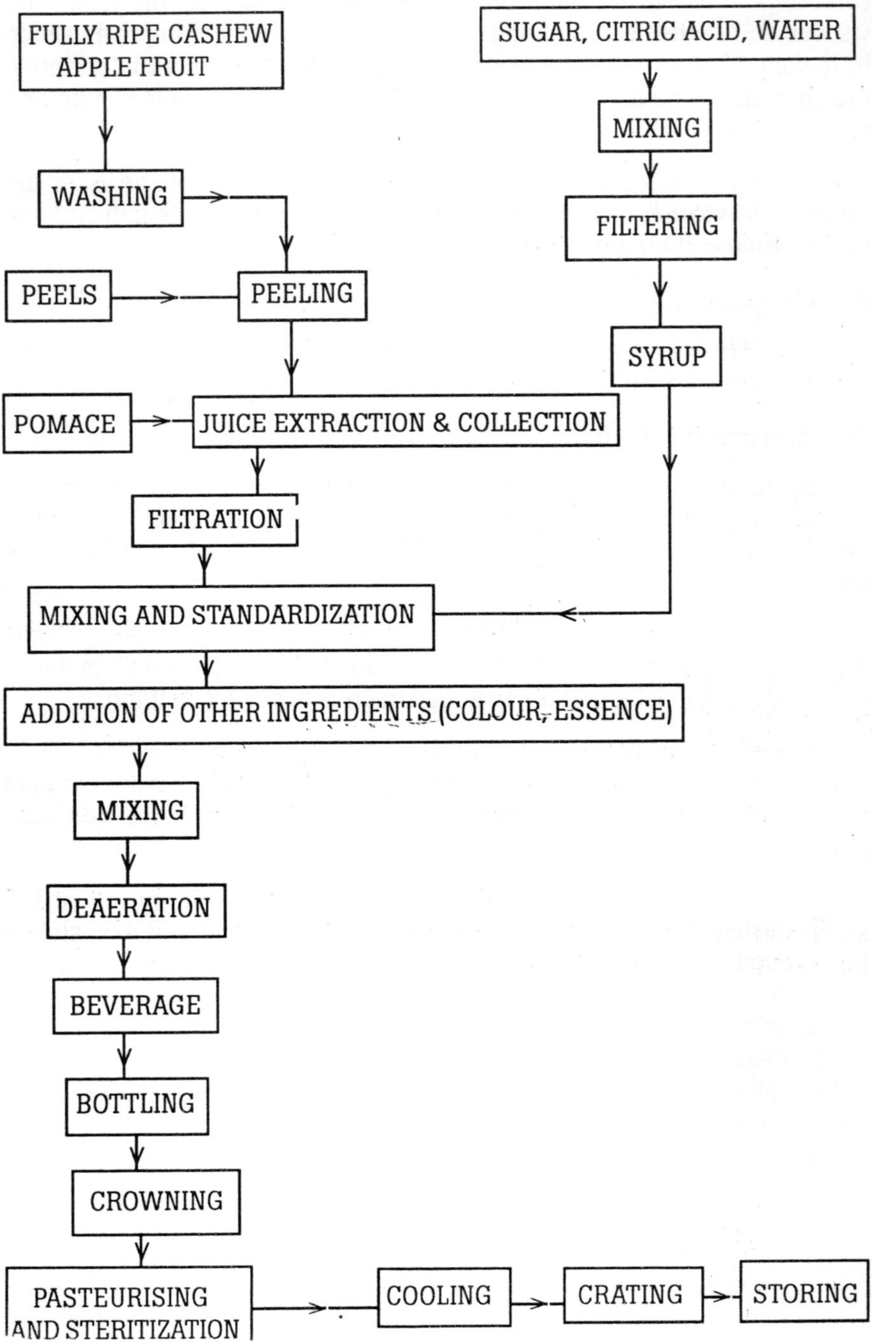

PLANT ECONOMICS

Rated Plant Capacity = 5.00 MT/Day

LAND & BUILDING

Land Area 1 acres = Rs. 30,30,000.00

PLANT & MACHINERY

1. Conveyor belt
2. Goose neck elevator
3. Fruit washing Unit
4. Automatic peeling machine
5. Pulping juice extraction unit
6. Filtration unit
9. Final Beverage blending tank,
10. Plate exchanger (S.S. plates)
11. Boiler (Oil fired)
12. PVC Sintex tank (for water)
13. Card board boxes sealing machine
14. Pipes, pumps, valves

FIXED CAPITAL

1.	Land & Building	Rs.	30,30,000.00
2.	Plant & Machinery	Rs.	43,65,000.00
3.	Other Fixed Assets	Rs.	18,50,000.00
	Total	Rs.	92,45,000.00

RAW MATERIALS

1. Cashew apple fruit,
2. Sugar,
3. Citric acid,
4. Colour (sun set yellow),
5. Essence,
6. Laboratory chemicals
7. Crown
8. Glass bottle (250 ml),

TOTAL WORKING CAPITAL/MONTH

1.	Raw Material	Rs.	11,86,250.00
2.	Salary & Wages	Rs.	3,97,537.00
3.	Utilities & Overheads	Rs.	3,77,000.00
	Total	Rs.	19,60,787.00

TOTAL CAPITAL INVESTMENT

Total Fixed Capital	Rs.	92,45,000.00
Total Working Capital for 3 Months	Rs.	58,82,361.00
Total	Rs.	1,51,27,361.00

TURN OVER/ANNUM

By sale of Cashew apple juice (RTS) beverage, 250 ml size bottle — Rs. 3,60,00,000.00

PROFIT SALES RATIO = Profit/Sales x 100 = 24.55%

RATE OF RETURN = Operating profit/T.C.I x 100 = 58.42%

BREAK EVEN POINT (B.E.P) = 45.41%

16

Dehydration of Fruits & Vegetables (Freeze Drying Method)

Dehydrated vegetables, however, lost some of their popularity owing to some undesirable changes in colour, taste and flavour during storage and distribution. Dehydration techniques have since been greatly improved to get over most of these defects so that the modern dehydrated food is really a first class product in every way. It is sometimes said that the dehydration industry will one day be the most important one among the food preservation industries employing various other well-known methods of preservation such as canning, freezing, addition of chemical preservatives, etc. There is scope for advanced scientific as well as development work in the field of food dehydration, especially of fruits and vegetables.

RAW MATERIALS

VEGETABLES:- Beans, Carrot, Cabbage, Cauliflower, Capsicum, Mushrooms, Peas, Coriander, Potatoes, Onions etc.

FRUITS:- Bananas, Papayas, Apples, fruit Juices, Guavas etc.

FREEZE DRYING IS ADVANTAGEOUS IN THE FOLLOWING WAYS :

(1) Retention of original shape, Colour, aroma and texture.
(2) Retention of freshness and nutritive value.
(3) Quick and complete reconstitution.
(4) Light weight and long shelf life
(5) No need of refrigeration during transport and storage.

MANUFACTURING PROCESS

1. Fruits and vegetables are sorted and graded.
2. Then these are washed with clean water by automatic washing machine to remove soil and attached pesticides.
3. The washed fruits and vegetables are peeled to remove outer skin.

4. These are then sliced or diced into thickness of 2mm - 4mm.
5. The diced fruits & Vegetables are steam blanched for 5 minutes.
6. The vegetables are dipped in potassium Metabisulfite solution for 3-5 minutes and fruits are dissolves in water containing L-Ascorbic Acid (Vitamin C).
7. These fruits & vegetable treated products are now freeze dryed by automatic freeze-drying by automatic freeze-drying.
8. These dryed products are now packed in pouches by automatic vacuum packaging form-fill-seal machine. These pouches are now packed in cartons or cardboards, stored and market.

PROCESS FLOW SHEET FOR VACUUM FREEZE DRYING OF FRUITS & VEGETABLES

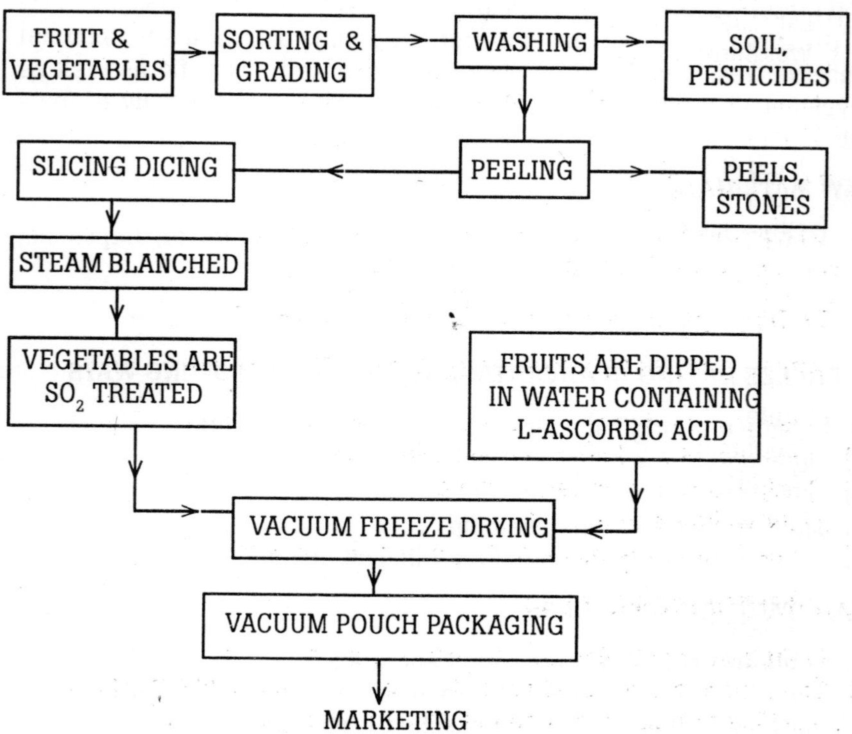

PLANT ECONOMICS

Rated Plant Capacity = 500.00 Kgs./Day

LAND & BUILDING

Total Land Area 2 Acres = Rs. 27,50,000.00

PLANT & MACHINERY

1. Automatic Washing machine
2. Automatic peeling machine
3. Blanching machine
4. Dicing or cubing machine
5. S.S. Tank
6. (S.S.) Strainer
7. Freeze Drying machine Model FDIT
8. Boiler
9. Automatic Vacuum pouch packaging machine
10. Laboratory testing equipment.
11. Weighing balance water pump valves motors

FIXED CAPITAL

1.	Land & Building	Rs.	27,50,000.00
2.	Plant & Machinery	Rs.	1,16,07,000.00
3.	Other Fixed Assets	Rs.	20,00,000.00
	Total	Rs.	1,63,57,000.00

RAW MATERIALS

1. Fruits
2. Vegetables
3. Chemicals as potassium metabisulfite, vitamin C etc.

TOTAL WORKING CAPITAL/MONTH

1.	Raw Material	Rs.	2,89,000.00
2.	Salary & Wages	Rs.	42,120.00
3.	Utilities & Overheads	Rs.	1,13,400.00
	Total	Rs.	4,44,520.00

TOTAL CAPITAL INVESTMENT

Total Fixed Capital	Rs.	1,63,57,000.00
Total Working Capital for 3 Months	Rs.	13,33,560.00
Total	Rs.	1,76,90,560.00

TURN OVER/ANNUM

By sale of 75000 kgs of Dehydrated Fruits Rs. 1,57,50,000.00

PROFIT SALES RATIO = Profit/Sales x 100 = 26.56%

RATE OF RETURN = Operating profit/T.C.I x 100 = 23.65%

BREAK EVEN POINT (B.E.P) = 62.53%

17

Frozen Foods

USES

Frozen foods is used to preserve fruits and vegetables and non vegetables.

Once they are kept in the cold storage, they do not get spoiled even after many months.

Some times, in production reason of certain vegetable or non vegetable, the demand for that thing decreases, which in Turn decreases the consumption the surplus amount of that particular item is kept in cold storage.

So this item, when needed, can be taken from the cold storage & can be made available to consumers very easily.

MANUFACTURING PROCESS

The rapidity with which fish decomposes has resulted in various process of prescription and curing which aim at preserving the fish from the attacks of putrefactive organisms. The method for this purpose are freezing drying, salting pickling and smoking.

Refrigeration fishes are kept in small refrigerators or ice boxes, which cool the air this preventing to a certain extent the growth of microorganisms. But the freezing of fish does more than this. They are often reduced to a temperature below zero, faha, and in this condition may be kept for long periods and transported considerable distances

As soon as the catch reaches the refrigeration plant, the fish are washed in cold running water to cleanse them from scime & dirt and fish that are heavy feeders or are of any oily nature are eviscerated coilest small fish, such as mackerel, whiting etc. are frozen in their natural slate in pans, in which they are placed head to tail. The pan when full is set upon the shelf of what is known as the quicker this is done the better favoured are the fish after thawing.

Large, fish like halibut, salmon cool, etc. are frozen separately until they are of the consistency of a coke of ice. It usually takes ten or twelve hours to freeze through a thick fish the next step is to give the fish an icy coat or greaze, and the manner in which this is carried out is most important, for unless properly geazed, the skins of frozen fin may twin white or get tractured whilst the bodies shrink owing to evaporation of moisture, from the flesh. Glazing is carried out for the purpose of giving each fish an airtight envelope of ice, which prevents the evaporation of moisture, deterioration of oils in the fush of salmen and other oily fish, and protects the fish from mechanical injuries. The method of doing it is as follows. The frozen fish enter the glazing room where the temp. is about 25°F and are quickly put through a trough of clean water, kept near to freezing point. This water forms a thin film over the surface of the fish, which solidifies almost instantly in the cold air of the room. The fish are passed through the trough two or three times, until the film is thick enough to protect the entire surface. In some refrigerating plants, brine is used for ice coating the fish then pass to cold storage, when they remain until required.

Harrings, in particular, are subjected to quick freezing at about -40°F followed by cold storage they are said to keep palatable for nine months.

Salman, after thawing, is sometimes found to be discoloured yellow near to the skin to possess a particular rank taste. This is due to disruption of the fat cells, caused by insufficient glazing of the surface of the fish thawing then sets the oil of the disrupted cells free which is subject to oxidation and rancidity and the taint spreads to surrounding flesh number of anti-oxidants, including vitamin (ascorbic acid) have been used from time to time on fish and fillet before freezing to retard this process.

Frozen fish, after thawing, can generally be distinguished from fresh fish by reason of its dull appearance and absence of sheen its softer and flabby condition, and also by small particles of ice which may often be seen on the fish.

CHEESE

Cheese varies considerably in its composition, depending upon whether it is made from or skimmer milk. The cheeses, (e.g. dutch cheeses) ore characterized by their hold and dry consistence, whilst those made from whole milk are softer and richer in flavour. These again are divided into pressed cheeses, Eleu-veined cheeses, and soft cheeses. Cheddas, caerpilly, and double and dingh gloucester are examples of the pressed cheeses, stilton blue dorest of the blue-veined variety and the French and Swiss cheeses are of soft variety.

American and Canadian cheeses are example of the whole-milk variety. Some falty and richly flavoured cheeses, such as Stilton, have cream added to the milk before making. The natural colour of cheese is pale yellow or straw coloured: the pink or orange hues of certain kinds are produced by the addition of annetto cream cheeses contain about 40% of butter fat, whole-milk cheese 34%, and those made from skimmed mill 10-22 percent.

Moisture content 23-25% for cream cheese 30-40% in whole-milk cheese is formed by the action on milk of rennet, a product of the fourth stomach of the calf, which, in combining with the phosphates produces precipitation and coagulation of the cascirion and varying proportions of fats and salts. When kept at a suitable temp. this undergoes a process known as 'ripening' changes in the casein and lactose, as well as the formation of certain salts and acids are the results of this ripening process.

The process of making is as follows milk, on reception at the factory, is strained into large vats which are jacketed for cooling or heating purposes, if the milk requires to the cooled (and this depends on time of the year) cold water is circulated through the jacket the milk constantly being stirred to prevent rising of the cream and ensure even cooling a quantity of 'starter' is added and evenly distributed through the milk, which is now by passing steam through the jacket and the temp. raised to 80-90 colouring matter is added, if the cheese required is the coloured variety, and the milk tested for acidity; if this a the correct percentage the rennet is added, the amount added and the temp. at which it is done varying with the class of cheese being produced. This effects coagulation are noticed. The card is then left until signs of wagulation are noticed. The card is ben left until it is ready for cutting. An operation performed with american knives, first with the vertical knife and then the horizontal knife until it is cut. Evenly into small cubes, after which it is again tested for acidity the curd is gain stirred to get it enter a loose condition and subsequent treatment depend upon the class of cheese being made. Cheddas cheese are scalded at this stage by passing steam through the jacket of the cheese vat, after which the card is pilled into a mass and the whydrown. If it is next cut into blocks and placed clothes on a rak and left for several hours, and tested for acidity before the ext. process, i.e. grinding after being ground and haging salt added the end is ready for processing. The moulds are lined with cheese clothes and weighed quantities of curd placed in them. Pressure is applied either by mechanical means or by chains or serious in the case of cheddards they are passed for 3 days being removed for turning etc. each day after which the cheese are removed from the moulds and placed in the repening room which is kept at a temp. of 56-65°F. The cheeses are turned daily for the first month and attain a good flavour in about 3 to 4 months cheese is not allowed to ripen to the same extent as was the practice years ago, a milder flavour being more popular now with the public repening is a bacterial process and it is interesting to note the cows given penicillin as treatment for mastitis or other conditions, excretes enough of the antibiotic in their milk to kill the bacterial essential for normal cheese making.

The repening of cheese, which is really a process of decomposition render it liable to the attacks of moulds and aminol parasites, including acari and the "cheerfly", the soft, greasy kin ds are more often attacked than the hard and dryskimmed milk cheeses Blue, black and red moulds are common on source check whilest the cheese acarus and the larvae of the cheese fly are common animal parasites. To prevent attacks of parasites, the rinds of cheese, which consist of the cloth passed into the exterior of the cheese, are flouring matters or antiseptic solutions. The curing and again of cheese needs special core to prevent surface defects appearing special valve ventilated cases for holding cheese have been introduced in recent years, lacquered internally to avoid surface sicoloration. Abhnorneal tastes, tall owiners being the most common, and internal discolorations are also found in cheese. Numerous taints have been observed and may be due to the presence of yeasts in the milk, faulty feeding of the cow, the use of dirty utensils, or some defet of temp., starter, renat etc., in the actual cheese making among the discolorations may be mentioned the brown patches existing in the interior of stilton cheese and some what prevalent a few years ago. There is nothing on the exterior of the cheese to indicate that it is so affected the cause is dere to the presence of discolouring organisms in the milk.

PREPARATION FOR FREEZING

Meat :

The preparation of meat for freezing is essentially the same as cutting for retail sales loin, ribs or round sections beef, pork loins or bomb racks, loins or legs are cut into steaks, chops, roasts or legs and other portions for cooling. These portions are placed in cartons or overwrapped hand in preparation for freezing.

Vegetables continued

Vegetables are brought to the processing plant in the whole or cut or vined state. Some products such as peas or beans may be size graded prior to further treatment corn may be judged for maturity orgenoleptically, on the basis of moisture content, or the refractive index of the kernel "milk" may be used as a criterion of maturity. Some vegetables are selected to includes a general maturity range butars not graded specifically.

Some vegetables are dryclined prior to washing peas and lina beans are passed through a fanning mill Broccoli is sorted and trimmed by hand or the batt end may be removed with a rotating knife, then the speers may be spilt with a hand knife to portions of suitable size. The bare of the brusels sprout is trimmed off by machine. Corn must be husked before it can be washed. This is done in machine which cuts off the stalk attachment and removes the husk as the ear posses over rubber rollers. Spinach is dry cleaned by passing it through rotating rels; dirt, stones, and other detritos passing through the spaces in the reel to the outside.

Prior to washing cauliflower, the base of the cluster and the leaves are trimmed off with a hand knife, the core is cut out and the individual flowerетts are broken off. The flowerettes are then passed through a cylindrical rod cleaner to remoke detritus. Peas and lima beans are washed in feotation-type, water-filled machines which pass them over stone traps in such a manner that dense materials sink to the bottom and are removed. The products pars over the top and are separated from water by means of a reel. Special washers may be used for bear in which case the product is passed through a mineral-oil detergent-water emulsion when tracated in this manner and passed into water, sound peas sink and are separated, thistle buls, nightshade berries, skin and other foreign material float and are then used to clean the sound peas.

Real-type washers with forced sprays may be used to wash some products prior to blanching soaker-types washers with agitating sprays may be used for brocoli, brussel sprouts and cauliflower flowerettes Carrots usually receive both spray/and soaker-type washings. Green beans are not washed before blanching spinach is washed in moving water in tanks fitted with a drum which immerses the product as it moves along. It is then passed through a wet reel where it is further washed with water sprays, then passed over a wire-mesh belt for drainage, inspection and removal of foreign material.

Other operations which must be carried out before the products are blanched include shape beans. Shipping by machine, cross-cutting or Frenching, also by machine, carots-steam peeling spray waghing, trimming and slicing: cut corn-cutting the kernels from the cob by machine if the product is to be beanched in this form.

All vegetables, except onion, must be blenched prior to freezing, to inactive enzymes, which would otherwise cause the development of offtlavours during frozen storage Blauching is carried out in hot water or in sterm. In water blenching the product is conducted through water at 190 to 210°F.

In steam blanching the product is carried on a belt through a hooded section into which live steam is injected

The time and temp are regulated in such a manner that the enzymes which could case off-flavour development are inactivated. Tests for calalase or peroxides are used to determine the adequacy of blanching. It is considered that a negative peroxidan test is better indication of the adequacy of blanching than a negative catalase test. After blanching, vegetables are quickly cold at least 70°F. This may do done by emptying the product from the blander into a fluve of running water which serves to cool the products and convey to the next operation. In some cases blanched products re emtied into a perforated or rod-type cylindrical reel fitted with forced water sprays or into a finnel-shaped tank, with a stream of cold coates.

Corn is blanched on the for or as cut kernels as it passes along on a hooded, wire-mesh belt. The cut product must be cooled on the belt with atomiged water sprays but corn on the cob may be cooled in a tank of slowly moving water.

After blanching and cooling, lima bear as passed through a quality grades or separator containing nearly saturated lrine (Nace John). The less mature beans float and can be removed from the surface while the corinkled, over-mature lbeans sink and are removed from an outlet near the bottom of the separation tank. Over-mature beans are discarded. Beans which float will become the frozen product and these must be washed to remove salt this done by flaming in water or by passing through a rod reel fitted with water sprays whole kernel (cut) corn is cleaned before packaging to remove silk and husk particules. This may be done in a quality separator containing water instead of brine. In this case corn kernels are removed at the bottom outlet, silk and foreign material floating off at the top. Peas are passed through a quality separator or grades as are lima bears.

However, the density of brine solution used to separate over-mature peas in lower than that used for lima beans. The more desirable (loss mature pear float and are removed at the top the more mature peas sink and are removed at the bottom outlet. Separated peas are washed to remove brine.

All vegetables are passed over inspection belts prior to packaging here small pieces of product, weeds and other unwented materials are removed by hand. Asparagns, French at green beans, broccali, brussels spronts and cauliflower may also be size granded at this time.

After blanching and cooling and prior to packaging spinach must be pressed and drained to remove water picked up during processing. This is done by passing the product over a wire mesh belt fitted with a weighted roller which rides on the spinach as it passes by, Packages are filled by hand.

Lima beans, cross cut string beans, cut corn and peas are filled into packages by automatic volumetric follers. A certain proportion of the filled packages are check weighed.

Carrots are often loose frozen as individual cubes prior to packaging this permits use in mixtures with peas after freezing they are packed "in bulk" in polyethylene bags and metal containers and stored at temp. near 0°F until mixed with other vegetables and packaged in retail or institutional size containers volumetric fillers my be used for placing the mixed, frozen products in packages.

Fruits

Frozen apple slices or sections are used for bakery products. Apples are peeled and cred by machine, then passed over a belt where trimming is done by hand. They are then sliced by machine passed over a vibrating screen to remove small pieces and then over an inspection belt prior to freezing, apples are treated to prevent browning due to enzyme action during freezing and storage. The apples are allowed to stand for at least 8 hours in a refrigerated room prior to breezing to allow the SO_2 to penetrate, otherwise browning will in the interior.

Blanching and cooling or soaking in solutions containing salt, sugar and/or ascorbic acid are also used to retord browning in frozen apples soaking may be combined with vacuum treatment.

Apple slices, to be frozen are usually packed in enamelled, slip-cover cans holding 30 to 50 lbs of product. The filled containers are placed in cold rooms or tunnels at temp blow 0°F for freezing.

The warehousing of Frozen foods Prefer Freezing alone will not is sure the successful distribution of frozen foods-successful storage is at least as important as freezing itself. Unless frozen foods are warehoused under proper conditions of storage and temperature, all of the careful production and quality control methods that a packer may have used could easily be lost control methods that a packer may have used could easily be lost before the product is delivered to the final consumer. To avoid endangering the quality and/or nutritive value of frozen foods, consideration must be give to numerous factors that are involved in the proper warehousing of frozen foods are temperature humidity methods of storing, and methods of handling.

Temperature: The proper storage temperature is a vital point in the storing of frozen foods. In the beginning of the industry, it was assumed by many that as long as the product was properly quick frozen it would remain unchanged indefinitely during long. During long-contained storage also, at that time there was considerable question investigators as to what was the proper storage temperature.

Today, no one questions the fact that frozen foods should be stones at 0°F or below. Many recognized authorities in the industry recommend temp. as low as-20°F. For the long time storage of certain products. It is the Universal opinion that most frozen products may be held in a satisfactory manner at a storage temp of 0°F. A few products, such as asparagus, corn on the cob, mushrooms, snap beans, apples, pickles, poultry and fatty fish, such as mackered and salmon should be stored at -50 F or lower.

All frozen foods should be reduced to a temperature of 0°F. In the centre of the product before being placed in a refrigerated room to be used for storage. Packers should make contain that their products are thoroughly frozen before moving then to storage in other words, a refrigerated room used for the storage food should be near used for frozing separations. In cold storage room freezing such as may be used by the cold pack fruit industry, or by some pacleers of loose frozen vegetables, it is recommended that freezing from those in which frozen foods are being stored.

Unless that recommendation is followed, it will be impossible to maintain constant, oniform temperature in any storage room. Every effort should be made to avoid fluctuations in temperature in cold storage room. Several a Uniform temperature.

The refrigeration system should have ample capacity and sufficient coil area or plate area in the cold storage room a vestibule or outer room should be constructed, preferably on the in side of the room it a vestibules or outer room is not feasible, a tarpaulin or piece of heavy canvas should be
hung on the inside of the storage room door.

The effect of fluctuating storage temperatures on the quality of frozen foods has been studied by numerous Investigators Hustratid and Winter stored snap beans, Corn, plas straw berries, raspberries and muskmelon for six months at a constant temperature of 5°F, and at temperatures fluctuating from 0°F to -20°F in comparing the two different storage conditions.

METHODS OF STORAGE AND HANDLING PRODUCTS

From a theoretical stand point, frozen foods should be stacked in solid piles in such a way as to reduce to a minimum air circulation around the products. Such system is practical only when the storage has a cold floor and the products are not piled against warm walls, and when all of the foods moved into the storage are as cold or colder then the storage itself. Under such conditions-desiccation and oxidation will be less than when considerable air circulation is permitted.

In actual practice, frozen foods are foten unloaded from trucks or refrigerated cars in which the products have warmed above the storage temperature in this case, it is important that the food temperature be quickly reduced to that of the storage.

Frozen foods are warehoused in a number of different types of containers. Permanent floor racks may be made by placing 2 * 45 on edge and mailing 1 * 45 at right angles to the length of the celling coils in order not to interfere with the nature of air circulation with in the cold storage room. The cases may be piled on fork type pallets or on floor rocks, so that the first layer of containers is at least two, and preferably four inches above the floor.

Permanent floor racks may be made by placing 2 x 25 of edge and mailing 1 x 45 or 1 x 65 at right angles and on top of the 2 x 45 at right angles to the length of the ceiling coils in order not to interfere with the natuin of air circulation with in the cold storage room. Strip of woods (dannage should be used to separate about every 2 or 3 ft. of layers of containers of frozen foods dannage streps should be not less than 3/4 in thick and not more than 4 in wide in this way, horizontal, air circulation is themselves, serve as damage strip can must be taken when using pallets, or floor racks and damage to avoid having the containers overlap the edges. If this precaution is not taken, part of the bottom layer of cases will crash down over the ends. In addition to damage to the containers, the crushed part may hinder air circulation.

One of the problems encountered in ware housing frozen foods is the poor stacking strength of some containers, annually referred to as shipping cartons frozen foods should not staclacl within fine feet of any non-refrigerated spaces, such as opening to stairs or elevator wells. When defrosting coils by scrapping, a tarpaulin must be placed over the stacks of frozen products and directly under the coils to prevent frost and ice from fulling on the cases.

In the handling of frozen foods today must ware houses use pellets and forklift tracks.

Aside from the basic consideration of temperature, humidity, and methods of storking and handling, other precautions should be observed in the storage of froze every care should be taken to prevent and delay what so ever the moving frozen foods from freezers to storage rooms and from storage rooms to refrigerator care and trucks. The length of that frozen foods are not in refrigerated space at 0°F. should be held to an absolute minimum.

PLANT ECONOMICS

Rated Plant Capacity = 15.75 MT/Day

LAND & BUILDING

Land area 800 sq. mt. = Rs. 27,38,520.00

PLANT & MACHINERY

FOR FROZEN FOODS AND VEGETABLES :

1. Ammonia refrigerating cabinet
2. Washing machine motor
3. Peeling machine
4. Water reservoir tank
5. Cutting machine
6. Automatic sorting machine
7. Automatic chopping machine
8. Freezing tank
9. Automatic packing machine
10. Depolluting equipments
11. Piping, valves and other fittings
12. Lab. testing equipments

FOR TOMATO PASTE (CONCENTRATE) :

13. pulper supreme equipped
14. Hydraulic juice press
15. Automatic weighing, filling and packing machine
16. Rotary fruits and vegetable washing machine equipped
17. Conveyor
18. Vacuum pan evaporator.
19. DU - 65 Double seaming machine
20. Reforming unit
21. Open pans for heating crushed tomatoes
22. Assorted vessels of aluminium stainless steel trays basin tanks
23. Testing equipment and instruments
24. Steam jacketed kettle

FOR DEHYDRATED ONION & ONION POWDER

25. Dryer
26. Direct oil fired burner
27. Conditioning bins
28. Stainless steel tables
29. Benches
30. Stainless steel trays
31. Automatic weighing, sealing and packing machine
32. Galvanised iron tanks

33. Water blancher
34. Peeler
35. Grinding mill
36. Cutting equipment

FOR POTATO AND POTATO POWDER :

37. Peelers
38. Slicers
39. Blancher trays
40. Electrically heated dryer
41. Wooden preparation tables
42. Micro-pulverizer
43. Heat sealing machine
44. Boiler
45. Piping & pipe fittings, electrical
46. D.G. Set

FIXED CAPITAL

1.	Land & Building	Rs.	27,38,520.00
2.	Plant & Machinery	Rs.	87,35,004.00
3.	Other Fixed Assets	Rs.	17,60,000.00
	Total	Rs.	1,32,33,524.00

RAW MATERIALS

FOR FROZEN FOODS AND VEGETABLES:

1. Liquid ammonia
2. Vegetarian foods, fruits and vegetables
3. Non-vegetarian foods
4. Chemicals, preservatives

FOR TOMATO PASTE (CONCENTRATE) :

5. Tomatoes
6. Chemicals/salts/basil leaf
7. O.T.S. Flattened
8. Labels
9. Cardboard boxes

FOR DEHYDRATED ONION & ONION POWDER

10. Raw wet onions

FOR POTATO AND POTATO POWDER :

11. Fresh potatoes
12. Sodium metabisulphite
13. Anti - Cooking material (Silicate, aluminium, calcium, magnesium etc.)
14. Packaging materials

TOTAL WORKING CAPITAL/MONTH

1.	Raw Material	Rs.	74,77,400.00
2.	Salary & Wages	Rs.	2,55,238.00
3.	Utilities & Overheads	Rs.	2,00,800.00
	Total	Rs.	79,33,438.00

TOTAL CAPITAL INVESTMENT

Total Fixed Capital	Rs.	1,32,33,524.00
Total Working Capital for 3 Months	Rs.	2,38,00,314.00
Total	Rs.	3,70,33,838.00

TURN OVER/ANNUM

By sale of Vegetarian Frozen Foods & Vegetables
By sale of Non-Vegetarian Frozen Foods (Miscellaneous foods) 500 tons
By sale of 24,00,000 cans of Tomato Concentrate of 500 gms each
By sale of 13,50,000 kgs of Dehydrated Onions
By sale of 4,50,000 kgs of Onion Powder
By sale of 225 tonnes of Dehydrated Potato
By sale of 225 tonnes of Potato Powder Rs. 13,37,75,000.00

PROFIT SALES RATIO = Profit/Sales x 100 = 20.73%

RATE OF RETURN = Operating profit/T.C.I x 100 = 75.28%

BREAK EVEN POINT (B.E.P) = 31.12%

18

Fruit Juices Making & Packaging In Plastic Containers & Pouches (Fruits-Juices: Mango, Pineapple, Apple, Litchi)

MANUFACTURING PROCESS

Juices of Mango, Pine apple, apple, Guava, Litchi, etc. on deliver to the plant, the fruit is passed over a roller conveyor or between revolving brushes to remove leaves or other debvis before entering a tank containing a chlorine rotations or detergent. Strong currents of wash solutions direct the flating fruit toward a roller elevator over which sprays of fresh water remove the wash solution. It is important that chlorine to removed from fruit containing polyphenols since they may react with chlorine to form chlorophinols which give a medicinal flavours to the Juice. In addition to removal of debvis or dirt, washing reduces the number of micro organisms on the fruit; thereby making subsequent Juice sterilization process move effective. Reduction in microbial content by washing as difficult where the interior of the fruit is open to the atmosphere apples. A second brushing is sometimes combined with fresh water sprays. The spud of brush rotation, alignment and stiffness of the livistles are varied with the rigidity of the fruit surface and the intent of the operation, as for example the removal of bruised tissues.

Sorting

The fruit receiver final inspection on ruler conveyors to ensure freedom from imperfection before it is regulated into different size grades. Spots of rot on a few apples can cause an adverse flavour in a large inspection samples are frequently analyzed.

Mechanically harvested grapes are dumped from collection bins into a hopper pan which individual barries and partial elusters are elevated to a stemmer - crusher on a woven wire belt. Foreign materials such as baves, cluster steams, etc. are removed manually, Juice drauning to the base of the hopper is combined with that from the crushed pulp.

Several types of sizing equipment have been used, e.g. inclined diverging belts or rolls, roller conveyors with varying space between the rolls or revolving drums located at different heights above a fud conveyor. The fruit of each size category is collected on a cross - conveyor and delivered to a temporary storage bin or directly to the extraction units. Stationary surfaces on the grader are usually converted with foam rubber to minimise brashing.

Communition

A variety of methods are used to break the fruit for Juices rebase depending as the struders of raw materials, the clarity desired in the final Juice, and enzymatic discolauation and destruction of pectin.

The most common disintegrator is the hammer mill or a variations of it where fixed or free - swinging hammer force the fruit particles through a screen.

In Europe the fruit is fed into the centre of a cylinder and propelled by lears past stationary knives. Graded fruit contains less fines and permits the formation of a more porous press cake.

For the production of tomato puree or concentrate the chopped material is dripped into a tank of stivved pulp where pectic enzymes are immediately inadivated. The bottom of tank provides agitation and maintains a pulp temperature of 93°C.

Many fruit pulps have a mucilaginous character that make Juice extractions difficult specially with continuous presses. The nature of this stifferiness of the pulp can be overcome somewhat by the addition of press aid. In Europe grand apple have been treated with commercial pectic enzymes following aeration of the pulp to facilitate Juice extraction on a belt press. As Press aids, fibrous materials, coarse wood floor, rice hulls and beached or unbleached wood pulp are used.

Owing to composition and structural differences in fruits a variety of procedures are used to extract - Juice. They are divide into two classes

1. Citrus &
2. Deciduous

The Citrus Juices from oranges, lemons or grape fruit are automatically conveyed to one of several types of intractors & processed.

Until a decade ago deciduous Juices were extracted with draped pressed,

Loosely forms were filled with comminuted fruit and the edges folded over to form cheeses that were separated by racks having square lattice openings. These racks permitted Juice drainage & provided stability to a stack of cheeses when it was moved into position between press platens. Juice started to flow during cheese formations and reached a maximum flow rate with a pressures of 25 lb p.s.i. on the cheese. The flow declined until the end of cake compression at 100 - 150 lbs p.s.i.

The Juice are classified & pasteurized before storage & packaging. Fruit Juices generally have a P.H of 4 or less and spoilage is usually limited to yeast and mold growth. Under such an acid condition, commercial sterility is achieved by filling the containers at 88°C followed by inversion for one minutes or slow cooling under water sprays. Chemical preservatives like potassium and sodium salts of sorbic Benjoic and sulfurous acids are also allowed up to 0.1% by weight.

Fruit Juices can also be preserved by freezing. Fruit Juices are concentrated by evaporation and ceromatic flavouring is collected from distillate for readying to concentrate.

All the steps such as cleaning, sorting, blanching, extractions, classification, & pasteurization etc. are similar except some differences in the peeling and pulping machines.

The Juices are packed ion Plastic containers, or bottles, tetrapacks containers or Pouches L.D.P.E by automatic machines as required.

Bottling

The bottling machine must be capable of being steamed for 20 minutes but it must be sterilised effectively, as the design of many internal parts makes it a happy hunting ground for years and other organisation.

Bottling Room It is quite possible to bottle in thoroughly adequate manner. The bottles should not be open to the air on their journey from the bottle steriliser to the filler a simple cover in all that is needed and glass sides enable the operator to follow the course of bottles within.

From the filler to the crowner the bottles must again be protected, but once the crown is fixed, after it has been sterilized by heat, So_2 or other means, they are safe from outside infection.

Elaborate precaution are taken to bottle, The bottling room is completely separated for the purpose and has are door, the only other exit being a narrow slit through which the conveyor belt takes the filled bottles out of the room. A cylinder of compressed air within the room maintain an internal pressure of about one atmosphere above normal so that a (instant leakages) of air takes place from the room for the outer air and not vice versa.

The Juice is sterilised in the usual type of filter and is led to the filter by a sterile house, the great point to remember is that in some products one single yeast cell can destroy Juice in bottle cleaning in most important efficiency can be combined with simplicity workmen in the room should be provided with rubber boots and gloves etc.

PLANT ECONOMICS

Rated Plant capacity = 12000.00 LTS./Day

LAND & BUILDING

Total Land Area 2 acres) = Rs. 42,80,000.00

PLANT & MACHINERY

1. Fruit Storage Tanks
2. Washing/Steaming/lye treatment vessel
3. Automatic pineapple processing machine
4. Comminutor
5. Blancher
6. Shredding M/c.
7. Juice Extractor (Vertical press master).
8. Filter press
9. Juice processing vessels
10. Intermediate Juice storage tanks
11. Deaeration Unit, with vacuum pump
12. Filling & Packing M/c. (Automatic)
13. Chilling Units
14. Weighing M/c.
15. Boiler
16. Laboratory Equipments
17. Pipe fittings, Pumps & valves etc.
18. Miscellaneous Expenses
19. Erection & Commissioning charge

FIXED CAPITAL

1.	Land & Building	Rs.	42,80,000.00
2.	Plant & Machinery	Rs.	56,00,000.19
3.	Other Fixed Assets	Rs.	14,45,000.00
	Total	Rs.	1,13,25,000.19

RAW MATERIALS

1. Mango Fresh Fruit
2. Apple Fresh Fruit
3. Pineapple/Orange
4. Litchi

5. Preservatives (like citric acid, sod. benzoate etc.), sugar, salt barley water essences etc.
6. Plastic Pouches (laminated) labels,

TOTAL WORKING CAPITAL/MONTH

1.	Raw Material	Rs.	75,71,000.00
2.	Salary & Wages	Rs.	2,09,375.00
3.	Utilities & Overheads	Rs.	5,48,300.00
	Total	Rs.	83,28,675.00

TOTAL CAPITAL INVESTMENT

Total Fixed Capital	Rs.	1,13,25,000.19
Total Working Capital for 3 Months	Rs.	2,49,86,025.00
Total	Rs.	3,63,11,025.19

TURN OVER/ANNUM

By sale of 9,00,000 litres of Mango Juice
By sale of 9,00,000 litres of Apple juice.
By sale of 9,00,000 litres Pine apple.
By sale of 9,00,000 litres Litchi Juice Rs. 12,42,00,000.00

PROFIT SALES RATIO = Profit/Sales x 100 = 12.96%
RATE OF RETURN = Operating profit/T.C.I x 100 = 44.33%
BREAK EVEN POINT (B.E.P) = 42.29%

19

Fruits & Vegetables Juice with Other Products

Procurement of Raw materials

Fruit and vegetables produce as raw materials both primary and secondary are available in abundants in vast surrounding area where the Project is located. With the best means of transport agro based raw materials availability to the Project will not be a problem, rather the abundants raw materials availability is enchancing to the Project.

Fruits

1. Guava
2. Banana
3. Plum/peach/Pears
4. Mango
5. Pineapple
6. Orange
7. Litchi

LIMITS FOR PERMITTED PRESERVATIVES IN FRUIT PRODUCTS

Permitted preservatives are

(a). Benzoic acid including salts thereof, and
(b). Sulphurous acid including salts thereof

The quantities of individual preservatives used in various fruit products shall be as mentioned in the table given below :

Fruit product	Preservative	Parts per million
1. Fruit and fruit pulp or juice (not dried) for conversion into jam or crystallized, glazed or cured fruit or other products		
(a) Cherries	Sulphur dioxide	3,000
(b) Strawberries and Raspberries	do	2,000
(c) Other fruits	do	1,000
2. Fruit juice concentrate	do	1,500
3. Dried fruits		
(a) apricots, peaches, apples, pears and others	do	2,000
(b) raisins or sultanas	do	750
4. Squashes, crushes, fruit syrups, cordials, fruit juice and barley waters	Sulphur dioxide	350
	or	
	Benzoic acid	600
5. Jam, marmalade, preserve and fruit jelly	Sulphur dioxide	40
	or	
Benzoic acid	200	
6. Crystallized, glazed cured fruit (including candied peel)	or	
	-	
	Sulphur dioxide	150
7. Fruit and fruit pulp not otherwise specified in the schedule	Sulphur dioxide	350
8. Sweetened ready-to-serve beverages	Sulphur dioxide	70
	or	
	Benzoic acid	120
9. Syrups and sherbets	Sulphur dioxide	350
	or	
	Benzoic acid	600

MANUFACTURING PROCESS

Mango Juice Manufacturing Process

The operation describes in this report are, where possible, performed by mechanical equipment, however, substitution of hand operations is not precluded if the same principles are followed.

WASHING

Washing fresh Mangoes accomplished one or more of the following purposes

a) Remove soil or earthy substances.
b) Remove mold, yeast, bacteria and/or spores of these micro organism.
c) Remove insects, insect eggs, larve of fragments.
d) Remove downy or spinery portions of skin.
e) Remove toxic and flavour or odour bearing residues of sprays and dusts.

To a soak tank into which raw Mangoes are discharged. Tank may contain cold or warm water (to 120°F) with or without addition of a harmless detergent. The time in soak tank to soak, is 2-3 minutes. Mangoes are elevated to brush washer with transverse revolving fibre or nylon brushes which fumable the product under sprays or water or high pressure. Washed fruit is now ready for final inspection and/or trimming.

SORTING AND TRIMMING

The sorting and trimming operations remove whole units by sorting, or portions of units by trimming with knives.

EXTRACTION OF JUICE

Washed, sorted and trimmed fruit drops into a juice extractor where paddles or brushes revolving inside a circular, perforated screen separate juices and pull (which flows through the screen) from the seeds, skin and tough tissues. The waste material is discharged from the end of the juice extractor.

Many other methods are also available for extraction of fruit juices and anyone of them can be adopted.

BLENDING OF JUICES

Juices are frequently packed with added sugar, salt, spices, harmless food colours, vitamins and citric or other fruit acids. It is also desirable at times to blend juices from several varieties of fruits to produce pleasant flavours or colours. The blending is normally accomplished in open kettles. The kettles may contains steam coils or be steam jacketed. Generally, they are equipped with mechanical agitators which thoroughly mix the contents without incorporating air into the product. All types of juices which requires this treatment are handled in exactly the same while the other is used for filling, after which the juice continues through the regular processing steps.

DE-AERATION

Where pre-heating is employed, de-aeration should follow immediately. This step is preferred by pumping the preheated juice into a closed container and drawing a vacuum of 10-15 inches on the vessel. This makes free the juice of any entrapped air. Removal of air which contains oxygen, aids in retention of colour and flavour and vitamin content. It prevents the oxidation of fruit juice and there by prolong the shelf life of product.

PASTEURIZING, FILLING. STERILIZING COOLING

These operations are considered because the acidity range of fruit dictates the types of operations and their order.

The PH is generally 4 and the spoilage is usually limited to yeast and mold growth. Under such acid condition, commercial sterility is achieved by filling the containers at 190°F, followed by inversion, for one minute or slow cooling under water sprays. In addition this heat treatment is usually sufficient to inactivate pectolytic and oxidative enzymes. The spores of some molds such as Byssochlamys and certain pencillium commonly found on fruit surfaces are more heat tolerate. This mold contamination can be greatly reduced by rejection of fruit-bearing rots, brushing the fruit surface with water sprays, or immersion in chlorine water followed by a fresh water rinses.

Preheated and de-aerated juice is filled into cans or bottles at temperature of near 160°F and caps or lids are applied. Containers are placed in crates and into boiling water. The cook time is measured from the time the water in the retort comes to a second boil. Cooking continues for the specified time, depending upon type and size of the container. Temperature of 195-200°F at centres of bottles is usually sufficient for a period of 6-8 minutes. The containers are then removed from boiling water and placed in cold running water until the contents of the containers, initial cooling water must be warm (130°-140°F) to temper the glass and prevent breakage from shock.

In some areas of the world the cost of cans and glass containers is prohibitive. For this reason other types of container must be considered. Juices can be packaged in plastic containers, tetrapacks container or pouches LDPE by automatic machine as desirable or heat sealed polyethylene bags if harmless preservatives are added. In the event this type of packaging is employed, the following procedure could be followed:-

(a) Extracted juice is pumped to blending kettles and all the ingredients added (sugar, acid, etc.) and the juices heated to 180oF to inactivate the enzymes.

(b) The juice is cooled to approximately 140°F and filled into polyethylene or other suitable plastic containers and sealed.

(c) Containers can be air or water cooled.

Extreme caution must be exercised in the filling, sealing, cooling and distribution of products packed in plastic containers to avoid rupturing them.

CHEMICAL PRESERVATIVES

The most common preservatives used in fruit juices are the potassium and sodium salts of sorbic, benzoic and sulfurous acids. The amount of sodium benzoate should not be greater then 0.1 wt% in any case and a common rate of addition of 0.08% may impart an objectionable odour. Potassium metabisulfite, and potassium Sorbate can also be used as preservatives. Instead of a sulfite salt, SO_2 can also be added as a gas (350-600 ppm) but So_2 must be removed before canning as it can be reduced by tin creating an H_2S odour and darkening the interior of the container.

The preservative used should be dissolved in a minimum amount of water before addition to juice to prevent the immediate precipitation resulting from its direct addition to juice it should be added after pasteurization.

LABELLING & CASING

Where production is small, labels are ordinarily applied to containers manually. Where labour costs are high, or where volume is large, the use of automatic labelling machine is necessary.

The containers are usually cased manually after labelling, the exception being in operations which produces large volume of a single container sizes. Automatic casers are not adjustable and therefore, usually confined to large volume operations.

Glass containers are hard cased normally to prevent breakages.

STORAGE

All caned and glass packed mango juice are subject to a loss of flavour, colour and vitamins during storage.

The most acceptable storage is that in which the temperature remains nearly constant at about 70°F. These conditions should be maintained within commercial practibility.

Consumption as an beverage as processed.

PLANT ECONOMICS

Rated Plant Capacity = 2.00 TONS./Day

LAND & BUILDING

Total Land Area 1600 sq.mt. = Rs. 48,28,000.00

PLANT & MACHINERY

FRUIT PROCESSING SECTION :

1. Working Tables
2. Aluminum Trays heavy duty,
3. Rotary fruits & vegetable washing machine
4. Water heating tank
5. Pulper Super Deluxe made of S. S.
6. Fruit Mill, all contact parts
7. Hydraulic juice press
8. Storage & mixing tank
9. Rosing machine
10. Water storage tank

BOTTLING SECTION :

11. Tubular pasteuriser
11. 4-Head Bottle washer
12. Rotary Bottle washing machine
13. Semi automatic Bottle filling machine
14. Semi automatic Crown corking machine
15. Super Refractometer
16. Pocket Refracto meter
17. ABBE Refractometer Table model
18. Laboratory Equipments
19. Boiler
20. Water Demineralizer
21. Pipes, pumps fittings, tanks, trolleys
22. Miscellaneous tools, jigs, fixtures

FIXED CAPITAL

1.	Land & Building	Rs.	48,28,000.00
2.	Plant & Machinery	Rs.	51,44,740.16
3.	Other Fixed Assets	Rs.	21,00,000.00
	Total	Rs.	1,20,72,740.16

RAW MATERIALS

1. Ripe Mango
2. Ripe Litchi
3. Orange and other fruit
4. Tomato
5. Coconut (green)
6. Sugar
7. Citric Acid
8. Colour (beta-carotene)
9. Essence
10. Salt
11. Spices
12. Potassium Meta bisulphite
13. Acetic Acid
14. Benzoic Acid
15. Laboratory chemicals
16. Glass bottle, crown
17. Glass Bottles for pulp and ketchup
    500 ml size, with sticker, tapes, caps, cartons

TOTAL WORKING CAPITAL/ANNUM

1.	Raw Material	Rs.	1,15,47,800.00
2.	Salary & Wages	Rs.	21,18,000.00
3.	Utilities & Overheads	Rs.	18,70,000.00
	Total	Rs.	1,55,35,800.00

TOTAL CAPITAL INVESTMENT

Total Fixed Capital	Rs.	1,20,72,740.16
Total Working Capital for 3 Months	Rs.	38,83,950.00
Total	Rs.	1,59,56,690.16

TURN OVER/ANNUM

By sale of Mango juice in (200 ml Bottle), (5,00,000 Nos.)
By sale of Litchi juice in 200 ml Bottle,
By sale of Orange and other fruit juice (200 ml size)
By sale of Tomato juice (200 ml)
By sale of Tomato Pulp (500ml)
By sale of Tomato Ketchup (500 ml)

By sale of Coconut water in bottle
(200 ml size) (15,00,000 Nos) Rs. 3,06,00,000.00

PROFIT SALES RATIO = Profit/Sales x 100 = 32.82%

RATE OF RETURN = Operating profit/T.C.I x 100 = 62.93%

BREAK EVEN POINT (B.E.P) = 39.72%

20

Guava Jam and Jelly

SPECIFICATIONS OF JAM & JELLIES

Specification for Jams :-

Product	Kind & Variety of fruit	Minimum % of fruit in the final product on fresh fruit basis w / w	Minimum % of soluble solids in the final product w / w	Special Characteristics	General Characteristics
Jams	Any fruit of suitable variety	45	68	The finished product shall have a heavy consistency	It may be a single or mixed fruit jam. The fruit used shall be mature, fresh, sound, clean & free from fermentation and mould. Dry or canned fruit, preserved pulp or juice may be used. Pectin derived from any fruit may be added, when necessary. The only substances that may be added are sugar, dextrose invert sugar or liquid glucose, flavouring matter, ascorbic acid, citric acid, permitted colours & preservatives. It shall have the

					flavour of the original fruit & shall be free from burnt or other objectionable flavours, crystallization, mould growth & shall show of no sign of fermentation.If packed in cans, it shall not show any positive pressure at sea level. No artificial sweetening matter shall be added.
Fruit	Any	45	65	Fruit jellies shall be made from clear strained fruit extract prepared by boiling the fruit with water.	The fruit shall be clean and free from fermentation and mould. The finished product shall be reasonably uniform & shall be of good keeping-quality & attract colour. The only substance that may be added are sugar dextrose, invert sugar or liquid glucose, ascorbic acid, citric acid, permitted colours & preservatives. fruit jelly shall be a product of gelationous consistency prepared by boiling by boiling strained fruit extract with sugar. It shall be clear sparkling, transparent and of an attractive colour. It should not be syrupy, sticky or gummy and should retain the flavour & aroma of the original fruit. No artificial sweetening matter shall be added. It shall show no sign of fermentation.

MANUFACTURING PROCESS

Ripe guavas, preferably with plenty of pulp and less seeds, are used for the preparation of jelly. The fruit is washed well and cut into thin slices. They are covered with an equal weight of water containing 2 grams of citric acid for every kg of guava taken. The mixture is heated gently for about 30 minutes to extract pectin from the slices. The extract is drained, and to the residue, water equal to 1/4th of the weight of slices is added, and a second extract is taken. The two extracts are combined and strained through a piece of thick cloth to remove the coarse particles. The strained extract is allowed to settle overnight in a tall vessel. Next day, the clear supernatant liquid is syphoned off without disturbing the sediment at the bottom of the vessel. The extract which is clear, is tested for its pectin content by the alcohol precipitation method or by the jelmeter. The required quantity of sugar (generally on equal quantity) is added to the extract and the mixture boiled down to the desired consistency. The finished jelly is packed in glass jars or in cans. Guava jelly with its attractive purplish red colour and pleasant taste and aroma, is a fairly popular product in this country and also in some other countries.

PROCESS FLOW SHEET

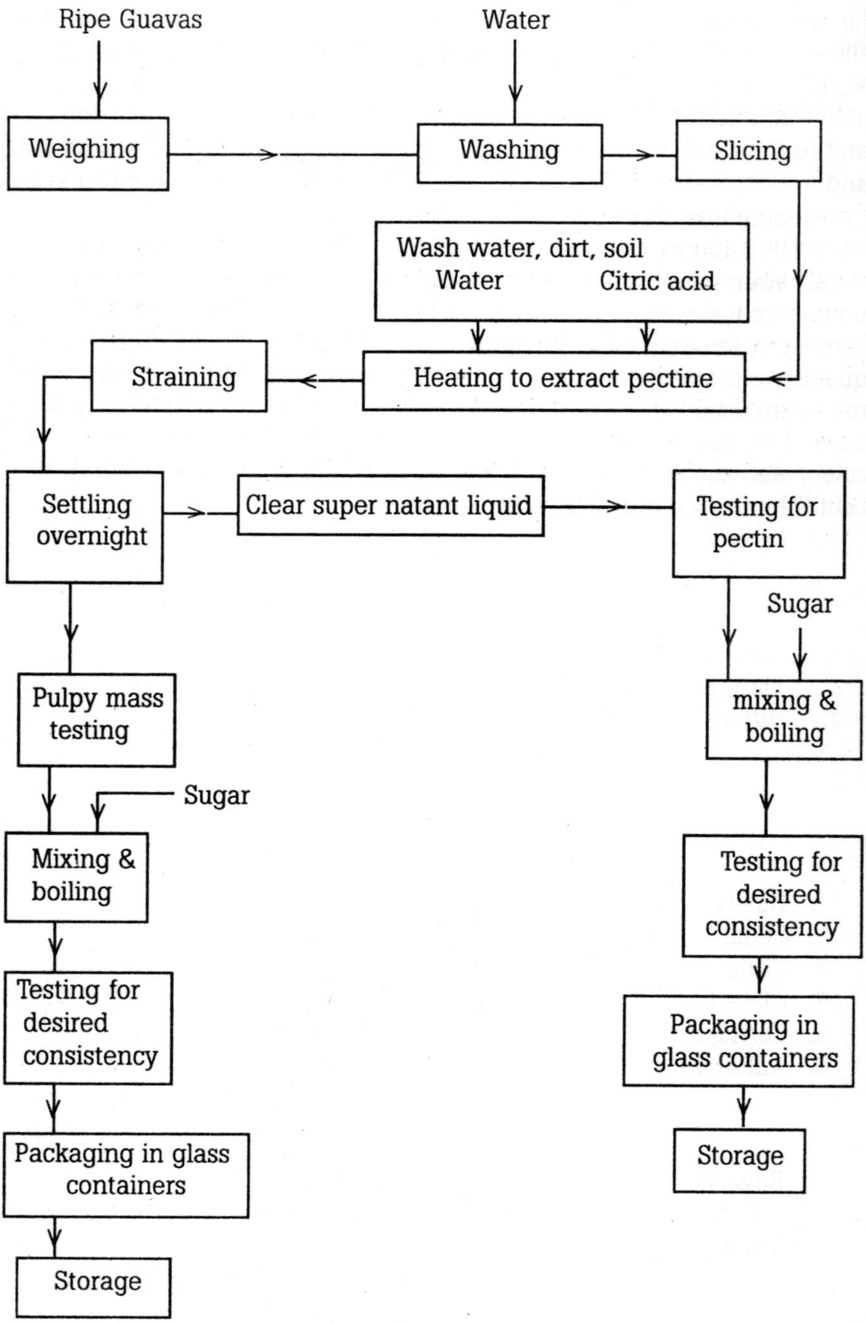

PLANT ECONOMICS

Rated Plant Capacity = 400.00 KGS/Day

LAND & BUILDING

Total Land Area 250 Sq. Mt. = Rs. 4,55,000.00

PLANT & MACHINERY

1. Stainless steel tank
2. PVC-Sintex tank
3. Water pump
4. Fruit slicer
5. Stainless steel semi circular tank
6. Heating furnace or chullah.
7. Stainless steel straining
8. Stainless steel water storage tank
9. S.S. filling tank
10. Bottle/jar sealing machine
11. Laboratory equipment

FIXED CAPITAL

1.	Land & Building	Rs.	4,55,000.00
2.	Plant & Machinery	Rs.	3,34,000.00
3.	Other Fixed Assets	Rs.	2,30,000.00
	Total	Rs.	10,19,000.00

RAW MATERIALS

1. Guava
2. Sugar
3. Citric acid
4. Glass bottles
5. Corrugated paper cartons
6. Adhesive tapes

TOTAL WORKING CAPITAL/MONTH

1.	Raw Material	Rs.	2,24,100.00
2.	Salary & Wages	Rs.	45,500.00
3.	Utilities & Overheads	Rs.	49,500.00
	Total	Rs.	3,19,100.00

TOTAL CAPITAL INVESTMENT

Total Fixed Capital	Rs.	10,19,000.00
Total Working Capital for 3 Months	Rs.	9,57,300.00
Total	Rs.	19,76,300.00

TURN OVER/ANNUM

By sale of 60000 Kgs of guava jelly
By sale of 60000 Kgs of guava jam Rs. 51,60,000.00

PROFIT SALES RATIO = Profit/Sales x 100 = 16.40%
RATE OF RETURN = Operating profit/T.C.I x 100 = 42.83%
BREAK EVEN POINT (B.E.P) = 52.63%

21

Jam, Jellies, Pickles & Squashes

MANUFACTURING PROCESS FOR SQUASHES

1. ORANGE SQUASH :

First of all oranges are peeled and rags sticking to the segments is removed. Now the juice from segments is extract by using screw type s juice extractor and juice is collected and sieved to remove coarse seeds etc. and if necessary heated and packed in bottles.

The formulation is given below:-

Orange juice 10° Brix	45 Kgs.
0.8% acidity	45 Kgs.
Sugar	74 Kgs.
Citric Acid	2.33 Kgs.
Essence of orange	1.125 Kgs.
Water	57 Litres.
Orange Colour	qs
Potassium meta bisulphite	110 gms.

From the above formula, the squash obtained will have the following specification :

Juice	25%
Brix	45°
Acidity	1.5%

2. FORMULATION FOR OTHER SQUASHES :

In all types of squashes the method is same that is extraction of juice and addition of ingredients. Therefore, it is needless to repeat the process but to be familiar with formulations is essential.

(a) MANGO SQUASH

Mango Pulp 18°	45 Kgs.
Brix 0.5% acidity sugar	62.6 Kgs.
Citric acid	1.2 Kgs.
Water	71.8 lit.
Preservative	110 gms.

SPECIFICATIONS :

Juice	25%
Brix	45°
Acidity	0.8%

(b) PINEAPPLE SQUASH

Pineapple juices 80° Brix	
0.5 acidity	45 kgs.
Sugar	74.8 Kgs.
Citric Acid	2.475 kgs.
Pineapple flavour	1.125 Kgs.
Water	56.5 Kgs.
Yellow colour	qs
Preservative	110 gms.

SPECIFICATIONS :

Juice	25%
Brix	45°
Acidity	1.5%

(c) LEMON SQUASH:

Juice 10° 5% acidity	45 Kgs.
Sugar	76 Kgs.
Citric Acid	460 gms.
Water	57.5 lit.
Essence of lemon	1.125 Kgs.
Preservative	110 gms.

SPECIFICATIONS

Juice	25%
Brix	45°
Acidity	1.5%

The equipments required for squashes are as under :-

1. Conveyor type juice extractor	1 No.
2. Mixer with heating arrangement	1 No.
3. Sealing Machine	1 No.
4. Buckets etc.	

MANUFACTURING PROCESS FOR SAUCES & KETCHUP

Sauce of any fruit can be prepared but the most popular sauce. It is also used as chutney. Manufacturing process of all varieties of fruits sauces is almost similar.

First, the fruits are peeled, sliced, and ground. The spices, and other additives are added. Thickening agents also are added to prevent or retard sedimentation of the solid particles in suspension. In India, apple pulp is often used for this purpose. Sometimes, the fruit, which is used for making sauce, is boiled pulped as a filler. The starches of maize potato, arrowroot, sago and rye also are used as thickening agents. The use of Indian gum locust, kernel gum tragacanth, karaya gum, glatin, irish moss, pectin and other similar substances is also advised. These are however, as good as the starches.

Formula for tomato Sauce

Tomato pulp (6% soluble solids)	29.250 Kgs.
Cardamom, pepper and cumin in equal quantities	8.5 gms.
Cinnamon, broken	10 gms.
Cloves, headless	8.5 gms.
Mace	5.7 gms.
Salt	5.7 gms.
Onions, chopped	154 gms.
Garlic ground	18 gms.
Sugar	2.140 Kgs.
White vinegar 100 grain	580 c.c.
Red Chilli powder	15 gms.

It is cooked to about half its volume i.e. about 28% solids, Eng point is determined by refractometer. It is filled into plain cans and processed for 45 min in boiling water.

CHILLI SAUCE

To 22.4 kgs. of peeled tomatoes, add 1 kg. of sugar 10 gm. of red chillies 0.9 Kg. of washed, peeled finely chopped onions, and the following spices tied loosely in a cloth bag.

Mace	7 gms.
Cinnamon broken	18 gms.
Cumin cardamom and black paper in equal quantities	22.5 gms.
Ground white paper	10 gms.
Ground ginger	10 gms.

Cook the whole mass in steam :- jacketed kettle to about 25.2 Kgs. crushing tomatoes with a ladle, if necessary. Add 2.14 Kgs. of kgs. of sugar and 0.675 Kg of salt and 1.57 Kgs (100 grain) vinegar. Continue the cooking of the mass further for about 5-10 minutes after which pack immediately in plain a cans seal and sterilize for half an hour in boiling water.

JAMS AND JELLIES

Jam is a product prepared from fruits. Jams should have 45% minimum of fruit in final product based on fresh fruit but in case of raspberry and strawberry, minimum percentage of fruit is be 25% minimum percentage of soluble solids in the final product is 68% and the finished product shall have a heavy consistency.

MANUFACTURE OF JAMS

They are generally prepared from almost all the fruits and from some vegetables. First, fruits are boiled in small quantity of water and thus pulp is made. Now the sugar is added to the pulp. The proportion of sugar to fruit varies with the variety of the fruit its ripeness, and the effect desired, although usually the amount of sugar used in equal to the amount of fruit in case of berries, plums, apricots, pineapple and other fruits. Sweet prunes require lesser sugar and in some cases even one fourth the amount of fruit is sufficient.

In manufacturing jams, boiling is essential so that fruit pulp and sugar are mixed intimately. Jams are concentrated to a boiling point of 102-105°C, and point varying with fruit variety, proportion of sugar and other factors. A jelly thermometer may be used with advantages to determine the end point of the boiling processes. The usual finishing point is 65 to 68% soluble solids as determined by abbe refrectometer.

At this stage jams are packed in cans or tins but sometimes, glass bottles of wide mouth may also be used. If the product contains a very high concentration of sugar (70% or above), it will not spoil in most climates. Most commercially prepared jams are not concentrated to this high density, however, and should be pasteurized at 80°C for 30 mins. or packed at 90 to 95°c in preheated glass containers, in order to prevent moulding or fermentation.

JELLY

In manufacturing unit, the essential substances are pectin, acid and sugar, of these pectin is most important. To obtain good quality jelly, proper proportions of substances may be used. Pectin and acid are added to those fruit juices which are deficient in these substances. Citric, tartaric or suitable acid are added to make up the deficiency of acidity in fruit juice.

MANUFACTURING PROCESS

Jellies are prepared from acqueous fruit extracts fruits are cut into slices so that pectin and acid may be extracted easily. Only a minimum quantity of water would be added to the fruit for a simple extraction of pectin. If necessary, a second or even a their extraction may also be taken and mixed with the first extract. If large quantities of water are used, jelly will be weak, and if too little water is used, the extract will be difficult to clarify. The length of boiling will vary according to the variety of and texture of the fruit. Apples normally require only 20 minutes or less and oranges from 30 to 60 min. The fruit should be heated only long enough to soften it sufficiently to permit through extraction of the juice by pressing and long enough to render it mushy.

In jelling making process, boiling is most important step because it dissolves the sugar and cause union of the sugar, acid and pectin to form jelly. Its principal purpose is to increase the concentration of the sugar too the point where jelling will occur. Prolonged boiling results in loss of flavour, injury to colour, and hydrolysis of the pectin consequently it is a frequent cause of jelly failure. The boiling is continued until on cooling the product will form a jelly of the desired consistency. The concentration of the mixture, when this point is reached will depend upon several factors viz the concentration of pectin concentration of acid, ratio of sugar to pectin and acid and texture desired.

Finally jelly is packed in cans or bottles near boiling point or nearly 95°C and sealed hot. Such procedure sterilizes the jelly glass and lid, and as the package is hermetically sealed, the product does not mould or foerment. It has been noted that at 0.05% acidity (as citric) 75 gms. of sugar per 100 gms of jelly was necessary to form jelly, while at 1.05% acidity jelly formed when the finished product contained only 53.5 gms of sugar per 100 gms of jelly.

PROCESS CONDITIONS OF MANUFACTURING JAMS & JELLIES

While manufacturing jams the most important observation is the PH of the material. Since the pH is the controlling factor is the setting of jams, it is sometimes necessary to adjust it the optimum. This is done by adding acid salts of citric or tartaric acids or alkalines like sodium bicarbonate or calcium carbonate. Teh addition of about 31 gms of the buffer salt to 50 kgs. of gam will generally change the pH about 0.1 of a unit.

The pH of the material has great influences on the inversion of sugar and the setting of jam of marmalade. The pH required to produce a good firm set in pectin jelly is 3.30 but in jams it varies with the kind of fruit used.

pH RANGE FOR DIFFERENT KINDS OF JAMS

TYPE OF JAM	PH RANGE	OPTIMUM pH
Apricot, Greengage, plum	3.2 - 3.5	3.35
Apple and Damson, Apple and plum	3.2 - 3.5	3.35
Apple and Raspberry	3.4 - 3.5	3.40
Orange marmalada	3.4 - 3.5	3.40
Gooseberry	3.4 - 3.5	3.40
Raspberry	3.5 - 3.7	3.60
Raspberry and Red Currents	3.5 - 3.7	3.60
Strawberry	3.7	3.7
Mango	3.3 - 3.6	3.4

MANUFACTURING PROCESS OF CHUTNEY

Apple Chutney

RECIPE - I	
Apple	18.1 kg
Sultanans	9.0 kg
Onion powder	226.7 g
Sugar	13.6 kg
Slat	28.3 g
Cassia, ground	28.3 g
Pimento, ground	28.3 g
Nutmeg, ground	14.1 g
Caramel	283.4 g
Acetic acid	0.9 kg
Malt vinegar	13.6 litres

RECIPE - II	
Apple	2.7 kg
Onions	to taste
Brown sugar	2.27 litres

Preservative sugar	2 heads
Cayenne (red chilli powder)	1/4 tea spoonful
Garlic	1/2 tea spoonful
Salt	3 tea spoonful
Vinegar	2 tea spoonful

Sweet Mango chutney

RECIPE

Peeled mango slices	0.9 kg
Sugar	0.9 kg
Slat	56.6 g
Mixed spices (cardamon, cinnamon, cumin etc. in equal quantities)	28.3 g
Garlic, chopped	6.0 g
Red chilli powder, finely ground	14.0 g
Vinegar	113.4 g
Onions, chopped	28.3 g
Ginger, green	113.4 g

Peach Chutney

RECIPE

Dried peaches	0.9 kg (equal to 4.5 kg of peeled peaches)
Onion	0.45 kg
Raisin	0.45 kg
Sultanas	0.22 kg
Cinnamon, powder	14 kg
Ginger, ground	14 g
Vinegar	1.1 litre

Plum Chutney

RECIPE

Plums, fully ripe	1.8 kg
Sugar	1.8 kg
Vinegar	0.45 kg
Mace (Jalvari) not ground	1 blade
Cloves (headless)	6 in number

Pepper, black, ground	10 in number
Chilli, Kashmiri, finely ground	7.0 g
Salt, finely powdered	14.1 g

Tomato Chutney

RECIPE	
Tomato	13.6 kg
Onions, chopped	9.5 kg
Sugar	18.1 kg
Salt	0.9 kg
Ginger	56.0 g
Chillies	14.1 g
Vinegar	20.4 litres
Garlic vinegar	9.0 litres

The chutneys are prepared from fruits, vegetables. The fruits or vegetables are cut into slices or pieces of suitable size and softened by boiling in water. Slow cooking at a temperature below the boiling point yields a better product than brisk heating at a comparatively higher temperature. Onion and garlic are added at the start to melow their strong flavours. Spices are coarsely powdered before they are added to the product. Sometimes a vinegar extract of spices is used instead of whole spices.

Sweet chutneys such as mango and apricot chutneys are generally cooked to consistency of Jam to avoid fermentation of product during storage. Where vinegar is used in large quantities, the amount of sugar reduce correspondingly because vinegar itself serves partly as a preservative.

Bottling

Only clean and dry bottles and jars earlier sterilized in boiling water should be used and they should be warm at the time of filling. If the bottles are jars are not properly clean, fermentation organisms adhering to the walls of the containers. It is safer to pasteurize the filled bottles after sealing them at 82°C for about 30 minutes in 0.45 or 0.5 kg size jars

PLANT ECONOMICS

Rated Plant Capacity = 416.66 BOTTLES/Day

LAND & BUILDING

Total land area 1000 sq.mt = Rs. 9,50,000.00

PLANT & MACHINERY

1. Screw type juice extractor made of aluminium & one sieve
2. Vacuum filling machine
3. Pulveriser/Grinder Machine
4. Pulper Super Deluxe
5. Steam Jacketed Kettle
6. Fruit Mill
7. Storage tank and mixing tanks
8. Drying/Heating/Dehydrator, Sturdily built fitted
9. Vacuum Tester
10. Working table stainless steel top
11. Boiler
12. Aluminium trays & trollies
13. Crown corking heavy duty
14. Bottle washing M/c.
15. Peeling knives made of stainless steel.
16. Fruit cutting knives
17. Fruit Cutting knives
18. Stainless steel knives, extra large
19. Sterlization tank with steam heating coil

FIXED CAPITAL

1.	Land & Building	Rs.	9,50,000.00
2.	Plant & Machinery	Rs.	4,01,760.00
3.	Other Fixed Assets	Rs.	1,25,000.00
	Total	Rs.	14,76,760.00

RAW MATERIALS

1. Pine Apple ripe
2. Mango Season,
3. Bamboo Shoot,
4. Citric Acid,
5. Lemon fully **pipe**
6. Sugar,

7. Pectin,
8. Common salt
9. Spices complete range
10. Chemical preservatives potassium metabisulfite sodium Benzoate etc.
11. Packaging materials Glass Bottle
12. Glass Bottle

TOTAL WORKING CAPITAL/MONTH

1.	Raw Material	Rs.	1,24,353.70
2.	Salary & Wages	Rs.	49,750.00
3.	Utilities & Overheads	Rs.	25,500.00
	Total	Rs.	1,99,603.70

TOTAL CAPITAL INVESTMENT

Total Fixed Capital	Rs.	14,76,760.00
Total Working Capital for 3 Months	Rs.	5,98,811.10
Total	Rs.	20,75,571.10

TURN OVER/ANNUM

By sale of 10,500 Bottle of 450 gm. Mixed Jam & Jellies
By sale of 21000 (250 gm) Bottle of Mixed Jam & Jellies
By sale of 10,500 (500 gm) Bottles mango pickles
By sale 21000 Bottles 250 gm) of mango pickles
By sale of 9000 Bottles (500 gm) of Mixed pickles
By sales of 18000 Bottles (250 gm) of Mixed pickles.
By sales of 9000 Bottles (500 gm) Bomboo shoot pickles
By sales of Tomato Products
(Ketchup, Sauces Etc.) 9000 Bottles
By sale of Squashes (Full range)
17077 Bottles of 650 ml each. Rs. 34,28,195.00

PROFIT SALES RATIO = Profit/Sales x 100 = 14.46%
RATE OF RETURN = Operating profit/T.C.I x 100 = 23.88%
BREAK EVEN POINT (B.E.P) = 64.45%

22

Lemon Juice Squash (Lime Squash, Cordials)

LEMON SQUASHES

Formulation - 1

(25 % Juice, 45° Brix, 1.5 % acidity)

Ingredients	(Kgs)
Lemon juice, 10° Brix 5 % acidity	45.4
Sugar	76.5
Citric acid	0.5
Water	57.5
Essence of lemon	1.300
Potassium metabisulphite	0.113

Formulation -2

(25 % juice, 65° Brix, 2 % acidity)

Ingredients	Kgs
Lemon juice (10° Brix, 5 % acidity)	45.4
Sugar	115.5
Citric acid	1.30
Water	26.50
Essence of lemon	1.30
Potassium metabisulphite	0.113

LIME SQUASHES

Formulation - 1

(25 % juice, 45° brix, 1.5 % acidity)

Ingredients	Kgs.
Lime juice 10° Brix, 6 % acidity	45.4
Sugar	76.5
Water	59
Potassium metabisulphite	0.113

Formulation - 2

(25 %, 65o Brix, 1.5 % acidity)

Ingredients	%
Lime juice	45.4
Sugar	113.5
Water	23
Potassium metabisulphite	0.113

LIME JUICE CORDIAL

Formulation - 1

(25 % juice, 35° Brix, 1.5 % acidity)

Ingredients	Kgs.
Clarified lime juice,10°Brix,6% acidity	45.4
Sugar	58.5
Water	77.1
Colour	q.s.
Potassium metabisulphite	0.113

Formulation - 2

(25 % juice, 50° Brix, 1.5 % acidity)

Ingredient	Kgs.
Clarified lime juice, 10o Brix, 6% acidity	45.4
Sugar	86.5
Water	50.0
Colour	q.s.
Potassium metabisulphite	0.113

PROCESS OF MANUFACTURING

Lemon Squash

European lemon, eureka lemon, and galgal are generally used for the preparation of lemon squash. Lemon squash requires addition of flavour to improve its taste.

Extraction of Juice

The tight skinned lemons are cut into halves with a halving machine having circular knife. The halves are pressed by rose fitted to a rosing machine.

These machines are of various sizes and capacities. The reamed juice is collected in a vessel. It contains plenty of coarse tissues, seeds etc. To remove these, it is filtered through a net cloth or passed through a sieving machine known as pulper, in which the juice gets brushed. The sieved juice is utilized for making squash.

Preparation of Squash

The above juice is taken in a stainless steel tank fitted with S.S. agitator/stirrer. Sugar, citric acid, flavouring materials, colour & preservative (potassium metabisulphite) are added to the juice in correct proportions.

Initially sugar, citric acid and water are mixed and heated. Any dirt is skimmed off. The syrup is cooled slightly and filtered through cloth. The clean syrup is blended with the juice. The edible colour, flavour also are added.

After mixing all the ingredients, the preservative, potassium metabisulphite predissolved in the little quantity of the juice or water, is added to squash.

The product is homogenized and packed in the sterile glass bottle with 1.2-2.5 cm head space. The bottles are then closed with crown corks or pilfer proof clousers, which have been dipped in 1 % potassium metabisulphite solution to sterilize them. The bottles are washed dried and labelled. Then packed in cartons and stored in a cool and dry place.

Lime Squash

Lime or kagzi nimboo is widely used for making lime squash. These limes are available in large quantities in Gujarat, Maharashtra, Andhra Pradesh, Karnataka, Tamil Nadu etc.

The fruit is cut into halves by means of halving machine. Then juice is pressed out by means of stone roller-type presses. Seeds are removed by sieving through cloth.

Sugar is first made into a syrup, which is filtered and added to the juice. The preserved squash is bottled as usual.

Lime Juice Cordial

Lime juice is extracted as above. It is stored in a large carboys or upright wooden barrels lined with microcrystalline wax. Fifty-six g of potassium metabisulphite is added to every 45 Kg of the juice to preserve it during storage. The juice settles gradually, and the sediment forms a compact layer at the bottom, leaving a clear juice at the top. This process takes 2 to 3 months. The clear juice is syphoned off. This method is rather slow and time-consuming. Clarification of the juice can also be achieved quickly by adding gelatin and tannin in proper proportion, based on preliminary laboratory trials. Sugar, water, colour, if necessary, and preservative are added to the clear juice, and the mixture is then filtered by means of a filter press. Filter aids are added in this process to facilitate filtration. The clear cordial is bottled as usual.

PROCESS FLOW SHEET

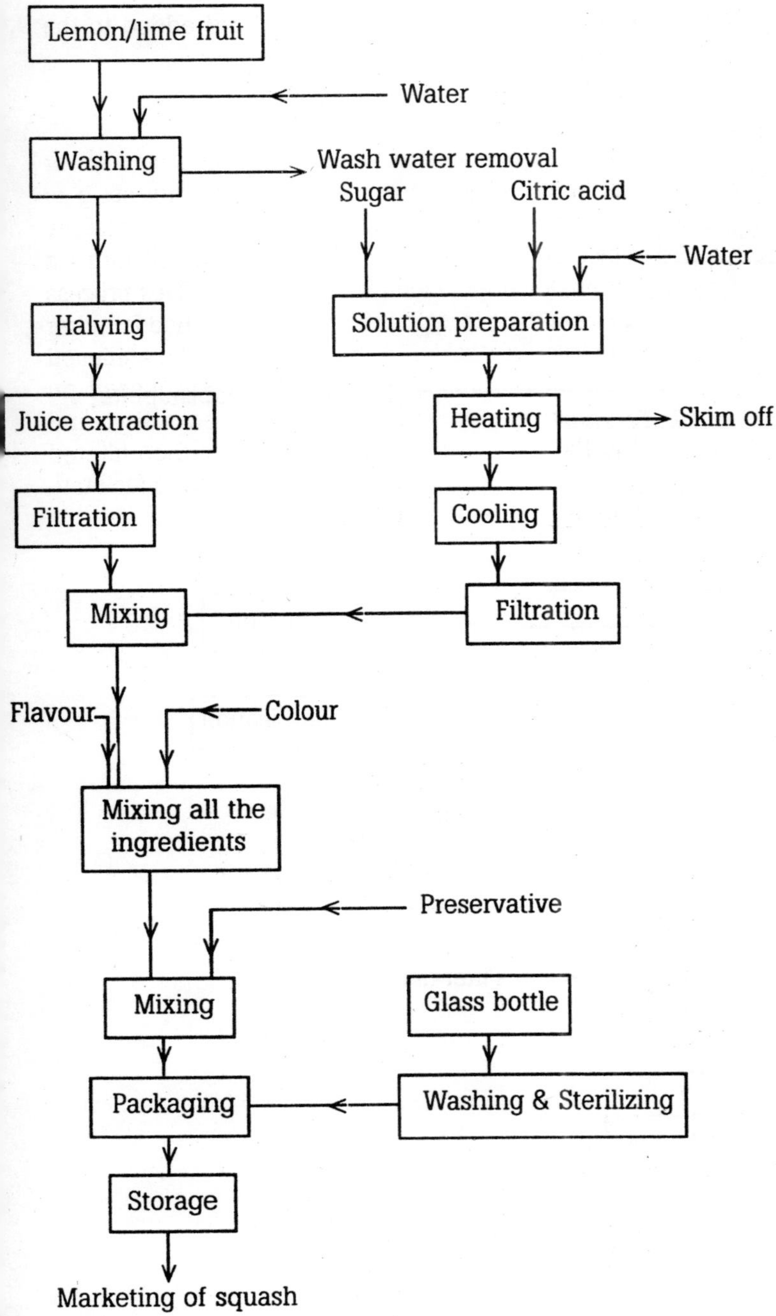

LIME JUICE CORDIAL

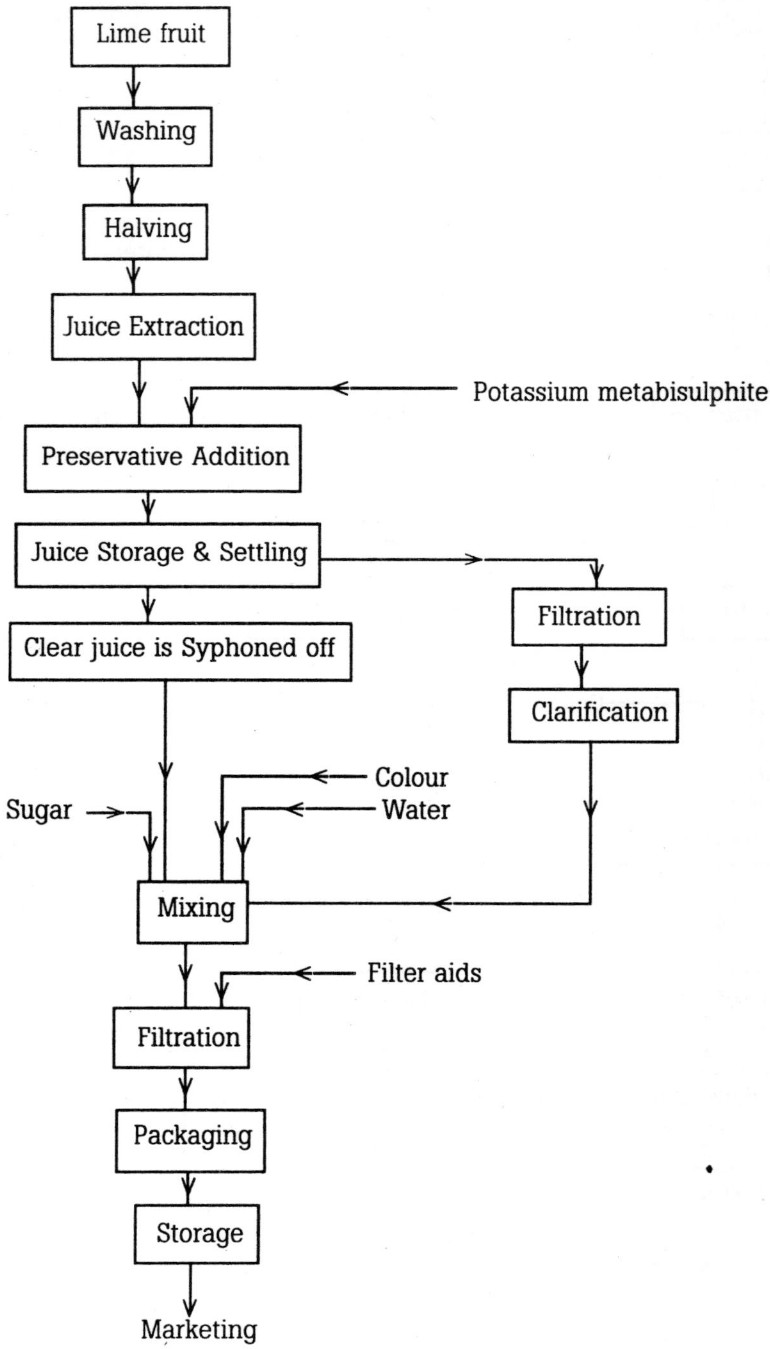

PLANT ECONOMICS

Rated Plant Capacity = 1000.00 KGS/Day

LAND & BUILDING

Total Land Area 500 Sq. Mt. = Rs. 10,75,000.00

PLANT & MACHINERY

1. S.S. Washing tank,
2. Halving machine
3. Ream type juice extractor
4. Plate & frame filter press (polypropylene plate)
5. Stainless steel tank
6. Stainless steel tank with stirrer, motor etc.,
7. Semi-automatic bottle filling & sealing machine
8. Laboratory equipment.
9. Pipes, pumps & fitting valves

FIXED CAPITAL

1.	Land & Building	Rs.	10,75,000.00
2.	Plant & Machinery	Rs.	12,10,000.00
3.	Other Fixed Assets	Rs.	8,00,000.00
	Total	Rs.	30,85,000.00

RAW MATERIALS

1. Lemon/lime fruit
2. Sugar
3. Citric acid
4. Potassium metabisulphite
5. Colour, essence
6. Glass bottle, & aluminium caps
7. Cartons, stickers
8. Adhesive taps.

TOTAL WORKING CAPITAL/MONTH

1.	Raw Material	Rs.	4,36,920.00
2.	Salary & Wages	Rs.	93,750.00
3.	Utilities & Overheads	Rs.	54,000.00
	Total	Rs.	5,84,670.00

TOTAL CAPITAL INVESTMENT

Total Fixed Capital	Rs.	30,85,000.00
Total Working Capital for 3 Months	Rs.	17,54,010.00
Total	Rs.	48,39,010.00

TURN OVER/ANNUM

By sale of lemon squash, lime squash
lemon juice cordials etc.
429000 bottle (700 ml), Rs. 1,15,83,000.00

PROFIT SALES RATIO = Profit/Sales x 100 = 28.33%

RATE OF RETURN = Operating profit/T.C.I x 100 = 67.81%

BREAK EVEN POINT (B.E.P) = 37.81%

23

Frozen Meat

PROCESS OF MANUFACTURE

All the sheeps are subjected to medical check up to be sure that they are free from any disease before they are slaughtered. The sheep is slaughtered by a sharp knife by removing half neck to cut the all the blood circulating nerves and vein and it is bled to death. Then the hides are removed. Before the viscera is removed they are again subjected to inspection by vetinary staff. Then the interior of the animal is thoroughly cleaned.

The quantity of field of dressed meat obtained per animal depends largely on its live weight, size and breed ,and also on topographical and climatic conditions. The average dressing yield in terms of the original live weight for indian sheep and goats calculated about 40% .

After the carcass of the sheep is divided into sides and quarters, it is further subdivided into recognised portions known as cuts. The bigger cuts, generally made at the points of articulation are known as joints. The value of meat depends to a great extent on the appearance and shape of these cuts. Mutton and goat meat cuts are the legs, loins, racks, breasts shank and shoulders. Besides the dressed meat certain parts of the carcass and their organs called offals are also sold as meat. Edible offals include tongue, sweet bread (pancreas) kidneys, heart, liver, tripe (the first and second stomach of cattle i.e. the rumen and reticulum), and tails.

In edible offals includes the hides, hair, bones, horns and hoofs. Blood and miscellaneous scraps of meat and fat may be used for both edible and inedible purpose.

Percent. For storing mear for long periods, frozen storage is used and the temperatures recommended are -23 deg to 18 deg. Meat may be frozen in whole carcasses, in large cuts or as consumer cuts. It is usually wrapped and packed in fibre board or wooden bases before freezing. The two methods of freezing and commercially adopted nowadays are blast freezing and plate freezing, the former being used for irregularly shaped items like material fast and are preferable to slow freezing of chilled meat in still air at -10 deg to 15 deg, since the drip on thawing and consequently the loss in soluble nutrients and consumer appeal, are much less in fast-frozen meat. Storage life of frozen meat and meat production kept at -18 deg is as follows: lamb, 6-16; liver, 2-4 months.

In India, raw meat is mostly sold fresh and is not ordinarily stored in any appreciable quantity while extensive cold storage facilities are available in western countries for the storage of meat and its products for long periods. Meat is sometimes stored for long periods. Meat is sometimes stored for 12-36 hr in ice during warm weather; mechanical refrigeration is resorted to only in major cities. Refrigeration results in the quick removal of body heat from the carcass and thus helps in slowing down rigor mortis and in achieving optimum preservative qualities .

Storage of meat at chilling temperature above the freezing point of meat (-2.2deg) is known as refrigerated storage and that below the freezing point as frozen storage is used and the temperatures recommended are -23 deg to -18 deg. Meat may be frozen in whole carcasses, in large cuts or as consumer cuts. It is usually wrapped and packed in fibre board or wooden boxes before freezing. The two methods of freezing and plate freezing, the former being used for irregularly shaped items like beef quarters and small carcasses and the latter for items of regular shape. Both these methods freeze the material fast and are preferable to slow freezing of chilled meat in still air at -10 deg to -15 deg, since the drip on thawing and consequently the loss in soluble nutrients and consumer appeal, are much less in fast-frozen meat. Storage life of frozen meat and meat products kept at -18 deg is as follows :lamb,6-16; liver,2-4 months.

Curing

Four methods are generally followed for curing meat, viz,

1) Sweet Pickle Curing
2) Dry Salt
3) Curing, dry curing
4) Injection curing.

Meat curing agents includes sodium chloride, nitrite, Ascorbate or erythorbate and possibly sodium phosphate, sucrose, dextrose, or corn syrup, and seasoning the salts content of processed meats varies 1-12 %, according to the type of product, salt is used for flavour,preservation and extraction of myofibriller protein, whereas nitrite per mole colour development, flavour and preservation by unhabiting the growth of microorganisms and fat oxidations. Erythorbate acts as color stabilizer, reduces fat oxidation, and inhabits undesirable.

Canning

Canned meat may be processed to be commercially sterile or semi-preserved. The objective of commercial sterilization is to destroy all harmful bacteria or bacteria that may cause spoilage of the products under normal unrefrigerated storage. However, the process does not kill the spores of all heat-resistant bacteria. Therefore, it is essential to cool the cans rapidly after processing and avoid storage above 33 deg C. The most persistant type of bacteria are performing organisms. The common vegetative and non performing pathogenic bacteria are killed with adequate processing and are of little or no importance in spoilage.

The amount of heat, time, and temperature required for a given degree of sterility depends upon the nature of the product, the pH, curing salts, shape and size of the can, and the type of heat-processing retort used. Some products are packed into the can hot and others cold. Hot filling eliminates the need to apply a vacuum during can closure. The vacuum is necessary to avoid excessive strain on the can and its seems during processing and to minimize oxidative spoilage of the product.

Semi-preserved or pasteurized products depend on during on curinga and chilled storage for their preservation.

Irradiations

Preservations of meat by irradiation methods is of recent introduction. The types of irradiations are known, viz, non-ionizing (making use of microwaves, inferred and ultra-violet rays),and ionizing (utilizing cathode and gamma rays). The former type has poor penetration characteristics, catalyses oxidative ranacity of the fat and causes discolouration of the meat pigments: bactericidal effect is obtained only with radiations near 2600 A. The use of the latter type of radiations otherwise known as cold sterlization, kills micro-organisms without producing heat but may cause some adverse effects like fat deterioration and unpalatable irradiation odours.

Irradiation doses lower than the sterilizing dosages are reported to be more practicable when used in conjunction with refrigeration, antibiotics and chemicals.

Nitrite reactions Phosphate facilitate myofibriller protein extraction, inhibit fat oxidation and improve colour development. Sugar and seasonings are used principally for flavour.

CONCLUSION

Large cut muttons are stored in freezer within the short period of time to change due to microorganism and enzymes. If the meat is to be kept for longer period, it should be frozen when the meat is thoroughly chilled it is then cut into suitable small pieces for packing into can. The prepared (cut dressed and trimed) meat is balanced if it is to be canned in brine to reduce or to kill the micro-organism. It is then filled into can and hot brine is filled upto the brim of the can. It is exhausted and sealed. The sealed cans are processed at 12lb pressure for a definite period of time depending upon the size of the cans.

PROCESS FLOW CHART FOR MUTTON PROCESSING

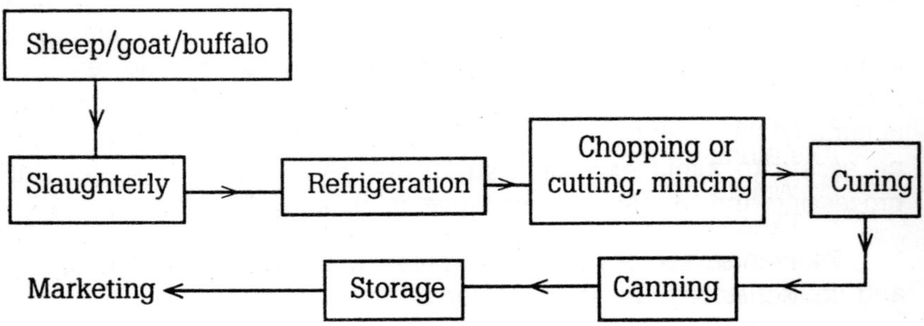

PLANT ECONOMICS

Rated Plant Capacity = 10.00 TON/Day

LAND & BUILDING

Total Land Area 2 acres = Rs. 51,10,000.00

PLANT & MACHINERY

1. Slaughtering equipments
2. Jet spray washing unit
3. Hangar made of Stainless steel
4. Electric rotating circular knife
5. Meat cutting and chopping machine
6. Jacketed Vessel (Stainless Steel)
7. Meat mincer
8. Bone separation Unit
9. Autoclave
10. Automatic weighing can filling and sealing unit
11. Weighing bridge
12. Exhaust Box
14. Preparation table stainless steel
15. Boiler
17. Conveyor Belt
18. Waste treatment Unit

FIXED CAPITAL

1.	Land & Building	Rs.	51,10,000.00
2.	Plant & Machinery	Rs.	33,01,000.00
3.	Other Fixed Assets	Rs.	18,30,000.00
	Total	Rs.	1,02,41,000.00

RAW MATERIALS

1. Buffaloes
2. Goats
3. Sheep
4. Packaging Materials
5. Chemicals, Preservative and salts, oils

TOTAL WORKING CAPITAL/MONTH

1.	Raw Material	Rs.	27,95,000.00
2.	Salary & Wages	Rs.	1,93,375.00
3.	Utilities & Overheads	Rs.	1,70,750.00
	Total	Rs.	31,59,125.00

TOTAL CAPITAL INVESTMENT

Total Fixed Capital	Rs.	1,02,41,000.00
Total Working Capital for 3 Months	Rs.	94,77,375.00
Total	Rs.	1,97,18,375.00

TURN OVER/ANNUM

By Sale of 3000 Tons of Processed Canned Meat — Rs. 6,00,00,000.00

PROFIT SALES RATIO = Profit/Sales x 100 = 29.05%

RATE OF RETURN = Operating profit/T.C.I x 100 = 88.39%

BREAK EVEN POINT (B.E.P) = 26.88%

24

Mango Processing & Canning (Mango Pulp)

MANGO PULP MANUFACTURING

The fruits of semi solid texture is taken and sorted by either manually or by automatic sorting machine. Then the fruits are washed either by detergent solution or clean water thoroughly to remove dirt, soils and other impurities sticking on the surfaces offruits. This washing or cleaning operation is followed by automatic washing machine or manually washed. The fruits are now ready for steaming operation. By steaming operation the fruits become soft. These are now passed through a pulper machine which is power driven and comprising of a perforated cylindrical sieve and revolving wooden or metallic paddles. The pulp passing through the sieve is collected in stainless steel or wooden barrels. The pulp is then Deacrated under vacuum of 27-28 ind. mercury pressure and heated in an vacuum pan evaporator at temperature 84-88°C. Then suitable preservative such as potassium metabisulfite (sulphur dioxide) or sodium benzoate at amount 350 PPM is added and mixed homogeniously. Then it is filled in sterilized cans, and the cans are passed through exhaust box heated with hot air. The cans are then sealed by double seaming machine. The sealed cans are pasteurized in boiling water for 15-35 minutes. After pasteurization process is complete the cans are taken out, cooled and stored in cool dry place. Then packed in cartons or cardboard boxes.

CHEMICAL PRESERVATIVES

The most common preservatives used in fruit juices are the potassium and sodium salts of sorbic, benzoin and sulfurous acids. The amount of sodium benzoate should not be greater then 0.1 wt% in any case and a common rate of addition of 0.08% may import an objectionable odour. Potassium metabisulfite, and potassium Sorbate can also be used as preservatives. Instead of a sulfite salt, So_2 can also be added as a gas (350-600 ppm) but So_2 must be removed before canning as it can be reduced by tin creating an H_2S odour and darkening the interior of the container.

The preservative used should be dissolved in a minimum amount of water before addition to juice to prevent the immediate precipitation resulting from its direct addition to juice it should be added after pasteurization.

LABELLING & CASING

Where production is small, labels are ordinarily applied to containers manually. Where labour costs are high, or where volume is large, the use of automatic labelling machine is necessary.

The containers are usually cased manually after labelling, the exception being in operations which produces large volume of a single container sizes. Automatic casers are not adjustable and therefore, usually confined to large volume operations. Glass containers are hard cased normally to prevent breakages.

STORAGE

All caned and glass packed mango juice are subject to a loss of flavour, colour and vitamins during storage.

The most acceptable storage is that in which the temperature remains nearly constant at about 70°F. These conditions should be maintained within commercial practibility.

QUALITY CONTROL

Consumers of food products are "brand" conscious and owners of established brands attempt to pack merchandise of uniform quality for this and other reasons.

In juice production where product is homogeneous less difficulty is achieving uniformity is encountered in many products. However in case of mango juice it is a bit difficult due to the numerous available variety of mangoes in market.

The flavour of juice is generally greatly dependent upon the acid and ugar present. Tests for these constituents are relatively easy to perform.

PLANT ECONOMICS

Rated Plant Capacity = 2.00 Tons/Day

LAND & BUILDING

Total Land Area 1000 Sq.mt. = Rs. 18,40,000.00

PLANT & MACHINERY

1. S.S. Tank for washing for mango
2. Pulp Extractor
3. Stainless Steel pulp collection tank
4. Dearator
5. Semi Automatic filling machine for can filling.
6. Boiler
7. Water Chiller
8. Can double seamer
9. Exhaust Box
10. Carton sealing machine
11. Conveyor Belt & elevators

FIXED CAPITAL

1.	Land & Building	Rs.	18,40,000.00
2.	Plant & Machinery	Rs.	23,60,000.00
3.	Other Fixed Assets	Rs.	6,50,000.00
	Total	Rs.	48,50,000.00

RAW MATERIALS

1. Ripe mangoes
2. Preservatives like sodium benzoate
3. Other like sugar, salt, flavours etc.

4. Cartons

TOTAL WORKING CAPITAL/MONTH

1.	Raw Material	Rs.	10,55,250.00
2.	Salary & Wages	Rs.	60,250.00
3.	Utilities & Overheads	Rs.	1,22,000.00
	Total	Rs.	12,37,500.00

TOTAL CAPITAL INVESTMENT

Total Fixed Capital	Rs.	48,50,000.00
Total Working Capital for 3 Months	Rs.	37,12,500.00
Total	Rs.	85,62,500.00

TURN OVER/ANNUM

By sale of 12,00,000 Nos. Cans of Mango Pulp (500 gms) Rs. 2,40,00,000.00

PROFIT SALES RATIO = Profit/Sales x 100 = 27.71%

RATE OF RETURN = Operating profit/T.C.I x 100 = 78.38%

BREAK EVEN POINT (B.E.P) = 33.65%

25

Pickles

Formulations & Preservatives for some important type of pickles

1. Apple Pickle:-

Recipe

A.	1.	Sour apples	1.8 Kgs.
	2.	Spritor cider vinegar	0.84 Litres.
	3.	Sugar	0.90 Kgs.
	4.	Cinnamon Stick	7.5 qm.
	5.	All Spices	1 Teaspoonful
	6.	Cloves whole	20 (in numbers)

Procedure : Peel, core and slice the apple place the slice in water to prevent their browning. Boil the vinegar, sugar and spices, for 5 minutes. Then add the slice and simmer the mass till the pieces become soft take out the fruit and pack into Jars. Reboil the vinegar and sugar to a syrupy consistency, pour it not on the slices and seal the Jars. It desired, spices may be added to the Jars.

2. Green Chilli Pickle

Recipe

1.	Green Chillies	500 grms.
2.	Tamarind	100 grms.
3.	Jaggery	100 grms.
4.	Corriander Leaves Salt, powdered red Chillies, mustard seeds.	Each two tea spoons
5.	Black gram dal	4 Tablespoon
6.	Turmeric Powder	0.25 Teaspoon
7.	Gingerlly Oil	0.25 Pint

Where 1 Pint - $4.732 \times 10^{-4} m^3$.

Procedure : Slice a hole in chillies taking core not to split them . Soak the tamarind in one pint of water for about half an hour. Finally strain the Juice.

Heat the oil and mustard seeds black gram and coriander leaves. Add green chillies and fry till chillies are dry. Add tamarind turmeric, chilli powder, salt and Jaggery. Simmer stirring constantly til liquid dries cool and preserve in air right Jar.

3. Mixed Vegetable Pickle :

Recipe :

1.	Turnips	4 lbs.
2.	Carrots	2 lbs.
3.	Cauliflower	1 lb.
4.	Garlic	4 lb.
5.	Green Ginger	100 grms.
6.	Onion	0.25 lb.
7.	Chilli Powder	2 table spoon.
8.	Garam Masala	1 table spoon.
9.	Jaggery	2 lb.
10.	Vinegar	0.75 Pint
11.	Mustard Oil	1 Pint
12.	Turmeric Powder	1 Tea spoon
13.	Ground mustard Seeds	1 Tea spoon
14.	Salt to taste	as per requirements.

Slice turnips into 0.25 inch. dises. Quarter corrots length wise and cut cauliflower into 2 inch. pieces. Boil water in a large sauce pan, add a the vegetable and cook for 5 minutes to soften. Drain of the water and spread on a clear towel to dry wipe off excess water.

Grind ginger onions and garlic together to a paste Heat oil and fry the paste add remaining spices and salt and fry till the oil floats to the pp. cool and add vegetables shake vessel to mix well put in a large jar and keelo in the sun for 2-3 days till vegetable turn a little sour shake the bottle well each day.

Heat vinegar will Jaggery and boil. Cool and add to the vegetables, place Jar in the sun for another two days till well blended and tender. Preserve in air tight Jars.

4. Mutton Pickle :

1.	Muttons	5 lbs.
2.	Ginger	1 lb.
3.	Onions	1 lb.
4.	Garlic	2 lbs.

5.	Mustard Oil	1.5 Pint
6.	Vinegar	1.5 Pint
7.	Cloves	15
8.	Cardamoms	12
9.	Nutmeg	0.75 tea spoon
10.	Salt	4 table spoon
11.	Chilli Powder	2 table spoon
12.	Ground Mace	1 table spoon
13.	Mango Powder	2 table spoon

Preparation :

Cut the meet into 1-5 inches cubes. Put in a large sauce pan to simmer without adding any water, till all liquid from the meat dries up keep on one side. Grind the onions, Garlic and ginger to paste. Heat oil and fry the paste till brown.

Add meat pieces, mix well and fry. Add 0.5 pint vinegar, all the remaining spices and cool for 5 minute stirring continuously remove from heat. Pour in remaining vinegar and cool. Put in air tight jars and keep for a week before use.

5. Mango Pickles

1.	Mango Slices	10 Kgs.
2.	Salt powders	2.5 Kgs.
3.	Methi Ground	1.25 Kgs.
4.	Kalaunji ground coarsely	
5.	Turmeric Powder	300 grms.
6.	Red Chilli Powder	300 grms.
7.	Aniseed	300 grms.

Preparation :

Mix the mango slices with the common salt powder place the mixture in a glazed Jar. Keep it in the sun for 4-5 days till the slices turn pale yellow. Then mix other ingredients with the slices and smear them with a little sarson (rape seed) oil. Then pack the pickle in a glass or glazed jar and cover with a thin layer of sarson oil the pickle will be ready in 2-3 weeks.

6. Turnip Pickle :

Sweet turnip pickle in oil are highly popular in India select sound turnips, preferably with a pink skin wash them thoroughly. Peel and slice them into pieces of convenient size. preferably 1/2 to 1/2 inch.

thickness.

1.	Prepared Turnip	10 kgs.
2.	Red Chillies	8 oz.
3.	Black Pepper	4 oz.
4.	Mustard	1/2 Kg.
5.	Spices (Caraway & Cinnamon)	2 oz.
6.	Dried dates	8 oz.
7.	Tamarind	8 oz.
8.	Ginger fresh chopped	8 oz.
9.	Onion fresh chopped	1 oz.
10.	Garlic chopped	4 oz.
11.	Salt	1 Kg.
12.	Vinegar	26 oz.
13.	Jaggery	1/2 Kg.
14.	Rape Seed Oil	1/2 Kg.

Blanch the turnip pieces for 5-6 minutes in boiling water chop the ginger, onions and garlic and fry then in a little oil soak tamarind and dates in water overnight. Prepare a thick extract of the tamarind by maceration and pass it through thin mustin cloth to remove. Seeds Removes the stones from the dates and slice them into small pieces. Grind black pepper, red chillies and all the other spices. Mix all these ingredients except gur and rap seed oil with the prepared turnip pieces. Fill the mass into the Jars and keep the letter in the sun for 5-6 days. Then add the gur in the form of a thick syrup and again place the Jar in the Sun for 3-4 days. Add the rape seed oil and pack the pickle in store Jars.

7. Cauliflower Pickle

1.	Prepared Cauliflower	20 kgs.
2.	Salt	1.25 kgs.
3.	Chilli Powder	0.75 kgs.
4.	Cumin	2 oz.
5.	Cloves	2 oz.
6.	Cardamom	1 oz.
7.	Cinnamon	2 oz.
8.	Ginger Green	2 oz.
9.	Onions chopped	0.75 kg.
10.	Mustard seeds	0.75 kg.
11.	Pape Oil Seed	2.25 kgs.

Take fully developed and compact heads of cauliflower. Remove the outer leaves and the central stalk cut the flowers into pieces, wash, drain and place them in the sun for 2-3 hours to remove surface moisture.

Take all spices except mustard and grind them into a fine powder fry them in the oil, when the spices turn brown add the cauliflower pieces and mix the whole mass thoroughly. When the cauliflower pieces turn slightly soft allow them to cool when the mass has cooled down to room temperature, add mustard and mix it thoroughly. Place the mixture in the sun for 5-7 days then add 2.5 kgs of vinegar and again place it in the sun for 3 more days.

8. Jack Fruit Pickle

1. Brined Jack Fruit slices	9.07 kgs.
2. Salt	0.56 kgs.
3. Chilli Powder	170 grms.
4. Cumin	28 grms.
5. Clove	28 grms.
6. Cardamom	14 grms.
7. Cinnamon	28 grms.
8. Dry Ginger	14 grms.
9. Onion chopped	283 grms.
10. Mustard Seed	28 grms.
11. Ginger Oil	1.12 grms.
12. Garlic	28 grms.
13. Vinegar	1.12 kg.
14. Sugar	1.12 kg.

Fry chopped ginger onion, garlic and mustard seeds in a little oil til they turn brown. Add these and the rest of spices to the Jack fruit slices and fill the mass into glazed Jars. Mix well and place the Jars in the sun for 3 to 4 days, stirring the mass occasionally. Add sugar and vinegar, again mix well and keep the Jar in the sun. The pickle will be ready in another into glass or glazed corthen Jars and pour sufficient oil an top to cover the pieces well.

MANUFACTURING DETAIL I.E. PICKLING PROCESS

Pickling Process

Pickling is done is two stages:- (i) By curing or fermentation with dry salting or fermentation in brine, or salting without fermentation; and (ii) by finishing and packing.

Dry Salting

In this method, the vegetable is treated with dry salt. The salt extracts the juice from the vegetable and forms the brine, which is fermented by lactic acid-forming bacteria. The method of dry-salting in general, is as follows.

The vegetable is prepared, washed thoroughly in running cold water, drained and weighed. For every 100 kg of the prepared vegetable, 3 kg of salt is used. The vegetable is placed about 2.5 cm. deep in the keg or barrel and is sprinkled with a small quantity of salt from the weighed amount. Another layer of the vegetable is added and again sprinkled with salt. The salt is added, layer by layer, in this manner till the keg is three-quarters full. Then one or two-folds of cheese cloth are spread over the salted vegetable, tucking in the cloth at the sides, and then placing a wooden board on the top of it. A clean stone, which is not acted upon by salt and organic acids, is placed on the board to press the vegetable so as to form a brine. Generally, a stone weighing about 4.54 kg will be sufficient in the case of a 22.10 litres keg. If necessary, additional weight may be placed, in case brine does not form after the material has stood for sometime. Generally, brine is formed in about 24 hours.

After packing the vegetable, the keg is placed in a warm and dry place and fermentation is allowed to proceed. In a short time, due to osmosis, juice from the vegetable forms the brine covering the whole mass. The weighted board helps to keep the vegetable submerged in the brine.

As soon as the brine is formed, fermed, fermentation starts and bubbles of carbon dioxide begin to rise from the liquid. Fermentation is usually completed in 8 to 10 days under favourable conditions which are attained in the temperature range of 27° to 32°C. In cold weather, however, it may take 2 to 4 weeks for the fermentation to be complete. When the fermentation is over, gas bubbles cease to form and rise. This may be confirmed by tapping the keg gently.

The product may now be preserved and kept by excluding air. If this is not done, 'pickle scum' a kind of wild yeast, appears on the surface. It soon destroys the lactic acid formed by fermentation with the result that the pickle is ultimately spoilt.

According to Round and Lang, air can be exhausted or expelled in the following manner:-

Method I. An air-seal on the surface of the brine can be made by pouring on top of it an edible oil-like rape seed oil or cotton seed oil. The oil, being lighter than the brine, floats on the surface and thereby prevents the access of air to the pickle below. A layer of oil about a 0.6 cm. thick is generally sufficient to keep the pickle indefinitely. The only drawback in this otherwise simple method is that the vegetable cannot be taken out from the container without getting covered with the oil. To overcome this, the oil may be removed from the surface by decanting, sysphoning or skimming, or by making it overflow by adding more brine to the deg.

Method II. After dry salting and fermentation, the barrel or keg is filled with the vegetable to its maximum capacity, and the cover replaced. A 1.25 cm hole is bored in the head. Then the barrel is filled to the brim with the brine so that very little air is left inside. It is allowed to stand for about 48 hours, or till such time that bubbles of gas cease to rise. If necessary, more brine is added at intervals to keep the barrel full. When the bubbling has stopped, the vent-hole is closed tightly and the barrel kept in a cool and dry place. The product packed in this manner will keep indefinitely.

Fermentation in Brine

Steeping of the vegetable in a salt solution of pre-determined concentration for a certain length of time is called brining. This type of treatment is adopted in the case of cucumbers and similar vegetables, which do not contain sufficient juice to form brine with dry salt.

Brine Preparation

Brine can be prepared by dissolving common salt in water and filtering it through jelly bags to remove insoluble impurities. The amount of brine necessary to cover the vegetable is usually equal to about half the volume of the material to be fermented. To be more precise, if a keg of 45.4 litres capacity is to be packed, the amount of brine required would be 22.7 litres. It is preferable to make the whole quantity of brine needed for the day in one lot.

Brining is the most important step in pickling. Although no set of conditions, ordinarily practicable in pickle-making will destroy or retard the growth of every kind of bacteria, yet the growth of a majority of them is checked in a brine containing 15 percent salt. Lactic acid bacterial, which are salt-tolerant, can flourish in a brine of 8 to 10 percent strength only.

Fermentation takes place fairly well in a brine containing approximately 5 percent salt (20° Salometer). In a brine containing appromixately 10 percent salt, fermentation proceeds somewhat slowly. To some extent fermentation takes place up to 15 percent also, but at 20 percent strength, all fermentation stops. It is, therefore, customary to place the vegetables in 10 percent salt solution to allow lactic acid fermentation to take place and then to increase the proportion of salt gradually, so that by the time the pickle is ready, salt concentration would have reached 15 percent level. It is to be borne in mind that vegetables contain a certain amount of moisture, which exudes from them in the presence of salt and lowers the strength of the brine. The brine strength can, however, be maintained by adding dry salt. The time required for proper fermentation is determined by experience.

Keeping Quality

Properly brined vegetables will keep well in vinegar for a long time. The duration of brining is of importance. If the vegetables are soaked for a short time of about 12 hours only, the curing of the vegetable tissues will be incomplete with the result that the pickle will not have proper textures and taste. Brining has, therefore, to be controlled properly. On curing, the vegetables become semi-translucent, and their colour changes from green to dark olive green or yellowish green. This is an indication of correct curing. This usually takes 4 to 5 weeks. By this method, the vegetables can be kept more or less for an indefinite period, provided the right storage conditions are maintained. If the vegetables is to be kept in brine of 10 percent or less, all air should be excluded from the containers. During curing, the vegetables lose their 'raw' flavour and become firm and crisp.

With salt. In this method, vegetables are packed with a large quantity of salt to inhibit fermentation. In practice, generally 25 kg of salt is mixed with every 100 kg of the prepared vegetables.

The cured vegetables are drained, and excess salt is removed by soaking them in cold or warm water, as may be necessary. After removing the salt, the vegetable are stored for several weeks in plain vinegar of 10 percent (100 grain) strength. This treatment reduces the tendency of the vegetable to shrivel when packed in sweetened and spiced vinegar and also helps absorption of vinegar by the vegetable tissues.

Spiced Vinegar. Spiced vinegar should always be kept ready so that it is available at the time of pickling. It is made as follows:-

Method I. The ground spices are soaked in vinegar and set aside for 2 to 3 months, stirring occasionally. The spices are then squeezed out, and the vinegar allowed to stand. When it has become clear, it is decanted or syphoned from the sediment.

Method II. The spices are boiled with the vinegar till the flavours are extracted fully. The extract is then filtered.

Method III. Essential oils of spices are used. This, however, does not always impart to the product the original aroma of the spices.

The kind and quantity of spices required depend upon the piquancy desired in the pickle. There are numerous recipes, each having its own adherants. A few of these are given here to serve as guidelines.

According to Poultney, sweet spiced vinegar is made as:

RECIPE

Sugar	213.1 kg
Clove, hole	4.9 kg
Coriander seed	5.8 kg
Mustard seed	7.2 kg
Cardamom seed	0.67 kg
Celery seed	0.56 kg
Ginger, whole	1.69 kg
Caraway seed	0.22 kg
Vinegar	227.3 litr.

The sugar is dissolved in vinegar by heating. The spices placed ir linen bags, are suspended in the vinegar. The batch is simmered gently for 6 hours and is then allowed to cool. The bags are removed and the vinegar filled into casks for storage.

According to him, spiced vinegar with essential oils is made as follows:

RECIPE

Oil of ginger	42 g
Oil of cloves	39 g
Oil of mace	8 g
Oil of coriander	85 g
Oil of mustard	49 g
Oil of cardamom	226 g
Oil of bay	28 g
Vinegar	908 litres.

The essential oils are stirred with the vinegar. For proper emulsification a little gum may be added. The oils may also be mixed with sugar and then dissolved in the vinegar.

According to Campbell, the following recipe gives a good spiced vinegar.

RECIPE

White vinegar (100 grains)	90.9 litres
Water	77.2 litres
Garlic	311g
Cayenne, finely ground	680 g
Cloves, headless, finely ground	1360 g

Mace, finely ground	226 g
Coriander, finely ground	1360 g
Mustard, finely ground	1360 g
Cardamom, finely ground	226 g
Bay leaves, finely ground	680 g
Caraway, finely ground	92 g
Ginger, finely ground	907 g

The spices should be leached in the vinegar for about a week.

Packing Methods

Pickled onions and mixed pickles should be packed finally into bottles or jars loosely so as not the damage the shape and appearance of the pieces. Fresh vinegar is then added to fill up the spaces between the pieces. The bottles or jars are then allowed to stand for a while, with the lids loosely on, covered again with more vinegar, if necessary and then closed air-tight. They are stored for a few days, the storage period depending upon the vegetable, etc., so as to ensure thorough absorption of the vinegar before the pickles are sent to the market.

Causes of Spoilage

Different kinds of spoilage occur in pickles. They are dealt with briefly in the following paragraphs.

Shrivelling

Shrivelling occurs when vegetables like cucumber are placed directly in a very strong solution of salt or sugar and even in very strong vinegar. To avoid this, weak solutions should be used to start with, increasing their strength gradually.

Bitter Taste

This results from the use of strong vinegar. It can also be caused by cooking the pieces for a long time and also by oversicing.

Blackening

This is caused by iron, which enters through the brine or from the equipment. Sometimes, specific organisms also cause blackening.

Dull and Faded Products

Pickles become dull and faded due to either insufficient curing or use of material of inferior quality.

Softness and Slipperiness

This is owning to the action of bacteria and is the most common form of spoilage. It is invariably owing to inadequate covering with brine or owing to the use of a weak brine. By using a brine of proper strength and by keeping the pickle well below the surface of the brine, this kind of spoilage can be eliminated.

PROCESS FLOW SHEET

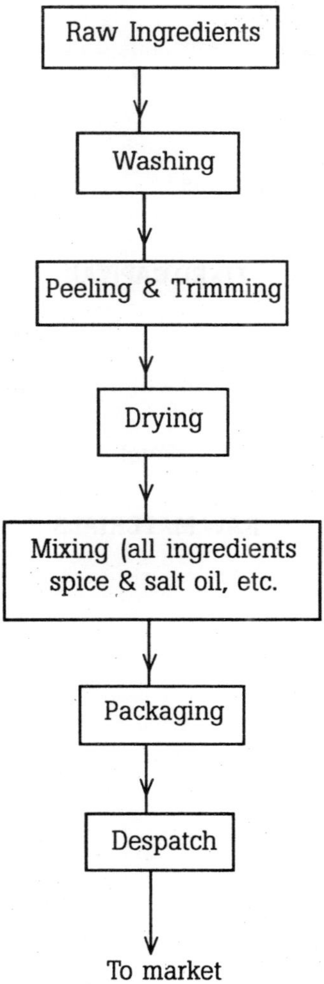

PLANT ECONOMICS

Rated Plant Capacity = 800.00 KGS./Day

LAND & BUILDING

Total Land Area 500 Sq. Mt. = Rs. 8,25,000.00

PLANT & MACHINERY

1. Fruit & Vegetables Washing tanks
2. Knives
3. Preparations Tables
4. Weighing balance
5. Chopping m/c
6. Grinder
7. Peeling & Cutting equipments.
8. Steam Jacked Vessels

FIXED CAPITAL

1.	Land & Building	Rs.	8,25,000.00
2.	Plant & Machinery	Rs.	2,85,000.00
3.	Other Fixed Assets	Rs.	1,13,500.00
	Total	Rs.	12,23,500.00

RAW MATERIALS

1. Mango
2. Mix Vegetable
3. Turnips
4. Jack Fruit
5. Apple
6. Green Chilli
7. Cauliflower
8. Muttan
9. Salt
10. Vegetable oil

TOTAL WORKING CAPITAL/MONTH

1.	Raw Material	Rs.	4,46,000.00
2.	Salary & Wages	Rs.	51,875.00
3.	Utilities & Overheads	Rs.	42,000.00
	Total	Rs.	5,39,875.00

TOTAL CAPITAL INVESTMENT

Total Fixed Capital	Rs.	12,23,500.00
Total Working Capital for 3 Months	Rs.	16,19,625.00
Total	Rs.	28,43,125.00

TURN OVER/ANNUM

By Sales of 800 X 300 = 2,40,000 Kgs.
per Annum Rs. 96,00,000.00

PROFIT SALES RATIO = Profit/Sales x 100 = 25.96%
RATE OF RETURN = Operating profit/T.C.I x 100 = 87.66%
BREAK EVEN POINT (B.E.P) = 30.23%

26

Processed Food

MANUFACTURING PROCESS FOR FRUIT JUICES

1. CLEANING:

Any species of fruit like those under the mandrin orange group from which juice is to be extracted after peeling can be simply cleansed by means of a rotary washer. Those citrus fruits from which juice is extracted by reamer without peeling are cleansed more scruplously, i.e. in two stage, by rotary brusher.

2. WARMING TREATMENT :

The second rotary washer is used as warm water tank, because fruits are easily peeled if they are warmed. In this case, temperature and warming time should be properly adjusted so that the temperature of warming treatment is so soften the peel only.

3. PEELING :

Warmed fruits with peels are received on a trimming table, on which they are peeled by female workers.

4. JUICE EXTRACTION :

Peeled fruits are cut into two or four pieces. Then the juice is extracted out of them by popular and finisher, with extraction yielding 40-50 per cent.

When they are put under extraction by reamer, fruits with peel are cut into two pieces of about the equal size, and the manually done so by applying them to the reamer head.

5. PRE HEATING:

Extracted juice is heated to about 90°C for the purpose of making inactivate enzyme and bacteria contained in it, and then is cooled down to about 40°C.

6. CENTRIFUGALIZATION :

Extracted fruit juice which contains a considerable amount of pulp is applied to the centrifuge for the purpose of re-separation of pulp. it is to be noted, however, that juice containing some amount of pulp has a better demand in which case pulp is of course left without being re-separated.

7. DEAERATION :

Fruit juice when applied to the pulper, finisher and centrifuge, is mixed up with a considerable amount of air. Therefore, it needs be dearrated to prevent the juice from bad effect to be caused after wards by the air. The suitable vacuum in the dearator is 60-100 mm Hgabs.

8. SEASONING :

Bottled soft drinks on the market are usually comprised of pure juice properly diluted and seasoned with essence colours, activators, citric acid, sweetenings, etc. in the proper degree.

9. STERILIZATION :

Fruit juice is before being canned or bottled, sterilized at a temperature of 90°C-95°C for 30 seconds, and then it is canned or bottled while it is hot.

10. FILLING INTO CANS :

Sterilized hot juice is delivered to the juice filler, whereby it is canned in No.2 cans or No.3 cans.

11. SEAMING OF CANS :

Cans filled with juice are delivered to the seamer, vacuum seamer in this case, by which they are seamed.

12. COOLING :

Seamed cans are cooled next for 3-5 minutes by the rotary cooler and are taken out of it. If the cans are excessively cooled, water drops are sometimes formed on the surface when they are exposed to the open air. Therefore, they need be taken out at the most appropriate degree of temperature.

The temperature is to be determined properly according to the atmospheric temperature, humidity etc.

13. MARKING ON CAN LIDS :

Can lids are to be impressed with marks by can maker beforhend.

14. LABELLING AND BOXING :

When printed cans are not used lables are affixed to the cans on their side, and 2 dox of No. 2 cans are packed in a box storage and delivery to the market.

SQUASHES :

Squashes are juices which are sweetened and have more fruit pulps. The squashes are prepared from all varieties of fruit by mixing strained juices with filtered heavy sugar syrup to contain about 35-40% sugar in the finished products.

MANUFACTURING PROCESS FOR SAUCES & KETCHUP

Sauce of any fruit can be prepared but the most popular sauce. It is also used as chutney. Manufacturing process of all varieties of fruits sauces is almost similar.

First, the fruits are peeled, sliced, and ground. The spices, and other additives are added. Thickening agents also are added to prevent or retard sedimentation of the solid particles in suspension. In India, apple pulp is often used for this purpose. Sometimes, the fruit, which is used for making sauce, is boiled pulped as a filler. The starches of maize potato, arrowroot, sago and rye also are used as thickening agents. The use of Indian gum locust, kernel gum tragacanth, karaya gum, gelatin, irish moss, pectin and other similar substances is also advised. These are however, as good as the starches.

Formula for Tomato Sauce:

Tomato pulp (6% soluble solids)	29.250 Kgs.
Cardamom, pepper and cumin in equal quantities	8.5 gms.
Cinnamon, broken	10 gms.
Cloves, headless	8.5 gms.
Mace	5.7 gms.
Salt	5.7 gms.
Onions, chopped	154 gms.
Garlic ground	18 gms.
Sugar	2.140 Kgs.
White vinegar 100 grain	580 c.c.
Red Chilli powder	15 gms.

It is cooked to about half its volume i.e. about 28% solids, Eng point is determined by refractometer. It is filled into plain cans and processed for 45 min in boiling water.

CHILLI SAUCE

To 22.4 kgs. of peeled tomatoes, add 1 kg. of sugar 10 gm. of red chillies 0.9 Kg. of washed, peeled finely chopped onions, and the following spices tied loosely in a cloth bag.

Mace	7 gms.
Cinnamon broken	18 gms.
Cumin cardamom and black paper in equal quantities	22.5 gms.
Ground white paper	10 gms.
Ground ginger	10 gms.

Cook the whole mass in steam :- jacketed kettle to about 25.2 Kgs. crushing tomatoes with a ladle, if necessary. Add 2.14 Kgs. of kgs. of sugar and 0.675 Kg of salt and 1.57 Kgs (100 grain) vinegar. Continue the cooking of the mass further for about 5-10 minutes after which pack immediately in plain a cans seal and sterilize for half an hour in boiling water.

TOMATO KETCHUP

Ketchup is a product obtained from properly prepared strained tomatoes with spices, salt, sugar and vinegar. The ketchup is made directly from the raw tomato pulp but it can be prepared from tomato paste, as the raw material, prepared elsewhere. In many case only clean wholesome tomatoes of intense red colour and of meaty not watery textury should be used for the purpose. High acidity and rich tomato flavour are the additional desirable qualities. Tomatoes are washed sorted, trimmed, cut and pulped.

The juice is then in some cases concentrated to 1.06 sp gravity, IN some plans, the juice is directly mixed with ingredients and then cooked. In majority of plants the partially concentrated pulp of 1.06 sp gravity is heated to boiling in open stainless steel or glass lined kettles, and cooked a short time final desired solid content with the required quantities of salt, vinegar, onion powder or chopped raw onions and a mixture of certain spices.

PLANT ECONOMICS

Rated Plant capacity = 10000.00 Bottle/Day

LAND & BUILDING

Total Land Area 2000 Sq. Mt. = Rs. 30,08,000.00

PLANT & MACHINERY

1. Hammer Mill
2. Neutralising vessel, equipped with jacket, agitator etc.
3. Filtration press
4. S.S. Lining mixers equipped
5. Pressure storage tanks & Sealing
6. Automatic bottling machine
7. Cooling/Conditioning Units
8. Clarification Vessels
9. Centrifuges
10. Evaporators
11. Deaerator
12. Pasteurisation units
13. Spray Drier
14. Motor pipes
15. Boilers
16. Generator

FIXED CAPITAL

1.	Land & Building	Rs.	30,08,000.00
2.	Plant & Machinery	Rs.	25,31,000.00
3.	Other Fixed Assets	Rs.	5,50,000.00
	Total	Rs.	60,89,000.00

RAW MATERIALS

1. Fruits
2. Sugar
3. Citric Acid

TOTAL WORKING CAPITAL/MONTH

1.	Raw Material	Rs.	12,21,750.00
2.	Salary & Wages	Rs.	1,42,500.00
3.	Utilities & Overheads	Rs.	1,66,000.00
	Total	Rs.	15,30,250.00

TOTAL CAPITAL INVESTMENT

Total Fixed Capital	Rs.	60,89,000.00
Total Working Capital for 3 Months	Rs.	45,90,750.00
Total	Rs.	1,06,79,750.00

TURN OVER/ANNUM

By Sale of 30,00,000 Bottles of Squash/Year — Rs. 3,00,00,000.00

PROFIT SALES RATIO = Profit/Sales x 100 = 28.28%
RATE OF RETURN = Operating profit/T.C.I x 100 = 79.45%
BREAK EVEN POINT (B.E.P) = 35.32%

27

Tomato Products Manufacturing
(Tomato Sauce, Ketchup, Tomato Puree & Tomato Powder)

MANUFACTURING PROCESSES

TOMATO PRODUCTS

Tomato Juice, Ketchup, sauce and soup, and chilli sauce are some of the important products made from tomatoes. The method of preparing these are described below :

TOMATO JUICE

For this product, only plant-ripened tomatoes should be used. All green, blemished and over-ripe fruits should be rejected as they adversely affect the quality of the pack. Juice made from over-ripe tomatoes is usually thin and unpleasant in taste and aroma.

The Yield, colour and flavour of the juice depend on the ripeness of tomatoes, the variety used and the place where grown. The following points should be kept in view to ensure good quality of the juice :

1. The juice should be of deep red colour. As the red colour in tomatoes is contained in the fibres, as much of the fibrous portion as possible should be incorporated in the juice.

2. The juice should have the characteristic flavour of tomatoes.

3. The acidity of the juice should be about 0.4 percent.

4. The vitamins present in fresh tomatoes should go into the juice. Their retention depends on the method of extraction employed. It has been found that while carotene is fairly resistant to heat and oxidation in the various processes of preparation. Vitamin C is lost appreciably, particularly during the screening of the juice, due to oxidation.

5. For uniformity in quality, either the tomatoes used should be from one stock and place or the juice should be suitably blended.

WASHING THE TRIMMING

More rinsing of tomatoes in water in not enough, because mould filaments and other micro-organisms, found in their cracks, wrinkles, folds and otem cavities, are not easily dislodged. For through cleaning, they should be washed in running water. For work on a large scale, rotary washers are used.

Great care should be taken in trimming. The loss on account of trimming etc. as worked out In India, various from 4.0 to 17.0 percent. With an average of about 8.0 percent. This heavy wastage is largely due to the absence of standard varieties and defects in picking, transport and marketing of the produce.

CRUSHING

After trimming, tomatoes are out into small pieces before boiling. Alternately, they may be crushed by means of wooden roller-crushers.

PULPING

Tomatoes can be pulped by the hot or cold process described below :

HOT PULPINGs

The crushed tomatoes are boiled in their own juice in steam jacketed kettles or aluminium pans for 3-5 minutes to facilitate pulping. The process has the following advantages;

1. The tendency of the juice to separate into liquid and pulp can be overcome if the natural pectin present in the seeds and the skin can be incorporated. During boiling, the pectin is released, and this thickens the pulp. The ectase enzymes, which would otherwise hydrolyse the natural pectins present in tomatoes and make the juice thin, are also destroyed during boiling.

2. Heating sterilizes the juice partly thereby checking to some extent the growth of living organisms which cause fermentation, etc. It also inactivates the oxidatie enzymes which destroy Vitamin C.

3. A light cooking release the colour present in the skin.

4. The yield of juice is higher than in cold to satisfy the market demand. The flavour of the cold-pulped juice is much sharper and more acidic. This is due to the pressure applied in this process whereby the juice surrounding the seeds which is richer in acid and poorer in sugar than

the other portions of the tomato is extracted first. On account of this, the cold-break juice is also of lighter consistency than that obtained from hot pulping. It has, however, a good fresh flavour.

EXTRACTION OF JUICE

There are two types of extractors in use, the continuous spiral press and the cyclone.

CONTINUOUS SPIRL PRESS

This consists of a long spiral screw which presses the tomatoes against a tapered screen of fine mesh having 25 holes per linear inch, each hole with a diameter of 20/1000 of an inch. The juice passes through the screen while the skin and seeds are expelled at the other end of the machine. When these machines are open.

COLD PULPING

The tomatoes are crushed and passed as such through a pulper. This process has the following defects:

1. As compared to the hot process, the extraction of juice is somewhat difficult. The yield also is smaller.

2. Air gets incorporated in the juice in the process of extraction and oxidizes Vitamin C there are, however, machines available now-a-days which considerably eliminate the mixing-up of air.

3. The juice extracted by this process in somewhat light in colour.

4. The process has to be finished quickly to avoid spoilage, especially during the initial stages of preparation.

Recently, Penfold has pointed out that pulping gives a juice whose flavour and consistency are different from those of the hot-break juice. The manufacturers have, therefore, to decide about the type most likely operated at a speed of about 250 revolutions per minute, there is little or no incorporation of air in the juice. The tomatoes passing through the hopper should have a jet of steam playing on them to prevent oxidation and destruction of the vitamins.

TOMATO PUREE

Concentrated tomato pulp without skin or seeds, with or without added salt and containing not less than 8.37 per cent. of salt-free tomato solids, is called 'Medium tomato puree'. If it is further concentrated so that it contains not less than 12 per cent, solids, it is called 'Heavy tomato puree'.

PREPARATION

The first step is the preparation of tomato pulp. This is made from plant ripened tomatoes in the same manner as tomato juice.

PULP CONCENTRATION

Concentration of the pulp is done in two types of vessels, namely, (i) open cookers and (ii) vacuum pans.

OPEN COOKERS

For work on a small scale, aluminium patilas will do. For large-scale production, glass-lined tanks or made of stainless steel, monel metal or nickel and fitted with flash coils are used. The open pan method although employed generally, has obvious disadvantages. During boiling, the juice comes into contact with the he oxygen of the air which not only destroys the Vitamin C in it, but also makes the juice brown. Lal Singh and Girdhari Lal have pointed out that unless special equipment is used to prevent the incorporation of air during the entire manufacturing process, a considerable loss of vitamin C takes place. Buytter or an edible oil is added to the juice during boiling to prevent it from foaming. boiling-over, sticking or burning. Incidentally it also helps in lessening oxidation. This method has now, however, been superseded by the vacuum pan method which gives a product of superior quality.

VACUUM PAN

The installation of a vacuum pans is rather expensive. Its main advantage is that the juice can be boiled at a much lower temperature, i.e. at about 160°F., thus helping in the retention of the original colour and flavour of the tomatoes to a marked degree. As air also is removed during boiling, there is very little likelihood of oxidation or Vitamin C losses. In order to sterilize the product, the vacuum is broken towards the end and the temperature raised to 212°F. for about 10 minutes.

PULP CONSISTENCY

The processes used for concentration of tomato pulp are as follows :

METHOD 1

The pulp is poured into the boiling pan till the heating coils are covered. Heating is then commenced more juice is added and the heating continued6 till the pan is full of pulp. Heaving is then stopped and the total solid content of the pulp is determined. If the solid content is higher than the required percentage, more juice is added to lower it : if it is lower, concentration is continued till the desired consistency is reached.

Manufacturers find this method easy to follows.

METHOD II

In this case, a known volume of the juice is concentrated to a known volume of the finished pulp. The juice is let into the boiling tank and, when the coils have been covered, heating is started and the tank is filled to capacity. Heating is continued till the pulp begins to boil vigorously. Steam is then shut off momentarily and the volume of hot pulp is measured with a measuring rod. Then a small sample is drawn for determining the tomato solids by the specific gravity method. While the determination of the solids is being done, boiling of the pulp in the pan is continued. By making use of standard Tables the pulp is boiled to the desired specific gravity. Since both the original and final measurements of volume are taken at the boiling point, temperature correction is not necessary or the reading.

THE END POINT

The total solids in the juice, at the start, during cooking and at the finishing point can be determined either with a specific gravity hydrometer or with an vacuum at 70°C. In practice, the first two methods are used as they are simple.

PACKING

Puree can be packed in plain as well as in enamelled cans. The cans are usually filled with scalding-hot puree at 180°F - 185°F and sealed without exhausting. Sixteen-ounce cans are processed at 212°F for 20 minutes. Larger cans are not generally processed, the temperature of the hot puree itself being sufficient for sterilization.

TOMATO PASTE

A concentrated tomato juice or pulp, without seeds and skins and containing not less than 25 percent of solids, is known as tomato paste. If the pulp is further concentrated so as to contain 33 percent. or more of tomato solids, it is called concentrated tomato paste. Common salt, basil leaf or sweat oil of basil leaf also may be added. Part of its acidity may be neutralised with sodium bicarbonate or carbonate. Ordinarily tomato juice can be concentrated to about 14-15 per cent. Tomato solids in open pans, but for higher concentration, vacuum pans are necessary. The initial concentration is generally carried out in open pans and the product is finished in vacuum pans.

Since the product is very thick, the total solids are determined by an Abbe refractometer.

TOMATO COCKTAIL

Tomato cocktail is gaining popularity in may high class hotels and restaurants. It is prepared just before serving and is also served from stock. In the latter case, the cocktail is preserved by pasteurizing it in bottles. Recipes may differ, but the main constituent is tomato juice to which common salt, vinegar, Worcestershirs sauce, lemon or lime juice, tabasco sauce, etc. are added in different proportions to suit the palate. Two typical formulas are given below :

FORMULA 1

Tomato Juice (Sp. Gr. 1.020)	10 lb.
Cloves (headless), whole	1.5 gm
Cumin, Black peeper and cardamom in equal quantities	4.5 gm.
Cinnamon, broken	1.5 gm.
Coriander seeds	1.5 gm.
Red chillies, Kashmiri (finely ground)	0.25 gm.
Vinegar (10 percent acetic acid)	10 oz.
Common Salt	45 gm.

Simmer the tomato juice with the spices loosely tied in a cloth bag for about 20 minutes in a covered vessel and then add lime juice, vinegar and common salt.

FORMULA II

Tomato juice (sp. Gr. 1.010)	10 lb.
Cloves (headless), whole	1.5 gm
Cumin	1 gm.
Black Pepper	1 gm.
Cardamon	1 gm.
Red Chillies, Kasmiri (finaly ground)	0.25 gm.
Ginger	1.5 gm.
Lime Juice	1.5 oz.
Vinegar (10 percent. acetic acid)	7.5 gm.
Common salt)	45 gm.

TOMATO KETCHUP

Tomato ketchup is made by concentrating tomato juice or pulp without seeds and pieces of skin. Spices, salt sugar, vinegar, onions garlic etc, are added to the extent that it contains not less than 12 percent tomato solids and 28 percent. total solids.

RAW MATERIAL

Select only sound ripe tomatoes of deep red colour. Cut off all green and yellowish portion. Green fruit should not be used as it will made the ketchup inferior in colour and flavour.

JUICE EXTRACTION

The juice is extracted in the same manner as in tomato juice or puree.

JUICE STANDARDIZATION

The raw juice is a thin water fluid and its specific gravity varies with the kind of fruit and the duration of boiling. It follows, therefore, that spices have to be added each time in varying proportions. This would, therefore, hot yield a standard product. Standardization can be achieved by using a recipe for juice of 1.0220 specific gravity (filtrate of pulp of 5.66° Brix). Keeping the other ingredients constant, and equivalent amount of juice of any other specific gravity can be coveniently added.

RECIPES

There are several recipes which give good ketchup. Recipe I given by Lal Singh and Girdhari Lal, with slight variation has become popular with the manufacturers in this country. the remaining three recipes are popular in other countries.

RECIPE I

Tomato Juice (Sp. Gr. 1.022 - 1.027)	6 gal.
Onions, chopped	375 gm.
Garlic, chopped	25 gm.
Cloves, whole, headless	10 gm.
Cardamom	4 gm.
Black pepper	4 gm.
Zira	4 gm.
Macc (Jalvatri), not ground	2.5 gm.
Cinnamon (broken)	17.5 gm.
Vinegar, 6% acetic acid	2.5 lb.
Sugar	2.0 gm.
Salt	312 gm.
Red Chillies	12.5 gm.

TOMATO SOUP

In preparing tomato soup, the first step is to make tomato pulp, in the same way as for tomato juice. The main constituents of this soup are : tomato juice, butter or cream, spices, arrowroot (a thickening agent) etc. These are added in various proportions to suit the taste.

The following typical formula yields a good soup :

Tomato juice (Sp. Gr. 1.0220)	7 gal.
Onions, finely chopped	13 oz.
Cinnamon, broken	5 gm.
Cloves whole, headless	5 gm.
Ground white pepper	7 gm.
Red chillies, ground (Kashmiri)	0.7 gm.
Cumin (Zira) cardamom and black pepper in equal quantities	5.3 gm.
Ginger dry ground	4.2 gm.
Cream (30 percent) or butter butter	1 1/4 lb or
Arrowroot starch	4 1/2 oz.
Sugar	17 oz.
Common Salt	1 1/2 oz.

PREPARATION OF TOMATO SAUCE

For the preparation of tomato sauce following recipe should be used.

TOMATO PULP

PREPARATION

Neutralize about 1/6 acidity of the juice by adding a thin paste of sodium bicarbonate made with water. Place 6 gallons of the juice in a boiling pan and heat it. While it is being concentrated, add spices tied loosely in a muslin bag as is done in the case of tomato ketchup. In the meantime, mix arrowroot and butter (or cream) with the remaining one gallon of juice to form a smooth paste. When the juice in the pan gets concentrated, add this mixture. Again boil to the desired consistency, stirring it continuously to prevent clotting of the starch, etc. At the end, add sugar and boil the mixture for about about two minutes to dissolve them. Fill the soup into cans.

STERILISATION

Sterilize at 240°F for 45 minutes in the case of A 2 cans and for 40 minutes in the case of 1 lb. milk or jam-size cans. Cool quickly after processing.

TOMATO SAUCE

PREPARATION OF TOMATO SAUCE

For the preparation of tomato sauce following recipe should be used.

Tomato pulp (6% Soluble Solids)	29484 gm.
Cardamon, Pepper and Cumin (Zir) in equal quantities	8.5 gm.
Cinnamon, broken	10 gm.
Cloves (head less)	8.5 gn.
Mace (not ground)	5.7 gm.
Common Salt	700 gm.
Onions (chopped)	200 gm.
Garlic ground	18 gm.
Sugar	2500 gm.
White Vinegar (100 grain)	580 c.c.
Red Chilli powder	15 gm.

Took the above ingredients in a kettle, heat it by steam to make a paste like product until it contains total soluble solids around 25% by refractometer.

When the product contains soluble solids around 25%., then stop steaming put the recipe in the packaging system for packing, then store and sale in the market.

PROCESS FLOW SHEET FOR SAUCES

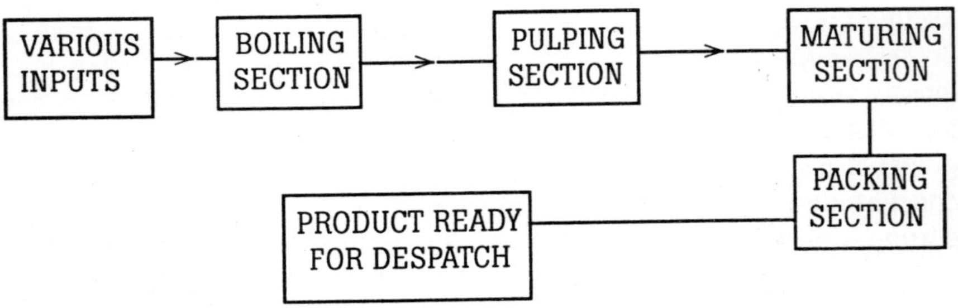

PLANT ECONOMICS

Rated Plant Capacity = 1100.00 PAC/Day

LAND & BUILDING

Total Land Area 195 Sq. Mt. = Rs. 5,32,000.00

PLANT & MACHINERY

1. Vertical Boiler
2. Hydraulic Juice Press,
3. Pulper
4. Juice Presturizer,
5. Steam Jacketted Kettle
6. Sterilization Tank
7. Super Crown Corking Machine
8. Rotary Fruit &Vegetable Washing Machine
9. Aluminium Trays
10. Storage And Mixing Tanks (S.S.)
11. Platform type weighing scale
12. Automatic Pouch filling machine
13. Automatic Pouch and Ketchup filling
14. Bottle Washing Machine
15. Vacuum filling machine
16. Portable stirrer
17. Preparation Tables
18. Testing equipments & Instruments
19. Blanching Equipment
20. Stainless steel peeling
21. Fruit and Vegetables Slicer
22. Fruit Crater,

FIXED CAPITAL

1.	Land & Building	Rs.	5,32,000.00
2.	Plant & Machinery	Rs.	9,17,500.00
3.	Other Fixed Assets	Rs.	1,60,000.00
	Total	Rs.	16,09,500.00

RAW MATERIALS

1. Tomatoes
2. Sugar
3. Chemicals/Salts spices
4. O.T.S. Flattened
5. Empty glass bottles
7. Crown Corks
8. Plastic Caps
9. Labels
10. Cardboard Boxes
11. Pouches

TOTAL WORKING CAPITAL/ANNUM

1.	Raw Material	Rs.	12,10,384.00
2.	Salary & Wages	Rs.	6,21,000.00
3.	Utilities & Overheads	Rs.	3,18,400.00
	Total	Rs.	21,49,784.00

TOTAL CAPITAL INVESTMENT

Total Fixed Capital	Rs.	16,09,500.00
Total Working Capital for 3 Months	Rs.	5,37,446.00
Total	Rs.	21,46,946.00

TURN OVER/ANNUM

By sale of Tomato Juice in 1,30,000 of 200 ml pouch pack
Tomato pure in 1,00,000 Pack 200 gms/pack
Tomato ketchup 1,00,000 pack 500 gms pack Rs. 37,15,000.00

PROFIT SALES RATIO = Profit/Sales x 100 = 22.46%
RATE OF RETURN = Operating profit/T.C.I x 100 = 38.87%
BREAK EVEN POINT (B.E.P) = 57.00%

28

Details of Plant & Machineries

1. TUBULAR PASTEURISER

For pasteurisation of the cashew apple juice from embient temperature to 90°C. The pasteuriser is consisting of bundle of stainless steel tubes, suitable jacketed with m.s. jacket. The unit is complete with necessary fittings.

Capacity	:	500 litres/hour.
Electric power	:	1 H.P.
Quantity	:	1

2. BOTTLING LINE-30 BOTTLES/MIN. OF 200 ML.

(a) 4 - Head Bottle Washer with Soaking Tank

The unit will be supplied with a suitable motor. A small s.s. tank is fitted on the machine for soaking of the bottles prior to the washing. A rinsing unit will be provided, having twelve rinsers with the machine for rinsing of the bottles after brushing. The unit is complete with motor and starter.

Capacity : 30 bottles per minute of 200 ml. Size depending upon the type and quality of the bottles and efficiency of the operator.

Electric Power	:	0.5 H.P.
Quantity	:	1

(b) ROTARY BOTTLE WASHING MACHINE

As per the detailed specification enclosed

Quantity : 1

(c) SEMI AUTOMATIC BOTTLE FILLING MACHINE (4 HEAD TYPE)

As per the detailed specification enclosed

Quantity : 1

(d) **SEMI AUTOMATIC CROWN CORKING MACHINE**

Semi automatic corking machine for crowning of the bottles. The unit will have a feed hopper, motor and starter.

Electric power	:	0.25 H.P.
Quantity	:	1

(e) **SLAT BAND CHAIN CONVEYOR**

With oxidised m.s. slats. The conveyor is suitable for inter-linking the above three machines. The conveyor will be with m.s. angle frame and will be driven with fixed drive of 1/4 h.p. Necessary inspection lights will be provided for inspecting the empty/filled bottles.

Quantity : 1

3. GOOSENECK ELEVATOR

Gooseneck elevator for elevating the product. The buckets of the elevator are of high density polypropylene with stainless steel side straps linked up with stainless steel rod. The height of the elevator from the ground level is approx. 3300 mm.

Electric power	:	1H.P.
Quantity	:	1

4. III WAY INSPECTION AND MANIPULATION CONVEYOR

As per the detailed specification enclosed.

Quantity : 1

5. PLATE & FRAME FILTER PRESS

Quantity : 1

6. FILLED BOTTLE STERILISER

Quantity : 1

SPECIFICATION

ROTARY BOTTLE WASHING MACHINE

Construction : The machine is arranged for left hand feed, having two mild steel side tanks. One for hot detergent solution and the other for hot water. Painted with alkali and rust resistant paint. The machine is provided with automatic device for centering jets underneath the bottle necks. Hot water and detergent tanks are provided with removable filter through which hot water and detergent water pass through before recirculation. The detergent tank only is fitted with suitable steam heating coils with suitable connections.

The total travel cycle is of 2 minutes 40 seconds and considering this travel cycle, capacity of the bottle washer will be upto 30 bottles per minute, depending upon the efficiency of the operator.

Operation : The new bottles or pre-soaked and rinsed used bottles are inverted over the holders by the operator and moved through the successive stages of washing and are treated with hot detergent water, hot water and cold water respectively from internal and external jetting. In the final rinse the bottles are washed from inside and outside with fresh water (to be supplied by the buyer at approximately 25 psi pressure at the bottle washer inlet). External steam ejector manually controlled will be provided for final rinse so that the bottles in final wash are washed with hot water at approximately 60°C.

Electric Power	:	2 HP.
Steam Consumption	:	For normal working, steam consumption is approximately 275 lbs per hour at 50 lbs/sq. inch pressure.
Water requirement	:	13 Imp. gallons per minute.
Capacity	:	30 bottles per minute depending upon the size, type and quality of the bottles.

SPECIFICATION

SEMI AUTOMATIC BOTTLE FILLING MACHINE

4 Head type, semi-automatic, Vacuum Filling Machine, suitable for handling bottles from the range of between 200 ml. juice bottling and 750 ml. squash round bottles. The machine is suitable for filling free flowing products like fruit juices based beverages, squash, ketch-up etc. and is also suitable for filling he product at 85°C. The valves in the machine are of go up and down by rotation so that except for manual operation of putting the bottles on the platform, all other operations are automatic. The valves as well as the platform are connected to a vacuum cum compressor pump through a manifold. The stainless steel liquid tank is at the bottom of the machine and is mounted on the machine and is provided with S.S. valve with glass interceptor. All metal contact parts are in stainless steel. The level in the liquid tank is controlled automatically by means of a float valve.

The machine will be provided with a water ring vacuum pump. This pump will be mounted outside the machine and will therefore, add to the overall dimensions.

Capacity : Upto 30 bottles per minute depending upon the size of the bottles, product to be filled and the efficiency of the operator.

Electric Power : 5 HP.

SPECIFICATIONS

3 WAY INSPECTION AND MANIPULATION CONVEYOR

3-way inspection conveyor, generally as per our G-A. drawing G/STD/42. The conveyor bely is food quality PVC coated belt - 900 mm wide X 10,000 mm long centre to centre distance and is driven by driving and driven rollers. The conveyor belt is supported on idler rollers to avoid sagging. The conveyor is also provided with an arrangement throughout its length on both the sides to enable operators to discharge waste material which falls on return side of the conveyor. The waste material on return side is collected at one end. The conveyor is provided with scrapping with spring loaded arrangement, brushing with spring loaded arrangement and fresh water spraying arrangement to keep the belt clean. The unit is complete with stainless steel feed hopper and discharge chute. The flat surface of the conveyor will be divided into 3 lanes. outer 2 lanes are for the material to be inspected and the centre lane is for the inspected and prepared material. The conveyor is designed to avoid spill, over of fruit pulp from sides. The unit is complete with motor and starter.

MACHINERIES USED FOR CANNING

Canning Retort
Available in 21, 90, 200, 300, 425 A2½ cans capacity

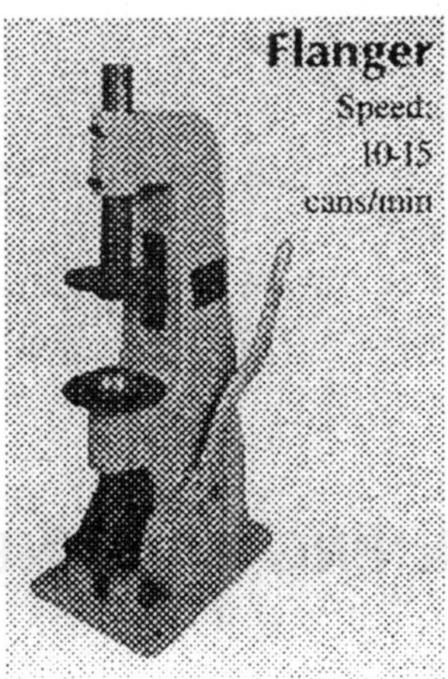

Flanger
Speed: 10-15 cans/min

Double Seamer BM 1 ADS
(Can Rotary Type)

Speed:
10-15 cans/min

Rotary Flat Can Body Reformer

Speed:
10-15 cans/min

BM Canning machines are designed to handle cans of the following specifications:

Can dia:	Max. 7 inches	Min. 2 inches
Can height:	Max. $9^{3/8}$ inches	Min. 7/8 inches

CANNING MACHINES

JUICE EXTRACTION EQUIPMENT

Fruit Mill

Available in following models:

C115	Junior	0.5 T/hr.	1 HP
C117	Senior	2.0 T/hr.	3 HP
C119	Twin	2.0 T/hr.	5 HP

C117

C 119

Rosing Machine

Available in 2 and 4 head models

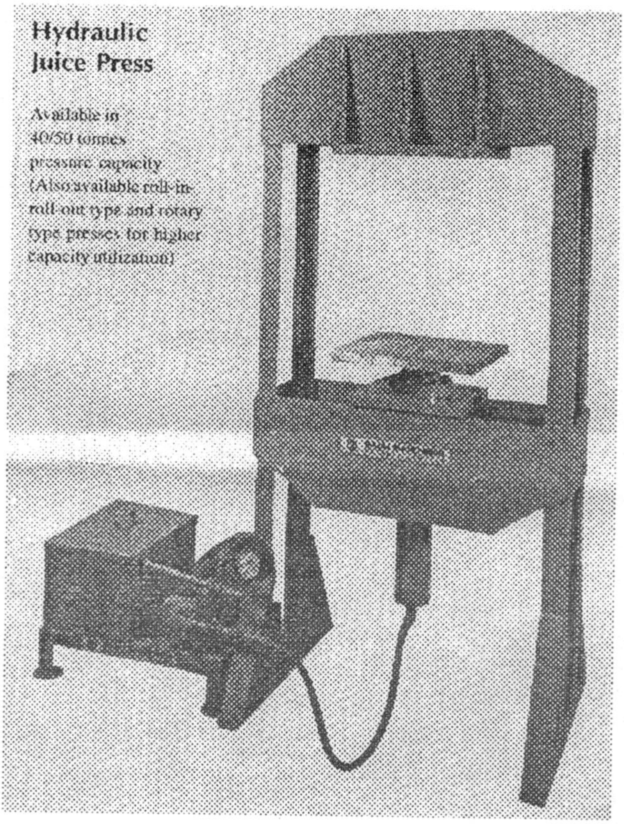
Hydraulic
Juice Press
Available in
40/50 tonnes
pressure capacity
(Also available roll-in-
roll-out type and rotary
type presses for higher
capacity utilization)

Screw type
Juice
Extractor
Available
in
¼, ½
and 1 HP
motor
model

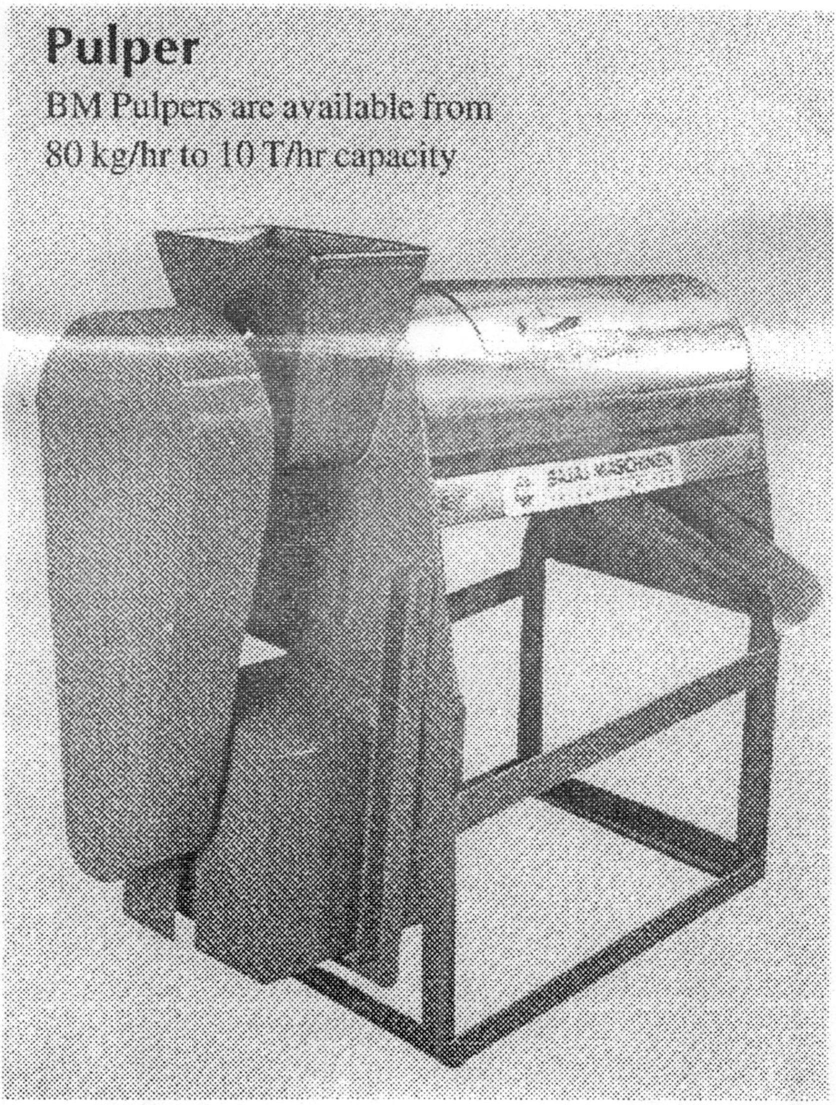
Pulper
BM Pulpers are available from
80 kg/hr to 10 T/hr capacity

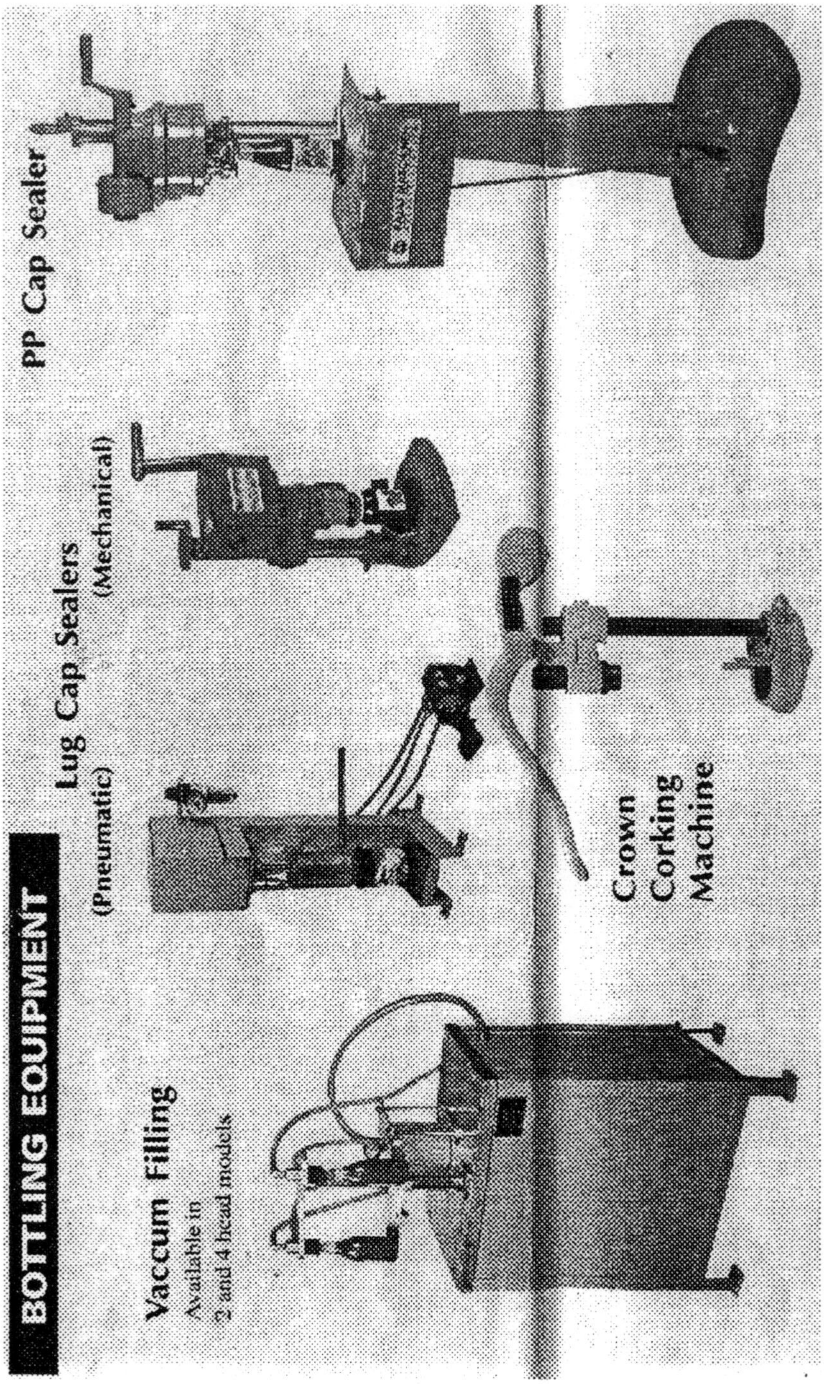
BOTTLING EQUIPMENT
Vaccum Filling
Available in
2 and 4 head models
Lug Cap Sealers
(Pneumatic)
(Mechanical)
PP Cap Sealer
Crown
Corking
Machine

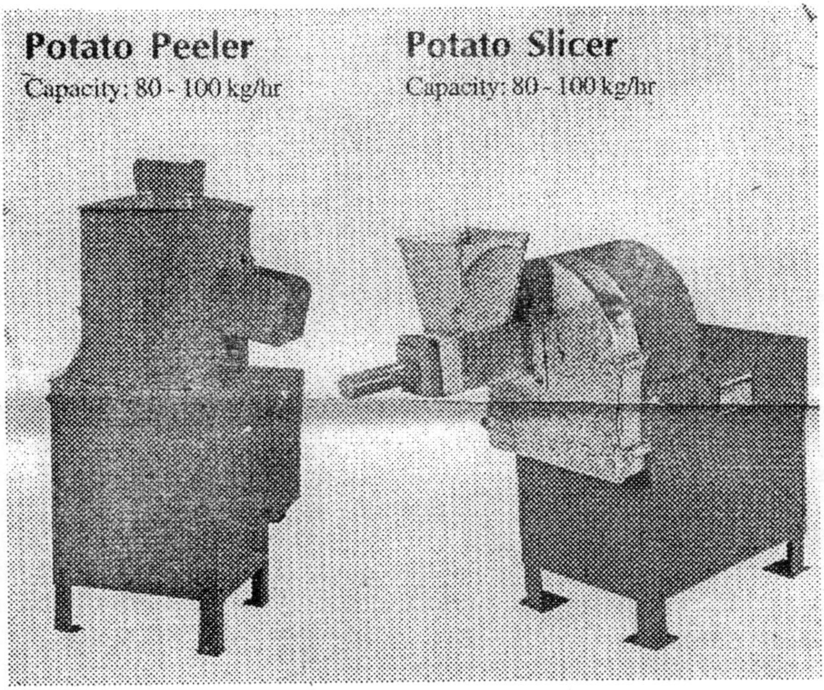

EFFLUENT AND DISPOSAL

The waste disposal in a non-urban plant does not pose much of a problem since the waste produced in such factories are organic and of a highly biodegradable in nature. The liquid effluents in such plants where there are no public drainage system can discharge the effluent after slight treatment into land where it can be used for irrigation purposes.

The waste from this fruits and vegetable processing plant generally consists of two types ; (1) Solid waste and (2) Effluents.

(1) Solid Waste

The solid wastes are peels, seeds, fibres etc. If these are thrown around it will harbour flies and also starts smelling after sometime. It is therefore, in the interest of maintaining sanitary conditions inside the factory it is desirable that these are properly disposed off away from the factory. These are dried in the yards and used for manure purposes. It may, therefore, be seen that the waste disposal do not pollute the area.

(2) Disposal of Effluents

The effluents in this factory consists of three types

(a) Effluent which could be recycled. This is normally used for cooling the sterilised cans and can be recycled and will not go into the drainage system.

(b) Wash water for pre-cleaning of fruits to remove dirt and adhering packaging material like straw leaves etc. Since this water does not contain any soluble solids, it will be just sufficient to filter off suspended solids and use it straight away for irrigation purposes.

(c) Plant clean up : At the end of every day's operation the plant has to be cleaned up and this water will generally contain some small quantities of pulp, fibre and may contain small amounts of soluble solids. The total solids would about 11,000 to 12,000 ppm are suspended solids and about 2000 PPMdissolved solids. The pH will vary anywhere from 6.0 to 6.9. The B.O.D. of this also is very low. This water will contain only edible matter and is not of the nature of effluents obtained in chemical and other processing factories which can be toxic. Since the suspended solids are higher than the soluble solids it will be just sufficient to screen the suspended solids either by filtration or adding coagulant to sediment the suspended solids and the clear effluent used for irrigation purposes.

Disposal of waste water which is not acidic or alkaline would not pose any problems. It is therefore proposed that the entire effluent coming from the factory is filtered and suspended solids removed before the effluent is let into the fields. The suspended solids after filtration and sun drying could be used as manure.

We therefore, propose, that this factory will have as settling tank for collection of the effluent for sedimentation purposes and sufficient space to sun dry the solid waste matter, which can be subsequently used as a manure.

Courtsey : *Bajaj Maschinen Pvt. Ltd., New Delhi.*

29

Suppliers of Plant and Equipments

Jwala Techno Engineering Pvt. Ltd.
Mr. Rahul Paharia (Director)
C-1/4, Tarapur MIDC, Camlin Road,
Boisar, Thane - 401506,
Maharashtra, India
Mobile: +(91)-9820197764
Tele: +(91)-(22)-65703038
+(91)-(22)-65702548
Fax: +(91)-(22)-26862622

Aguapuro Equipments Private Ltd
Mr. Jitendra Rane (Director)
416/417, Jogani Industrial Complex,
Building No. 9, V. N. Purav Road,
Chunabhatti,
Mumbai - 400022, Maharashtra, India
Mobile: +(91)-9987154980
+(91)-9004618072
+(91)-9870078929
+(91)-9821078929
Tele: +(91)-(22)-24052813
+(91)-(22)-24052814
+(91)-(22)-24052816
Fax: +(91)-(22)-24052813
Email: jcr@aguapurosystems.com
jitendra.rane@aguapuro.com
sales@aguapurosystems.com

Repute Engineers Private Limited
12/23 D-1 Block MIDC Chinchwad,
Pune - 411 019. Maharashtra, (India)
Tel. No: +(91)-(20)-27481687
Mobile: +(91)-9422020943
Telefax : +(91)-(20)-27481368
Email : info@reputeindia.net
Visit Us : www.reputeindia.com

Shiva Engineers
Mr. Arun Kulkarni (CEO)
T- Block, Plot No.- S 33,
MIDC, Bhosari,
Near Pavana Industrial Complex
Pune - 411026, Maharashtra, India
Mobile: +(91)-9822499586
+(91)-9011021839
Tele: +(91)-(20)-27129610
+(91)-(20)-27127104
Fax: +(91)-(20)-27127104
Email: shivaengineers1@gmail.com

Deepak Engineers
Mr. Sunil Gaiwal (Proprietor)
Hengade Building, 3rd Floor,
Behind Santosh Mangal Karyalaya,
Santosh Nagar, Thergaon
Pune - 411033, Maharashtra, India

Mobile: +(91)-9552251400
+(91)-9975152732
Tele: +(91)-(20)-27277663

Dhanvanthri Engineers Pvt. Ltd
Mr. Anil Athri / Mr. Vivek (Director)
A- 440, TTC Industrial Area,
Mahape MIDC,
Off Thane-Belapur Road, Navi Mumbai - 400710,
Maharashtra, India
Mobile: +(91)-9819058905
+(91)-9611225432
+(91)-9820081661
Tele: +(91)-(22)-27781891
+(91)-(22)-27781918
Fax: +(91)-(22)-27782536

Sujay Industries
Mr. K. S. Jayarama / Mr. Sudhir Kumar
Shed No. A-267, 6th Main,
2nd Stage, Peenya Industrial Estate
Bengaluru - 560058,
Karnataka, India
Mobile: +(91)-9845195720
+(91)-9845201201
Tele: +(91)-(80)-28362210
+(91)-(80)-28362211
Fax: +(91)-(80)-41171329
Email: Info@sujayindustries.com
jayarama.ks@gmail.com
sujayind@airtelmail.in
foodfab@gmail.com

Bimal Water Solutions
Mr. Barun Kumar Singh (Proprietor)
D - 64, 1st Floor, Sector - 10
Noida - 201301,
Uttar Pradesh, India
Mobile: +(91)-9958547779
+(91)-9310068423
Tele: +(91)-(120)-4562520
+(91)-(120)-4232520

YSM Biotech International
Mr. S. M. Mishra (Managing Partner)
UL - 30, EF - 3 Mall, Plot No.-12,
Sector - 20 A, Faridabad - 121006,
Haryana, India
Mobile: +(91)-9810005609
+(91)-9990016952
+(91)-9990016153
Tele: +(91)-(129)-2220669
Fax: +(91)-(129)-2220669
Email: info@ysmbiotech.com

Eskimo Refrigeration Industries
Mr. Anil. S. Upalaikar (CEO)
S. No. 85/1, Shree Shankar Nagar,
B-Building, Ground Floor, Poud Road,
Kothrud, Pune - 411038, Maharashtra,
India
Mobile: +(91)-9822403226
+(91)-9822206070
Tele: +(91)-(20)-25381934
+(91)-(20)-25382124
Fax: +(91)-(20)-25381934

Mech - Air Industries
Mr. Sandip Shah (CEO)
3/16-A, BIDC Industrial Estate Gorwa,
Vadodara - 390016, Gujarat, India
Mobile: +(91)-9428507684
+(91)-9426416803
Tele: +(91)-(265)-2285751
+(91)-(265)-2290728
Fax: +(91)-(265)-2291613

Aguapuro Equipments Private Limited
Mr. Jitendra Rane (Manager)
416/417, Jogani Industrial Complex,
Building No. 9, VN Purav Road,
Sion Chunabhatti, Mumbai - 400022,
Maharashtra, India
Mobile: +(91)-9987154980
+(91)-9322247922
+(91)-9870078929
Tele: +(91)-(22)-24052813
+(91)-(22)-24052814

+(91)-(22)-24052816
Fax: +(91)-(22)-24052815
Email: rashmy.rane@aguapuro.com
sales@aguapurosystems.com,
jcr@aguapurosystems.com

Guru Engineers
Mr. Raj Kumar Patil (Proprietor)
Plot No. 232,
Sector - 10, P. C. N. T. D. A.,
Bhosari, Pune - 411026,
Maharashtra, India
Mobile: +(91)-9822230912
+(91)-9890862251
Tele: +(91)-(20)-66126051
Email: guruengineers9@gmail.com

Santosh Engineering & Fabricators
Mr. Ram Naval Yadav (Proprietor)
A. No. 33, Bhandup Industrial Estate,
Pannalal Silk Mill Compound,
Bhandup West,
Mumbai - 400078,
Maharashtra, India

Mobile: +(91)-9820423150
+(91)-9867360172
Tele: +(91)-(22)-25962117
+(91)-(22)-67038334
Fax: +(91)-(22)-25962117

Pennwalt LimitedMr. Ravi Khosla
D- 221, M. I. D. C , T. T. C.
Thane- Belapur Road, Nerul,
Mumbai - 400706, Maharashtra, India
Mobile: +91-9833525208
+91-22-27632503
+91-22-27632644
+91-22-65166631
http://www.pennwalt.com

Clean Green Biosystems
Dr. S. Prem Mathi Maran (CEO)
No. 2872, Sun Shelters,
Susheela Nagar,
1st Street, Kovilambakkam
Chennai - 600117, Tamil Nadu, India
Mobile: +(91)-8056126827
Tele: +(91)-(44)-64627337

ALL FOLLOWING PROJECT REPORTS ARE READILY AVAILABLE

- Condenser For Motor Using Mpp Film
- Control Panel Board
- Cooling Coil For Air Conditioners
- Copper Strip Coil From Scrap
- Cordless Telephones
- Cyber Cafe
- Cyberkiosk
- Data Processing Centre
- D.C. Micro Motors
- D.G.Sets
- Display Systems (Led Type)
- Dish Antenna And Cable T.V. Network Equipment
- Distribution Transformers & Repairs
- Domestic Electrical Appliances-Room Cooler, Washing Machine, Water Heater, Electric Room Heater
- E-Commerce/Business
- Electric Energy Meter
- Electric Fans
- Electric Horn For Automobile
- Electric Lamp/Gls (Incandescent Lamp)
- Electric Mixer
- Electric Motors Up To 10 Hp. Rewinding Of All Types Of Motors Water Pumps
- Electric Motor Winding (For Fan, Mixies, Etc.)
- Electric Steam Iron
- Electrical Appliances
- Electrical Fixtures
- Electrical Stamping
- Electrolytic Capacitors
- Electromagnetic Relay
- Electronic Balast/Chok
- Electrical Choke
- Electronic Digital Watches
- Electronic Digital Weighing Machine
- Electronic Fire Alarm
- Electronic Gas Stove Lighters
- Electronic Phones, Dry Battery Packs And Chargers/Adapters
- Electronic Pressure Indicators, Electricals, Electronic Liquid Level Indicators, Electronic Temperature Indicator, Digital Tachometer
- Electronic Telephone Instruments
- Electronic Toys
- Electronic Watches & Clocks
- Fax Machines
- F.H.P Motors
- Floppy Diskettes
- Fluorescent Lamp Starter
- Fluorescent Tubular Lamps With Introduction To Mercury Vapour Lamp
- Franchisee Computer Education Centre (Rs. 10000)
- Gas Detector (L.P.G)
- Generator Set & Pump Sets
- Generator (Battery Operated)
- Gis Service Centre (Geographical Information Systems)
- Hardware Fitting For Transmission Line (Overhead Line Material
- Headers For Transistor Ics Semi Conductor
- H.T & L.T Insulators
- H.T & M.V Industrial Cubical Switch Board
- Information Moving Display (L.E.D Type)
- Insurance Claim Processing Centre (Eou) (Rs. 10000/-)
- Integrated Circuits
- Internet Based Stock Trading (Rs. 10000/-)
- Internet Service Provider (I.S.P.)
- Jelly Filled Telephone Cables
- Lap Top Computers
- Lead Acid Batteries
- Lead Acid Battery Plates And Assembling Of Battery
- Legal Transcription & Secretarial Services Center (Eou)(Rs. 15000/-)
- Light Emitting Diodes (L.E.D)
- Linear Ics Trainer Kit
- Loud Speaker
- L.T Transformer Repairing
- Medical Transcription Centre
- Metal Film Resistors
- Metallised Polypropylene, Polyester Film Capacitor
- Mica Base Electronic Components
- Mica Paper Waste Paper From Mica Waste
- Micro Processors Trainer Kits Based On Micro Processors
- Mini Computer (Personal Computer)
- Miniature Circuit Breaker (M.C.B)
- Miniature Watch Batteries (Button Cell)
- Mixer/Grinder (Mixi)
- Mono Chrome Computer Monitor
- Motor Start Electrolytic Capacitor
- Multi Layer P.C.B
- Multiple Relay For Low Voltage
- Neon Indicator
- Neon Sign Manufacture
- Optical Fibre Cables
- On Line Shopping Mall (Rs. 10000/-)
- Opto Mechanical & Electrical Equipments
- Photo Colour Lab
- Picture Tube (B/W)
- Plain Paper Copier
- Plastic Film Capacitors
- Polyester Capacitors
- Portable Generator Set
- Portal
- Portable Television(Tv)
- Power Capacitors

- Power Inverters
- Power Plant (Gas Based)
- Fower Plant (Hydro Based)
- Power Transformers Up To 600 Kva
- Printed Circuit Board
- Pvc Wires & Cables
- Pvc Pipe And Fitting
- Re-Conditioning Of Picture Tube
- Resin Cast Ct & Pt (1 Kv)
- Semi Conductor Device
- Semi Conductors For Transistors & Diodes
- Setting Up Of A Video Studio
- Smoke Detectors
- Solar Cells
- Solar Modules
- Solar Power Plant (Energy)
- Solar Photo Voltaic System
- Solder Fluxes
- Solar Water Heating Panels
- Steel Furniture & Electrical Appliances
- Stereo Amplifiers
- Stereo Cassette Recorders/Players
- Street Light Fittings Surge Suppressor
- Tantalum Capacitors
- Teflon Coated Electric Cable
- Telemedicine (Distance Health Care) (Rs. 10000/-)
- Telephone Cord/Cable
- Telephone (Push Button Type)
- Telephone (Push Button & Cordless)
- Television (Ctv & B/W)
- Television (3-D)
- Television Deflection Components
- Television Signal Boosters
- Television Tuners
- Traction Batteries
- Training Institute Of Medical Transcription
- Transformer For B/W Tv
- Transformer For Voltage Stabilizer & E.H.T
- Transmission Power Line Fitting
- Transmission Tower Fitting
- T.V. News Channel
- Tv Audio Equipment Cabinets & Their Assembling Unit
- Un-Interrupted Power Supply (U.P.S)
- Variable Frequency
- Variable Voltage A.C. Drive
- Video Cassettes (Complete Manufacturing & Assembling)
- Video Cassettes Recorder (V.C.R)
- Video Film Studio
- Voltage Regulator For Automobiles
- Voltage Stabilizers
- Voltage Stablizer & T.V. Gain Booster
- Wax And Chemical Coated, Braided Tinsel Wire
- Website Design & E-Mail Registering
- Welding Electrodes
- Wind Energy Power Project (10 Mw)
- Wire Wound Potentiometers
- Wire Wound Resistance

Market Survey Cum Detailed Techno Economic Feasibility Report on all Projects are available Contact.
"ENGINEERS INDIA RESEARCH INSTITUTE". 4449, Nai Sarak (D), Main Road, Delhi-110006 (India)
Ph. : 09811437895, 91-11-23918117, 23916431, 45120361, 64727385 Fax : 91-11-23916431
E-mail : eiriprojects@gmail.com, eiribooks@yahoo.com • website: www.eiri.in, www.eiriindia.org